The Poetic Way of Xie Lingyun

Ping Wang

THE POETIC WAY OF XIE LINGYUN

LITERARY EXPRESSION AND THE NATURAL WORLD

University of Washington Press | *Seattle*

The Poetic Way of Xie Lingyun was made possible in part by a grant from the Traditional Chinese Culture and Society Book Fund, established through generous gifts from Patricia Buckley Ebrey and Thomas Ebrey.

Support for this book was also provided by the China Studies Program, a division of the Henry M. Jackson School of International Studies at the University of Washington.

This book will be made open access within three years of publication thanks to Path to Open, a program developed to bring about equitable access and impact for the entire scholarly community, including authors, researchers, libraries, and university presses around the world. Learn more at https://about.jstor.org/path-to-open/.

Design by Ani Rucki

Composed in Minion Pro, typeface designed by Robert Slimbach

UNIVERSITY OF WASHINGTON PRESS   /   *uwapress.uw.edu*

LIBRARY OF CONGRESS CATALOGING-IN-PUBLICATION DATA

Names: Wang, Ping, 1973 March 6– author

Title: The poetic way of Xie Lingyun : literary expression and the natural world / Ping Wang.

Description: Seattle : University of Washington Press, 2025. | Includes bibliographical references and index.

Identifiers: LCCN 2025006294 | ISBN 9780295753720 hardcover | ISBN 9780295753737 paperback | ISBN 9780295753096 ebook

Subjects: LCSH: Xie, Lingyun, 385–433—Criticism and interpretation | LCGFT: Literary criticism

Classification: LCC PL2666.H75 Z88 2025 | DDC 895.11/24—dc23/eng/20250614

LC record available at https://lccn.loc.gov/2025006294

For EU product safety concerns please contact Mare Nostrum Group B.V. at Mauritskade 21D, 1091 GC Amsterdam, The Netherlands, or gpsr@mare-nostrum.co.uk.

♾ This paper meets the requirements of ANSI/NISO Z39.48-1992 (Permanence of Paper).

To my great-grandmother,
a Uyghur woman whose name was lost to time

Contents

Acknowledgments *ix*

Conventions *xi*

Chronology of Chinese Dynasties,
    with Major Writers from Han through Sui *xiii*

Map of Xie Lingyun's Travels *xviii*

Introduction *1*

PART I / A Political and Poetic Life

1. Xie Lingyun in Place and Time *11*

2. Performing Literary Friendship *31*

3. The Untrammeled Hero *48*

PART II / Steps toward a Literary Revolution

4. A Home in the Mountains *67*

5. Poetic Loneliness *84*

6. The Hillside Garden *107*

7. A Life in Natural and Political Times *124*

8. Patterning the Dragon *142*

9. A Buddhist End *165*

Conclusion *186*

Appendix 1
   Notes on Roaming Famous Mountains 191

Appendix 2
   Xie Lingyun's Poems in the *Wen xuan* 199

Chinese Character Glossary 203

Notes 207

Selected Bibliography 257

Index 275

Acknowledgments

This book would not have been possible without the support and encouragement of many individuals and institutions.

I would like to express my deepest gratitude to the University of Washington, particularly the Department of Asian Languages and Literature, the China Studies Program, and the Walter Chapin Simpson Center for the Humanities, for providing the intellectual and financial support that made this work possible. The resources and community at the University have been instrumental throughout the research and writing process.

My deepest gratitude goes to David R. Knechtges, whose mentorship has been invaluable. I am grateful to Wendy Swartz, whose dedication to supporting sinologists was important in shaping the direction of this work. The annual Chinese Medieval Studies workshops she hosted at Rutgers University provided a platform to receive criticism and feedback on the manuscript. I am especially thankful to Sarah Allen, Robert F. Campany, Jack Chen, Alexei Ditter, Meow Hui Goh, Christopher Nugent, Michael Puett, Antje Richter, Matthias Richter, and Xiaofei Tian for their intellectual insight as well as camaraderie.

Special thanks are due to Lorri Hagman, my editor at the University of Washington Press, whose meticulous editing and keen eye for detail have improved the clarity and coherence of the manuscript. I also wish to thank the UWP manuscript reviewers, whose constructive criticism has greatly enriched this book.

An earlier translation and study of Xie Lingyun's imitation poems of the Jian'an era appeared in my essay "Making Friends with the Men of the Past (*shangyou* 尚友): Literati Identity and Literary Remembering in Early Medieval China," which was included in *Memory in Medieval China: Text, Ritual, and Community*, coedited by Wendy Swartz and Robert Ford Campany (Leiden: Brill, 2018), 82–123. I have revised and updated the translations and discussions of the poems in chapter 2 of the current volume. Chapter 6 contains material in my article "Contemplating 'Return" (*gui* 歸): Xie Lingyun's 謝靈運 (385–433) 'Hillside Garden' (*qiuyuan* 丘園)," *Journal of Chinese Humanities* 7 (2021): 286–309. Revised translations and discussions are incorporated as well. I wish to acknowledge Brill for allowing the reuse of this content in this volume.

I am deeply indebted to my family and friends for their patience and encouragement. Their support has been a constant source of motivation and strength.

Lastly, I acknowledge the contributions of all those who have been part of this journey, whether through direct collaboration or through their work, which has inspired and informed my own. Any errors or shortcomings in this book are entirely my own.

Conventions

Poems in *The Classic of Poetry* (Shijing) are referred to by their numbers as arranged in the Mao version, which is the received text of that work (i.e., the version passed down through millennia, as opposed to other versions discovered in recent excavations). The Mao text represents a tradition of interpretation that originated in the third or second century BCE. The 305 poems are grouped in four sections: Mao 1–160 are the "Airs of the States," Mao 161–234 the "Lesser Elegantiae," Mao 235–265 the "Greater Elegantiae," and Mao 266–305 the "Eulogia." Titles usually are the first bisyllabic phrase taken from a poem's first line. For example, Mao 154, titled "Seventh Month," refers to a poem in the "Airs of the States" section of the received text, which begins, "In the seventh month, the Fire Star sinks westward."

Translations in this volume, except when noted otherwise, are my own. Square brackets in translations mark insertions or supplementary information necessary for clarification in rendering the often terse classical Chinese texts.

Romanization of Chinese terms is rendered in modern pinyin spelling. Quotations that contain other styles of romanization, such as Wade-Giles, have been silently changed to pinyin.

Xie Lingyun's own poetry is presented in this volume in enface Chinese and English format. Excerpts from the work of other writers usually is quoted in English translation only, with citation in a note directing the reader to the Chinese source.

Chronology of Chinese Dynasties, with Major Writers from Han through Sui

Xia (legendary)   ca. 2100–ca. 1600 BCE

Shang   ca. 1600–1046 BCE

Zhou   1045–256 BCE

    Western Zhou   1050–771 BCE

    Eastern Zhou   770–256 BCE

    Spring and Autumn (Chunqiu)   770–476 BCE

    Warring States (Zhanguo)   475–221 BCE

Qin   221–207 BCE

Han   206 BCE–220 CE

    Western Han   206 BCE–9 CE

      Major Writers:

        Sima Qian (ca. 145–86 BCE)—Historian and author of *Records of the Historian* (Shiji)

        Liu Xiang (79–8 BCE)—Scholar and editor of classic texts

    Xin   9–23 CE

      Established by the usurper Wang Mang, briefly interrupting the Han dynasty

    Eastern Han   25–220 CE

      Major Writers:

        Ban Gu (32–92 CE)—Historian and author of *The History of Han* (Han shu)

        Cai Yong (132–192 CE)—Scholar, calligrapher, and musician

        Seven Masters of the Jian'an reign period   (196–220 CE)

Three Kingdoms Period   220–280

    Cao Wei   220–265

      Major Writers:

        Cao Cao (155–220)—Warlord and poet

        Cao Zhi (192–232)—Poet known for his lyrical style

Shu Han   221–263

Eastern Wu   229–280

    Major Writer:

        Lu Ji (261–303) — Poet and writer of "Rhapsody on Literature"
        (Wen fu)

Jin   265–420

    Western Jin   265–316

    Major Writers:

        Pan Yue (247–300) — Known for his elegies

        Zuo Si (250–305) — Known for "Rhapsody on the Shu Capital"
        (Shudu fu)

    Eastern Jin   317–420

    Major Writers:

        Guo Pu (276–324) — Known for "Rhapsody on Roaming
        Mount Tiantai" (You Tiantai shan fu)

        Tao Yuanming (365–427) — Poet known for his pastoral
        themes

        Xie Lingyun (385–433) — Pioneering landscape poet

Southern and Northern Dynasties

    Southern Dynasties   420–589

    Liu-Song   420–479

    Major Writers:

        Shen Yue (441–513) — Poet and literary critic

        Bao Zhao (414–466) — Poet known for expressive lyrics

    Southern Qi   479–502

    Liang   502–557

    Major Writers:

        Xiao Yan (464–549) — aka Emperor Wu of Liang

        Xiao Tong (501–531) — Compiler of the *Wen xuan* (Selections
        of refined literature)

        Xiao Gang (503–551) — Poet known for the Palace Style

    Chen   557–589

    Northern Dynasties   386–581

    Northern Wei   386–534

    Eastern Wei   534–550

Western Wei   535–557

Northern Qi   550–577

Northern Zhou   557–581

Sui   581–618

Tang   618–907

Song   960–1279

Northern Song   960–1127

Southern Song   1127–1279

Yuan   1279–1368

Ming   1368–1644

Qing   1644–1911

Selected Jin–Liu-Song Reign Periods

Yonghe (345–356)—Emperor Mu of Jin

Shengping (357–361)—Emperor Ai of Jin

Longxing (397–401)—Emperor Xiaowu of Jin

Yixi (405–418)—Emperor An of Jin

Yuanxi (419–420)—Emperor Gong of Jin

Yongchu (420–422)—Emperor Wu of Liu-Song

Jingping (423–424)—Emperor Shao of Liu-Song

Yuanjia (424–453)—Emperor Wen of Liu-Song

The Poetic Way of Xie Lingyun

Xie Lingyun's travels, 385–433 CE. Xie's age (in SUI, counting from one year at birth) at different locations on the map was: 1–4 in Guiji (modern Shaoxing); 4–15 in Qiantang (modern Hangzhou); 15–38 in the capital Jiankang (modern Nanjing), as the Duke of Kangle; 38–39 in exile in Yongjia (modern Wenzhou); 39–42 in Guiji; 42–44 in Jiankang; 44–47 in Guiji; 47–48 in Jiankang; 48–49 in exile in Linchuan (modern Fuzhou, Jiangxi); 49, executed in Nanhai (modern Guangzhou). Map by Ben Pease.

Introduction

The Chinese have been idealists, and experimenters in the making
of great principles; their history opens a world of lofty aim and
achievement, parallel to that of the ancient Mediterranean peoples.
We need their best ideals to supplement our own—ideals enshrined
in their art, in their literature and in the tragedies of their lives.
—ERNEST FENOLLOSA, *The Chinese Written Character as a Medium for Poetry*

Xie Lingyun (385–433) is best known as China's first nature poet, but his influence extends beyond literature. Drafts of his poetry were highly sought after by his contemporaries, partly because of the beautiful penmanship. His maternal great-grandfather was Wang Xizhi (303–61), China's most celebrated calligrapher. Xie contributed significantly to the development of Chinese thought and religion in the fifth century through his Buddhist activities as a scholar-translator and patron. His self-professed passion was landscape design. Both in exile and while serving in office, he initiated land surveys and led construction projects. Xie was also admired and emulated for his sense of fashion. Examples of his sartorial design included a pavilion-shaped sun hat, hiking clogs with removable cleats, and an elaborate outfit that required four or five assistants for donning and moving about. As an explorer and experimenter, Xie expressed his innovative spirit through poetry. He is remembered as a great stylist of words and as the father of landscape poetry for presenting for the first time a vivid verbal picture of the remote southeastern coasts of China.

Xie Lingyun was also said to have been arrogant and self-absorbed. Reportedly uncooperative, he incurred displeasure from those in power. The larger-than-life character that Xie came to be associated with was not atypical among Eastern Jin (317–429) aristocrats.[1] Forced to abandon the Central Plains, these landed émigré elites projected their status and family history in their vocal and gestural performances. Exchanges of bons mots, often accompanied with ostentatious body language, were common among the educated class. Xie Lingyun's deployment of words was peer-less. He not only captured nature's manifold appearances with precision, but was also able to convey intimate and poignant emotions, expressing the thought processes and spiritual yearnings of a community in crisis. He elevated lyric poetry (*shi*) by making nature its central subject for the first time. Xie's intense focus on "mountains and waters" (*shanshui*, often translated as "landscape") created a distinctly new poetic vision, through which he crafted a fresh language for describing the natural world, driven by a passionate pursuit of the mysterious principles underlying all visible phenomena.

Eastern Jin culture was largely shaped by the émigré elites whose encounter with the southeastern lands gave rise to brilliant cultural expressions in calligraphy, painting, and poetry. Yet the glory was short-lived. Chinese writers would recall this era as "vulnerable and exquisite" (*kelian*). Not only did the high-minded and accomplished men of culture perish quickly and often tragically, but their arts also disappeared, leaving behind few traces. Due to Xie's popularity as a poet and celebrity as an aristocrat, his writings, including a few dozen or so poems, were preserved in the *Wen xuan* (Selections of refined literature), a comprehensive anthology compiled by Xiao Tong (501–531), an imperial disciple of Shen Yue (441–513), who was a prominent statesman, scholar, and historian. The latter's assessment of Xie as a pivotal figure in literary history proved astute.

In religious life, this period witnessed the spread of Buddhism. Although the elite families were devout followers of the Daoist sect known as the Heavenly Celestial Masters, conversion was not uncommon. Elites demonstrated intellectual curiosity about Buddhism as a foreign religion. Xie Lingyun participated in important Buddhist events throughout his life, and he left behind communications with Buddhist teachers that explored the subtleties of the notion of "sudden enlightenment" (*dunwu*). As a patron and donor, Xie constructed meditation halls for monks in his mountain estates, transforming the religious and natural landscape of an area that had been, up to the turn of the fifth century, dominated by Daoism. He had been raised in the family of a Daoist priest, but that didn't limit the scope of his pursuit of a universal law (*li*) that supposedly governed the world at large. Buddhism was particularly appealing with promises of enlightenment and an afterlife.

Through Xie Lingyun's works, one glimpses the sophisticated introspection of an educated person living through momentous changes in a politically tumultuous but intellectually stimulating era. Much of his writing reflected the musings not of an individual poet, but the pulse of his times. Xie, with his linguistic talent, expressed complex concerns in transparent verse. His poetic descriptions of real and imagined relationships, familiar and strange landscapes, and religious and spiritual visions reveal the inner workings of a curious and creative mind. Always searching, and continuously experimenting, Xie invented new ways of saying things that unveiled a new way of seeing the world. His landscape poetry (*shanshui shi*) departed from earlier works filled with "arcane philosophical discourse" (*xuanyan*) by revealing nature's wonders through precise description rather than preaching about its omnipresence. His accessible yet elegant writings appealed to his contemporaries in their articulation of the south's beauty. While displaced northern émigrés felt deep nostalgia for their homeland, often expressing the clichéd lament that "this beautiful land is not ours," Xie achieved unprecedented emotional clarity and aesthetic precision in his poetry. He even turned complex classical allusions into crystalline themes and vivid images, an achievement that made landscape poetry the dominant mode among his admirers and helped usher in Chinese poetry's golden age in the Tang dynasty. This book examines how Xie reimagined poetic language by turning mountains and waters into meaningful symbols that could represent both the ephemeral and the ultimate truth of the Way (Dao). While Xie grappled with the same fundamental questions about the Way that preoccupied his predecessors and contemporaries, he charted a different course. Instead of relying heavily on established Daoist terminology, he crafted a new path through poetic form.

A common topic of Xie Lingyun's verse is a journey that begins in a dark, difficult, and entangled state of mind. Following the movement of the body and the eye, the spirit is then lifted and mental clarity regained. His voice is often intimate, as if speaking to a friend. As the poet narrates his own story, he also offers advice and shares his wisdom and insight. Lyric poetry, through Xie Lingyun, morphed into an adaptable vessel. Classical learnings and cumbersome historical knowledge were filtered through the poetic form. Simplicity turned out to be the key to a complicated conundrum. For contemporaneous readers, this was not only refreshingly appealing, but also liberating. Xie's poetry was a most welcome consolation for those facing impending paradigm change. As one of the last members of Eastern Jin aristocracy, Xie prominently and haplessly stood between military strongman Liu Yu (363–422) and his ambition to take over the throne. Ill health plagued Xie throughout his life. As the sole male descendant of the Xie clan, he symbolized the imminent extinction of Eastern Jin and its high culture. Teachings and memories of the past sustained the émigré group that withstood the onslaught of the rising military class. The parallel between the collapse of Eastern Han during the Jian'an era (196–220) and the threatened state of Eastern Jin was evident. Jian'an poets that had played a key role in popularizing lyric poetry, bringing a more personal, emotional, and expressive style to Chinese verse during the turbulent end of the Han dynasty, constituted a beacon of light for Xie Lingyun as he navigated political crises similar to theirs. Xie also drew lessons from the past by populating his poems with moral paragons and spirited personalities from his own family whose heroism and wisdom inspired and sustained their offspring.

Poetic works of Xie Lingun showcase a rich tapestry of literary, historical, and other classical references, of which *The Classic of Poetry* (Shijing; 11th–7th c. BCE) and *Songs of Chu* (Chu ci; 4th c. BCE) are two important examples. Allusions culled from these fountainheads of lyricism are often juxtaposed, showing an affinity between the two traditions that furnished patterned expressions of sorrow and joy. Although Xie frequently speaks from the heart, his poems abound in metaphysical musings. Like his contemporaries, his intellectual interest in the so-called Three Mysteries (Sanxuan)—namely, the *Laozi*, *Zhuangzi*, and *The Classic of Changes* (Yijing)—informed his literary output. He departed significantly, however, from earlier poets by avoiding monotonous rephrasings of these philosophies. Xie translated abstract ideas into concrete images. That he seldom mentioned the philosophers Confucius and Mencius is unsurprising, since this was a mark of fourth- and fifth-century Chinese thinkers preoccupied with the "mystic" (*xuan*) and "remote" (*yuan*), tenets denoting the ineffable, unapproachable, and the abstract Way. Emerging fascination with distant mountains and remote areas was a factor of the literati's pursuit of a higher plane in mind and spirit. Significantly, Xie had been brought up and educated in a Daoist household. His outlook represented that peculiarly glorious but brief era of Chinese history when the Confucian grasp on the literati lifestyle and thinking pattern was at its weakest.

Copious studies of Xie and his poetry exist in Chinese and Japanese, and he is assumed by Western scholars of Chinese literature to have been a literary giant. Stephen Owen has famously referred to Xie as "the least read major poet."[2] Wendy Swartz, in her 2018 book on the intertextuality of early medieval Chinese poetry, highlights the use of *The Classic of Changes* in Xie's landscape poetry.[3] J. D. Frodsham's 1967 biography of Xie remains unsurpassed as an English-language historical examination into the poet's life.[4] Francis Abeken Westbrook's close attention to Xie's "landscape poetry" led him to observe in 1972 that, in spite of Xie's "excessive use of allusion, antithesis, and recondite vocabulary," the poet transformed the conventions of his time to create lyric poetry that combined "passionate personal statements" with "mystical visions of the mountain landscape."[5]

The current study, having benefited from and absorbed insights of these and other scholars, argues that Xie Lingyun reinvented lyric verse, especially in the formal features of the five-syllable line. He wrote poetry as a means of personal discovery, creating a poetic language that bridged the gap between external reality and inner experience. Within the space of a single line of five characters, each pronounced as one syllable, Xie used concrete images to reveal the mysteries of the world. Mundane objects such as grass and trees proffer profound lessons. He turned taxing and tortuous travel into verbal landscape paintings in which change and movement are palpable. Xie inspired later poets, ultimately creating a literary revolution by establishing *shi* poetry as the sanctioned and preferred means for expression of private as well as public sentiments. Firmly entrenched by the Tang dynasty in the iconic poetry of Du Fu (712–770) and Li Bo (701–762), *shi* remained the dominant Chinese poetic form until the twentieth century.

Lyric poetry broke the earlier modes and limitations thanks to Xie Lingyun, whose intervention was in both subject and form. While championing Xie as a nature or landscape poet, premodern and modern critics neglected to pinpoint his innovation was in lyric form. In his poetry, nature's revelations came through not only in imagery, but also in where images are placed in each five-syllable line and how they make meaning beyond their sources and between the lines. His poetry refers to universal mysteries in a self-referential scheme, approaching and mimicking the Way through the construct of language. His nature is often kinetic, portending a moment of change, the only constant cosmic law. His poetic journey may begin in a depressive mood but always ascends to appreciative clarity. Emotional catharsis is a salient function of his poetic exercises.

Xie's most distinctive formal in(ter)vention lies with what I call the "pivot verb"—a dynamic word in the middle position, the third syllable of the five-syllable line. This position allows nouns or even adjectives to play the role of a verb, serving the nouns before and after. The pivot verb acts as a free agent in its central position, empowered to violate rules and thwart expectations. In chapter 8, I discuss how Xie's deployment of the pivot verb, with its unpredictability, dispelled the monotony and woodenness brought about by excessive parallelism, which was the basic syntactic design of lyrical verse. As a result, Xie found a way out of this conundrum encountered by earlier generations of poets. The new verbal design expanded the syntactic space of the five-syllable line and diversified the inter- and intralinear semantic mirroring. The expressive and associative space of the lyrical form was thus widened, opening a path for transfiguring the small and originally lowbrow five-syllable line into a sophisticated form that Chinese writers and readers have come to enjoy for almost two thousand years.

Part I of this book focuses on Xie Lingyun's family background and his poetic influences that constituted the bedrock of his creative energy. It begins with a complete translation of Xie's official biography, which covers his political life and his place in literary history. From there, it considers a set of poems through which he expresses the ideal relationship among literati in the Jian'an period, highlighting his belief that like-minded friends and camaraderie functioned through the arts as necessary antidotes to unfortunate times. Xie's response to political banishment involved the articulation of a new type of hero garnered from the Daoist text *Zhuangzi*.

Part II presents close readings of Xie's works, including examination of the logic and aesthetics behind the poetic construction of his mountain

home, the paradox of loneliness as found in his nature poetry, the theme
of reciprocity in his vision of nature, his translation of the notion of cosmic
time into natural images, his pathbreaking use of formal poetic features
such as the pivot verb and the parallel couplet, and his life-long interest in
Buddhism, as evident in his death poem and its many afterlives.

Part I

A POLITICAL AND POETIC LIFE

CHAPTER 1

Xie Lingyun in Place and Time

Xie Lingyun's life straddled two dynasties: the Eastern Jin and the Liu-Song (420–79). A scion of the Xie clan, which played an instrumental role in the survival of the Jin house following the invasion by the Former Qin (350–94), he remained an exalted figure and a symbol of refined culture when the Jin house finally succumbed in 420. The founding emperor of Liu-Song, Liu Yu (Emperor Wu, 363–422; r. 420–22), treated Xie Lingyun with deference, and his son Liu Yilong (Emperor Wen, 407–53; r. 424–53) described Xie's calligraphy and poetry as "twin jewels" (erbao).[1] Calligraphic art spread in the fourth century among the aristocratic families who practiced religious Daoism.[2] Xie Lingyun's mother was a niece of the renowned Eastern Jin calligrapher Wang Xianzhi (344–88), the youngest and most talented son of the even more famous Wang Xizhi. Although no examples of Xie's calligraphy survived, he was a fine artist whose work was highly sought after during his lifetime.[3] Equally renowned was his poetry, as reported in *The Liu-Song History* (Song shu): "Whenever a poem of Lingyun's arrived in a town or city, copies were made and spread among the high- and low-class readers. Within days it would have reached all admiring readers from near to far. Lingyun's fame made resounding waves in the capital area."[4] Born in Guiji County (modern Shaoxing, Zhejiang), Xie Lingyun was sent to Hangzhou at age three and raised in the home of a Daoist master. When the Sun En (?–402) rebellion against the Jin broke out in 399, Xie, at age fifteen, fled to Jiankang (the southern and final capital of the Jin dynasty), where he was taken under the wing of his uncle Xie Hun (?–412), an imperial son-in-law.[5]

It was at Xie Hun's literary salon that Xie Lingyun first demonstrated his talent as a poet.[6] At the time, the young Lingyun probably harbored political ambitions given the influence and reputation of the Xie clan. Any hopes he had would be dashed in 412, however, when Xie Hun was executed following Liu Yu's ascension to power. By 420, Jin was no more. A new Song dynasty stood in its place. Liu Yu, however, ruled as emperor for only two years before passing away from ill health in 422. Xie's enemies seized this opportunity to drive him out of the capital. Having served at the Jin and then Liu-Song courts for two decades, Xie was reluctant to embark on a tortuous journey toward the destination of his exile, the remote town of Yongjia (modern Wenzhou, Zhejiang) in the sparsely populated southeast. It was around this time that he began writing meditative poems about his travel. He visited the Xie estate in Guiji before journeying on and arriving at Yongjia in 423, where he spent less than a year. His early departure was described in his official biography (as we will read later in the chapter) as negligent and self-indulgent. His sightseeing and aimless roaming, the main subject of his poetic works from this period, support this criticism. After returning to Guiji, Xie continued with his rambling, now with the purpose of developing the Xie family estates. He supervised the construction of lodges, belvederes, and religious retreats in the depths of the Guiji mountains. In some of these places, he entertained friends and associated with monks. In the late 420s, following a short stint in the capital, a disenchanted Xie seemed to withdraw more and more into the world of intellectual reflection and literary production. Yet his mere presence, accompanied by a large entourage and ostentatious development projects, still proved too much for local officials. A falling-out with one powerful man in 431 drove Xie out of his mountain home, to which he would never return. Reading Xie's poems sometimes gives the impression that he was constantly traveling in exile. The emotions are often poignant, but the descriptions of scenery never fail to be striking, leading historians to call Xie Lingyun the "father of Chinese landscape poetry."[7]

Dangerous river journeys and arduous treks through the mountains took a toll on Xie's health. For instance, the first stretch of his journey into exile was from Jiankang to Guiji, 250 miles mostly by boat. He treated the trip as an excursion in his poetry, mixing representations of business and pleasure for the first time by focusing on nature while his mind was apparently occupied by matters of life and death. Such keen observations would earn Xie his sobriquet as China's first nature poet. The second stretch of this journey, from Guiji to Yongjia, extended for about 126 miles. Upon arrival, Xie fell ill and was bedridden for much of the winter season. When he opened the curtains in spring, Xie reported renewed hope upon seeing nature's rejuvenation. He seemed to be saying that human drama was insignificant and mundane compared to great natural forces. Indeed, every time Xie was forced to travel, he found marvels on the road. For instance, after he returned to Guiji from Yongjia, he reluctantly made two additional trips to Jiankang: in 426 to answer Emperor Wen's summons, and again in 431 to defend himself against Meng Yi's accusations. Xie's final journeys took him through China's southern provinces all the way to Guangzhou, a thousand miles from the mountains of Guiji where he had wished to live out his years in peace. Xie's remarkably exquisite poems were the product of his extensive travels, some of which must have been undertaken with a heavy heart.

After Xie's death, Bao Zhao (ca. 414–66), a Liu-Song poet of renown, likened his poetry to "a fresh lotus blossom emerging out of [muddy] water."[8] This is apt. Based on what we know of Xie's life, his art is a far cry from murkiness. The poems, whatever we call them—landscape poetry, travel poetry, nature poetry—survived the "dusty things" of a life caught up in a unique historical moment.[9] The fifth-century critic Zhong Rong (467?–518) placed Xie Lingyun in the top rank of his *Gradation of Poets* (Shi pin): "During the Yuanjia era [424–53], there was one Xie Lingyun, whose talent had no match. His language was posh, his vocabulary profuse, and his style extravagant—all quite impossible to imitate."[10] Although imitating Xie was the path to literary excellence for generations of aspiring poets in the second half of the fifth century, few succeeded, according to Prince Xiao Gang (503–51), the future Emperor Jianwen of the Liang dynasty (502–57).

> The poetic expressions of 'Xie the Sojourner' [Xie Ke] are plucked from heaven, naturally arising from things portrayed.[11] Occasionally, his language was overly ornate, which constituted the dregs of his art. . . . This is probably why in imitating Xie, many failed to achieve the essence of his art, but only obtained its verbosity. . . . Therefore, the ingenuity of Xie's poetry can't be reached through a step-by-step mimicry.[12]

The Liang prince's observation probably had a basis in personal frustration born out of trying to imitate Xie's masterly art.[13] Xie's influence reached well into the Tang dynasty (618–907), which is considered to be the pinnacle of classical Chinese poetry. Both Li Bo (701–62) and Du Fu (712–70), China's two greatest poets, professed their indebtedness to Xie Lingyun.

The Official Portrait

Any study of Xie Lingyun needs to go back to the oldest and original source, the official account of Xie's life and career in *The Liu-Song History*, which was compiled by Shen Yue (441–513). This two-part account takes up an entire *juan* (fascicle) and consists of over 20,000 characters in classical Chinese. A full annotated English translation would amount to a hefty volume.[14] The abridged translation here focuses on major events in Xie's adult life, highlighting his importance in the cultural-intellectual and political arenas during the Jin-Song transition (396–420), the last twenty-five years of Eastern Jin. The two *fu* (rhapsody) texts are omitted.

> Xie Lingyun was a descendant of the Xie clan that hailed from Yangjia County of Chen Commandery [modern Henan]. His grandfather was Xuan, the [Jin] General of Chariot and Horse. His father was Huan, who was unintelligent. Huan attained the rank of Secretary of the Imperial Library and died young. Lingyun, from an early age, displayed signs of intelligence and brilliance. Xuan was extremely surprised and used to marvel to his friends and relatives: "If I begot Huan, how is it that he begot Lingyun?"
>
> As a child, Lingyun was fond of learning. He became well-versed in a variety of canonical texts. His literary style was unmatched in elegance. His uncle Hun appreciated his talent. From his grandfather, Lingyun inherited the title Duke of Kangle [Kangle Gong], which gave him revenues from two thousand households. As a duke of a state, he was customarily appointed Extra-Officiary Junior Chamberlain, a post he declined. He acted as a personally appointed administrator to the grand marshal, Prince of Langye.[15] By nature, Lingyun was extravagant and unrestrained. His chariots and appurtenances were gorgeous. In ritual garments, objects, and utensils, Lingyun brought about many changes to existing stipulations. Everyone followed suit. They all referred to him as "Xie Kangle."
>
> When Liu Yi, the general director of the army, was stationed in

Gushu [modern Dangtu, Anhui], Lingyun was appointed as administrator of the redaction office.[16] When Liu Yi governed Jiangling [modern Hubei], Lingyun acted as an Executive Gentleman of the Household of the General of the Guardian Army. After Liu Yi committed suicide, the Exalted Ancestor appointed Lingyun as administrator to the commander-in-chief.[17] Upon entering the capital, he was given the post of assistant director of the Imperial Library.[18] He was then dismissed due to an offense.[19]

The Exalted Ancestor embarked on a northern campaign in the autumn of 416 to reclaim Chang'an.[20] Liu Daolian, who was general of light cavalry, stayed to guard the capital.[21] Lingyun was appointed as his administrative counselor. Later, Lingyun was transferred to other posts— vice president of the imperial secretariat, counselor to the general of the central army, and Gentleman in Attendance within the Yellow Gates. In these capacities, Lingyun was dispatched as an envoy to receive the Exalted Ancestor in Pengcheng. For this occasion, Lingyun composed "Rhapsody on the Northern Punitive Campaign" [Beizheng fu].[22]

Lingyun continued as Gentleman in Attendance within the Yellow Gates, while taking up the post of Executive Gentleman of the Household of the Prime Minister and, later, Captain of the Left Guard of the Crown Prince.[23] After he was implicated in the death of a retainer, Lingyun was stripped of his appointments.

When the Exalted Ancestor received the Mandate of Heaven, Lingyun's title was reduced from that of duke to marquis with an income cut accordingly from the tax revenue of two thousand to five hundred households.[24] He was appointed to the rank of Officer of Irregular Cavalry in Constant Attendance on the Emperor and reinstated as Captain of the Left Guard of the Crown Prince.[25]

Lingyun was, by nature, headstrong and incautious. More than once he violated the law and went against regulations. The court treated him according to the stated ritual terms but didn't grant him actual power. Lingyun, however, regarded himself as talented and hence suitable for participating in advisory matters of considerable political importance in the court. Having not received an acknowledgment, Lingyun often held grudges.[26]

Liu Yizhen [407–24], Prince of Luling, was fond of texts and documents from a young age.[27] He struck up an unusually amicable relationship with Lingyun. When the young emperor [Liu Yu's eldest son Liu Yifu (406–24), Yizhen's older brother] ascended the throne, authority remained in the hands of several ministers. Lingyun, through his "forming alliances" and "fanning dissonance," denigrated those in power.[28] Director of Instruction Xu Xianzhi [364–426] and his clique, regarding Lingyun as a cause for concern, exiled him to Yongjia.

The land of Yongjia Commandery has beautiful mountains, something that appealed to Lingyun immediately. As his ambition was thwarted in exile, Lingyun abandoned himself to roaming about aimlessly. His footprints covered all of the neighboring counties in Yongjia. Each excursion lasted ten days or more. As a result, he failed to tend to court cases presented by the local people. Everywhere he went, Lingyun composed poems to convey his thoughts and feelings. Before his term was up, Lingyun left his post on account of ill health, despite the dissuasion letters from his cousins Hui, Yao, and Hongwei.

Lingyun's father and grandfather had been both buried in Shining County, where there were old houses and estates.[29] Lingyun subsequently transferred his registration to Guiji and began to renovate these residences. Nestled in the mountains and circled by rivers, the constructions fully exhibited the beauty of a secluded life.

In the company of local recluses such as Wang Hongzhi [365–427], Kong Chunzhi [372–430], and others, Lingyun freely enjoyed himself and desired to live like this to the end of his days.

Whenever a poem of Lingyun's arrived in a town or city, copies were made and spread among the high- and low-class readers. Within days it would have reached all admirers from near to far. Lingyun's fame made resounding waves in the capital area, eliciting a response from the intellectual elite. He composed "*Fu* on Dwelling in the Mountains," to which he also attached a commentary.

[The full text and commentary of the *fu* are omitted here.]

When the Grand Ancestor ascended the throne, he executed Xu Xianzhi and members of his clique.[30] Lingyun was summoned [back to court] with the appointment of director of the Imperial Library. The summons was sent again. Lingyun still didn't accept. Emperor Wen then entrusted Fan Tai [355–428] to send a letter to Lingyun, urging him with words of encouragement and praise. After this, Lingyun came out of retirement and took up the post in the Imperial Library where he was charged with ordering documents and archives and supplying whatever was missing or lost. In addition, because there had not yet been a complete history compiled for the Jin dynasty from the beginning to end, Emperor Wen thereupon ordered Lingyun to compile an official version. For this, Lingyun drafted a rough outline. In the end, it was not brought to completion.[31]

[Shortly afterward,] Lingyun was transferred to be the vice-president of the Imperial Chancellery. Day and night, he was given an audience by the emperor, who treated Lingyun with gracious appreciation and generous support. In calligraphy as well as poetry, Lingyun was peerless. Whenever he finished composing a poem, Lingyun would himself copy it out in [his own] calligraphy. Emperor Wen referred to the work as "twin jewels." Privately, Lingyun thought he ought to be included in Emperor Wen's inner circle of advisors, considering his personal renown, the ranking of the Xie clan, and his numerous talents. When the court initially summoned him, Lingyun had secretly expected such an honor. Upon his final arrival, Emperor Wen received Xie on account of his literary talent. When attending court banquets, Lingyun was included only in casual conversations about art and literature [i.e., without sharing confidence in matters of important administrative discussions about personnel appointment or policy-making]. Yet Wang Tanshou [394–430], Wang Hua [385–427], Yin Jingren [390–441], and others, who did not surpass him in reputation or ranking, were consulted and treated with confidence and honor.[32]

Feeling uneasy, Lingyun would often absent himself from court audiences on account of ill health. He busied himself with projects to dredge pools, erect hedges, plant bamboo, and grow pansies. In deploying corvée labor, Lingyun allowed no remission in meeting the deadline or completion of the task. He would leave town and roam aimlessly. Occasionally he covered 160 or 170 *li* [fifty to fifty-three miles] in a single day.[33] Sometimes he left for weeks without an official report or excuse. Emperor Wen, reluctant to injure a grandee, issued an edict allowing

Lingyun to remove himself. Upon this, Lingyun submitted a memorial requesting a leave of absence on account of ill health. Emperor Wen granted his return to the east [i.e., Guiji]. Before his departure, Lingyun presented a memorial urging a punitive expedition against the north.

[The full text of the memorial is omitted here.]

After Lingyun returned east on grounds of ill health, he occupied himself with socializing with friends, hosting banquets and parties that continued into the morning hours. Once again, he was censured by Fu Long [369–451], who was the vice-president of the censorate.[34] [In 428,] Lingyun was relieved of his titles and appointments. This was the fifth year of the Yuanjia reign.

After Lingyun returned east, he associated with his cousin Huilian [407–33], He Changyu [?–443] of Donghai, Xun Yong of Yingchuan, and Yang Xuanzhi of Taishan.[35] They gathered to examine documents and roam about in the mountains. Their contemporaries gave them the sobriquet the "Four Friends" [siyou].[36] Huilian had demonstrated talent and perspicacity from a young age. However, because he was frivolous, his father Xie Fangming didn't appreciate him. When Lingyun had initially returned to Shining from Yongjia, Fangming was the governor of Guiji. On one occasion, Lingyun paid a visit to Fangming on his way from Shining to Guiji. Lingyun passed by to see young Huilian and greatly adored him and appreciated his talent. He Changyu, Huilian's tutor, was living in the commandery. Lingyun also thought of Changyu as most outstanding. Lingyun told Fangming: "A'lian [Huilian] is so extraordinary and yet Your Honor treats him as an ordinary child; He Changyu is the Zhongxuan [Wang Can (177–217)] of our time and yet you feed him with the foods befitting a mere retainer. Since Your Honor has been unable to treat the worthy with ritual propriety, you should return Changyu to me." Upon this, Lingyun took Changyu with him, and they rode in the same carriage.

Xun Yong, style name Daoyong, held the post of Extra-Officiary Junior Chamberlain.[37] Xuanzhi, style name Yaofan, served as the Inner Officer of Linchuan and was [later] treated with honor by the minister of works, Prince of Jingling, Liu Dan.[38] When Dan's plot of rebellion failed, Xun Yong was executed. Elegant and graceful, Changyu's writing was second only to Huilian's. Yong and Xuanzhi were not his match. [Later,] the Prince of Linchuan, Liu Yiqing, recruited men of letters. Changyu was promoted from Secretary in Service of a Prince to Administrator in the Redaction Office of the General Pacifying the West. Once in Jiangling, he sent a letter to his clansman He Xu [n.d.], in which Changyu used rhymed verse in a memorandum addressed to Yiqing's court assistants and entourage: "Lu Zhan dyed his temples, / to please his young consort. / In black and blue, his hair shimmers, / yet soon streaks of gray rose like stars." Like this, there were five or six lines. Frivolous young men then elaborated on the poem, which spread widely with ever more exaggerated words and lines. Yiqing was enraged and reported it to the Grand Ancestor, who then demoted Changyu to magistrate of Zeng-cheng under the governorship of Guangzhou. When Yiqing had passed, the gentlemen at court paid respect at his residence and shared memories of regrets and sorrow. He Xu told Yuan Shu: "Now it's time Changyu was returned to office." Shu said: "The state is still mourning the loss of the august prince. It is not yet time to consider a man on exile." When Liu Shao [432–52], Prince of Luling, was stationed in Xunyang, he appointed Changyu as Acting Administrator to Adjutant of the South to take charge of keeping court records.³⁹ On his river journey to Xunyang, Changyu encountered a thunderstorm and drowned near Banqiao.

Lingyun, building on the wealth passed down by his father and grandfather, made a livelihood through enterprise. In addition to [owning] a large group of slaves, several hundred retainers had served the family since before Lingyun's time. They tunneled into the mountains and dredged lakes. Projects of construction went on ceaselessly. They followed mountain paths to ascend the peaks. They always explored untraveled and forbidding places. They reached deep into the mountains, past a thousand layers of craggy peaks. They wore a type of wooden sandal during climbing. In hiking up, the front cleats were removed; in hiking down, the back cleats were taken off. Once, they opened a path from South Peak in Shining [southwest of modern Shangyu, Zhejiang] that reached all the way to Linhai [modern Taizhou, Zhejiang]. Grand Warden Wang Xiu was greatly alarmed, taking them to be bandits. After realizing it was Lingyun's group, Xiu felt relieved. Lingyun then extended an invitation to Xiu to go on an expedition together. Xiu demurred. Upon this, Lingyun presented a poem to Xiu that read: "The Lord of the Region balks at dangers of the road; I, the guest traveler, have made the mountain path easy."

In Guiji, Lingyun had a large entourage of retainers who often caused alarm in towns and counties. Grand Warden Meng Yi served the Buddha with great earnestness, yet was belittled by Lingyun, who once said to him: "To obtain the [Buddhist] Way, one ought to be refined and intelligent. You may die before me. But in achieving Buddhahood, you will have to follow me." Yi deeply resented these words.

On the eastern outskirts of Guiji was Lake Huizhong, which Lingyun wished to drain and turn into land. The Grand Ancestor issued an order for the commandery to carry it out accordingly. The lake, right by the city wall, was a source of aquatic products. Local people valued it. Meng Yi protected the lake and prevented Lingyun [from carrying out his] project. Having failed to drain Huizhong, Lingyun, in turn, requested Lake Peihuang to be drained and turned into land. Yi held firmly to his disapproval once again. Lingyun stated that Meng Yi was not acting in the interest of the local people, but rather [acting out of his concern as a devout Buddhist, because] draining the lake would harm many living creatures [and thus hurt his chances of achieving Buddhahood]. These caustic comments from Lingyun injured Meng Yi, and hence their feud.

Stating that the local population were disturbed by the reckless and unrestrained activities of Lingyun, Meng Yi issued a public proclamation accusing Lingyun of rebellious intention and dispatched troops on the grounds of defensive needs.

[Upon this,] Lingyun hurried off to the capital city, where he went to court to plead his case with the following memorial [submitted to Emperor Wen]:

"Since your humble servant carried his sickly body to return to the Eastern Mountain, it has been three years. His dwelling has not been any place close to towns or city walls; his affairs have not interfered with the human realm. In seclusion he roosts on the farthest cliffs. He is severed from all outside *pratyaya* [conditions or causes]. Keeping to his lot and nourishing his life, he was prepared to end his remaining years in the mountains. All of a sudden, a memorial from the grand warden of Guiji arrived on the twenty-eighth day of last month, saying: 'Recently, there have been much disconcerting rumors and talk [about your rebellious intention]. Even if I wish to ignore them, the common folk will not allow me to not defend [by dispatching troops].'

Reading this put me in utter terror. Unable to understand its cause, I immediately, under the starlight, set out to the capital to return my bones to Your Majesty. When passing through Shanyin, I saw guards on horses, armed with shields and spears. Prominently placed, they blocked thoroughfares and barricaded alleyways, patrolling here and searching there. Weaponry and armor choked the roads. Yet what I couldn't understand was the exact crime this lowly servant had supposedly committed. When I finally saw Meng Yi in person, I was given the chance to declare my innocence. Still, this whole military deployment left me in horrified bewilderment.

In the past, this humble servant had been in close attendance to Your Majesty and covered in your heavenly grace. If there was a crime with clear evidence in writing, not only should there have been court judgment [and] public humiliation, I would also have been set as an example for the whole realm to chastise to rectify the law of the state. Now they've charged me on false pretext. How ruthless!

Since antiquity, even the worthy have not been able to stay away from slanderers and detractors. For any slandering case, there is always a cause. There are those daredevils who form cliques and amass crowds; there are bravadoes who dominate a region with their sword. Yet it is unheard of that a ritual-minded erudite would ferment the atrocity to topple the state; or a mountain-dwelling gentleman would design a scheme to affront the emperor. Now their hearsay evidence is fabricated from thin air; their false accusations are all but baseless. The cruelty in this is unprecedented. It's not that I crave life, but that I am pained by the excessiveness of this matter. I have honestly examined my heart and found no fault therein. Holding on to the truth, I have nothing to confess. It is for this reason only that I dragged my sickly body and packed up my skeleton, which I now return to you. I beg Your Majesty to reflect on this with the heavenly mirror. I shall regard the day that I die as my time of rebirth. In fear and anxiety, your humble servant has endured for days on end. His chronic pains and old aches are flaring up. Confused and befuddled, he walks about like a corpse, not knowing what is being said here."

The Grand Ancestor understood that Lingyun had been wronged and didn't fault him. Still, he forbade Lingyun to return east. Instead, Emperor Wen appointed Lingyun to serve as the Inner Officer of Linchuan [modern Jiangxi] with a full salary of two thousand bushels [of grain per year].

Lingyun roamed about and abandoned himself while serving in the commandery, not unlike how he had been in Yongjia. He was then censured. The minister of instruction dispatched an envoy to accompany the local administrator Zheng Wangsheng to arrest Lingyun. Lingyun instead held Wangsheng captive. He raised troops for an insurrection. Subsequently, he revealed an intent to rebel [against the court], which is revealed in his poem: "When the State of Han perished, Zifang rose to action;[40] / when Qin established himself as the First Emperor, Lulian felt ashamed.[41] / I, too, a wanderer of rivers and oceans;[42] / have long admired those gentlemen principled in loyalty and righteousness."[43]

Lingyun was chased down and captured. In front of the commandant of justice, Lingyun was granted a trial. The commandant of justice submitted to Emperor Wen a memorial stating that Lingyun instigated a rebellion and recommended capital punishment. Emperor Wen valued Lingyun's talent and wished to simply relieve him of his post and appointments. The Prince of Pengcheng, Liu Yikang [409–51], insisted that Lingyun not be pardoned.[44] Emperor Wen subsequently sent down an edict reading: "Lingyun has committed offenses repeatedly and should receive the utmost punishment by law. Still, Xie Xuan established considerable merit that should be sufficient to shelter his offspring. It is permissible that Lingyun's death sentence be mitigated by one degree. He shall be exiled to Guangzhou."

Later, when Zong Qishou, a general from the commandery, came to Tukou by way of Taoxu village, he saw seven men yelling by the roadside. Suspecting that they were not the usual locals, he returned to report to the commandery. Coming back with troops, Zong Qishou ambushed the group. Fighting ensued and all were arrested. One named Zhao Qin originated from Shanyang [modern Huai'an, Jiangsu]. He confessed, "My fellow villager Xue Daoshuang made the plan with Xie Lingyun. At the beginning of the ninth month of the previous year, Daoshuang informed me through another villager Chengguo, who told me, 'the former inner officer of Linchuan committed an offense and was exiled to Guangzhou; he provided funds for purchases of bows and arrows, swords and shields, and so on; he asked Daoshuang to gather young strong men from his region to come and rescue Lingyun at Sanjiangkou; once successful, each would be rewarded accordingly.' Subsequently, I gathered a group to rescue Xie, but without success. On our way home, we encountered famine and thus turned to banditry."

Those in charge submitted a memorial to Emperor Wen, asking him to send down punishment accordingly. The Grand Ancestor then ordered Lingyun to be executed in the marketplace of Guangzhou.

Before his death, Lingyun wrote a poem:

> Gong Sheng could not live out his life;[45]
> Li Ye also plunged to his death.[46]
> Lord Xi was hard-pressed because of his principle;[47]
> Master Huo, for his part, lost his life.[48]
> Solemn are the frostbitten autumn leaves;
> soaking wet are the storm-braving day mushrooms.
> How much time does one have for this "chance meeting"?[49]
> Such brevity is not what I grieve.
> Now I deliver my heart before the self's awakening.[50]
> Such pain has been endured for a long time.
> I most resent that my gentlemanly wish
> to "expire on the cliff" is not to be attained.[51]

Literary Legacy

In Xie Lingyun's death poem, he evokes historical personages to make sense of his own circumstances. Gong Sheng, Li Ye, Zifang, and Lulian are all mentioned elsewhere in Xie's poetry. Their collective appearance in this death poem is particularly poignant, revealing to a certain extent how history is used in poetry to express personal emotions. *The Liu-Song History* reports that Xie Lingyun died in the tenth year of the Yuanjia reign (424–53) at the age of forty-nine. He left behind a son named Feng (Phoenix), who died at a young age. In that sense, Xie Lingyun's works are thus his only legacy.[52]

Shen Yue's account of Xie Lingyun's life highlights a few important pieces of information: Xie was a child prodigy and a cherished scion of the Xie clan. At the tender age of fifteen, he inherited the title Duke of Kangle from his grandfather Xie Xuan (343–88). His uncle and patron Xie Hun was killed by Liu Yu in 412. Xie's life was spared due to his talents in art and literature, but his subsequent close relationship with the Prince of Luling caused the ire of his political enemies, who managed to oust him from the court. Xie spent less than a year in exile in the town of Yongjia before returning, against the council of his cousins, to the Xie family estate in Guiji in 424. In 426, Xie answered the call of Emperor Wen and returned to the capital where he stayed until 428, and then returned to Guiji once again. Meng Yi, a local official in Guiji who had powerful connections in the capital, leveled an official complaint against him in 431. Xie left for the capital the same night that Meng dispatched troops to arrest him. Xie then appealed his case in person before Emperor Wen. The emperor decided against capital punishment, but forbade Xie from returning to Guiji; Xie was ultimately sent to Linchuan in exile. While in Linchuan, Xie's enemies in the capital brought a treason charge against him; Xie went into exile a final time and was executed in Guangzhou in 433.

Despite his noble lineage, Xie's official biography reveals a pattern of conflict with authority figures, from local officials to the central court. Personal tragedy and the struggles revealed in Xie's biography contrast with the elegance and smoothness of his prose style, as seen in the quoted memorial. Two rhapsodies are preserved in his official biography, as if to serve as proof of Xie's literary grandiosity. Moreover, it is through the subtle spins and tone in his writing that the reader catches a glimpse of Xie's talent at work. For instance, Xie's "Rhapsody on the Northern Punitive Campaign," written around the year 418, was commissioned by Liu Yu as a propaganda piece to aggrandize a military endeavor to recover the northern capital of Luoyang, a potential final step in the usurper's consolidation of power.[53] Xie's rhapsody departed from the expected epideictic eulogy. A tone of reservation and even caution, in addition to the effervescent praise of Lingyun's own forefathers, their military achievements, and their moral fortitude, would have been quite deflating to Liu Yu. Through this piece, Xie made his stance clear as an old guard of the Jin house. The aloof tone and the theme of "return" (more on this in chapter 6) may be read as a strong disapproval of Liu Yu.

It is little wonder that Xie Lingyun's career path, as reported in Shen Yue's account in *The Liu-Song History*, turned out to be a downward spiral, with repeated exiles and demotions. His reputation was marred by numerous court cases brought against him. To a large degree, Xie Lingyun's life exemplified the decline of the nobility's influence at the Liu-Song court. Members of the so-called major clans once played an instrumental role in the political life of the Han and post-Han eras. By the mid-fifth century, however, their presence was reduced primarily to the cultural arena. Although talented in more than one field, Xie was unable to shape the trajectory of his life. His defiance of the Liu-Song rulers and death by public execution turned him into a sort of maverick martyr of a bygone age.[54] In that sense, he was the opposite of his grand uncle Xie An—the hero of the Eastern Jin in the quasi-history *A New Account of Tales of the World* (Shishuo xinyu), a collection of anecdotes and memorable stories compiled under the auspices of Liu Yiqing, the literary-minded Liu-Song prince. Liu filled his court with writers such as He Changyu, who cherished memories of his dead friend Xie Lingyun's boastful arrogance, which contrasted with Xie An's tasteful restraint.[55] Xie Lingyun's daring spirit marked the end of the noble idealism universally pursued by Wei-Jin intellectuals.[56] What made Xie Lingyun a unique member of the Xie clan was his literary production, especially poetry. Through his works we gain an insight into the rational and emotional workings of a cultured class and their way of seeing and understanding their natural and social surroundings. Although a negligible player in the Jin-Song political transition, Xie Lingyun was an eloquent spokesperson for the zeitgeist of the third and fourth centuries. He stood for the losing side, yet in his poetry the lost culture of the Eastern Jin intellectuals was reflected and preserved.

Shen Yue, like his subject, was a literary giant of his time. An instigator of literary reform, Shen is now remembered for his advocacy of strict prosodic regulations, which can be seen in the penultimate paragraph of his evaluative essay translated below. Like Xie Lingyun, Shen came from a learned family.[57] His father was executed for supporting Liu Shao (424–53), the fratricidal son of Emperor Wen, and yet Shen, through quiet prudence, survived the violent revolutions and served at the high court of three dynasties. His career culminated at the Liang (502–57) court, where he devoted himself to the education of the Crown Prince Xiao Tong (501–31), whose literary interests led to the compilation of China's earliest extant and most comprehensive anthology, a work including several dozen genres, spearheaded with rhapsodies and *shi* (poems mostly in tetrasyllables and pentasyllables). Shen's silent endurance stands in stark contrast to Xie's dangerous candor. If Shen had any sympathy for his subject, it was completely muted. Practical and capable, he and the new generation of courtiers who served the military lords learned to separate official duties from personal matters, including literary pursuits. Poetry, for example, came to be practiced as a hobby or even private obsession. The focus on technique gave rise to the impersonal "palace style" that treats life and worldly matters from a distance. By the mid-sixth century, China saw the production of a few monumental works on poetry and poetics. The precipitous development of *shi* poetry in the decades following Xie's death was nothing short of a miracle. It is in this way that Xie became an undisputed major figure in the literary and cultural history of premodern China.

One may get the impression that Shen's sketch of Xie's life as a courtier reads like a pastiche of court records. However, Shen's evaluation of Xie in the "historian's remarks" attached at the end of the biography is original and illuminating. In this section, Shen in essence composes a literary history in which Xie is accorded the status of an epochal poet. By laying out the theoretical foundations and recent developments of the *shi* tradition, Shen, a passionate and accomplished poet himself, pays the ultimate homage to Xie, whom he considers here as the culminating figure in the genre transformation of the *shi*. The evaluation reads:

People are endowed with the *qi* of heaven and earth; they are imbued with the potency of the five constants [elements of nature]. What is enabling alternates with what is yielding; joy and petulance divide the inner being. When the will is stirred inside, songs and laments issue forth. This is the basis of the "six principles" [*liuyi*] and the linchpin of the "four beginnings" [*sishi*] of *The Classic of Poetry*. Rising and falling are [the tones of] the songs and ballads; profusely lingering are the "decades of airs."[58] Before the times of the sage-kings Shun and Yu, no patterned writings were passed down. In principle, there ought to be no difference, since people should be endowed with the vital force and hence embrace the *qi*. However, in terms of that which is aroused through singing and chanting, "The Birth of the People" [Shengmin; Mao 250] was the beginning of it all. After the Zhou [Western Zhou (1046–771 BCE)] house became weakened in its influence, critical trends rose to be ever more prominent. Qu Yuan [ca. 340–278 BCE] and Song Yu [fl. 298–63 BCE] are the leaders of the pure stream; Jia Yi [ca. 200–168 BCE] and Sima Xiangru [ca. 179–17 BCE] are but the echoes and followers of their fragrant dust. Outstanding words embellish the metal and stone instruments; lofty overtones soar beyond the clouds. Ever since, ambitions and aspirations have been broadened. Wang Bao [fl. 61–58 BCE], Liu Xiang [77–6 BCE], Yang Xiong [53 BCE–18 CE], Ban Gu [32–92], Cui Yin [30?–92], Cai Yong [132/133–92], and others, via different courses, head in the same direction. In turn, they use [the "airs"] as their example. Although pure-sounding words and ornate tunes occasionally emerge from their compositions, there are too many clustered sounds and belabored tones. Zhang Heng [78–139] produced gorgeous writings that emanated from and followed the contour of emotions. Such extraordinary chanting, with its lofty traces, lacked an echo for an extended period.

During the Jian'an era [196–220], the Cao family held the mandate. The two emperors and the Prince of Chen were all richly endowed with flourishing talent in the art of letters. Unprecedentedly, emotive expressions came to be the structure of the writings and literary embellishments superseded substance. From the Han [206 BCE–220 CE] to Wei [220–66], for over four hundred years, literary forms thrice developed in the hands of writers and talented wordsmiths. [Sima] Xiangru is known for being crafty with phrasing in verisimilitudes; Ban Gu is good at discourses based on factual argumentation. [Cao] Zijian [192–232] and [Wang] Zhongxuan [177–217], through their vital force, are embodiments of literary refinement. In all cases, they flaunt their capability and display their excellence, shining forth through their time. As a result, writers of their generation are admired and imitated.

In tracing the origins of poetry, there is nothing that cannot be traced back to the "Airs" of *The Classic of Poetry* or *Songs of Chu*. It is only due to their varied proclivities that poets differ in their creative work. During the Yuankang era [291–99], Pan Yue [247–300] and Lu Ji [261–303] in particular were representative of their time. Their pitches differ from Ban Gu and Jia Yi. Their style has now deviated from that of Cao Zhi and Wang Can. Complex ideas multiply like stars; convoluted patterns come together like the intricate patterns on an embroidery. They patch together the fleeting sounds from the Level Terrace and adopt the lofty rhymes from the Seven Masters of Jian'an.[59] Through lingering influence and blazing effects, they reach the pinnacle of literary refinement in the Western Jin [266–316].

During the restoration era of the Jin house, "mystical criticism" suddenly appeared. Advocates and followers studied the *Laozi*, and in broad knowledge they arrived only at the seven chapters of the *Zhuangzi*. In galloping their literary dictions, the purport resided solely with these [i.e., the philosophical ideas and discursive patterns of Lao-Zhuang]. From Jianwu [317–18] to Yixi [405–19], for one hundred years, in patching together sounds and joining dictions, waves billowed and clouds gathered.[60] In expressing their intention, all were devoted to the "supreme virtue" or the "dark pearl."[61] Writings of vital force were unheard of. Yin Zhongwen [?–407] was the first to reform the influence of Sun Chuo [314–71] and Xu Xun [fl. ca. 358]. Xie Hun greatly altered the literary trend during Taiyuan [376–96]. When it was the Liu-Song dynasty, Yan [Yanzhi, 384–456] and Xie [Lingyun] vaunted their fame. Xie Lingyun propagated compositions inspired by literary companions; Yan Yannian wrote in a dense style. Together they matched the previous talents and set examples for later learners. If I could utter my heartfelt and sincere remarks about literature from former times, there is still more to be said about their levels of craftiness and clumsiness. Five colors coordinate each other; eight tones harmonize themselves. Similar to opaque and bright colors or yin-and-yang pitch pipes, each portends to its proper kind. One would like to have the lead note [*gong*] and end note [*yu*] played in alternation; falling and rising pitches regulate each other.[62] When a floating tone appears earlier, then a deflected tone should follow. Within the same line, sounds and rhymes should be varied; with two lines, light and heavy should be different. When one wondrously grasps this rule, then it is time to talk about literary writing.

Among the magnificent writings produced by writers of the past, [there are] Zijian's poetic presentations to Ding Yi [170?–220] and Wang Can, Zhongxuan's "Seven Sorrows" [Qi'ai], Zijing's [Sun Chu, 218–98] "Drizzling Rain," and Zhengzhang's [Wang Zan, d. 311] "Northern Wind" [Shuofeng].[63] Those who received critical acclaims invariably created from what was in their heart, not elaborations of historical sources. Exactly due to their lofty words and wondrous sounds, such writings exceeded their previous models. Beginning with Qu Yuan, many a generation of writers refined their styles of writing. Still, there had been no secret discovered for this art. As for lofty sounds and marvelous lines, euphony was achieved intuitively. All unwittingly conformed to the rules and seldom was there much conscious design. Zhang-Cai-Cao-Wang had no prescience. Pan-Lu-Xie-Yan were even farther removed. Those who understood the tone or could achieve tonal euphony would agree. Any wise person in the future who disagrees with what was said is worth waiting for.[64]

In this critical literary history, Shen Yue outlines the development of major literary trends, laboriously listing names of notable authors and titles of unforgettable pieces. At the very beginning, Shen posits that literary expressions, poetry in particular, are natural responses imbued with human "energy" (*qi*) and "spirit" (*ling*). This naturalist abstraction of literature is then followed with a chronologically arranged list of master writers and works of monumental status. *The Classic of Poetry* and *Songs of Chu* are the earliest sources of poetry. Qu Yuan, Jia Yi, and Sima Xiangru have been singled out for their literary accomplishments. Under Liu Che, Emperor

Wu of Han (156–87 BCE; r. 141–87 BCE), literature flourished for over half of a century. The language for poetry, a vocabulary of embellishment and dictions of ornamentation, was created. And then, as Shen Yue notes, there was a respite in refined writing during the second half of the Latter or Eastern Han (25–220), when Zhang Heng was a prolific writer. During Jian'an, the twilight years of Han, literati poets began composing with the five-syllable line. The development of poetry, however, stalled during the fourth century when ideas from *Laozi* and *Zhuangzi* dominated and confined literary creation.[65] Shen credits Xie Hun for turning the tide and Xie Lingyun for carrying the torch to advance lyric poetry, finishing what Jian'an writers had started.[66]

In this piece, arguably China's first literary history, Shen Yue emphasizes human emotion as the natural and driving force behind poetry. He identifies it as a common thread behind anonymous landmark works as found in *The Classic of Poetry* and *Songs of Chu* and authors such as Qu Yuan, Jia Yi, Zhang Heng, and the Jian'an writers. Shen places Xie Lingyun at the culmination of this history, while noting tonal euphony needs more deliberate design, a task he himself took on.[67] Shen's evaluation of Xie was echoed by other contemporary critics such as Zhong Rong, who traced Xie's influence to Cao Zhi, who lived two centuries earlier[68] In a widespread anecdote that similarly underscores this connection, Xie reportedly said: "If All-Under-Heaven has only ten pecks of talent, then eight of them have gone to Cao Zijian [Cao Zhi].[69] I have obtained one peck. The other one peck is to be shared by the rest of the world."[70] Cao Zhi, of course, is the poet-prince of Jian'an, standing for the literary glory of that era. To fully appreciate Xie Lingyun's affinity for the Jian'an style, we must focus on his emulation of the era's five-syllable-line lyric poetry.

CHAPTER 2

Performing Literary Friendship

During the Jian'an era (196–220) of the Eastern Han, major changes took place in the social identity and intellectual activities of the educated elite. The Jian'an master writers exerted unprecedented influence in later eras, especially in the field of literary production. A study of Xie Lingyun's transformation of *shi* poetry must therefore begin with his multifold emulation of the Jian'an poets, a group that included literary prodigies, erudite philosophers, ascetic scholars, and moral exemplars. Xie was inspired by their example to seek refuge and answers in art. Although two hundred years had passed, the sociopolitical unrest was not over. The Jian'an experience had much to teach for a descendant of a noble clan from the Central Plains.

Writers of the Jian'an Era

Thinkers of the twentieth century, such as Lu Xun (1881–1936) and Qian Mu (1895–1990), regarded the third century as a period that witnessed "the rise of individualism," "the awakening of literature," and "the liberation of the scholar-class."[1] Recent scholarship, however, has questioned the application of "individualism" and suggested instead "group" and "social circles" as more appropriate and effective analytical lenses for considering the changes in the intellectual identity of the scholar-class.[2] In literary production, the center had shifted from the imperial court to the local in the twilight years of the Han empire. The talented men of this era had lost institutional support. Foremost among the Jian'an masters was the military leader Cao Cao (155–220), who emerged in the late 190s as a patron of the arts and literature. A talented poet in his own right, his was the voice of a friend rather than an overlord, a mode of expression that harkened back to the Zhou meritocracy sanctioned in the Han Confucian texts.[3] Cao Cao's evocation of the Duke of Zhou as a model regent appealed to the disenchanted scholars who had recently witnessed the dissolution of the Han dynasty, and his restoration of Han court music promoted the development of lyric poetry.[4] In this environment, the five-syllable-line verse (*shi*) emerged as the preferred form of literati communication and restored friendship as a prevalent motif.[5] These literary tools gave writers the freedom to cross sociopolitical boundaries, creating an intimate and supportive milieu where personal voice and private feelings could be valued rather than eschewed.

Xie Lingyun's Poems of Emulation

One of Xie Lingyun's most widely appreciated works is "Eight Poems Reconstructing the Wei Crown Prince's Gathering in Ye" (hereafter, "Eight Poems"). Each poem is identified with the name of a Jian'an author and prefaced with a brief biography.[6] In these poems, Xie depicts a literary meritocracy associated with the Jian'an era.[7] Through carefully crafted personas and poetic voices, he envisioned and brought to life a court gathering where talented writers engaged in elegant discourse with the receptive prince mentioned in the title. In the general preface to the suite of poems, Xie adopts the voice of Cao Pi, the Wei crown prince.

> Toward the end of Jian'an, I took up residence in the Palace of Ye, where I hosted banquets and excursions to honor talented writers. Unreservedly, I indulged in the pleasure of their companionship. In this life, [there is] a fine hour, a beautiful sight, an appreciative mind, and a joyful event—[but] it is rare that all four elements come together. Now, with the presence of my younger brother [Cao Zhi], my literary companions, and a number of scholars, I have encountered and experienced the convergence of [the four pleasures of life]. Such perfect enjoyment has not been recorded in earlier documents. Why is this? In the times of King Xiang of Chu, there were Song Yu, Tang Le, and Jing Cuo.[8] At the court of King Xiao of Liang, there were Zou Yang, Mei Sheng, Yan Ji, and Sima Xiangru.[9] Those literary associates were refined, yet their ruler-patrons were not cultivated. At Emperor Wu of Han's court, Xu Yue and several other talented men were fully capable of furnishing responses in polite conversation and providing answers with regard to policymaking, yet there was suspicion on the part of the emperor and envy among the

members of the group.[10] How could they have obtained utterly candid communications? I do not wish to presume about future generations, as they surely will be worthier than today. Days and months rush along like flowing currents. Among the fallen, many were my friends. With this composition, I wish to remember them. Moved by events of those bygone days, my grief begins to mount.[11]

In Cao Pi's voice, Xie Lingyun explains the perfect harmony of literary friendship between the Wei prince and his talented scholars. Together they enjoyed precious moments of intellectual exchange and political consultation in Ye, where Cao Cao had established his power base and governed as Lord of Wei. Harmony depended on an enlightened ruler-patron relationship as well as talented people who trusted each other and openly shared private feelings and intimate thoughts. While lauding the conviviality of Cao Pi and his associates, Xie Lingyun mentions King Xiang of Chu (329–263 BCE) and King Xiao of Liang as inferior examples for being "uncultivated" (*buwen*) and lacking an "appreciative mind" (*shangxin*). He even faults Emperor Wu of Han for withholding trust, therefore causing jealousy and rivalry among his court gentlemen. Xie wryly comments that he shall refrain from making any slanderous remarks about his own time. Borrowing the voice of a dead prince, he safely suggests that harmony between prince or lords and talented men is missing at the Liu-Song court.

In style, Xie's preface imitates Cao Pi's famous letter to Wu Zhi, written in 215 and titled "Letter to Magistrate Wu Zhi," in which Cao longs nostalgically for the more enlightened past.[12] Although Cao Pi's vision of harmonious friendship may have been magnified over time, it reveals the importance the Wei rulers ascribed to a lord-courtier relationship built on the principles of equality and reciprocity.[13] Literary events, accompanied by other activities such as feasting, hunting, and sightseeing, symbolized the scholar-class and gave them a collective identity. As the classical archaeologist and Egyptologist Jan Assmann posits: "The elements of collective identity are underpinned by factors that are purely symbolic, and the social body is simply a metaphor—an imaginary construct. As such, however, it has its own position in reality. The collective or 'we' identity is the image that a group has of itself and with which its members associate themselves."[14]

Cao Pi's fond recollection of the Jian'an masters placed them outside the political and social hierarchy. As associates and friends, men of letters were valued for their talent in literature, which was, for the first time, elevated as a pillar of the state in Cao Pi's "Treatise on Literature" (Lun wen): "Literary refinement is the greatest endeavor by which to govern a state, a splendid activity that does not decay."[15] Like his father Cao Cao, Cao Pi was invested in the power of *wen* (literature) and made it a guiding principle in governance. The scholar-class were thus granted an independent place in sociopolitical life. This important change in post-Han intellectual life, however, was challenged in the politically tumultuous times that followed. Two centuries later, Xie Lingyun found himself lamenting the disregard for cultivated virtues. Liu Yu was the first of a slew of usurpers in the fifth century who oversaw the most barbaric regimes in Chinese history, and many men in the Xie family were killed during Liu Yu's path to the throne.[16] Xie Hun's execution was a mere premonition of Xie Lingyun's own fate.[17]

CAO PI

Jian'an writers for the most part did not live to fifty. Ruan Yu (ca. 167–212) passed away in the year 212.[18] A deadly plague ravaged northern China in 217 and killed Ying Yang (170?–217), Liu Zhen (ca. 170–217), Xu Gan (170–217/18), Chen Lin (160?–217), and Wang Can.[19] The Cao rulers, however, extended their influence beyond death via literary creation. Cao Pi, "while residing in the Eastern Palace [the residence for Crown Prince], composed over a hundred pieces of writing."[20] Xie Lingyun, through prosopopoeia, partakes vicariously in the Wei's prince's construction of an ideal moment in the past. In the first poem of the set, Xie rekindles the voice of Cao Pi:[21]

	百川赴巨海	All streams proceed to join the vast ocean;[22]
	眾星環北辰	myriad constellations circle the North Star.[23]
	照灼爛霄漢	Gleaming and shining, they light up the Empyrean Han;[24]
4	遙裔起長津	far and distant, they rise from the "Long Ford."[25]
	天地中橫潰	Between heaven and earth there were traverse flows;[26]
	家王拯生民	the King of the Cao Clan raised the common folk.[27]

	區宇既滌蕩	He scoured clean areas under the eaves;[28]
8	羣英必來臻	men of talent came to him in throngs.
	忝此欽賢性	This humble person is endowed with reverence for the worthy;[29]
	由來常懷仁	all along I have cherished the principle of benevolence.[30]
	況值眾君子	Now that I have encountered these many gentlemen,[31]
12	傾心隆日新	whole-heartedly, I devote to "Daily renewing [of virtue]."[32]
	論物靡浮說	In discourses about the physical world, we avoid empty talk;
	析理實敷陳	in analyzing the "principle," we lay out "actuality."[33]
	羅縷豈闕辭	In listing minute details, there never is a shortage of terms;
16	窈窕究天人	into the subtle and profound, we investigate heaven and humankind.
	澄觴滿金罍	Clear ale fills the bronze vessels to the brim;
	連榻設華茵	joined couches are decorated with magnificent mattresses.
	急弦動飛听	Agitating strings stir up high-flying sounds,
20	清歌拂梁塵	clear singing sweeps dust on the beam.[34]
	莫言相遇易	Don't say that our meeting is easy—
	此歡信可珍	such joy is rare indeed.

The first section of the poem, couplets 1 through 4, focuses not on Cao Pi, but on his father Cao Cao, who is praised here as a savior of the world and a worthy ruler who offers protection and patronage to the talented and worthy in the tumultuous twilight days of the Han empire. Couplets 5 through 8 portray Cao Pi as a humble and benevolent patron-prince who follows in the footsteps of his father and serves the scholar class. The last section, couplets 9 through 11, describes a banquet scene and stresses the rarity of the harmonious relationship between the prince and his advisors.

It is worth noting that Xie Lingyun's description of the historical context from which the Cao family rose to power and played a significant role in restoring sociopolitical order bears resemblance to the 380s, when the Xies stabilized the Eastern Jin court and prevented foreign invasion and internecine conflicts. The same prideful tone of a scion from a noble family characterizes Xie's two-part poem "Narrating My Forebears' Virtue" (Shu zude shi), which will be discussed in the next chapter.[35] In terms of intertextual usage, Xie alludes to the *Analects*, the *Mengzi*, *The Classic of Changes*, and the *Zhuangzi* for notions on benevolent government and moral cultivation, two apt traits for the future founder of the Wei dynasty.

WANG CAN

No writer of Jian'an gave us a more visceral account of the death and devastation the period had witnessed than Wang Can, who is the second impersonated subject in Xie Lingyun's poetic set.[36] With a preface, Xie provides an elegant tetra-syllabic summary of Wang Can's life: "Coming from a household in Qinchuan [a region consisting of modern Shaanxi and Gansu], I am the noble offspring of a ducal clan; now that I have encountered chaos, I am driven to exile and in search of a home. Bemoaning my fate, I have much sorrowful emotion."[37]

	幽厲昔崩亂	Kings You and Li of Zhou experienced turmoil and downfall;
	桓靈今板蕩	Emperors Huan and Ling of Han now are experiencing the quaking earth.[38]
	伊洛既燎煙	Between the rivers Yi and Luo there was conflagration and smoke;
4	函崤沒無像	over Hangu Pass and Mount Yao, all were sunken and sightless.[39]
	整裝辭秦川	With my luggage packed, I took leave of the Qin River Basin;[40]
	秣馬赴楚壤	foddering my horse, I departed for the land of Chu.[41]
	沮漳自可美	The Ju and Zhang rivers were truly gorgeous;
8	客心非外獎	yet to the heart of a sojourner, their appeal was naught but an appearance.[42]

	常嘆詩人言	Often, I would sigh over what is said in the Odes:
	式微何由往	"When good times are over, where can I go?"[43]
	上宰奉皇靈	The Supreme Chancellor, in reverently serving the August Divinity,[44]
12	侯伯咸宗長	was widely honored by lords and noblemen.[45]
	雲騎亂漢南	Cavalry thick as clouds disrupted the area south of the Han River;
	紀郢皆掃蕩	the lands of Ji and Ying were swept clean.
	排霧屬盛明	Eliminating the pernicious vapor, Splendorous Luminescence is revealed;
16	披雲對清朗	separating clouds, I faced the Lucid Brilliance.[46]
	慶泰欲重疊	Felicity and great harmony arrived in multiplication;
	公子特先賞	the young lord was particularly appreciative of the talented.[47]
	不謂息肩願	It was not that I wished to take refuge,[48]
20	一旦值明兩	but that I encountered the Double Brightness.[49]
	並載游鄴京	Sharing a chariot, we roamed the capital of Ye;
	方舟泛河廣	in linked boats, we sailed across the Yangzi.
	綢繆清燕娛	Intimately, we enjoyed the pleasures at the lord's feast;
24	寂寥梁棟響	on quiet nights, there were clear sounds encircling the beams.
	既作長夜飲	Having had our night long drinking,
	豈顧乘日養	how could we fret over the daily sustenance?[50]

The first five couplets of this poem recall the theme and semantics of Wang Can's famous works: the "Seven Sorrows" poems and the "*Fu* on Ascending the Tower,*" in which the poet speaks about the fall of the Han capital Chang'an and his subsequent displacement in the south. Couplets 6 through 10 reflect Xie's penchant for using vocabulary of a high register, appropriate for grand historical events. The final three couplets eulogize the triumph and subsequent patronage of the Cao court, where Wang Can was able to take refuge.

The third poem of this set is titled after the writer Chen Lin who served as an administrator under several military generals in the chaotic last decades of Han. The preface reads: "Chen Lin was a scholar-official who served in the secretariat of Yuan Benchu [aka Yuan Shao; 154–202] and, therefore, his writings were mostly about matters of death and devastation.[51]

	皇漢逢屯邅	August Han encountered adverse difficulties;
	天下遭氛慝	all under heaven suffered from "poisonous miasma."[52]
	董氏淪關西	Dong Zhuo ransacked the area west of the Hangu Pass;
4	袁家擁河北	Yuan Shao held the area north of the Yellow River.[53]
	單民易周章	People were exhausted from turbulent transferences;[54]
	窘身就羈勒	in straitened circumstances, I was tethered in service.[55]
	豈意事乖己	Who could have predicted that affairs would go awry?
8	永懷戀故國	in constant yearning, I longed for the old state.
	相公實勤王	The prime minister toiled earnestly on behalf of the emperor;[56]
	信能定蚤賊	for certain, he could pacify the pestilent bandits.
	復覩東都輝	Once again, we would witness the glory of the Eastern Capital,[57]
12	重見漢朝則	time again the precepts of Han shall manifest.
	余生幸已多	For this life of mine, there was abundant good fortune,
	矤乃值明德	how much more so now that I have encountered His Luminous Virtue.[58]
	愛客不告疲	With such care for his guests, he seldom complained of weariness;[59]
16	飲燕遺景刻	drinking and feasting, we lost track of the water clock's notches.

	夜听極星闌	The evening concerts lasted till stars faded;

夜听極星闌　The evening concerts lasted till stars faded;
朝游窮曛黑　our morning excursions ended when light gave way to darkness.

哀哇動梁埃　Sorrowful singing stirred the dust on the beams;
20　急觴蕩幽默　encouragements to drink replaced silence and reticence.[60]

且盡一日娛　Allow us to enjoy pleasures of this day to the full—

莫知古來惑　and forget about all the age-old worries.

The first four couplets of the poem describe the disaster that had befallen the Han toward the end of the second century. Couplets 5 and 6 mention Cao Cao's rise, which brought peace and order to the world. The poet then devotes the final five couplets to praising the patronage of the Cao court and describing convivial parties and social gatherings hosted by Cao Pi. Through a tripartite structure, Xie's poem weaves together a narrative in the Jian'an style that laments Han's collapse, lauds the patronage of Cao Cao, and culminates in a verbally and emotionally glorifying banquet scene.

XU GAN

The fourth poem is written in the name of Xu Gan, the author of *Balanced Discourses* (Zhonglun), an acclaimed philosophical text.[61] Around 207, Cao Cao invited Xu Gan to join his staff and appointed him as a consultant to the army in the Ministry of Works.[62] In 208, Xu Gan accompanied Cao Cao on a southern expedition and participated in the battle of Red Cliffs. It was around this time that Xu Gan composed "*Fu* on Recounting the Expedition" (Xu zheng fu), which calls to mind Xie's "Zhuan zheng fu." Xu's secretarial role also bore similarity to that of Xie in eulogizing an overlord's military feat to stabilize and unify the empire.[63] In 211, when Cao Pi was appointed Leader of Court Gentlemen for Miscellaneous Uses (Wuguan Zhonglang Jiang), Xu served as his secretary.[64] Around the year 214, Xu was made an instructor to Cao Zhi, who had been enfeoffed as Marquis of Linzi (modern Zibo, Shandong). Around 216, Xu Gan became ill and died the next year in the epidemic. In the preface to the poem "Xu Gan," Xie praises the philosopher for his pure-mindedness: "Xu Gan had lacked ambition for official trappings since a tender age.[65] Instead, he harbored thoughts for Mount Ji and River Ying.[66] Because of the troubles of the world, he emerged to serve in order to save the masses. His writings were noted for a chaste quality."[67]

	伊昔家臨淄	Previously I had lived in Linzi,
	提攜弄齊瑟	where, with a like-minded friend, I played the zither from Qi.[68]
	置酒飲膠東	Setting out jars of ale, we drank in Jiaodong;[69]
4	淹留憩高密	during a long sojourn, I respited in Gaomi.[70]
	此歡謂可終	In pleasure such as this, I could end my days;
	外物始難畢	external things, however, would not cease.
	搖蕩箕濮情	Buffeted about, shaken was my Ji-Pu resolve;[71]
8	窮年迫憂慄	in a straitened year, I was hard pressed by worries and apprehensions.
	末塗幸休明	In dire circumstances, fortune led me to Blessed Illumination,[72]
	棲集建薄質	[allowing me to] rest and apply my meager talents.
	已免負薪苦	Already exempted from the work of bearing firewood,
12	仍遊椒蘭室	I rambled in chambers scented with fagara pepper and thoroughwort.
	清論事究萬	In our pure conversations, we investigated myriad matters;
	美話信非一	of our dialogues, there were more than one that was truly remarkable.
	行觴奏悲歌	As we passed the cups, an impassioned song was performed;
16	永夜繫白日	an endless night morphed into the light of the day.
	華屋非蓬居	Gorgeous chambers were certainly not my previous thatched hut;
	時髦豈余匹	how could my humble person match the luminaries of our era?

| 中飲顧昔心 | Deep in the cups, I recalled my original intention— |
| 20　恨焉若有失 | rueful, I felt as if something had been amiss. |

The poem on Xu Gan departs from the previous three poems with its emphasis on the named literatus's aspiration for reclusion. The first part, composed of four couplets, describes Xu's life before he served the Cao court. He enjoyed music and preferred the companionship of like-minded friends to court service. But contrary to Xu's wish to live out his life as a recluse, he ended up serving at Cao Cao's court. Couplets 5 through 9 describe the convivial activities enjoyed by men of letters and their newfound stability. The poem ends with a lament where Xie, through the impersonated voice of Xu Gan, seems to be expressing his own thwarted wish to return to the life of a recluse, a thinly veiled criticism of an unenlightened regime.

LIU ZHEN

The fifth poem is on Liu Zhen (style name Gonggan), a distant offspring of the Han dynasty Prince of Liang. As a writer, Liu Zhen was best known for his achievement in the five-syllable-line verse.[73] In the preface, Xie Lingyun describes Liu Zhen as "eccentric," "yet demonstrating a most vigorous writing style," and that "his attainments reflect a familiarity with the classics and also an extraordinary quality."[74] This evaluation probably had an influence on the fifth-century critic Zhong Rong's praise for Liu's "vigor" (*qi*) in the following terms: "His style shows an affinity with the *Odes*. Relying on his vigor, he was fond of the unusual. . . . However, his personal vigor dominated his literary style, resulting in a regrettable lack of embellishment.[75] *Qi* as an important critical valence was first raised explicitly in Cao Pi's "Treatise on Literature," where the prince-critic regarded *qi* as the key element of a literary work, for it stands for the vitality and individuality of a writer.[76] Xie Lingyun begins the "Liu Zhen" poem with an account of his humble origin.

| 貧居晏里閈 | In poverty, I lived in the "low gate" village of Yanzi,[77] |
| 少小長東平 | I grew up in Dongping.[78] |

	河衰當衝要	Yanzhou, by the Yellow River, was located at a major crossroads;
4	淪飄薄許京	drifting about—I found myself in Xu.[79]
	廣川無逆流	In the broad stream, there was no adverse current;[80]
	招納廁群英	summoned, I was placed among the ranks of talented people.
	北渡黎陽津	Northward we crossed the Liyang ford;[81]
8	南登紀郢城	southward we ascended the walls of Jiying.[82]
	既覽古今事	Having observed events of past and present times,
	頗識治亂情	I came to recognize the true nature of order and chaos.
	歡友相解達	Close friends understood and supported me;
12	敷奏究平生	through writing, I investigated matters of this life.
	矧荷明哲顧	Further, I was obliged to the favor from the Enlightened One;[83]
	知深覺命輕	his appreciation was deep; my heaven-ordained life was inconsequential.
	朝遊牛羊下	In the morning, we roamed until cows and sheep came down;
16	暮坐括揭鳴	at dusk, we sat around till the roosters crowed.[84]
	終歲非一日	Throughout the year, many days went by like this,
	傳卮弄清聲	over goblets of wine, we played clear tones.
	辰事既難諧	Times and events hardly converged in harmony,
20	歡願如今并	yet my wishes and desires were completely fulfilled on this day.
	唯羨肅肅翰	I could only envy the feathered kind, swooshing by;
	繽紛戾高冥	in throngs, they reach beyond the remote heavens.

The impersonated self-narration of Liu Zhen focuses on his service to Cao Cao during the latter's military campaigns. Xie's adoption of the voice of a soldier by citing "Broomcorn Millet Hangs Heavy" (Shu li; Mao 65) in lines 15 and 16 gives the narrative a reflective tone, echoing the lament songs in *The Classic of Poetry*. Through Liu Zhen, who had served on Cao Cao's military staff, Xie made known his reservations about war. In the final couplet, the imagery of flocks of high-flying birds disappearing into the firmament may be interpreted as a wish to live a life free from service. The revelation of such a subtle standpoint is only possible through the use of *The Classic of Poetry*, the canonical corpus showcasing the gamut of human emotional expression. Readers respond to the pensive reflection evoked through the familiar lines from "Broomcorn Millet Hangs Heavy." This piece adds to the rich dimensions of the collective experiences of Jian'an, a momentous time when historical players were challenged and galvanized. These master writers were heroes who harbored lofty aspirations, ready to give their lives, but they were also humans whose yearning for freedom and pathos over the loss of life was all too compelling.

YING YANG

The sixth poem in Xie Lingyun's Jian'an collection is "Ying Yang." Ying Yang came from a family of writers and was initially appointed to serve under Cao Zhi because of his literary talent.[85] He later joined Cao Pi's staff in 211. Xie's preface reads: "Originating from the vicinity of Ru and Ying, where the two rivers flowed through the Han Commandery of Runan [modern Henan] into the Huai River, [Ying] met with dispersal and separation due to the events of his day. He expressed much lament about instability and impoverishment."[86] The poem proper begins where the "Liu Zhen" piece leaves off, with imagery of soaring birds.[87]

	嗷嗷雲中鴈	*Ao, ao* cried the goose in the clouds;[88]
	舉翮自委羽	raising its pinions, it took leave of Mount Tucked Wings.[89]
	求涼弱水湄	Seeking coolness—it arrived on the banks of Weak Water,[90]
4	違寒長沙渚	eschewing the cold season—it alighted on the sandbars of Changsha.
	顧我梁川時	Thinking back to my days in Liangchuan—[91]
	緩步集潁許	there I paced leisurely, arriving in Ying and Xu.[92]
	一旦逢世難	One day, I met with the catastrophe of our age;

8	淪薄恒覊旅	buffeted about, a life on the road became my constant.
	天下昔未定	The world was unstable;
	託身早得所	I had given myself a place to perch.
	官渡厠一卒	At Guandu, I had been a foot-soldier;[93]
12	烏林預艱阻	at Wulin, there had been anticipated hardships.[94]
	晚節值眾賢	Late in life, I joined in the crowd of worthy men;
	會同庇天宇	together, we were protected under Heaven's Canopy.[95]
	列坐廕華榱	Sitting side by side, we were sheltered under the floral pillars;
16	金樽盈清醑	bronze goblets were presented with clear wine filled to the brim.
	始奏延露曲	In the beginning, there was the performance of "Receiving Dew,"[96]
	繼以闌夕語	then we carried out conversations deep into the night.
	調笑輒酬答	Asides from jesting repartee, we exchanged poems;
20	嘲謔無慙沮	teasing and laughing, there were no insults or hurt feelings.
	傾軀無遺慮	Even if one had to give up his person, there would be no regrets;
	在心良已敘	it was from the heart that trust had been expressed.

In this three-part poem, the opening bird imagery alludes to "Great Geese" in *The Classic of Poetry* (Hong yan; Mao 181)—an ode to King Xuan of Zhou (862–782 BCE), who restored stability in the tumultuous final decades of the Western Zhou. This allusion sets Xie's eulogistic tone, in which he pays tribute to Cao Cao, who similarly brought stability to the Han noble families and masses. The poem mentions battles with Yuan Shao and Zhou Yu before Cao Cao unified the Central Plains. The second part, consisting of five couplets, is an account of how the Cao court offered refuge for the displaced scholar. The conviviality and harmony restored trust among the different groups that were congregating under Cao Cao's leadership. The banquet scene culminates with a vow of loyalty and ultimate dedication.

The penultimate piece in this set is titled "Ruan Yu."[97] An older scholar in the group, Ruan Yu studied with the Han polymath Cai Yong (133–92), who was forced into an alliance with Dong Zhuo and later executed. In the preface, Xie Lingyun characterizes Ruan Yu's literary language with a mimicking binome, *youwo*, meaning "rich and abundant."[98]

	河洲多沙塵	Over the land of the Yellow River, there was much sandy dust;
	風悲黃雲起	in the mourning wind, brown clouds rose.
	金羈相馳逐	Chariots drawn by metal-bridled horses chased and galloped;
4	連翩何窮已	in close succession, their race went on with no end in sight.
	慶雲惠優渥	Felicitous clouds sent down abundant moisture and rain;
	微薄攀多士	with a meager talent, I clambered to the rank of "various officers."[99]
	念昔渤海時	Thinking back on those years in Bohai,[100]
8	南皮戲清沚	in Nanpi we frolicked in the limpid streams.[101]
	今復河曲遊	Now we roam along the bend of the Yellow River;[102]
	鳴葭汎蘭汜	sounding the reed pipes, we bob on the thoroughwort stream.
	躍步陵丹梯	Walking leisurely, we climb the vermilion steps;
12	並坐侍君子	side by side, we serve our lord,
	妍談既愉心	We engage in conversations that delight our heart;
	哀音信睦耳	mournful tones indeed are pleasant to the ear,
	傾酤係芳醑	We pour ale and then some fine wine—
16	酌言豈終始	deep in the cups, we forget about time.
	自從食蓱來	Since I became an invited guest,[103]
	唯見今日美	today is most enjoyable.

An account of Ruan Yu's military service and celebratory feasts, the penultimate poem of Xie's set is yet another display of the poet's skillful use of imagistic language, which depicts grand historical events in a reve-latory personal voice.

CAO ZHI

Xie's set of poems dedicated to the Jian'an masters culminates with "Cao Zhi," who was the son of Cao Cao and brother of Cao Pi, and also known as the Marquis of Pingyuan.[104] Born into a political family, Cao Zhi was a pure-minded artist. His literary talent earned him the highest accolades from Xie, a proud poet who saw himself as second only to the Wei prince. Xie's preface reads: "The prince did not care for worldly matters. He only prized making friends and roaming with his associates. His writings were tinged with sorrowful laments about life."[105]

	朝遊登鳳閣	Roaming in the morning, we ascended the phoenix tower;
	日暮集華沼	at dusk, we gathered by the floriated pond.
	傾柯引弱枝	From drooping boughs, tender twigs hung down;
4	攀條摘蕙草	pulling on the branches, we plucked patchouli.
	徒倚窮騁望	Pacing to and fro, we gazed far into the distance—
	目極盡所討	what our eyes could see were all that had been conquered.
	西顧太行山	Looking west, it was Mount Taihang;
8	北眺邯鄲道	To the north, we saw the thoroughfare to Handan.
	平衢修且直	Smooth roads were long and straight;
	白楊信裊裊	white poplars waved gently in the wind.
	副君命飲宴	The Heir Apparent ordered a drinking feast;[106]
12	歡娛寫懷抱	joyfully we released and let out our emotions inside.
	良遊匪晝夜	With good friends we roamed, forgetting day or night—
	豈云晚與早	who cared whether it was morning or evening?
	眾賓悉精妙	All guests were well-versed in refined subjects;
16	清辭灑蘭藻	their pure words sprinkled forth like fragrant ornaments.
	哀音下迴鵠	Mournful music brought down circling geese;

餘哇徹清昊　　　lingering songs pierced the pure heaven.

中山不知醉　　　Over the ale from Zhongshan, we didn't know to
　　　　　　　　　　get drunk;

20　飲德方覺飽　　　only in the nectar of virtue could we feel sated.

願以黃髮期　　　We wish we could grow old like this,

養生念將老　　　nourishing our lives as we approach old age.

This piece culminates in the theme of convivial friendship among the Cao family patron-prince and the literary masters of Jian'an. Written in the voice of Cao Zhi, it begins with a scenic description with a metaphorical dimension. The images of "ascending phoenix" and "gathering blossoms" in the first couplet stand for the talented people. So do the drooping boughs that join with tender twigs and fragrant herbs. Also interconnected and offering mutual support is the society at the Cao court. Couplet four refers to Cao Cao's military campaigns. Couplets five through ten offer an account of the banquet scene. The literary impersonation of Cao Zhi is a fitting summary of the whole set. It both highlights the virtue and harmony of the Cao court and accentuates the court's culture of cherishing literary talent, which is rooted in the patrons' own "refinement" (*wen*). Cao Zhi was the most talented writer of the Cao family and his entire generation. Xie envisions an unattainable immortal land where literary companions roamed and associated with Cao Zhi—the uncrowned king of literature and refined culture.

Throughout this set of eight poems, Xie finds aspects of the poets with which he identifies. Each poem has a distinctive tone. The shared component of the set, constituting an overarching theme throughout the eight poems, is the description of a gathering and banquet held under the auspices of the court. Xie, by remembering and literarily reconstructing the Jian'an court, hopes to restore a lost ideal, in which he sees himself as part of a literary society that transcends time.[107] In the 420s, as the power of noble families waned, the sociopolitical status and identity of Xie Lingyun and his class faced real threats. As if to brace for what was coming, Xie looked to the Jian'an masters and the moral paragons in his own family for inspiration.

CHAPTER 3

The Untrammeled Hero

One century after the Jian'an period came to an end, turmoil again embroiled the Central Plains. In the 310s, Chang'an and Luoyang fell to the invading Xiongnu nomads from the Eurasian steppe. One of the Jin princes, supported by the Wang clan of Langye (modern Shandong), set up a court south of the Yangzi, and Jiankang (modern Nanjing) was established in 317 as the southern capital. For much of the Eastern Jin, "prominent families" played an important role in stabilizing the court, where weak emperors were threatened by military strongmen who plotted usurpation.[1]

The Legend of the Xie Clan

The Xie clan's influence began to rise in the middle of the fourth century. Xie An, Xie Lingyun's great-granduncle, emerged as the "savior" of Jin in both domestic affairs and foreign relations. He was remembered as the "strongest character" out of the 623 notable personalities mentioned in *A New Account of the Tales of the World* (Shishuo xinyu), a collection of anecdotes and quasi-historical events about real people from the second to the fourth centuries.[2] Xie An orchestrated the legendary Fei River Battle in 383, with Xie Xuan, Xie Lingyun's grandfather, serving as a general.[3] Although victory in that conflict secured both the Jin house and the Xies' political clout, they distanced themselves from the court to avoid a power struggle.[4] In 385, Xie An passed away and Xie Xuan returned to Guiji.[5]

The Xie family estate in Guiji is famously referred to as Eastern Mountain (Dongshan)—a name associated with the Duke of Zhou, who played an instrumental role in assisting the young King Cheng in spite of vicious rumors spread by his enemies about the Duke's intention to usurp the throne. In *The Classic of Poetry*, the poem "Eastern Mountain" (Dongshan; Mao 156) commemorates the duke's military campaign to the east to pacify the insurrections.[6] Aside from being considered a loyal and trustworthy minister, Xie An was valued among fourth-century elites for his eremitism. Eastern Mountain emerged as a multivalent symbol, speaking to Xie An's moral, political, and spiritual prowess. In *A New Account of Tales of the World*, Xie An's courage and composure when facing life or death situations are presented as examples of transcendent behavior. As the late East Asian historian Michael Rogers posits: "Xie An's legend . . . does not depict an isolated great man, hurling a challenge into the teeth of fate and commanding the tides of history; his heroics are of a gentler order, and seem to be predicated of him more as a member of a collectivity than as an individual." The Xies represented a great cultural ideal that Rogers calls "the inevitable triumph of spirit over brute force."[7]

This "way of the gentleman" (*junzi zhi dao*), as exemplified in Xie An and emulated by other members of the Xie clan, was lauded in *New Account*, compiled about two decades after Xie Lingyun's death. In the twilight years of the Jin, military strongmen and ruthlessly practical administrators dominated the court. As a result of his first-hand experience with this irreversible decline of the noble way, Xie Lingyun wrote "Recounting Ancestral Virtues" (Shu zude shi; hereafter, "Recounting Virtues"), likely as an admonishment to Liu Yu. The two-part poem begins with a preface:[8]

In the middle of the Taiyuan reign (376–97), my grandfather [Xie Xuan] pacified Huainan. He bore the family heritage handed down through generations. He revered the ruler and uplifted the people. When the Worthy Minister [Xie An] suddenly encountered his demise, the way of the gentleman waned. He [Xie Xuan] gathered his robes and left for his estate. He made divinations at the Eastern Mountain. In actuality, his deeds equaled those of Scholar Yue; his aims matched those of Fan Li.[9]

太元中。王父龕定淮南。負荷世業。尊主隆人。逮賢相徂謝。君子道消。拂衣蕃岳。考卜東山。事同樂生之時。志期范蠡之舉。

PART I

	達人貴自我	A man of penetrating vision values the self;
	高情屬天雲	his lofty sentiments extend to heavens and clouds.
	兼抱濟物性	Simultaneously, he is disposed to assist the world,
4	而不纓垢氛	and yet he does not get entangled in dirt or grime.

	段生蕃魏國	Master Duan protected the state of Wei;[10]
	展季救魯人	Zhan Ji saved the people of Lu.
	弦高犒晉師	Xiangao rewarded the [Qin] troops in Jin;
8	仲連卻秦軍	Zhonglian repulsed the army of Qin.
	臨組乍不緤	When bestowed silk sashes, they at once declined to wear;
	對珪寧肯分	when offered a jade tablet, they decidedly refused to share.
	惠物辭所賞	Benefitting the world, they eschewed rewards;
12	勵志故絕人	by steeling their resolve, they rose above others.
	苕苕歷千載	Far-reaching, their stories were passed down for a thousand years;
	遙遙播清塵	over a great distance, their pure dust has spread far.[11]
	清塵竟誰嗣	Their pure dust—who in the end would inherit it?
16	明哲時經綸	The perspicacious and sagacious one in time managed state affairs.[12]
	委講綴道論	Quitting debates and discourses, he set aside disquisitions into the Way;
	改服康世屯	he altered his attire to bring stability to a world in adversity.
	屯難既云康	After adversity and hardship gave way to stability,
20	尊主隆斯民	he then revered the lord and raised the masses.

PART II

	中原昔喪亂	The Central Plains suffered from chaos and disorder;
	喪亂豈解已	could the chaos and disorder ever be dispelled?
	崩騰永嘉末	Collapsing and crumbling happened at the end of Yongjia [307–13];
4	逼迫太元始	pushing and pressing occurred at the beginning of Taiyuan [376–96].
	河外無反正	East of the Yellow River, there was no turning the tide;
	江介有蹙圮	on the banks of the Yangzi, the land became cramped and ruined.
	萬邦咸震懾	A myriad states shook in fear;

	橫流賴君子	in a time of turmoil, the world relied on the gentleman.
8	橫流賴君子	in a time of turmoil, the world relied on the gentleman.
	拯溺由道情	Rescuing those in need accorded with the essence of the Way;
	龕暴資神理	to quell violence, he followed the divine principle.
	秦趙欣來蘇	Qin and Zhao were happy to be restored;
12	燕魏遲文軌	Yan and Wei waited for unification.
	賢相謝世運	The Worthy Minister took leave and left the world behind,[13]
	遠圖因事止	his far-reaching plans were thwarted because of the circumstances.
	高揖七州外	With a deep bow, he left the Seven Regions;
16	拂衣五湖裏	gathering his robes, he descended to the Five Lakes.
	隨山疏濬潭	Along the mountain, he drained deep ponds;
	傍巖藝枌梓	against the cliffs, he planted elms and catalpa.
	遺情捨塵物	Foregoing worldly passions, he cast aside dusty things;
20	貞觀丘壑美	with undivided attention, he investigated the beauty of mountains and valleys.

The significance of this piece is reflected in how it is anthologized in the *Wen xuan*, which altogether has twenty-three categories of *shi* poetry. The "Recounting Virtues" (Shude) category occupies second place, and Xie Lingyun's "Recounting Ancestral Virtues" is the only example, suggesting that this category was created specifically for Xie. Before "Recounting Virtues" is "Supplying for the Missing" (Buwang)—a group of six reconstructed eulogistic poems from *The Classic of Poetry*. Because that canonical text lacked authors, Xie Lingyun became the first named poet in the *Wen xuan*, whose compiler, Xiao Tong, had probably been influenced by Shen Yue. Xie thus towered over all named poets from the Han to the turn of the sixth century, an honor consistent with the critical evaluations of Zhong Rong and others. The status of the piece may also have been a factor of the veneration associated with the Xie clan after the Liu-Song. A few other "Recounting Virtues" poetic works were written by poets before Xie Lingyun's time, but they are not included in the *Wen xuan*.[14] Two examples include Lu Ji's (261–303) "Recounting Ancestral Virtues: A *Fu*" (Zude fu), and Cai Yong's and Yu Jun's (?–273) "Recounting Ancestral Virtues: A Eulogy" (Zude song).[15] Lu Ji's work, a eulogy for his grandfather, the Wu state general and minister Lu Xun (183–245), is most famous among these. Part of the work is preserved in the early Tang miscellany *Classified Extracts from Literature* (Yiwen leiju).[16]

	咨時文之懿祖	Alas, such refinement of my venerated grandfather!
	膺降神之靈曜	His [brilliance] matched the Numinous Dazzle of a descending god.[17]
	栖九德以弘道	Abiding in Nine Virtues, he propagated the Way;[18]
4	振風烈以增劭	spreading his moral influence, he added to its advancement.
	彼劉公之矯矯	How arrogant was that Lord Liu![19]
	固雲網之逸禽	He was but a bird set loose from the cloud net.[20]
	既憑形以傲物	Relying on Shu's topography, he slighted others;
8	諒傅翼而栖林	riding on the imperial wing, he settled in the grove.[21]
	伊我公之秀武	Our lord was truly superior and mighty;
	思無幽而弗昶	there was no tenuity that his thinking did not penetrate.
	形鮮烈於懷霜	His distinctive figure was more intense than frost;
12	澤溫惠乎挾纊	his beneficence was warmer than a quilt.
	牧希世之洪捷	He orchestrated an exceptionally grand victory;[22]
	固山谷而為量	its impact was measurable only by mountains and valleys.
	西夏坦其無塵	Western Xia was pacified without dust of war;
16	帝命赫而大壯	he propagated the emperor's charge, making it prominent.[23]

登具瞻於太階　　Ascending high, regarded by all, he was on the
　　　　　　　　　　Grand Stairway;

濯長纓乎天漢　　he cleansed the long tassel in the Heavenly
　　　　　　　　　　River.

解戎衣以高揖　　Shedding the armor, he bowed reverently;[24]

20　正端冕而大觀　straightening his black cap, he broadly
　　　　　　　　　　surveyed.

戢靈武於既曜　　He gathered numinous might while it shone;

恢時文於未煥　　he aggrandized civil virtue to make it vibrant.

騰絕風以逸鶩　　He revived distant customs and made them
　　　　　　　　　　soar again;

24　庶遐蹤于公旦　and followed the remote footsteps of the Duke
　　　　　　　　　　of Zhou.

Lu Ji's eulogy is written in what I call a hybrid mode—combining diction that recalls the Zhou temple hymns from *The Classic of Poetry* and prosody of the Chu *sao*-style. The ancestor-god who receives the praise here is Lu Xun, grandfather of Lu Ji. The Lu clan's service to the state of Wu was instrumental, especially in vanquishing the threat coming from the western state of Shu. Lu Xun personally led the final battle and was later honored as a minister. In this piece, the poet compares his grandfather to the exalted Duke of Zhou—the minister famous for loyalty and statesmanship.

This motif of "ancestor-praising" is refreshed in Xie Lingyun's rendition that utilizes the five-syllable line that muted the innate hybridity as seen in Lu Ji's piece. The effect is a compact and clear delivery with intriguing intertextual layering and play. The two-part poem is prefaced with a succinct narrative that embodies Han Confucian historiography, where terseness and subtlety are prized over explicit value judgment. The poet first uses three four-word phrases to sum up his grandfather Xie Xuan's meritorious deeds. More importantly, the Xie clan's collective loyalty to the Jin house is highlighted. The Xies had become the moral paragon of Eastern Jin. In the next part of the preface, the poet adopts four four-word phrases, creating an incremental argument. Here it is explained that along with Xie An's passing, the "way of the gentleman" (governance through the power of virtue instead of brute force) disappeared. Xie Xuan's timely withdrawal from a court that had lost its way is likened to historical exemplars of the Zhou, including an implicit reference to the Duke of Zhou, the fourth son of King Wen and the younger brother of King Wu.[25] Although dedicated to assisting the young King Cheng after King Wu died, the Duke of Zhou's loyalty was questioned. The rumors spread by other princes forced him to leave the capital. He divined the fortune of the state with oracle bones and led a three-year campaign to the east. The Duke of Zhou, after having vanquished the rebellions, reunited with King Cheng. The poem "Eastern Mountain" (Dongshan; Mao 156) from *The Classic of Poetry* was dedicated to the Duke of Zhou. In Xie Lingyun's poem, the term "Dongshan," while referring to the mountains in eastern Zhejiang where the Xie family estate was located, evokes the Duke of Zhou, whose name was associated with the poem. Xie's choice of words, as seen here and elsewhere, creates crossroads into canonical texts, generating rich historical associations and a layered reading experience.

Additional allusions to history are found in the main text. Lines 5 through 10 of Part I tell the stories of four historical men from the Eastern Zhou (770–256 BCE). Duangan Mu (ca. fl. 475–396 BCE) was a famous recluse during the Warring States period. His reputation as a worthy man helped thwart Qin's aggression against Wei.[26] In line 6, Zhan Ji (720–621 BCE), also known as Zhan Qin or Zhan Huo, a distant descendant of the Duke of Zhou, lived in the state of Lu. Because he was enfeoffed at a place known as Liuxia, Zhan Ji was posthumously known as Hui of Liuxia (aka Liuxia Hui or the "Gentleman from Liuxia"). Thrice dismissed from office, Zhan Ji lived as a recluse and yet gained a reputation for his noble character.[27] Zhan Ji's brother Zhan Xi (fl. 634 BCE), through a proactive reward ceremony, thwarted the troops of Qi.[28] Xiangao (in line 7), a merchant of Zheng, became a hero for turning back an invading Qin army by feigning a reward ceremony.[29] Line 8 praises Lu Zhonglian (ca. 305–245 BCE), a man from Qi who was talented yet unemployed, and saved Zhao with a persuasive speech.[30]

These allusions share a common thread that is made evident with a uniform syntax as well as an undertext that delineates the meritorious deeds of Xie Xuan. The rich contextualization, made succinct via the five-syllable line and parallel structure, allows the poet to present complex and intricate information with clarity. While tales from the Zhou are on the surface of the poem, references to Xie Xuan's battle in recent history are evoked through place names such as "Jin" and "Qin." The Battle of the Fei River was fought between the Eastern "Jin" and the Former "Qin." In lines 7 and 8, by placing Jin in the first line of the couplet and Qin in the second, matching "rewarding Jin" with "repulsing Qin," the poet calls attention to the heroic deeds of his forefathers.

Beyond Sagehood: Reaching a Higher Plane of Greatness

In presenting his forefathers as larger-than-life figures, Xie Lingyun highlights the guiding principle behind their heroic deeds of "rescuing the drowning" (*zhengni* 拯溺) and "subduing the violent" (*kanbao* 戡暴) with two key terms: *daoqing* 道情 or "the essence of the Way" (line 9, Part II) and *shenli* 神理 or "the divine principle" (line 10, Part II). The Way (Dao) is a conceptual term used by all schools of thought that denotes how things *naturally* exist, evoking teachings found in the *Laozi*. The constant (i.e., true) Way is invisible and ineffable. Nevertheless, it rules. *Li* (principle) is often used to complement Dao in Xie Lingyun's poetry, and thus may also refer to the governing principle of the universe. When referring to human affairs, *li* denotes order and reason. With these abstract concepts, the poet reveals the intellectual reasoning buttressing the behavior, deeds, and choices made by the Xies. They led by example and their pursuit of the superior Way made them spiritual leaders whose influence extended far beyond the fourth century among the émigré communities. In this sense, their "virtue" was as much in the realm of the mind as in moral practice. They reached a higher plain of understanding and ferried others across. At the beginning of the first poem, we find the phrase *da-ren* 達人, which may be translated as "a person of penetrating vision."[31] To understand the semantic range of *da*, a detour into the canonical texts is necessary. The following passages from *The Analects* may shed some light.

> In any particular case, to be *da*, one needs to be upright and fond of righteousness. He discerns what others say and observes their emotions.

He is considerate so as to remain humble. [When such a person] exists, the state necessarily *prospers*; [when such a person] exists, a clan necessarily *prospers*.[32]

In any particular case, to be benevolent, one strives to establish others before he establishes himself; one strives to *prosper* others before he *prospers* himself.[33]

In the context of these passages, *da* could be translated as "to succeed" or "to prosper"—the figurative sense of "to arrive or reach [a height of prosperity or accomplishment]." The Han dynasty dictionary *Explaining the Graphs* (Shuowen) defines *da* as "going without meeting [obstacles]."[34] *Da*, when juxtaposed with *qiong* 窮 ("to be blocked"), forms an idiomatic compound *qiongda*, which could be translated as "in success or failure" or "in prosperity or destitution."[35] *Mengzi 7A/9*, for example, gives the following admonishment: "In destitution, one should strive to improve the self; in prosperity, one should strive to benefit the entire world."

The literal and figurative connotations aside, *da* is seen as denoting "unobstructed understanding of the abstract and abstruse world." A person with this ability is referred to as a *da-ren*. In *Zuo Tradition* (Zuozhuan), the phrase *da-ren* exhibits a synonymic function to the ubiquitous term *shengren*, that is, a "sage" or "the sagacious one:" "If a sage, with his bright virtue, does not meet his time, among his offspring, there necessarily will emerge a *da-ren*."[36] "Sage," in the Chinese canonical texts, refers to only a handful of culturally holy figures such as Confucius, Mencius, and the mythological demigods such as Yao, Shun, and the Yellow Emperor. Etymologically speaking, the basic quality of a sage resides with a remarkably acute sense of "listening" (*ting*).[37] Aural receptiveness, synecdoche to human perception and sentience, is prerequisite to true understanding. To be sagacious, one needs to have an open mind. Such is the message from a description of Shun's governance as recorded in *The Book of Documents* (Shangshu): "On the first day of the first month, sage-king Shun consulted with the Cultured Ancestor and the Four Sacred Mountains. He opened the four gates, brightened the four eyes, and made the four hearings unobstructed."[38] What I translate here as "unobstructed" is in Chinese none other than the word *da*. Therefore, *da-ren*, as construed alongside the "sage," refers to "one whose senses are open or unobstructed." *Da* thus denotes the kind of profound understanding and penetrating vision that only a superhuman can have.[39] Such a person can see beyond what is close at hand: gain or loss, peril or felicity, or success or failure, and, as a result, rise above the usual calculations, cravings, and other causes of suffering.

In modern parlance, *da-ren* is one who operates with an uncluttered mind. In Han and post-Han China, philosophical notions are often inseparable from the practical wisdom of religious Daoism. The Daoist Ge Hong (283–343), for instance, defines *da-ren* as: "To comply with any circumstances, to be undisturbed in favorable or treacherous situations, to allow life to run its course without being bogged down—such a person may be called *da-ren*."[40] Here, the implicit focus goes back to the literal meaning of "to arrive," "to travel unobstructed," and "to reach." "Spirit-journeying into the heavens" (*shenyou*) in literary texts reflects the popular Daoist beliefs and practices during the Han. Through breathing exercises and diet, practitioners of the Dao may hope to transform and transport the body beyond,[41] and, most importantly, "to arrive" at the "Very Beginning" (Tai Chu) or "Ultimate Clear" (Zhi Qing) where Nothingness abides.[42] The "arrived one" is an immortal who is one with the Way. The secular notion of "transcendence" or "arrival" has to do with a practicable savviness that grants freedom and security to a mortal being traveling through the treacherous tides of human affairs, which are considered inevitably "muddy" or "dusty." Xie Lingyun's use of *da-ren*, when examined in the discursive convention and the immediate context of the poem, remains largely in its secular sense, yet not without a religious overtone. The descriptive *qing* or "clarity" (Part I, line 14), for example, although not necessarily referring to the Daoist heaven beyond heavens known as the "Ultimate Clear," does generate an image of the Xie forefathers rising above worldly entanglements and achieving moral and physical purity. Likewise, "white clouds" (line 2), while signifying the far-reaching influence of a hero, conjures up a pious admiration of the otherworldly and the superhuman. Finally, note the paradox that is innate in the notion *da*: "to arrive" is to travel ceaselessly and smoothly, and without stopping or being blocked.

Xie Lingyun's characterization of *da-ren* is complicated with a variant reading. Li Shan's commentary reads: "A man of penetrating vision values [*gui* 貴] the self," whereas the Dunhuang manuscript version of the text reads: "A man of penetrating vision abandons [*yi* 遺] the self."[43] The apparent antonyms of *gui* and *yi* are cognates in Middle Chinese, meaning their overlapping semantic range allowed them to be treated as synonyms. In addition, their phonetical affinity compounds with the Zhuangzian paradox: *to value is to abandon*. Life and death, loss and gain, are essentially parts of the same whole.[44] The philosophical resistance to conventional value and wisdom prepared post-Han Chinese thinkers to absorb Buddhist teachings, giving rise to a new personality trait dubbed *fengliu*.[45] The term can be roughly translated as "gracefully detached." Its imagistic invocation of "wind" (*feng*) and "flow of water" (*liu*) denotes a condition that is not dissimilar to *da*: to move smoothly without attachment. Both *da-ren* and *fengliu* convey a metaphysical triumph over the physical; this was the aspiration of many Eastern Jin intellectuals, and the members of the Xie clan were the most eloquent spokespersons for this ideal. In this poem, Xie Lingyun uses the language of poetry to delineate the key traits of a detached mind and its power to elevate one from the evils of the world and the failings of humankind.

Zhuangzi's Influence

The idea that an aloof mind is a prerequisite for *perfected being* is repeatedly expounded in the *Zhuangzi*. The earliest literary iteration of this Zhuangzian principle is found in Jia Yi's (200–169 BCE) "*Fu* on the Owl" (Funiao fu; hereafter, "The Owl").[46] The influence of this predecessor on Xie Lingyun's piece is significant, as it illustrates the philosophical abstraction that can be called "graceful detachment." In particular, Xie's notion of *da*, as seen in the opening line—"A man of penetrating vision *values* the self"—seems like a conscious response to Jia Yi's *fu*. In addition, the paradox of "self-valuing" and "self-casting"—that is, "ridding worldly attachment"—can be traced to "The Owl," especially the following lines:

55	天不可與慮兮	Heaven cannot be predicted;
	道不可與謀	the Way cannot be planned.
57	遲數有命兮	Tardiness or speediness, each has its determinant;

	惡識其時	how can one know the [opportune] time?[47]
59	天地為鑪兮	Heaven and earth constitute the furnace,
	造化為工	the great fashioner works like an artisan.
61	陰陽為炭兮	Yin and yang function like charcoal,
	萬物為銅	the myriad things are the copper.
63	合散消息	In their gathering and dispersing, waxing and waning,
	安有常則	rarely is there a constant rule.
65	千變萬化兮	Only a thousand changes and ten thousand mutations.
	未始有極	Never is there a beginning; nor is there an end.
67	忽然為人兮	Suddenly something turns into the human form,
	何足控摶	hardly the reason for control or manipulation.
69	化為異物兮	In transforming into some other thing,
	又何足患	why then is it worth vexation?
71	小智自私兮	Small knowledge, self-centeredness;
	賤彼貴我	belittling others' valuing the self.
73	達人大觀兮	A person of penetrating vision has a broad view;
	物無不可	regarding all things being equal.
75	貪夫徇財兮	A greedy man dies for money;
	烈士徇名	a martyr dies for fame.
77	夸者死權兮	A braggart dies for power,
	品庶每生	the common folk cling to life.
79	怵迫之徒兮	Those who can be lured or intimidated
	或趨西東	dash about east and west.
81	大人不曲兮	The great person does not bend.
	意變齊同	Millions of changes are all the same.
83	愚士繫俗兮	A foolish man sticks to convention,
	窘若囚拘	restrained like a prisoner.
85	至人遺物兮	The ultimate person abandons the world.
	獨與道俱	Alone he is with the Way.[48]
87	眾人或或兮	The masses are befuddled and confused;
	好惡積億	affections and aversions burst inside.

89	真人恬漠兮	The true person is quiet and unconcerned.[49]
	獨與道息	Alone he abides by the Way.
91	釋智遺形兮	Releasing knowledge, shedding the outer form,
	超然自喪	aloof and unperturbed, he vanishes.
93	寥廓忽荒兮	Boundless, vast, murky, and indistinguishable—
	與道翱翔	he roams with the Way.
95	乘流則逝兮	Over a current, it flows;
	得坻則止	obtaining a mound, it respites.
97	縱軀委命兮	Cast away the body, commit to the ordained;
	不私與己	never be partial to the self.
99	其生兮若浮	Life as such is a flow;
	其死兮若休	death as such is a rest.
101	澹乎若深泉之靜	How tranquil—the stillness of a deep pool.
	泛乎若不繫之舟	Bobbing, it is like that untethered boat.

Anchored in the Daoist notion of compliance and noninterference, this passage performs a literary explication on how to live without fear or worries about death.[50] The numerous intertextual references to the *Zhuangzi* formulate what sinologist James Robert Hightower calls "a statement of a philosophy of life."[51] To live well is to know death, according to Zhuangzi. At his wife's funeral, he reportedly explained his bizarre behavior as such:

Observing her origin, there had not been an original form of life. Not only had there been no original form of life, there had not been even a form. Not only had there not been a form, there had been no life-breath. Mingled among the murky and hazy, some change had given rise to her life-breath. Only then had a form taken shape. The form then morphed into her life. Then upon further transformation, there came death. All of this is but a matter of her moving along with the four seasons of spring, summer, autumn, and winter.[52]

Such knowledge of death, together with many of its latter-day reiterations,[53] cautions against greed, folly, and other ills and vexations rooted in mortal beings' instinctive servitude to "things" (*wu*), or external matters.

Lines 70 through 90 of "The Owl" bears a similarity to the following chastisement found in the *Zhuangzi*.

> From the Three Dynasties on, there were none who did not alter their nature to suit the world. The petty person was devoted to profit; the loyal person was devoted to fame; the grandee was devoted to his clan; and the sage was devoted to the world. Of these different devotions, although their causes varied and their reputations diverged, they were all the same in that they sacrificed their person and damaged their nature.[54]

In this denigration, Zhuangzi doesn't even spare the sage, whose service to the world is considered fundamentally similar to other forms of harming nature, which in this context refers to the basic condition of humankind as endowed by heaven. Heaven is the Way. Semantically overlapping and sometimes interchangeable, heaven (*tian*), the Way (Dao), the human nature (*xing* 性), and the pristine (*ziran* 自然) constitute some of the important discursive labels for exploring Daoist ideas on the true way of life and death. The Confucian sage is often found wanting in the metaphysical realm, due to inflexibility and sometimes rigid attachment to social norms. The sage's self-certain and self-righteous stance provides a springboard for the Zhuangzian spokesperson to reach for the higher ground of ultimate truth and transcendental being (*ji*). As an alternative to the busy government of Yao and Shun, Zhuangzi proposes the idealized personhood of the True One (Zhenren), who rises above the mundane human heroism.

> The True One of antiquity was not aware of life's pleasures; nor did he detest death. He emerged without delight; he entered without resistance. He came easily, he went easily. And that was all. He didn't forget where he had begun, nor did he seek where or how he should end. At the moment of receiving [life], there had been joy. Then he became oblivious and returned to the state [before life]. He didn't use his intelligence to harm the Way. Nor did he use the human to assist with heaven. Such was the True One: his heart still, his countenance tranquil, his forehead relaxed; his coolness was that of the autumn, his warmth that of the

spring, his joy and anger channeled by the four seasons and in proportion with things, his limits unknown.[55]

Zhuangzi's message is that oblivious flow is the state of true being. The sense of self, consciousness of the physical body, and perceptions of things fade away through unconscious unity with the Way. Elsewhere in the text of the *Zhuangzi*, "oblivion" grants entrance to heaven: "Be oblivious of things, be oblivious of heaven—this is called self-oblivion. Who can be oblivious of that human form thought of as the self enters the realm of heaven."[56] Heaven here refers to the abstract Way; entering heaven is tantamount to becoming unified with the Way and residing with the pristine conditions of "all there is" (*you*), which is, according to the philosophical development of *Zhuangzi* in the Eastern Jin, the ultimate nothingness (*zhiwu*).[57]

Couched in the Zhuangzian perspective, Xie Lingyun's *da-ren* offers a solution to the dilemma that the scholar-official class had had to confront since the Han: the "entanglement" (*lei*) of a set of incompatible worldly obligations such as filiality, loyalty, and personal integrity. Under the weight of these social, political, and familial burdens enforced by the absolute power of Han sovereignty, writers such as Sima Qian made existential inquiries, among which was the ethicality of noble suicide.[58] Jia Yi also reflected upon the suicide of Qu Yuan—the archetypal nobleman who had "encountered sorrow."[59] The loyal but slandered minister from the state of Chu failed in his counsel to the king, couldn't disentangle himself from the web of petty court politics, and so ended up drowning himself, according to the popular legend as laid out in Sima Qian's *Records of the Historian* (Shiji).[60] Qu Yuan's fate loomed large in the consciousness of Han intellectuals when they were faced with similar insurmountable challenges. There was no shortage of sympathy for Qu Yuan, who had exemplified the virtue of integrity and loyalty, but his alleged choice to take his own life became questionable when familial relations were emphasized. Joining with Jia Yi was the Confucian-minded Han philosopher Yang Xiong (53 BCE–18 CE), who referred thirteen times to Qu Yuan as the "entangled one" (*lei*) in his "Refuting *Sao*" (Fan *Sao*).[61]

Following the dissolution of the Han empire, elite thinkers poured over the so-called mystery texts such as the *Zhuangzi* and *Laozi* to search for answers about the true conditions of being. The intellectual trend formed in the ensuing century is sometimes called neo-Daoism. It promoted the value of life at the physical and metaphysical level, guiding decision-making in times of impossible social hardship and political complication. The wisdom encapsulated in the concept of *da-ren* or "person of penetration vision" reflects Daoist contemplations on grave matters such as death and prevalent devastation. To lift life—a dignified mind and an intact body—from the dusty net of the embattled world became a shared vision. Xie An was the undisputed example of the truly enlightened in the eyes of those who lived during the Jin-Song transition and the turmoil thereafter. Echoing contemporary attitudes, Xie Lingyun's praise concludes a resounding couplet: "Foregoing worldly passions, he cast aside dusty things; with undivided attention, he investigated the beauty of mountains and valleys." This image of Xie An elevates the Jin statesman to that of a Daoist immortal made familiar in the first chapter of *Zhuangzi*, "Free Roaming" (Xiaoyao you):

> In that distant Guye Mountain, there lived the divine one. His flesh and
> skin were like ice and snow. Supple and flexible, he was like a maiden.
> Abstaining from the five grains, he merely breathed in the wind and
> drank the dew. Riding on clouds and vapors, he yoked a soaring dragon
> to roam beyond the four distant boundaries.[62]

The modern historian Tian Yuqing posited: "The Xie clan of the Eastern Jin did not appropriate the ruler's power, advance themselves through the distaff members, or constitute pressure or threat to the throne."[63] *The Southern Dynasties History* (Nan shi) praises the Xie clan for their transmission of the "lofty way" (*yadao*).[64] This lofty way, as Wang Yongping correctly insists, must be understood within the cultural context of the Eastern Jin and denotes specifically the philosophical teachings of Laozi and Zhuangzi. The Xie clan thus upheld the "natural way" and a spontaneous attitude toward the self and the world at large. They preferred reclusion to service and pursued mindful unconventionality.[65] It was their higher moral plane and aloofness to fame and gain that made the Xies the most "famed" clan of the Eastern Jin.[66]

Xie Lingyun, in concluding "Recounting the Virtues of My Forefathers," expresses his desire to emulate his forefathers by returning to the east and dwelling in the mountains. "Mountains" here denote more than just the physical landscape of eastern China. More importantly, to the mind of the Jin poet and his contemporary readers, mountains stood for the natural Way, which held the key to transcending the constraints of time and place. Xie Lingyun, in his exile, explored the economic and aesthetic dimensions of the coastal mountains. He developed a way of exhibiting the multifaceted beauty and understanding that mountains offered. The close attention Xie paid to the phenomenal world and the natural principle evinced therein yielded unprecedented ideas and images in a language that would change how nature was to be portrayed and beheld for centuries to come.

Part II

STEPS TOWARD A LITERARY REVOLUTION

CHAPTER 4

A Home in the Mountains

Xie Lingyun explored the coastal mountains of what is today Zhejiang and Fujian provinces, and he is remembered as the most eloquent spokesperson for the area's natural wonder. Impressed by the mountains' majestic beauty, he spoke of his desire to become one with the land—to live out his life and be buried there after death. Such passion for nature, especially the mountains, struck a chord with Xie's contemporaries who, after much political turmoil, yearned for a place they could call home. The following passage, part of a letter written by a family friend of the Xies in the 530s, conveys both Xie's ability to articulate concerns of the émigré communities and the indelible mark the gorgeous landscape of Guiji had left on them.[1]

> The beauty of mountains and rivers has been a topic of discussion since antiquity. High summits pierce the clouds; the riverbeds are seen through clear currents. Rock cliffs hugging the river are reflected in variegated colors. Verdant bushes and halcyon bamboo groves—vegetations of all seasons thrive at the same time. At dawn, when the fog is about to recede, gibbons and birds cry in chorus; at dusk, when the sun is about to set, fishes of all kinds leap out of the water. This indeed is an immortal land in the realm of human desire. Since the passing of Duke Kangle [Xie Lingyun], there has never been another who knows how to partake of its wonder.

> 山川之美，古來共談。高峰入雲，清流見底。兩岸石壁，五色交暉。青林翠竹，四時俱備。曉霧將歇，猿鳥亂鳴。夕日欲穨，沈鱗競躍。實是欲界之仙都。自康樂以來。未復有能與其奇者。[2]

Xie's travels took him deep into rarely visited mountain areas and provided him with a firsthand glimpse of the coastal area's amazing geographical features and ecological diversity, which he later described vividly in his writings. While the latter chapters in this book focus on how Xie's poetry manifests breakthroughs in genre, this chapter considers the poet as a self-conscious environmentalist. His philosophy and visionary understanding of the intricate connections between humans and their environment surpassed previous nature writing in depth and breadth.

Xie's rarely studied geographical work *Notes on Roaming Famous Mountains* (You mingshan zhi; translated in appendix 1) provides context for his celebration of the land and its resources. This one-*juan* work is preserved in the Sui dynasty "Bibliography" and classified under "geographical records" (*dili ji*).[3] Nineteen mountains, three brooks, and two belvederes are mentioned in the work, which shows Xie's interest in documenting edible plants, medicinal herbs, and trees such as camphor, varnish, sweetgum, and spruce. Herbs include wild ginger, purple aster, black leek, peony, mountain basil, and parsley root, most of which can be used in health tonics. Purple aster, for example, was reported to be a cough suppressant, parsley root is beneficial for the female reproductive system, and black leek benefits both women and men. Also included in this "explorer's diary" are descriptions of the unique topography, which contain symbolic importance. For example, Xie mentions a cavernous chamber in the shape of a turtle shell and a secret cave on top of a lone rock standing in the middle of a lake. Poetically, a lone rock recalls the uncompromising stance of a dissident-martyr.[4] This association, further supported by historical-political lore, extends to denote religious yearnings for freedom and immortality.[5] One of Xie's "famous mountains" promises a passageway to the immortal land.

> Next to Pink Cloud Mountain, there is a lone pinnacle, standing resolutely and piercing into the clouds for two hundred *zhang* [2,187 feet], looking down on the water on three sides, with a circumference of 160 *zhang* [1,750 feet]. On the top, there is a lake where lotus flowers bloom. Nearby is a cliff known as Treading Void. Gazing at the pinnacle from afar, it is lower than Treading Void. Seeing it up close, Treading Void is beneath it.[6]

"Treading Void" (Buxu) refers either literally to "stepping into the void"—an immortal nether land—or a Daoist ritual chant that leads to a trance-like state of oblivion. In this entry from *Notes on Roaming Famous Mountains*, Xie claims to have discovered the secret path to eternity: an unnamed pinnacle that only reveals its easy access to Treading Void upon a closer look. Such religious fascination with new lands and frontiers that promise entry into paradise was patently Daoist; Xie championed humanity's return to nature in the preface to his explorer's diary:

> Food and clothing are what humans need for living; mountains and waters are what humans naturally gravitate toward. Now we are entangled in the necessities of life, which block the path of our natural inclinations. It is commonly believed that joy and fulfillment can be found only in the Grand Hall [i.e., public service] and that those who sleep on the cliff [i.e., dwell in the mountains] and drink from a stream lack great ambition and, therefore, can only care for their mortal selves. I disagree with this. If a gentleman is inclined to care for the world and is also endowed with the ability to save the world, then, in times of turmoil and disorder, which call for someone with special talents, he should go against his natural disposition, but only out of expediency, to ferry across those in need. Surely the arena of fame and profit is inferior to nature's sphere, which is chaste and boundless. I can speak of a ruler of myriad chariots [i.e., a large state] who let go of his reins and ascended to heaven [i.e., became an immortal] from Tripod Lake.[7] I can also name an heir apparent, who found freedom on Mount Song.[8] Additionally, there was one Tao Zhu who declined to serve as the minister to the king of Yue; the Marquis of Liu resigned as preceptor to the Han emperor.[9] Judging from these examples, it is evident [that the chaste and free realm of nature is superior to the arena of fame and profit].[10]

In the preface, which is composed of parallel distiches, Xie Lingyun connects human nature and the natural world, whose mystery is approachable through an immersion in "mountains and waters." He starts by saying that the human life is naturally drawn to the natural world and its Way. Further, he argues that human nature may at times yield to worldly affairs, but that is just for expediency, not necessity. It is in this light that the poet explains his forefathers' political engagement. He rationalizes his own adherence to the law of nature as manifested in "mountains and waters" by citing classical authority: an ancient sage-emperor, an intelligent crown prince, and two worthy ministers.[11] The poet thus argues that nature promises not only a better life, but also a mysterious delivery after life.

Similar arguments are found in "*Fu* on Dwelling in the Mountains," where Xie delineates and distinguishes four modes of disengagement from society, ranging from primitive cave-dwelling to suburban retirement.[12] His preference for nature is rooted in an aesthetic, not ascetic, need. Therefore, man-made structures, as long as they follow the law of nature, are perfectly acceptable. As sinologist Wendy Swartz points out, in building his mountain dwelling, Xie consulted *The Classic of Changes*, including the images in the hexagrams as well as the commentarial texts.[13] Once again, Xie avoids mechanical or slavish adherence to what is conventionally deemed virtuous or moral. Instead, he regards "change" or flexibility as essential. There is no real difference among the various modes or choices of disengagement. What matters is the state of one's mind.

In his "*Fu* on Dwelling in the Mountains," Xie describes himself as "Master Xie sitting atop the mountain, sick in bed yet engaged in browsing the texts left behind by the ancients; occasionally he would find delight in those ideas that are in accordance with his mind and then he would remark: 'The Way is to be valued; things are insignificant. The law [*li*] shall always prevail; worldly affairs always pass.'"[14] The natural law, he says, has stood true since time immemorial. Xie then cites exemplary figures of the past and concludes that "they were able to discern a distinction between their person and their reputation; they found the balance between glory and simplicity, knowing that nothing ever stays."[15] Xie's philosophical musing is eclectic. For example, the "ultimate law" (*zhi li*) may refer to the Daoist principle, the Confucian order, or the Buddhist absolute truth: *prajñāpārmitā*. In the Eastern Jin, the intellectual quest was to identify and articulate the ultimate truth while recognizing its evasiveness or mystery. This mysterious *li* was called *xuan li*. The late sinologist Richard Mather explains the intellectual notion as follows:

> It is a kind of mysticism, if you will, whose ultimate reality, called *li*, the innate principle of things, unites the empirical world with the transcendental world. By this mysticism all worldly experience may be viewed *sub specie aetenitatis* as an extension of what lies beyond it, and any duty performed in the state chancellery is not basically different from sitting in forgetfulness in some mountain hermitage.[16]

As a poet-thinker, Xie Lingyun contributed to the collective mind of his time by investigating ancient texts and weaving them into the phenomenal world, which he passed through and described. He shows us cosmic law and its mystery through representations of the ever transforming and transformative "mountains and waters." He communicates with his readers about the ultimate truth with poetic imagery, literary patterning, and confessionary self-examination. Self-awareness as a thinker and observer led him to prioritize not form (*xing*), but the spirit or spiritual or even divine (*shen*), which approximated the mystery of the Way.[17] At times, he used the term "divine principle" or "divine truth" (*shenli*). For humans, the body was but a temporary lodge for the spirit. For the natural world, objects and phenomena such as sights and sounds were merely the locale of ultimate truth. By divine principle, humans and the natural world are united.

For all his inventiveness in literature and intellectual thought, Xie Lingyun placed himself in a long line of ancient exemplars. This included his forefathers, who wished to return to a more chaste state of living in the mountains in order to enjoy a life free of official trappings. Li Si, the high minister of Qin, or Lu Ji, a general for the Western Jin, served as examples of the danger of changing political tides.[18] Since mountains are the "resting place for the remote-minded" and a home therein ought to be "constructed along the contour of the land," to return to the mountains is to live according to the law of nature.[19] Xie's mountain-dwelling and his declaration of its significance were intentionally epochal.[20] The Chinese appreciation for mountains in art and life began with Xie Lingyun.

Mountain-Dwelling Poems
"ASCENDING THE SUMMIT OF STONE GATE"

Xie Lingyun's professed mountain-dwelling philosophy is best understood through his poetry. His poems reveal how "mountains and waters" manifest the cosmic truth and to what extent humans can find their own truth by passing through the natural landscape. They also illustrate the perceived value of reclusiveness and loneliness, as Xie typically presents himself as lone traveler. To that end, let us begin with "Ascending the Summit of Stone Gate" (Deng Shimen zuigao ding 登石門最高頂; hereafter, "Ascending the Summit").[21]

	晨策尋絕壁	At dawn, with a hiking stick, I embarked on the cliff path;
	夕息在山棲	at dusk, I rested on the mountain top.
	疏峰抗高館	On the peak stood a lofty gallery;
4	對嶺臨迴溪	facing the ridge, I looked over the winding river.
	長林羅戶穴	Tall groves form gates and windows;
	積石擁基階	boulders gather and pile up to make stairways.
	連巖覺路塞	Layers of cliffs hide the road;
8	密竹使徑迷	dense bamboo blots out the path.
	來人忘新術	Visitors forget a newly discovered route;
	去子惑故蹊	upon leaving, they become confused about the old way.
	活活夕流駛	*Huo-huo*, the river rushes along;
12	噭噭夜猿啼	*Ao-ao*, gibbons wail throughout the night.
	沉冥豈別理	Sunk in silence—how could I deviate from the truth?
	守道自不携	Abiding by the Way, I shall betray myself.
	心契九秋幹	My heart engraves [the rings of] the tree that has endured many autumns;
16	目翫三春荑	although my eyes dally with tender shoots in warm spring.
	居常以待終	Dwelling with the constant law, I attend upon life's full span;
	處順故安排	staying and complying, I befriend all that comes and goes.
	惜無同懷客	If there is any regret, it is the lack of a fellow traveler,
20	共登青雲梯	with whom I shall ascend the stairs leading to the heavens.

This poem recalls the literary traditions known as "summoning the recluse" (*zhao yinshi*) and "roaming immortals" (*youxian*), which came to be established *shi* categories in the *Wen xuan*.[22] Nature, as seen in this poem, is portrayed as beautiful and mysterious. Humans, in exploring unpopulated landscapes, can find truth. Unlike the trappings of wealth and honor, nature is restorative and safe. In the third and fourth centuries, "nature-loving" (*ai shanshui*) in literature emerged alongside intellectual explorations of life's true meaning. A need to free the body and soul from suppressive social obligations and dangerous political participation led educated men to turn their attention to their private lives. In the pursuit of art and the search for the sublime, we see a change of attitudes toward nature. In *Songs of Chu*, "Summoning the Recluse" expressed a salient fear of the wilderness. The unknown and inhospitable aspects of nature are evoked to inspire awe if not sheer terror, as the shaman-priest methodically coaxes the wandering soul back to the human realm: "O Prince, return! In the mountains, you cannot stay long."[23] Mountains were thought to be the territories of wild animals and menacing creatures, and not a place for humans. Trees, as faces of nature, are described in *Songs of Chu* as having a gnarled appearance, implying a world that was torturous and a place that was dangerous.

In "Ascending the Summit," mountains are habitable and even hospitable. The poet describes nature with verbs such as *luo* 羅 and *yong* 擁 (lines 5 and 6): trees "gather" to form windows and gates; boulders "cluster" to make stairways. Consciously collaborating, nature houses dwellers of all kinds and welcomes visitors. Xie offers a wilderness that protects, not prohibits. Lines 7 through 10 suggest that it is the human mind, or consciousness (*jue* 覺, line 7), that blocks (*se* 塞), causes confusion (*mi* 迷), forgets (*wang* 忘), and doubts (*huo* 惑). Nature as a habitat has existed since time immemorial. Humans have abandoned their home and alienated themselves. Such eternal truth is echoed in the constant sounds of nature: the nightlong calls of the gibbons and the ceaseless murmuring of the river (lines 11 and 12). One can tune in to nature's rhythm by ridding the conscious mind of noise (line 13). Only then does one become nature: the heart-mind of an old tree that is firm, the limbs of young branches in warm spring that grow tenderly. In nature, life is sustained and rejuvenated. There is, importantly for Xie, proper care for old age. To die means to live out one's natural lifespan. The end doesn't just end, but becomes the beginning of a new life cycle. Fear (line 17) is thus replaced with hope (line 18). The natural Way is the abiding place for human existence (line 14).

Xie Lingyun's faith in and praise of nature is framed in a criticism of the political order or the lack thereof in human society. Professing "loneliness" in the ending couplet (line 19), Xie hearkens back to a literary trope established in the famous lament attributed to Qu Yuan: "The state has no one who understands me."[24] This powerful ending echoes an opening that calls to mind another political figure from the Warring States. Lu Zhonglian (ca. 305–ca. 245 BCE), a near contemporary of Qu Yuan, thwarted the invasion of Qin on behalf of the state of Zhao and then left the world without accepting the reward.[25] *Records of the Historian* cites the following speech from Lu: "That which is valued among men of honor is to lend one's helping hand in times of grave danger and yet not accept anything in return. To receive a reward would reduce one to a merchant. I would not bear the thought of it."[26] The code phrase for Lu Zhonglian's story is *zhangce* or "departing with nothing but a bamboo staff," which, as noted by the Tang commentator Li Shan (630–89), stood for the virtue of incorruptibility.[27]

In Xie's writing, the figure of Lu Zhonglian appears more than once as a hero who stood apart from a profit-driven society where the morally superior man was exiled and sent away. In "Ascending the Summit," the concept of lone hero intertwines with Xie Lingyun's fascination with nature's "singular beauty" or, to use the poet's own word, *qi*, which can be translated as "strange," "otherworldly," "extraordinary," or "wondrous." Although the poet seeks the singularity in both aesthetic and ethical terms, nature seems to respond with reciprocity, as seen in the descriptive couplets 2 through 4. Nature's quietude and solicitude stir kindred feelings in the human heart, transforming his attitude toward loneliness. Hence the paradox at the end: the persona who seeks to transcend the world wishes to have the company of a "like-minded sojourner."

"A NEWLY CONSTRUCTED LODGE"

Xie Lingyun strikes many readers as a lonely traveler trudging through the mountains by himself. This could not be further from the truth.[28] The "solitary sojourner" motif as played out in Xie's poetry peaked in Eastern Jin arts and culture, which paradoxically also accentuated the importance of appreciation from a "like-minded friend" or "fellow traveler." Specifically, Xie adopts the *Songs of Chu* tradition known as "pungent herbs and noble character" (*xiangcao meiren*) to comment on his social and political associations.[29] The following poem is a case in point. In celebrating the completion of a lodge on the Stone Gate cliff, Xie mentions an "absent friend," with whom he wishes to share his amazement about nature's glory. The title of the poem is "On Stone Gate—A Newly Constructed Lodge—There Are High Mountains on All Sides, Winding Streams, Rocky Shallows, Slender Bamboo, and a Thick Grove" (Shimen xin ying suozhu simian gaoshan huixi shilai xiuzhu maolin 石門新營所住四面高山迴溪石瀨修竹茂林; hereafter, "A Newly Constructed Lodge").[30]

	躋險築幽居	Treading the precipice, I have built this secluded lodge;
	披雲臥石門	draped in clouds, I recline on the Stone Gate.
	苔滑誰能步	Over the slippery moss, who can walk?
4	葛弱豈可捫	Kudzu, still tender, cannot be used as support.
	嫋嫋秋風過	Gently whispering, the autumn breeze passes by;[31]
	萋萋春草繁	lush and green, spring grass grows ever denser.[32]
	美人遊不還	The one I admire roams without returning;
8	佳期何由敦	a much anticipated reunion, whence to come?[33]
	芳塵凝瑤席	Fragrant dust has congealed on the jade mat;
	清醑滿金尊	translucent ale is filled to the brim in a golden goblet.
	洞庭空波瀾	Waves on Lake Dongting billow on;
12	桂枝徒攀翻	nonchalantly I pluck a cassia branch and turn it in my hand.
	結念屬霄漢	My yearnings build up as high as the cerulean sky;
	孤景莫與諼	alone with my own shadow, with whom can I commiserate?
	俯濯石下潭	I bend down to wash in the pond below the rocks;
16	仰看條上猿	looking up, I see gibbons among the trees.
	早聞夕颼急	At dawn, I hear the evening gusts howling;
	晚見朝日暾	at dusk, I watch the morning sun in a hazy glow.[34]
	崖傾光難留	Cliffs are too steep for the daylight to stay;
20	林深響易奔	the forest is so deep that sounds easily flee.
	感往慮有復	While feelings subside, contemplative thoughts arise;
	理來情無存	when the true order comes, passion loses its hold.

	庶持乘日用	Only by riding the chariot of the sun;
24	得以慰營魂	Can I comfort the beleaguered soul.
	匪為眾人說	This is not a conversation that I have with the crowd,
	冀與智者論	only for the wise with whom I hope to further discuss.[35]

The long and detailed title of this poem gives weight to the event mentioned: the completion of a lodge above Stone Gate, which was an architectural wonder in the fifth century.[36] However, the significance of this secluded location may be symbolic of the poet's "turning away" from society. Now a mountain dweller, he portrays himself as a reclining immortal draped in clouds (line 2). The second couplet stresses the inaccessibility of his new abode, which is constructed on the face of a cliff.[37] In the next section, lines 5 through 12, we come across a series of references to *Songs of Chu*. Together, they conjure up the motif that British sinologist David Hawkes calls *tristia*, sorrowful expressions over an absent friend or lover. Line 5 adopts a nominal sentence from "Lady of the Xiang River" and adds a verb at the end, turning a *sao*-style distich into a pentasyllabic line.[38] In line 6, "lush and green, spring grasses grow ever denser" is an image from "Summoning the Recluse": "lush and green, spring grass grow."[39] Line 8 recalls again "Lady of the Xiang River": "Having set a date to meet with my beloved, I now make preparations."[40] Line 9 contains imagery from "Sovereign of the East": "A jasper mat with a jade weight."[41] Line 10 borrows the description of a banquet scene from "Summoning the Soul": "Jasper-colored drink, flavored with honey, fills the winged goblets; iced ale, made from glutinous-rice, is strained of impurities; clear beer is cool and refreshing; floriate-patterned jars are filled with translucent juice."[42] Line 11 refers yet again to "Lady of the Xiang River": "Over Lake Dongting, leaves flutter and fall."[43] Line 12 cites from "Summoning the Recluse": "I pluck the cassia branch."[44] This last image became the familiar trope of lovesickness or remembering a loved one who is far away or otherwise absent.

The concentrated intertextual borrowing from *Songs of Chu* conveys the experience of a lone mountain-dweller (lines 13 and 14), accompanied only by his own shadow. His senses and perceptions of the natural surroundings are enhanced. Exhilarated by the unusual temporal-spatial configurations made possible by the otherworldly realm, the poet envisions a thorough communion with nature at a cosmic level (couplets 8, 9, and 10). His intense observation of the world, as denoted with the phrase "bending-down and looking-up" (*fuyang*), has physical as well as mental dimensions. Musing and meditating, the poetic figure allows himself to dance in the rhythm of nature's formative and transformative energy. The word "wash" (*zhuo*) indexes an ancient lesson: "When the water in the river is muddy, wash your feet in it; when the water runs clear, wash your hatstring."[45] As in nature, there is a time for everything. Service and action must be in tune with the political trend. The act of "washing" evokes a moment of reckoning in line 15, whereas the image of monkeys in trees suggests a sense of good order in line 16. Lines 17 and 18, according to modern commentator Gu Shaobo, captures an altered sense of time in the deep mountains.[46] A different explanation from the Ming dynasty poet-scholar Yang Shen (1488–1559) points out the plausible chiasmus of "dawn" and "dusk" to avoid conceptual repetition.[47] In the next couplet, the poet describes how steep cliffs block the daylight and how echoes scurry in dense forests. The dynamic use of altered temporal sensations elevate Xie's poem from a mundane repetition of old wisdom, as it constructs a different reality. From the top of a summit, Xie, now cut off from the world below, has the license to imagine an inverted image of the times.

The poem ends with a section (couplets 11, 12 and 13) in which Xie reflects on human emotions and how their fleeting existence, like everything else, is to be taken at a measured pace—similar to how the sun moves through the sky every day at an unhurried pace. To calm the soul, one ought to practice conscious living on a daily basis or, in Xie Lingyun's words, "ride the chariot of the sun" (*cheng riju*, line 23). This alludes to a tale from the *Zhuangzi*, part of which reads: "The herd-boy said [to the Yellow Emperor], . . . when I was young, I had roamed every corner of the world until my eyes grew blurry. An elder then advised me to ride in the chariot of the sun to travel in the wilderness of Xiangcheng. Now I have recovered from my eye disease and again am able to roam beyond the six bounds of the world."[48] The advice offered by the herd-boy to the sage-emperor, who sought active solutions for complicated problems in governing all-under-heaven, is simple and straightforward: allow things to unfold in their time and act accordingly. It evinces the profound naturalist principle expounded in the *Zhuangzi*. To roam the "wilderness" means to let things go their own way. This includes allowing human life to take its natural course, which, in this case, is signified by the chariot of the sun. Unreflective human intentions, designs, and endeavors bring harm as they interfere with nature's rhythm. Xie arrives at an unassuming lesson toward the end of the poem, saying that the "beleaguered soul" (line 24) is only cured through conscious daily living.

The final three couplets of "A Newly Constructed Lodge" are what some scholars call the "tail of metaphysical discourse" (*xuanyan weiba* 玄言尾巴)—adulterating poetry with philosophical discourse.[49] The influence of Daoist canons such as the *Laozi* and *Zhuangzi* became so widely spread in the Eastern Jin that poetry was only used as a vessel to pass on their teachings. The result was so-called metaphysical poetry (*xuanyan shi*), a trend that literary histories considered a setback. A dynamic intellectual of his time, Xie Lingyun participated in and arguably pushed the development of both old and new philosophies and teachings. The ubiquitous presence of Dao and *li* in his poetry, although proof of his metaphysical preoccupation, doesn't prevent a distinctively different kind poetry from emerging.[50] With his lyrical ordering, the evasive cosmic principle is signified through a transparent vision of a nature that is at the same time textual and realistic. As such, Xie's poetry clarifies, cutting through the density and opacity of the metaphysical discourses prevalent in the works of his contemporaries. Bao Zhao, a poet inspired by Xie's landscape representation, aptly characterized it with the metaphor of "a fresh lotus blossom emerging from the water."

"COMPOSED ON THE LAKE"

A persistent theme in Xie's poetry is that nature has the power to inspire and rejuvenate the weary soul. As shall be seen in the next poem, "mountains and waters" cleanse and lift one's spirit. Momentary bewilderment dissipates as one focuses on "seeing" the world; the labyrinth of emotional difficulties can be navigated through mentally engaging with what meets the body and mind. For Xie, writing a poem is the means and end to achieve order. Constructing the landscape is a process of patterning that extends from the ephemeral external world to the invisible and unknowable inner world. Nature, presented in a framework textual and natural imagery, has the power to clarify and delight. Consider the following piece, "Returning from the Stone Cliff Retreat: Composed on the Lake" (Shibi jingshe huan huzhong zuo 石壁精舍還湖中作; hereafter, "Composed on the Lake"):[51]

	昏旦變氣候	Between dawn and dusk, the climate has changed;
	山水含清暉	mountains and waters are imbued in a clear glow.
	清暉能娛人	The clear glow may delight the traveler,
4	遊子憺忘歸	who dallies and forgets to return.[52]
	出谷日尚早	It was early when I departed from the valley;
	入舟陽已微	when I moor the boat, the sunlight has faded.
	林壑斂暝色	Dimming hues gather about forests and ravines;
8	雲霞收夕霏	evening mists cluster into rosy clouds.
	芰荷迭映蔚	Lotus leaves incessantly shine in their luxuriance;
	蒲稗相因依	waving in chorus are the cattails and sweet flags.[53]
	披拂趨南逕	Brushing against them, I approach the southern path;
12	愉悅偃東扉	filled with joy, I close the eastern gates.
	慮澹物自輕	Rinsed free from worries, the burden of the world is lifted;
	意愜理無違	when the mood is light, order arrives without hindrance.
	寄言攝生客	Let me present these words to those who nourish life,
16	試用此道推	who may try to reason like this.

"Composed on the Lake" is considered a prime example of Xie's artistic achievement in depicting the natural landscape.[54] "Mountains and waters" (line 2) is used as a signifier for nature, whose transformative effect on humans is two-fold. While the mountain breathes air, water sustains different stages of life. The poet-observer "travels" through the miraculous play of light and shadow, becoming more and more mindful of each present moment and forgetting about what has weighed on his "conscious mind." When the unconscious takes over, he loses track of human time. Delightful oblivion is made possible through an immersion in the landscape. The physical body is transformed; the traveler is lost (line 4).

The poet-speaker reemerges from the ellipsis and describes what appears to be the finale of a splendid display of color and light (lines 7 and 8). The lush lotus leaves (line 9) and waving sweet flags (line 10) represent the dense real world and overwhelming phenomenon that surround the human. Blinding and intruding, they are to be brushed aside (line 11). The poet concludes that his heart is joyful and his mood light, free from the worries of the world. This piece categorically redefined lyrical poetry by erasing the philosophical. The "tail of metaphysical discourse" is no more, as the deeper message, as the poet indicates in the last line, can be reached through "this way," referring to a communion with "mountains and waters."

The category under which the *Wen xuan* compilers assigned this poem was "excursions and sightseeing" (*youlan*).[55] Of the twenty-four poems by eleven writers, almost 40 percent—nine pieces—were by Xie Lingyun. Three other members of the Xie clan—Xie Hun, Xie Huilian 謝惠連 (406–33), and Xie Tiao 謝朓 (464–99)—are represented with one poem each. Preceding the Xies are two titles by Cao Pi and Yin Zhongwen (d. 407).[56] Following the Xies are five poets, each represented with one piece except Yan Yannian, who has four and Shen Yue who has three. Xie Lingyun was clearly the leading poet in this category.

"Composed on the Lake," at only sixteen lines, reveals nature's mystery with a poetic solution. The striking depiction of nature with the term "clear glow" (line 2) reveals Xie's new way of seeing the world, which served as a reflection of the cosmic light. In other words, mountains and waters convey the truth. In early poetry, "clear glow" is seldom associated with mountains and waters. Instead, it is used to describe the sun, the moon, or the all-mighty ruler.[57] Xie Lingyun's use is an anomaly. Replacing these visible powers in the natural and human worlds with the invisible force of mountains and waters crowns nature as the reigning force of the universe. Through poetry, Xie is instigating a revolution that is at the same time intellectual and institutional. His "turning away" was not a concrete or incidental act, but symbolic and paradigmatic. In the natural world presented in Xie's poetry, there is no hierarchy. The myriad things are all in harmony with the cosmic law. The presence of this law can be approached by approximation (*qin*; literally, "treating as kin") to mountains and waters. The mystery of nature is the paradox. One can reach for the ultimate principle, but one cannot attain it. Hence, Xie omits some things while highlighting others. The descriptor "clear glow" is a paradox, clarity and haziness wrapped in one.

"GAZING FROM LAKE SHAMAN"

An epiphany is sometimes what our poet seeks on his excursions. The lake that seems to give him magical revelations was aptly called Wu (Shaman). A comparable poem to "Composed at the Lake" is "Gazing from Lake Shaman while I Traveled from the Southern Mountain to the Northern Mountain" (Yu Nanshan wang Beishan jing huzhong tiaowang 於南山往北山經湖中瞻眺; hereafter, "Gazing from Lake Shaman").[58]

	朝旦發陽崖	At dawn, I depart from the sunlit cliffs;[59]
	景落憩陰峰	at dusk, I respite by the shaded peaks.[60]
	舍舟眺迴渚	Leaving my boat, I gaze at the winding islets;[61]
4	停策倚茂松	planting my walking stick, I lean against a majestic pine.
	側逕既窈窕	The roundabout trail meanders like a maze;
	環洲亦玲瓏	the curving sandbars are intricate and labyrinthine.
	俛視喬木杪	Looking down, I see the tips of the towering trees;
8	仰聆大壑灇	turning my head, I listen to the roar of the ravine.
	石橫水分流	Boulders block, water parts;
	林密蹊絕蹤	thickets thicken, the path loses its track.
	解作竟何感	Releasing: what is the effect?[62]
12	升長皆丰容	Rising: all are exuberantly lush and luxuriant.[63]
	初篁苞綠籜	First shoots are enveloped in green shells;
	新蒲含紫茸	new cattails are imbued in purple fuzz.
	海鷗戲春岸	Seagulls frolic by the verdant shores;
16	天雞弄和風	sky-pheasants dally in the balmy wind.
	撫化心無厭	Embracing the transformations, one's heart shall never grow weary;
	覽物眷彌重	surveying the world, my attachment ever increases.
	不惜去人遠	I lament not that I am cut off from others;

20	但恨莫與同	it is only regrettable that I have no one to share [the moment].
	孤遊非情歎	Solitary journeying is not what my heart desires;
	賞廢理誰通	no one to appreciate; no one to relate to!

Comprising eleven couplets—the average length of Xie Lingyun's five-syllable line-verse—this poem's lyrical representation of nature is informed with two complementing rules for cognition that came to be established during the Han. First is the binary rule or yin-yang principle, which provides the underlying structure of lyrical poetry organized by the parallel couplet. The second rule is the constant law of change and transformation, on which *The Classic of Changes* was based. Under these laws, the poet's bodily immersion in nature constitutes movements along parallel axes of time and space. Nothing is static, as everything transforms along with the sun. The *yang* (sunlit/southern) cliffs stand across from the *yin* (shaded/northern) peaks (lines 1 and 2). The horizontal boat alternates with the vertical walking stick as means of travel (lines 3 and 4). Winding islets complement the upstanding pine. The sights of nature rival that of a kaleidoscope (lines 5 and 6). Possibilities of "reading" and "ordering" nature are endless, depending on where one gazes and how one sees. Looking down, the tip of a tall tree must be an unusual sight (line 7). Listening without looking, what does the roaring water sound like (line 8)? The orderliness created through the binary principle is but an ephemeral illusion, since nothing is static. That the cosmic force of change is powerful is expressed through two allusions to *The Classic of Changes* in lines 11 and 12. Scholars such as Francis Westbrook and Wendy Swartz have argued that in Xie Lingyun's depiction of nature the line between the textual and real landscapes disappears when the poet incorporates images from the text. Commenting on lines 11 and 12, Swartz points out how Xie highlights "the way of heaven" that is "reified in meteorological phenomena" and that "effects regeneration in the sphere of terrestrial processes"—the "way of earth."[64] In other words, Xie's gaze is guided by an internalized pattern of the universe as informed by canonical texts such as *The Classic of Changes*. This intricate and seamless weaving together of the experiential and the cognitive is perhaps Xie's greatest achievement.

Nature is reconfigured, as the poet travels to trace the Way and roams to reveal the law. Commenting on "Gazing from Lake Shaman," Westbrook posits: "The poem hangs somewhere between morning and evening, the shore and the summit, and to speculate on the poet's exact position would be to misread his intent to escape normal time and space relationships."[65]

Indeed, the poet erases himself from the scene in line 10 where the forests thicken. The two hexagrams Release and Rising have embedded commentaries that become part of the natural scenery. The "Commentary on the Judgments" for Release reads: "When Heaven and Earth allow Release, thunder and rain play their roles; when thunder and rain play their roles, all the various fruits, shrubs, and trees burgeon forth."[66] The "Commentary on the Images" for Rising reads: "Within the Earth grows the Tree: this is the image of Climbing. In the same way, the noble man lets virtue be his guide and little by little becomes lofty and great."[67] Also illuminating is the "Commentary on the Judgments" for Rising: "The soft and weak climb at their proper time. When obedience is practiced with compliance and when the hard and strong respond in such a way that the Mean is preserved, great prevalence is achieved."[68] The messages and images conveyed through hexagrams 40 and 46 lead to a springtime scene where life in all forms is celebrated. In the second part of the poem, the mood and tone, although joyful, quickly give way to a familiar lament of loneliness (lines 19 through 22), recalling the final couplet of "Ascending the Summit of Stone Gate:" "I only regret that there isn't a like-minded sojourner; / with whom I shall ascend the stairs leading to the heavens."

Xie revolutionized nature poetry by viewing the world through classical wisdom. His poetry weaves together ethical lessons from history, emotional depth from *Songs of Chu*, and philosophical insights from *The Classic of Changes*. His work moves between the personal perspective and the cosmic yin-yang duality, transcending surface observations. By seeing with his mind's eye, he explores the universe freely. His poetry reveals the mysteries of existence with unprecedented clarity, while the themes of solitude and human connection in his poetry reflect deeper principles of singularity and duality. As we will see in the next chapter, his lyric expressions of loneliness and appreciation for others mirror these universal patterns.

CHAPTER 5

Poetic Loneliness

Obi Kōichi, a renowned Japanese sinologist, subtitled his 1983 monograph on Xie Lingyun *The Lonely Landscape Poet* (Sha Reiun: Kodoku no sansui shijin). Many lines from Xie's poetry may be cited to support this view. Passages celebrating enlightening and even epiphanous traveling and sightseeing often end with him lamenting the absence of a like-minded friend. But to what extent is loneliness a literary trope? What early traditions does our poet perform? In what ways does his lyricism conform to or depart from them? How much can these confessions of loneliness be read biographically, in light of his belief system and social interactions? This chapter will examine some of these questions.

Reified Traveling

The last lines of "Ascending the Summit of Stone Gate" use the phrase "fellow traveler" (*tonghuai ke*) to refer to a friend with whom he wishes to ascend the "stairs leading to the heavens" (*qingyun ti*). These images and ideas take us directly back to *Songs of Chu*.[1] The Chu ritual songs dedicated to the gods of the heavens, masters of life, and nymphs of mountains and rivers invariably mention, in different degrees of detail, shamanistic journeys. These prosodically *sao*-style renditions of the heavenly travels were later appropriated by *fu* writers at the Han court in their sometimes satirical portrayal of the religious transcendence of the Daoist adept, a much-envied profession during the Han. "Far Roaming" (Yuanyou) and "The Great One" (Daren fu) are notable examples.[2] During the Jian'an period, the motif known as "roaming immortals" (alternatively, "wandering into transcendency"), rendered in the form of lyric poetry, appeared.[3] Eastern Jin writers furthered the tradition in both *shi* poetry and *fu*. Sun Chuo's (314–71) "*Fu* on roaming the Celestial Terrace Mountains" (You Tiantai shan fu) describes the mountains of Zhejiang through an amalgamated linguistic lens of Buddhism and Daoism.[4] Guo Pu's (276–324) set of fourteen pentasyllabic poems on "roaming immortals" (*youxian* 遊仙), in contrast, paraphrase the discourse of disengagement.[5] For example, the first piece of the set reads:

	京華游俠窟	The bustling capital is the lair of knights errant;
	山林隱遯棲	in mountains and forests, hermits may dwell.
	朱門何足榮	Vermilion Gates—why envy?
4	未若託蓬萊	Better still, commit to the immortal islets of Penglai.
	臨源挹清波	Facing a stream, you drink from clear ripples;
	陵崗掇丹荑	scaling the ridge, you gather cinnabar shoots.
	靈谿可潛盤	In an efficacious gorge, you can roam and ramble;
8	安事登雲梯	why trouble yourself to ascend the stairs to heavens?
	漆園有傲吏	From the lacquer garden hailed a prideful officer;
	萊氏有逸妻	a man from Lai boasted an unconventional wife.
	進則保龍見	Advancing—the dragon is to appear;
12	退為觸藩羝	withdrawing—an antelope gets his horn caught in the fence.
	高蹈風塵外	High and above, you shall tread beyond the dust and wind;
	長揖謝夷齊	with a long bow, you bid farewell to Bo Yi and Shu Qi.

Comprising a medley of complementary and at times contradictory platitudes of turning away, hiding, and fleeing, Guo Pu's roaming immortal rambles freely in a familiar discursive space. Such meditative chant maintains its universal relevance for the politically disenchanted throughout Chinese history. Lines 3 through 6 describe Penglai, the famous islands of the immortals, only to be followed with advice against pursuing immortality in line 8. Line 9 gives Zhuangzi as an example for "self-obscuring while serving" or the so-called obscuring-in-court (*chaoyin*).[6] Line 10 cites a recluse who took the advice from his lofty-minded wife to leave the world of glory and fame. The penultimate couplet (lines 11 and 12) recommends "advancing" and cautions against "withdrawing," while the concluding lines ask one to leave the service of a violent government. Bo Yi and Shu Qi (line 14) chose to starve themselves in political protest, but the poem argues against such sacrifice. Instead, it advocates for emotional detachment and finding fulfillment in private life.

This poem suffers from the weaknesses of metaphysical discourse poetry, mechanically stacking references without rising above them through a clear vision. Themes of immortality, disengagement, and mountain-dwelling are scattered without coherence, reflecting the deliberate obscurity found in metaphysical debates. In contrast, Xie Lingyun treats these same themes with a clear focus. A reader, as a result, may expect a lucid poetic vision rather than a jumbled set of topics. Take, for example, "Ascending the Lone Islet in the Ou River" (Deng jiang zhong gu yu 登江中孤嶼).[7]

	江南倦歷覽	South of the river I have exhaustively traveled;
	江北曠周旋	north of the river I have neglected to visit.
	懷新道轉迥	Yearning for something new, I turn on a path that is remote;[8]
4	尋異景不延	for my search for the unusual, the sun doesn't stretch.
	亂流趨正絕	Against a torrential current, I head directly toward a cliff-bank;
	孤嶼媚中川	a solitary islet beckons charmingly in mid-stream.
	雲日相輝映	Clouds and sun concur in their shining glory;
8	空水共澄鮮	sky and water coalesce into a purifying splendor.
	表靈物莫賞	Efficacy hereby manifested, but without appreciation;
	薀真誰為傳	the perfected but hidden ones—who tells their stories?[9]
	想像崑山姿	Its visage mimics that of Mount Kunlun,[10]
12	緬邈區中緣	far and away, it is cut off from the causality of this realm.
	始信安期術	Now I come to believe in Anqi's art;
	得盡養生年	may it assist with my heavenly ordained lifespan.

This poem, categorized under "traveling" (*xinglü*) in the *Wen xuan*, has a striking description of a river scenery in lines 7 and 8 where the natural world offers the beholder a sublime revelation. Without curiosity or willingness to take risks (lines 3 and 4), our poet wouldn't have embarked on this river trip. He describes how he cut through an impassable chaos (*luan*), symbolized by treacherous waters, before a magical lone islet revealed itself in otherworldly glory. There, the poet sees the legendary Mount Kunlun where the Queen Mother of the West dwells. In the last couplet, Xie claims to have been converted to a true believer in the art of immortality. The tripartite structure of poem is evident: an opening that states the poetic occasion, a main part that describes a journey and its sights, and a conclusion. Lines 7 and 8 constitute a pivotal couplet where "the spiritually realized" (*ling*) and "the perfected one" (*zhen*) point to a belief in mysticism. The reader can hardly miss the poet's self-reference with the word *ling*, which is part of Xie Lingyun's Daoist moniker. As is noted in *The Liu-Song History* biography, Xie Lingyun was raised and schooled in the household of Celestial Master Du in Hangzhou. When the poem ends with a reference to the art of Anqi, a fabled immortal, the demoted duke's new conversion (*shixin*, "begin to have faith") is probably a return to a version of his neglected younger self.

The truth found in this encounter echoes Daoist wisdom: live naturally and embrace life's full span. What distinguishes Xie's versification lies in how he makes this abstract admonition concrete through vivid travel descriptions. By weaving together carefully chosen images and words, he reveals nature's spiritual power more clearly than any religious teaching or philosophical argument could. As such, Xie reified traveling through his poetry.

The Solitary Traveler

Sojourner (Ke), another Daoist nickname Xie received at a young age, reflects a worldview frequently represented in early medieval poetry: life is brief and humans are but fleeting visitors to this world. It is through this lens that Xie writes about his travels. Often, the poet assumes the persona of a solitary and weary traveler, yearning for companionship. But Xie invariably takes these conventional tropes further. See, for example, "Traveling to Auburn Rocks, Advancing to the Ocean of Sails" (You chishi jin fanhai 遊赤石進帆海).[11]

	首夏猶清和	At the beginning of summer, the air is clear and balmy;
	芳草亦未歇	spring grasses are not yet done growing.
	水宿淹晨暮	Living on a boat, dawns and dusks have passed,
4	陰霞屢興沒	evening and morning clouds have come and gone;
	周覽倦瀛壖	having extensively seen the seaside,
	況乃陵窮髮	now I am about to cross the ocean.[12]
	川后時安流	The River Lord has calmed the currents;[13]
8	天吳靜不發	the Water God is quiet and hushed.[14]
	揚帆采石華	Raising the sail, I set out to collect rock blooms;[15]
	掛席拾海月	lifting the curtains, we will gather the ocean moons.[16]
	溟漲無端倪	The dark surging waves are boundless;
12	虛舟有超越	an empty boat can ferry me across.[17]
	仲連輕齊組	Zhonglian cared little for rewards from the state of Qi;[18]
	子牟眷魏闕	Zimou glanced toward the Tower of Wei.[19]
	矜名道不足	His pursuit of fame diminished Zimou's connection to the Way;
16	適己物可忽	Following his natural inclinations, Zhonglian detached himself from worldly concerns.
	請附任公言	I wish to mark the words of Master Ren,[20]
	終然謝天伐	so as to avoid being cut down first.

This is an account of a boat journey to the edge of the civilized world. The use of a *hapax legomenon*, the seaside (*yingruan* 瀛壖) in line 5, conveys the poet's sense of exploration, while defamiliarizing the landscape and transporting the reader into uncharted territory ripe for discovery. The professed sense of weariness in lines 3 and 4 paradoxically energizes the poem with its linguistic novelty The term *qiongfa* 窮髮 in line 6, echoing *Zhuangzi's* image of barren borderlands leading to the "heavenly lake," transfers its lexical novelty into the claimed unknown terrain.[21] The scenic description that follows in the next three couplets, lines 7 through 12, takes the reader to an exciting world imbued with a sense of wonder. The "rock blooms" and "ocean moons"—poetic names for shellfish—deliver the weary traveler from dreary contemplation to a realm of hope and possibility. As the poet dissolves into the scene, his consciousness emerges as an "empty boat"—the Zhuangzian state of transcending ego. Now "ferried across" (*chaoyue* 超越; literally, "transcending"), Xie concludes the poem with a clear vision of choosing between worldly fame (*wu*) and the authentic, natural self (*ji*). He populates the last three couplets of the poem with historical examples, notably Lu Zhonglian, who chose coastal seclusion over court life. Lu's selfless deeds and his rejection of reward, as discussed earlier in this volume, mirror the examples set by Xie Lingyun's own ancestors, Xie An and Xie Xuan.

In this poem, the rationalization that helps the weary traveler navigate into the open is a distinctive performance of the *Zhuangzi*. The unburdened "empty boat," together with the "straight tree" and "sweet spring" embedded in the allusion to Master Ren in the penultimate line, contains the lesson of how to live life naturally. Do not allow external things to interfere with the equilibrium of the inner world. Sail through life on an empty boat: a mind free of clutter. Self-voiding (*xu* 虛), letting go of the self, is the path to enlightened being. Cast away vanity; chase not what the common world values.

Xie excelled at transforming abstract wisdom into lasting insight through carefully crafted poetic moments. "Seven-League Rapids" (Qili lai 七里瀨) is an apt example.[22]

	羈心積秋晨	The tethered one—his heart heavy with autumnal thoughts at dawn;
	晨積展遊眺	at dawn, heart heavy—his eyes roam and he gazes.
	孤客傷逝湍	A solitary traveler is saddened by the rushing torrents;
4	徒旅苦奔峭	a lone wayfarer is troubled by the sliding rocks.
	石淺水潺湲	Over the stony shallows, water burbles and gurgles;
	日落山照曜	when the sun sets, mountains are illuminated.
	荒林紛沃若	In the desolate forest—a profusion of bright-colored leaves;

8	哀禽相叫嘯	pathetic birds shriek and whistle, calling out ceaselessly.
	遭物悼遷斥	Encountering these external things, I grieve my own demotion;
	存期得要妙	to preserve and persist, one ought to grasp the essential way.
	既秉上皇心	Holding fast to the mind of sage-kings from high antiquity;
12	豈屑末代誚	the jeering from the late-age is not worthy of my concern.
	目覩嚴子瀨	Now that I have witnessed Yanzi's rapids;[23]
	想屬任公釣	my thoughts extend to Master Ren— the fisherman.[24]
	誰謂古今殊	Who says that past and present share no path?
16	異代可同調	Living in different times—I concur in their tune.

"Seven-League Rapids" begins with Xie's exile-induced melancholy. Composed in the autumn of 422 during his journey to Yongjia, the poem captures his depression while navigating this treacherous section of the Qiantang River.[25] The first stanza builds a mood of despair through vocabulary like "tethered," "heavy-hearted," "lonely," "solitary," "painful," and "lamentable." The autumn season and dawn setting reinforce these themes of loss. The anadiplosis in lines 1 and 2 possibly implies an episode of insomnia where the poet has sat through the night. The rushing torrents (line 3) and sliding rocks (line 4) intensify the journey's bleakness. Yet the second stanza introduces order through the water-mountain duality—the middle pivot syllables of lines 5 and 6. Nature reveals its sounds and sights—gurgling spring water flowing over the rocks (line 5) and an illuminated silhouette of a mountain range (line 6). The somber tone of the poem, however, persists with its mixture of desolation and activity. In lines 7 and 8, the poet sees evidence of robust life in wilderness and hears calls for companionship from the birds. In the next stanza, the poet indicates the cause of his woes—he was banished from court (line 9). Now, he seeks solace through the teachings of Laozi and Zhuangzi.[26] He finds inspiration in the lives of ancient men such as Yanzi and Master Ren. The poem concludes on a reassuring note: a man rejected by his contemporaries shall find worthy companions beyond his own time.

In the next poem, "Following Jinzhu Gully, I Cross the Mountain and Travel along a Brook" (Cong Jinzhu yue ling xi xing 從斤竹澗越嶺溪行), Xie envisions an uncanny encounter with a spiritual being while tangled in the wilderness.[27]

	猿鳴誠知曙	Gibbons calling, I know then it is dawn;
	谷幽光未顯	the valley, in seclusion, is late to receive sunlight.
	巖下雲方合	Beneath the cliff, clouds are just gathering;
4	花上露猶泫	over the petals, dewdrops still glisten.
	逶迤傍隈隩	Twisting and turning, the path follows along nooks and crannies;
	苕遞陟陘峴	winding and meandering, the trail ascends into passes and peaks.
	過澗既厲急	Crossing the gulley, I wade through rapid currents;
8	登棧亦陵緬	climbing the plank-path, I hover over the abyss.
	川渚屢逕復	Stream islets frequently come and go;
	乘流翫迴轉	following the waves, I trifle through the whirling currents.
	蘋萍泛沈深	Water-clovers bob on the surface, then sink deep;
12	菰蒲冒清淺	wild rice shoots and cattails pierce the clear shallows.
	企石挹飛泉	Standing on tiptoes on a boulder, I reach toward cascading water;
	攀林摘葉卷	grabbing at branches, I cull the tendrils.
	想見山阿人	A figure seems to appear by the mountainside.
16	薜蘿若在眼	Clad in figs and lichen, he emerges before my eyes.
	握蘭勤徒結	A clasp of thoroughwort—I have earnestly knotted in vain;
	折麻心莫展	a snap of hemp flowers—my heartfelt feelings are not conveyed.
	情用賞為美	Sincerity is reserved for the one who appreciates me;

20 事昧竟誰辨　　human affairs are too obfuscated to judge.
觀此遺物慮　　Facing this sight, I shall forget my concerns for
　　　　　　　　the world;
一悟得所遣　　suddenly enlightened, I am able to dispel my
　　　　　　　　doubts.

Here, much of the poetic space is devoted to a detailed description of the sights and sounds a traveler may encounter as he treks across mountains and wades through streams, including natural phenomena such as dewdrops and clouds, and distant views of trails, flora, and fauna. The reader can follow the movement of the poet to experience all the elements of nature. Nature appears dynamic in the poem as Xie shows us not just what exists, and most importantly, how it comes to be. The water plants, for example, are thriving and playful (lines 11 and 12), beckoning the poet who reciprocates by turning his affection toward the trees and grasses. They trigger memories of a friend, stirring a desire to share the pleasure with this beloved companion. Yet these thoughts only deepen his sorrow. His mention of "affairs" in line 20 remains deliberately vague. We never learn who Xie misses or what troubles him. But these personal details matter less than the universal truth they reveal: worldly matters (*wu*) are entanglements that burden the spirit. To free oneself from such entanglements, one shall follow the Way. Like the poet, one should turn to nature both for clarity and refuge from the complexities of human society.

In the poem's main section, nature presents itself clearly, forging a deep connection with the poet who travels through its embrace and encounters its inhabitants. He hears the gibbons, then he knows the time; he sees clouds and dewdrops, he senses kinship; he follows the trails; he frolics with the spring water. The movement of the water evokes graceful ease, despite the descriptive binomes that recall the difficult language employed in Han rhapsodic writing. Xie's structural and syntactic balance reflects a belief that the deep mountains can be navigated with an understanding of the topography. The impression of a well-charted road that unfolds under his feet is achieved through imagery, phraseology, and structure. The use of four binomes in lines 5 and 6—two rhyming and two alliterative—contribute to a rhythmic flow that mimics the described scene and is one of Xie's signature styles. In addition, the focus placed on water as nature's essential element follows its metamorphoses from dewdrop to cloud to spring water to stream. Water balances and cleanses with an invisible yet incessant movement. It has no form and yet it penetrates the intractable. It is fluid, from which freedom arises. Water can even fly, as seen in line 13, which can be called the "eye of the poem."[28] In the scene, the poet, standing on his toes, reaches for the soaring waterfall. Flight from the world is the palpable sensation coming at the reader. The pivotal verb *yi* (to grasp) conveys an age-old human desire to flee from the world. Parallelism, moreover, frames nature, highlighting its fluidity and connectedness, while embodying its fundamental principle of reciprocity.

Also evident in this poem is the influence of *Songs of Chu*.[29] Most notably, the "person by the mountainside" in line 15 alludes to the Mountain Spirit, part of the shamanistic ritual ensemble known as the "Nine Songs."[30] The reference to a winsome otherworldly being in this poem remains debatable. Some scholars believe this spectral being is a reference to Liu Yizhen, the Liu-Song prince.[31] It is also plausible that the secluded apparition is the image of an idealized spiritual self that is pure and unpolluted by society, because "loneliness" often appears in Xie Lingyun's poetry as a theme denoting an insistence on impractical virtue. To a great degree, it is an extension of the *sao* tradition where the "fair one" is lamentably elusive. An enlightened prince, a like-minded friend, and an appreciative patron are hard to come by. Under the pressure of social conformation, good men go into hiding. The practice of and belief in solitary cultivation grew popular following the dissolution of the Han Confucian institution. Those who escape the net of the world are promised with a life in the mountains, where nature provides for both body and spirit. Xie, while drawing from the *Songs of Chu*, expanded the *sao* tradition for friendship poetry, although not all of the specific references can be identified.

Poems of Friendship

Scholars who identified Liu Yizhen in the previous poem may have erred on the side of biographical interpretation without sufficient evidence. However, there are poems in Xie Lingyun's oeuvre that spell out exactly with whom he spends his time, or on whom he lavishes his affection, or for whom he mourns. Poetic representation of Xie's social relations are explicitly and firmly grounded in historical records in the following piece, "Composed Reverently at the Prince of Luling's Tomb" (Luling wang muxia zuo 盧陵王墓下作), which is dedicated to Liu Yizhen.[32]

	曉月發雲陽	Under the moon at early dawn, I set out from Yunyang;[33]
	落日次朱方	by sunset, I arrive at Zhufang.[34]
	含悽泛廣川	Harboring sorrow, I sail across the broad river;[35]
4	灑淚眺連岡	with tears flowing, I gaze at the mountain range.
	眷言懷君子	With a pang of feeling, I think fondly of the noble prince;
	沉痛切中腸	deep pain rends my heart.
	道消結憤懣	"The Gentlemanly Way waned!" Indignation fills my chest.
8	運開申悲涼	Now that change has arrived, I can state my sadness.[36]
	神期恒若存	The prince's spirited countenance is vivid in my mind;
	德音初不忘	his virtuous tone I still can hear.
	徂謝易永久	Since his passing, days have gone by;
12	松栢森已行	pines and cypresses are forming into rows.
	延洲協心許	Prince Jizha in his heart pledged the sword to Lord Xu;[37]
	楚老惜蘭芳	the old man of Chu lamented Gong Sheng's passing.[38]
	解劍竟何及	Untying his sword, to whom could Prince Jizha present the gift?[39]
16	撫墳徒自傷	Stroking the tomb, I alone grieve.
	平生疑若人	Throughout my life, I have regarded the Prince of Luling as my peer;[40]
	通蔽互相妨	between good fortune and bad, harm is incurred.
	理感心情慟	Its reason now I can see, but my heart feels the pain;

20 定非識所將　　This is beyond anyone's comprehension.
　　脆促良可哀　　Vulnerable and short is his life! How truly
　　　　　　　　　　mournful!

　　天枉特兼常　　Even more so considering he is innocent and so
　　　　　　　　　　young.

　　一隨往化滅　　Once gone, he vanishes into oblivion;
24　安用空名揚　　what use is there to spread an empty name?
　　舉聲泣已瀝　　Sobbing loudly, my tears stream and flow,
　　長歎不成章　　with long sighs, how can I complete this piece?

To properly read this difficult and yet touching poem of heartfelt emotion, it's best to learn more about the relationship between Xie Lingyun and Liu Yizhen, and the consequences that relationship had for both parties. The Prince of Luling, Liu Yu's second son, was born in 407, and was thus twenty-two years younger than Xie. When Liu Yu fell ill in 422, Liu Yizhen became a rival successor to his brother Liu Yifu, who was one year older. Court members formed factions on behalf of the two young princes in bidding for their own power and influence. Xie, having served as a literary companion and tutor to the Prince of Luling, joined the side opposing the more powerful clique led by Xu Xianzhi, who forcibly installed the older brother Yifu as emperor on the same day Liu Yu died (June 26, 422). Xie Lingyun, among others, was quickly removed from court. In early 424, Liu Yizhen was subsequently demoted to the status of commoner. In the summer of 424, both Liu Yizhen and then emperor Liu Yifu were murdered separately, although probably on the same day.[41] Xu Xianzhi then placed Liu Yu's third son, Liu Yilong, on the throne. By early 426, the nineteen-year-old Emperor Wen was able to assert his authority by putting Xu Xianzhi to death and summoning the exiled officials back to court. Among them was Xie Lingyun, who, after repeated court invitations and following the encouragement of old friends, embarked on a journey to the capital Jiankang in the third month of 426.[42] Xie took a detour to pay condolences to Liu Yizhen. The piece he composed at this time was included in the *Wen xuan* under the category of "Elegies and Laments" (Aishang). The tone of indignation and sadness is palpable throughout the entire work. Xie Lingyun does not hold back

in expressing his disappointment with the Liu-Song court. The preface
to the poem testifies to its historical significance:

> Yizhen, son of Emperor Wu of Liu-Song, was enfeoffed as the Prince of
> Luling. Before he was established in his fiefdom, Emperor Wu passed
> away. The Prince of Luling was highly intelligent and fond of learning.
> Oftentimes, he associated with Xie Lingyun. Due to the lack of virtue on
> the part of the Young Emperor [Liu Yifu], court officials schemed about
> succession. Because Luling was second in line to succeed the throne,
> they spread rumors accusing him of being frivolous and incapable of
> shouldering the duties expected of a ruler. Later still, due to conflicts be-
> tween the Prince of Luling and the Young Emperor, Xu Xianzhi and his
> ilk proposed to demote him and send him away to Xin'an Commandery.
> [Still later,] Xu Xianzhi sent an assassin and had the Prince of Luling
> killed. Earlier, slandering charges had been leveled against Xie Lingyun,
> accusing him of attempting to install the Prince of Luling on the throne.
> For this, Xie Lingyun was exiled. Later, Emperor Wen [Liu Yilong],
> with knowledge of Xie Lingyun's innocence, summoned him back to
> court. When he arrived at Qu'e, Xie Lingyun made a detour to Danyang
> [to visit Yizhen's tomb]. Emperor Wen, during his audience with Xie
> Lingyun, asked: "Since you left for the south, what new compositions
> have you made?" Xie Lingyun [reportedly] replied: "I wrote this one
> piece during my visit to the tomb of the Prince of Luling."[43]

The preface sheds light on how the *Wen xuan* compilers, one century
later, viewed the events surrounding the Prince of Luling's death, Xie
Lingyun's exile, and the latter's subsequent return.[44] They delivered a verdict
of innocence for both Xie Lingyun and Liu Yizhen. Their relationship—as
described here and elsewhere, such as in Xie Lingyun's *Liu-Song History*
biography—is that of an erudite tutor and a literary-minded prince. This
type of relationship, parallel to that of the minister and ruler, recalls the
convivial political-intellectual milieu at the court of Jian'an, an era of enlightened rulers as well as flourishing literary activities. As discussed in
chapter 2, Xie Lingyun in his set of eight poems of emulation imagined
himself as part of the Cao court, where the protection and promotion of
literati fostered friendship between men from different backgrounds, age

groups, and sociopolitical status. Recognition of talent constituted the key to a noble and orderly society where a healthy meritocracy was the foundation of civil government. Xie Lingyun referred to this system as *shang*, a key word in his poetry that can be rendered as "to appreciate," "to recognize," "to value," or "to gift."

Shang is the cornerstone of the homosocial governing body whose members cultivate inner virtue and demonstrate external refinements through the pursuit of arts and literature. Appreciation of talent, recognition of merit, and the valuation of goodness underlie virtuous rule. Unfortunately, by Xie's time, the system was broken. The Prince of Luling, a talented and literary-minded man, was murdered at the tender age of seventeen. Xie's sorrow, mixed with palpable anger, receives direct expressions in the second and third couplets. Through allusions in lines 13 and 14, Xie compares his friendship with Liu Yizhen to the classic example of the ancient Wu prince Jizha, who befriended and patronized Lord Xu with utter sincerity. Yanzhou, the enfeoffed town of Jizha, stands in line 13 for the prince himself.[45] Knowing Lord Xu desired the precious sword that signified the prince's person, Jizha, having fulfilled his official duties, returned to present the gift to his friend, only to find that Lord Xu had passed. Dismayed, the prince mourned his friend and hung his sword on the tree by Lord Xu's tomb.[46] Line 14 alludes to Gong Sheng and how his "fragrance," or virtue and good reputation, drew mourners to his tomb.[47] Both allusions suitably enhance the theme of intense male bonding that was formed on the basis of appreciation and dedication. These allusions speak about Xie's appreciation of the Prince of Luling.

In the same year Liu Yizhen was killed, Xie Lingyun returned to Guiji where he had the chance to meet his cousin Xie Huilian, a talented young poet who was of the same age as the Prince of Luling.[48] The friendship between Xie Lingyun and Xie Huilian led to poetic exchanges that bore witness to homosocial bonding as a support system for young and orphaned (literally and figuratively) talents who relied on patronage from senior scholars in turbulent historical and political moments.[49] The Jin-Song transition during the first quarter of the fifth century was such a time. The poems Xie Huilian sent Xie Lingyun during his boat journey to the capital describe ominous weather and foreboding natural scenery: mountain-like clouds, overshadowed peaks, gusts of wind, rushing torrents, lingering rain, and even falling snow.[50] Understanding how anxious his young cousin may have felt before arriving in the capital, Xie Lingyun responded with empathy in the following five-part poem: "Presented to My Cousin Huilian" (Chou congdi Huilian 酬從弟惠連).[51]

I.

	寢瘵謝人徒	Lying sick in bed, I had turned away all visitors;[52]
	滅迹入雲峰	erasing my traces, I had entered the peak among the clouds.[53]
	巖壑寓耳目	Cliffs and ravines became lodges for my ears and eyes;
4	歡愛隔音容	my dear friend—his face and voice were gone.[54]
	永絕賞心望	Forever dashed—my wish to have a like-minded friend;
	長懷莫與同	my endless feelings—with whom could I share?
	末路值令弟	At the end of my road, yet I met you—my fine cousin;[55]
8	開顏披心胸	for your sake I was happy again and I opened my heart.

II.

	心胸既云披	I opened my heart.
	意得咸在斯	My wish [to have a friend] was fulfilled.
	凌澗尋我室	You crossed the ravine to visit my chamber;
4	散帙問所知	spreading out scrolls, you inquired of what I knew.
	夕慮曉月流	At night we worried about the moon that faded at dawn;
	朝忌曛日馳	during the day we dreaded the sun that galloped away so fleetingly.

悟對無厭歇　Face to face, we talked without stop or feeling tired.

8　聚散成分離　Too soon, our meetings gave way to separation.

III.

分離別西川　Separation took place by the banks of the Western River;

迴景歸東山　with the sun's shadow moving west, I returned to Eastern Mountain.

別時悲已甚　When we parted, my sorrow was unbearable;

4　別後情更延　after parting, my emotions lingered on.

傾想遲嘉音　I waited intensely for your message, which felt slow to arrive;

果枉濟江篇　finally, you sent me the piece on crossing the river—

辛勤風波事　Recounting your hardship on wind and waves,

8　款曲洲渚言　I could understand how you felt, being stranded in mid-stream.

IV.

洲渚既淹時　You were stranded in mid-stream, as time went on;

風波子行遲　by wind and waves, your journey was delayed.

務協華京想　Make firm your resolution to reach the capital;[56]

4　詎存空谷期　how could you fancy a rendezvous in the empty valley?

猶復惠來章　If you grace me with more of your verses,

祇足攬余思　they would be sufficient to stir up my feelings.

儻若果歸言　If you indeed return,

| | 8 | 共陶暮春時 | we shall have a delightful gathering in late spring. |

V.

	暮春雖未交	Late spring has not come to cross;
	仲春善遊遨	mid-spring is also a good time for excursions.
	山桃發紅萼	Mountain oleanders spit forth their pink blossoms;
4	野蕨漸紫苞	wild ferns gradually grow purple shoots.
	嚶鳴巳悅豫	Chirping birds are now happy and delighted;
	幽居猶鬱陶	living in seclusion, I am still deeply depressed.
	夢寐佇歸舟	I dream of waiting for your boat to return;
8	釋我吝與勞	so that I may be released from the bitter torture.

The five-part structure of Xie Lingyun's lyrical piece is arguably an imitation of Cao Zhi's iconic work "To Biao, Prince of Baiba," whose intimate tone, unchecked emotional expressions, and use of anadiplosis earned it an inclusion in the *Wen xuan* as the model for polite expressions of brotherly affection.[57] Beginning each new stanza with the final line from the previous stanza creates a wave-like verbal tapestry that mimics continuous longing. Cao Zhi wrote the piece after the premature death of Cao Zhang 曹彰 in 223. Xie Lingyun's choice to follow Cao Zhi's poetic model shows that his admiration for Jian'an poets extended to the symmetrical and balanced relationship among men that *shi* poetry had come to embody.

The five-part poem exhibits a coherent narrative flow. In part I, the poet speaks of his severance with the world and solitary living in the mountains after his exile. His existential crisis was then compounded by the death of the Prince of Luling. Meeting Xie Huilian, his young and talented cousin who surely reminded Xie Lingyun of the dead prince, was an unexpected turn of events that ameliorated his grief. In part II he recounts Xie Huilian's visit, their night-long conversations, and shared interests in classics and learning. These happy times were brief. Part III mentions Xie Huilian's departure for the capital and the delay due to "wind and waves," a metaphor for an unfavorable political climate. In part IV, Xie Lingyun encourages his cousin to persist on his journey despite the "treacherous waters." He asks him not to return east for the prospect of a joyful reunion. Yet this advice seems to be offered with conflicted feelings, because in the final part of the poem, the poet describes a future meeting in the spring and shares a dream where he summons his cousin's boat. In the Tang miscellany *Classified Extracts from Literature* (Yiwen leiju), a short poem from Xie Lingyun to his cousin upon the latter's arrival in the capital reads: "The one on my mind traveled a thousand leagues; / my heart labored for a hundred days. / When we parted, flowers were burning bright; / now the leaves are lush and verdant."[58]

Sinologist Nick Williams aptly posits that the friendship between Xie Lingyun and Xie Huilian was based on "recognition of talent" and "appreciation of virtue."[59] Poems are gifts. They are reifications of homosocial reciprocity and brotherly filiality. *Shang*—to recognize, to value, and to gift—was the last sanctuary for the threatened noble class during the Jin-Song transition. An emotional safehouse, poetry opened existential space for lives that are "vulnerable."[60] Like the Prince of Luling, Xie Huilian died prematurely. He was only twenty-six when he passed in 433, the same year Xie Lingyun was publicly executed more than a thousand miles away in the remote south.[61] Xie Huilian's official biography in *The Liu-Song History* describes his writings as "beautiful," "exceptionally ornate," and "uncommon."[62] "Autumnal Thoughts" (Qiu huai 秋懷), an autobiographical lyrical piece, is perhaps one of Xie Huilian's best known works.[63]

	平生無志意	Since I was young, I have lacked ambition;
	少小嬰憂患	from an early age, I was tormented by ill health.
	如何乘苦心	How do I last with this suffering heart?[64]
4	矧復值秋晏	as once again it's this season of late autumn.[65]
	皎皎天月明	Illuminating is the moon in the sky;
	弈弈河宿爛	bright are the stars in the Milky Way.
	蕭瑟含風蟬	In the sighing wind, cicadas chirp;
8	寥唳度雲鴈	honking geese skip over the clouds.

	寒商動清閨	A cold gust stirs my desolate chamber;
	孤燈曖幽幔	a solitary lamp dims the dark curtains.
	耿介繁慮積	Upright yet misunderstood, my manifold cares accumulate;
12	展轉長宵半	tossing and turning, I am unable to sleep for much of the night.
	夷險難豫謀	Peaceful or perilous—life is hard to predict;
	倚伏昧前筭	good fortune or bad—no calculations can reveal.
	雖好相如達	Although I am fond of Sima Xiangru who was unimpeded;
16	不同長卿慢	I cannot agree to Zhangqing's impetuousness.
	頗悅鄭生偃	I in particular admire Scholar Zheng who withdrew from service;
	無取白衣宦	but I do not approve of service in "commoner's clothes."
	未知古人心	I have not yet fully comprehended the minds of the ancients;
20	且從性所翫	for now, I shall follow what suits my nature.
	賓至可命觴	When guests arrive, I will order drinks;
	朋來當染翰	when friends come, I will moisten the writing brush.
	高臺驟登踐	Tall belvederes I have occasionally climbed;
24	清淺時陵亂	in limpid streams, I have sometimes waded.
	頽魄不再圓	A waning moon will not be full again;
	傾羲無兩旦	a toppled sun-chariot does not rise twice.
	金石終消毀	Metal and stone, ultimately, will erode;
28	丹青暫彫煥	cinnabar and azurite only glow briefly.
	各勉玄髮歡	Each of us should make merry as our hair is still black;
	無貽白首歎	do not wait to sigh in vain when your hair turns gray.
	因歌遂成賦	For this reason, I have composed this song-poem;
32	聊用布親串	to present to my dear friends.

This is one of the five poems by Xie Huilian included in the *Wen xuan*. Its insistence on and indulgence in a pessimistic view on life is bold, incurring criticism in a culture that values emotional restraint and moderation.[66] The poet portrays himself as leading a lethargic life, languishing in illness, and passively waiting for the inevitable. In lines 5 through 8, he describes seasonal change in cosmic as well as climatic terms, presenting heavenly phenomena and earthly creatures whose response to the end of the warm season recalls death. In the next stanza, lines 9 through 12, he takes us into his immediate surroundings. Invaded by the cold autumn air, his room is dim and dark. Pathetic and restless, the persona suffers from insomnia. Accompanied by a dim lamp, he contemplates his ill fortune. Whereas he takes some measure of comfort in Daoism, allusions to two Han officials in lines 15 through 18 reveal his perplexity over the conflict between one's public role and private life. Sima Xiangru, although a model for aloof equanimity, was too impetuous as a person; to claim court emolument without service sounded dubious as well. Failing to find a model, Xie Huilian decides to follow his own natural disposition (lines 19 and 20). Determined to rid himself of the disconcerting notes emanating from the universe, he ends the poem on a carpe diem theme and takes things in stride. With friends, he can enjoy good company, hearty drinking, and refined pursuits such as poetry. These lines remind us of the social scene of the Jian'an era, which Xie Lingyun also strove to re-create.

Finding Strength in the Past

Xie Huilian's pessimistic view on life as seen in the previous poem exceeds the literary convention. The last round moon and a toppled sun chariot—are these ominous images hints of suicidal intention? His poem appears to give readers a glimpse of his most intimate thoughts. And unlike Xie Lingyun's compositions, it lacks allusions to historical or textual precedents and models. Take, for example, the following poem, "Upon First Leaving the Commandery" (Chu qu jun 初去郡), in which Xie Lingyun uses verse as a means to find strength in exemplars of the past.[67]

彭薛裁知恥	Peng and Xue in lateness showed a sense of shame;[68]
貢公未遺榮	Duke Gong, after all, was not able to cast away the glory.[69]

	或可優貪競	Perhaps they are better than the greedy and contentious,[70]
4	豈足稱達生	yet not sufficient to be called "understanding life."[71]
	伊余秉微尚	This humble self adheres to a modicum of goodness;
	拙訥謝浮名	clumsy and tongued-tied, I shall decline ephemeral fame.
	廬園當棲巖	A hut in the field may match a perch on the cliff;
8	卑位代躬耕	a lowly position replaces toiling and ploughing.
	顧已雖自許	Examining myself, although I find reasons to agree,
	心迹猶未并	yet my heart and deeds have disagreed.
	無庸方周任	Lacking utility [to the court], I am with Zhou Ren [in knowing to stop];[72]
12	有疾像長卿	plagued by ill health, I am similar to Zhangqing [in our curtailed career].[73]
	畢娶類尚子	In marrying off my children, I am like Master Shang [who lived untethered];[74]
	薄遊似邴生	in roaming and traveling, I resemble Master Bing.[75]
	恭承古人意	Respectfully I receive instructions from the ancients;
16	促裝返柴荊	I hasten to return to my brushwood hut.
	牽絲及元興	During the Yuanxing reign [402–4], I was tied with silk cords;[76]
	解龜在景平	it was in Jingping [423–24] when I was relieved of the turtle seal.[77]
	負心二十載	For twenty years, I betrayed my heart;
20	於今廢將迎	now I shall cease the receptions and farewells.[78]
	理棹遄還期	Oars ready, I embark on my journey;
	遵渚騖脩坰	following the riverbanks, we pass speedily by the outskirts.
	遡溪終水涉	Sailing upstream, we arrive at the end of the waterway;
24	登嶺始山行	ascending the ridges, the trek in the mountains is about to start.
	野曠沙岸淨	Fields in the distance are laced with neat sandbars;

天高秋月明	the sky is remote, with an autumn moon shining bright.
憩石挹飛泉	Resting on the rock, I draw water from a flying spring;
28　攀林搴落英	trudging in the forest, I gather fallen blossoms.
戰勝臞者肥	Having won the battle inside,[79] I gain back my weight;
鑒止流歸停	a still mirror is formed when the stream returns to a stop.[80]
即是羲唐化	it is through the instructions of Fuxi and Yao[81]
32　獲我擊壤情	that I find my tune in "Beating the Pot."[82]

Xie Lingyun places himself here alongside men from the past in order to validate his decision in leaving court service. Historical examples of various official resignations are evoked in the poem. Some, according to Xie, unwisely stayed in office for too long. He then recalls his own career of twenty years when his heart and actions diverged. Lines 21 through 28 describe a serene sight as he embarks on the return journey. The image of the mirror-like surface of the water reflects the poet's mental calmness. He is now at peace with his difficult choice. Xie even cites his gained weight as a sign of freedom from conflicting thoughts. Body and mind finally agree. The ancient song quoted in the last line refers to a naturalist society where people live in harmony by following the course of the sun: "I rise at sunrise; I rest at sunset; digging a well, I have water; toiling in the field, I have food. Yao is certainly powerful, and yet what does he have to do with me?"[83] This embedded text is from the *Zhuangzi* chapter "Yielding the Throne"; a slightly different version of the song is presented as the exegesis to a recluse's reasons for declining an offer of the throne.

Shun proposed to yield his throne to Shanjuan, who declined by saying: "I stand in the middle of the universe; in winter I wear skins and furs; in summer I wear hemp and linen; in spring I plough and sow; my body is strong enough to labor; in autumn I collect my harvest; my person is ready to cease and feed; I rise at sunrise; I rest at sunset. Free and at ease, I roam in between heaven and earth. My heart is content, my mind is fulfilled. What do I need the throne for? How sad that you are not the one who knows me!" Without accepting Shun's offer, he left and went deep into the mountains. No one knew of his whereabouts.[84]

By evoking this ancient wisdom, Xie Lingyun seems to be proposing a different possibility of harmony in social coexistence. The "lonely poet" is not a loner per se but seeks to restore a vision of society and human relations that dates to high antiquity. It is worth noting that the recluse Shanjuan's complaint regarding Shun was that the king "didn't know" or "didn't understand." This takes us back to the core of what Xie Lingyun found to be lacking in his time—*shang* or "appreciation" and "mutual understanding" based on shared human values. To put it bluntly, Shun was not a kindred spirit.

Xie Lingyun's discourse on "loneliness" brings to light ideals of reciprocal relationship between the noble gentlemen and their support of the ruling class. Their shared interests in the common good at the humanistic and naturalistic levels should ensure a peaceful and self-sufficient society that is free from individual or collective afflictions, artifice, or extraneous formalities. The natural way of living, in Xie Lingyun's mind, can be realized through a return to the mountains, which are the original and final home for humans, especially the weary, vulnerable, and marginalized.

CHAPTER 6

The Hillside Garden

The poet Du Fu (712–70) once pondered whether he could achieve true literary greatness: "How could I ever aspire to write like Tao Yuanming [365–427] and Xie Lingyun?"[1] Though historical records suggest there was no direct contact between these two fifth-century poets, literary history links them as the preeminent voices of the Jin–Song transition. Their reputations evolved along divergent paths: Tao became celebrated as the ideal recluse who avoided political entanglements, while Xie's involvement with Liu-Song rulers drew criticism that overshadowed his literary achievements. The question of martyrdom remains contentious. Readers struggle to reconcile Xie's tragic end, questioning its purpose while finding reassurance in Tao's poetry of private contentment. This has rendered Xie the more challenging poet to interpret. Yet his work's complexity rewards careful analysis. Xie's use of allusions, in particular, reveal the darker undertones of this transitional period through their deliberate complexity.

In the winter of 416–17, the military leader Liu Yu embarked on a northern campaign, making yet another attempt to retake the old capitals of Luoyang and Chang'an. This act was politically symbolic for Liu, whose hold on the Jin had become ever firmer. Xie Lingyun, in his capacity as the top literary talent, was commissioned to compose a congratulatory *fu*—a long and elaborate presentation.[2] But instead of heaping praise on Liu Yu and his military achievements, Xie lauded his ancestors Xie An and Xie Xuan and their heroic deeds that saved the Jin house from the ravages of Fu Jian's army. Whether he purposely missed the mark on this commission is impossible to fathom, but the fact that the work was preserved as part of his official biography shows the significance of this commission and its pro forma nature. Liu Yu returned from his campaign in 418 to make a stop at Pengcheng (modern Xuzhou, Jiangsu), a military outpost two hundred miles northwest of the capital. Here, the general hosted a gathering to assert his authority. By this time, Liu Yu had secured the title Duke of Song. New appointments were also distributed to his followers and other dignitaries, anticipating an imminent change of dynasties. Xie Lingyun received the largely ceremonial titles Gentleman Attendant at the Palace Gate and Gentleman Councilor of the Inner Court.[3] Although these were decorative positions, it was through them that Xie came closest to the usurper Liu Yu. For instance, the poet was commissioned to mark the occasion with the grace of his words and, as a result, we have the following poem: "On the Double Ninth Day, Attending the Farewell Assembly Hosted by the Duke of Song at the Cavalry Terrace in Honor of Secretariat Director Kong" (Jiuri cong Songgong Ximatai ji song Kongling shi 九日從宋公戲馬臺集送孔令詩; hereafter, "On the Double Ninth Day").[4]

	季秋邊朔苦	In the last month of autumn, there are strong winds on the northern border;[5]
	旅鴈違霜雪	migrating geese struggle against the onslaught of frost and snow.
	淒淒陽卉腓	Withering and wilting, all grass has turned sallow under the sun;[6]
4	皎皎寒潭潔	bright and glistening, the frigid pool is immaculate.[7]
	良辰感聖心	On this fine day, his sagacious mind has been stirred;[8]
	雲旗興暮節	cloud-pennants are hoisted to celebrate the late-season festival.[9]
	鳴葭戾朱宮	The sound of reed pipes arrives at the vermillion palace;[10]
8	蘭巵獻時哲	fragrant ale is presented to the savant of our day.[11]
	餞宴光有孚	The banquet is hosted to inspire confidence and trust;[12]
	和樂隆所缺	harmonious conviviality fortifies the lost principle binding lord and vassal.[13]
	在宥天下理	Letting Be—All-under-heaven is in order;[14]
12	吹萬群方悅	Breezing the Myriad—people from all borders are delighted.[15]

歸客遂海隅　　The returning sojourner follows the river course
　　　　　　　to the ocean;[16]

脫冠謝朝列　　taking off his cap, he bows out of the ranks at
　　　　　　　court.[17]

弭棹薄枉渚　　Oars rested, the boat is moored by the winding
　　　　　　　sandbars;[18]

16　指景待樂闋　looking at the sun, he waits for the band to
　　　　　　　announce the hour.[19]

河流有急瀾　　River currents rush forth torrentially;

浮驂無緩轍　　the chariots press forward without pause.[20]

豈伊川途念　　How can I only be pensive about the parting of
　　　　　　　our ways?[21]

20　宿心愧將別　I regret also my cherished aim not being fulfilled.[22]

彼美丘園道　　That marvelous Way of the Hillside Garden![23]

喟焉傷薄劣　　Alas! How I bemoan my paltry virtue and lame
　　　　　　　pursuit![24]

The title of the poem provides the date of the composition: the Double Ninth Festival in the fourteenth year of Yixi reign period, which corresponds to October 24, 418. The title also mentions one Magistrate Kong. This is Kong Jing 孔靖 (347–422; style name Jigong 季恭), a long-time counselor and supporter of Liu Yu.[25] During Liu Yu's campaign to recover the northern capitals of Chang'an and Luoyang, Kong Jing had served as the libationer for the army.[26] Upon Liu Yu's triumphant return, he rewarded Kong Jing with the appointment of director of the imperial secretariat (*shangshu ling*). Declining the honor, Kong Jing requested instead to return to his estate in Guiji. Liu Yu granted the request and hosted a farewell banquet at the Cavalry Terrace (Xima Tai).[27]

Kong Jing's voluntary departure might invite speculation about his disapproval of Liu Yu's imminent takeover, but a ceremonial public gathering would hush any detrimental rumors.[28] In *The Liu-Song History* we read: "[Kong Jing] declined the appointment to return east. The emperor hosted a banquet to bid him farewell at the Cavalry Terrace. All officials [were asked] to present poetry of praise for this."[29] This historical narrative was written after Liu Yu had usurped the throne, as he was referred to as Emperor

Gaozu (Exalted Ancestor). It speaks openly on the function of the banquet, which was to give all officials an opportunity to present "beautifying" poetry about the event. Xie Lingyun employs intertexts to make meaning. But is this an ode? And how does the poet elaborate on the "return" by weaving together a sophisticated intertextual tapestry studded with references from *The Classic of Poetry* and *The Classic of Changes*?

The Classic of Poetry as Meaning-Making Intertexts

Xie Lingyun's poem is included in the *Wen xuan* under the "Lord's Feast" (*gongyan*) category, reflecting the conventions of this banquet poetry tradition.[30] For example, the opening stanza (lines 1 through 4) describes the occasion: a grand gathering in a desolate frontier town in autumn. Nature is portrayed to reflect human experience and emotion. Late autumn in line 1 implies a deterioration in the "kingly way."[31] Frost and snow denote the difficulties endured by campaign soldiers (*zhengfu*). The images of migrating geese and withering grass serve as "evocative imagery" (*xing*), reflecting underlying themes of displacement and social decline.

The poet evokes a rich set of intertexts from *The Classic of Poetry*, such as "The Fourth Month" (Siyue; Mao 204), which is a lament about "turmoil and troubles" (*luanli*), according to the exegesis in the "Lesser Preface."[32] Line 3 of Xie's poem sets the critical tone by bringing readers to the troubled times of the Zhou, which mirrors the last years of the Jin.[33] For those who are familiar with *The Classic of Poetry*, this line will evoke the woeful cry of displaced soldiers—"Alas, where can we return?"[34] Other songs would certainly come to mind as well.

In *The Classic of Poetry*, the soldiers' complaint, together with a set of related type-scenes such as "distressed/deserted wife, abandoned woman" (*sifu*, *qifu*), "yearning but failing to return" (*sigui*), and "hardship on the campaign" (*xinglu nan*), make up some of the most striking examples of the Zhou experiences with war. Famously, "The East Mountain" (Dongshan; Mao 156) gives a wistful account of the Duke of Zhou's arduous three-year campaign.[35] Other songs about the Zhou military actions include "Gathering Bracken" (Cai wei; Mao 167),[36] "Dispatching War Chariots" (Chu ju; Mao 168), "Lone Red Pear Tree" (Di du; Mao 169),[37] "Sixth Month" (Liu yue;

Mao 177), "Gathering Bitter Vegetables" (Cai qi; Mao 178), "Our Chariots Are Mighty" (Ju gong; Mao 179), and "What Grass Does Not Go Yellow" (He cao bu huang 何草不黃; Mao 234).[38] Traditional interpretations from the following (Mao numbered) odes, which were indispensable for later readership, illustrate how Xie Lingyun might have incorporated themes or imagery in his intertextual borrowing:[39]

156 — Soldiers and officers who had returned from the Eastern campaign sing of their grief.

167 — Chastisement of a military campaign.

168 — Commiseration of the sufferings of soldiers and officers who had returned from the frontier campaign against the Xianyun tribe.

169 — Yearnings to return.[40]

177 — King Xuan of Zhou's (?–782 BCE) northern campaign.

178 — King Xuan of Zhou's southern campaign.

179 — Praise of King Xuan of Zhou's restoration of authority and power.

204 — The travail and troubles of war.

234 — Satire of King You of Zhou's (781–70 BCE) time, when all neighboring tribes invaded the Central States, military actions never stopped, and people were treated as animals. Hence the lament from a gentleman-officer.

Although a majority of these poems contain criticism and satire, a few can be read as praise of notable Zhou leaders such as the Duke of Zhou and King Xuan of Zhou whose military achievements helped restore the way of early Zhou founders. Xie Lingyun's reference to Mao 204 in line 3 is intertextually striking, as it counters the required "celebratory" (*mei*) purpose of the poetic occasion.

Mao 204 is the fourth in a suite of ten songs. Its title piece, "Valley Wind" (Gu feng; Mao 201), is a wife's complaint.[41] According to the Han dynasty commentarial tradition, "Valley Wind" satirized King You of Zhou, during whose reign customs of conviviality and friendship declined.[42] The elegiac tone of the entire "Valley Wind" suite culminates in Mao 204, in which the "withering grass" theme gets its own elaboration in "What Grass Does Not Go Yellow" (He cao bu huang; Mao 234):

What grass is not yellow? On which day are we not marching? Which one of us has not been taken to toil on the four borders?

What plant does not turn black? Which one of us has not sickened? Alas! We soldiers alone are not treated as humans.

We are not the gaur; nor are we tigers. Yet we ramble in the vast wilderness. Alas! We soldiers have no respite day or night.

That fox, with its luxuriant tail, rambles through the dark grass. Those carts, like boxes, move along the Zhou roads.

The "grass" in this poem is an omen and a sign. Signifying wilderness and death, as suggested in the last line with the "boxes"—coffins carried along the Zhou roads. The king's epithet "dark" (*you*) appears in the last stanza, modifying "grass," accompanied by the curious image of a fox with bushy tail, rambling through the grass. Perhaps this refers to the king's favorite consort, the notorious Bao Si (?–771 BCE). As commentators have noted, "What Grass Does Not Go Yellow" is a song about the end of the year and the end of an era. Adopting the "withering grass" image, Xie sets an unmistakably critical tone of his piece. The imagistic evocation of King You, the "Dark King," and his doomed era, may not have been appropriate for the poetic occasion that calls for a felicitous arrangement of words as seen in the following example:

	公子敬愛客	The Lord pays his respect to the guests;
	終宴不知疲	throughout the banquet, he knows no fatigue.
	清夜游西園	On this clear evening, we roam the West Garden;
4	飛蓋相追隨	flowing canopies follow one another.
	明月澄清景	The moon is bright, the air crisp;
	列宿正參差	stars and constellations, each in their rightful position.
	秋蘭被長坂	Autumn thoroughwort covers the long slope,
8	朱華冒綠池	vermilion blossoms fill the green pond.
	潛魚躍清波	Submerged fish leap out of the limpid water;
	好鳥鳴高枝	fine birds chirp from the tall branch.
	神飆接丹轂	A numinous gust lifts the red wheel;

12　　輕輦隨風移　　　swiftly, our chariots sail with the wind.
　　　飄颻放志意　　　Soaring, we set our mind free;
　　　千秋長若斯　　　may it be like this for eternity![43]

This piece by Cao Zhi leads the Lord's Feast category as first established in the *Wen xuan*. The banquet for which the work was commissioned was held in honor of Cao Pi's promotion to the General of the Gentlemen-of-the-Household of All Purposes, which placed the older brother on the path to rule as the emperor of the new Wei dynasty. Cao Zhi, the long-time contender for the heir apparency, gracefully congratulates the winner. Xie Lingyun's piece, written for an arguably comparable occasion, lacks the decorous and congratulatory tone. Nor does it include paradise-like surroundings composed of a bright moon, shining stars, leaping fish, singing birds, blossoming flowers, and an auspicious breeze. In Cao's model of banquet poetry, the human experience and the natural environment are matched perfectly with the supposed blessing of the unseen but ever-present divine power. Such is the affective power of Cao Zhi's poem, leaving an indelible mark on how the Jian'an era was to be remembered. Xie's literary departure from Cao Zhi's approach reveals the darker thoughts that haunted the poet and his contemporaries, regarding Liu Yu's ascension to power and the imminent end of the Jin.

Divining the Unknown: Making Meaning through the Hexagrams

Xie Lingyun's banquet piece is opaque and somber; it has none of the magic of Cao Zhi's Lord's Feast poem. In the poem "On the Double Ninth Day," line 4's "frigid pool" image suggests the opacity of the poet's true feelings. His use of "sagacious mind" (*shengxin*) to describe Liu Yu in line 5 creates ambiguity—is this genuine respect or subtle criticism? By turning to another poem composed for the same occasion, which also contained the same use of the phrase *shengxin* (sagacious mind), we may find a basis on which to make an educated guess.[44] The author is Xie Lingyun's cousin Xie Zhan (387–421; style name Xuanyuan). His work was the only other poem read on the Cavalry Terrace that was preserved in the *Wen xuan*.[45] Just four lines shorter, Xie Zhan's poem covers similar poetic ground, but conveys a different mood and tone.[46]

	風至授寒服	Autumn winds have arrived—the time to distribute winter clothing;[47]
	霜降休百工	frost has descended—all work has stopped.[48]
	繁林收陽彩	The exuberant forest takes in all the sunlight;
4	密苑解華叢	out of a dense garden, an assemblage of flowers come forth.
	巢幕無留鷰	Over the Tent-Nest, no swallows dally;[49]
	遵渚有來鴻	following the sandbars, there are geese arriving from afar.[50]
	輕霞冠秋日	Wisps of rosy cloud crown the autumn sun;
8	迅商薄清穹	a swift west wind flits by the firmament.[51]
	聖心眷嘉節	His sagacious mind turns affectionately toward this fine season;
	揚鑾戻行宮	with bells ringing, the entourage has arrived at the traveling palace.[52]
	四筵霑芳醴	In front of all seats and mats, a fragrant brew is served;[53]
12	中堂起絲桐	in the middle of the hall, music arises from the string and paulownia instruments.[54]
	扶光迫西汜	When the sun presses on toward the western shore;[55]
	歡餘讌有窮	our joy lingers while the feast has come to an end.
	逝矣將歸客	Departing now! The returning sojourner!
16	養素克有終	Cultivating the "unadorned" virtue, he will achieve a fulfilling end.[56]
	臨流怨莫從	Facing the stream, I regret not being able to follow;[57]
	歡心歎飛蓬	in spite of the convivial heart, I bemoan myself—a blowing tumbleweed.[58]

To introduce the seasonal setting, Xie Zhan opens the poem with an allusion to "Seventh Month" (Qi yue; Mao 154), which is traditionally interpreted as a eulogy for the Duke of Zhou's eastern campaign.[59] The choice of citing a song from *The Classic of Poetry* that recalls the Duke of Zhou sets Xie Zhan's poetic intention far from Xie Lingyun's, who evokes the "Dark King" of Zhou. Xie Zhan's allusion suggests a favorable stance toward Liu Yu. In line 5, he alludes to *Zuo Tradition* to further praise Liu Yu for his military success in eliminating the competing regimes in the northern plains. Line 6 alludes to Mao 159, another eulogy for the Duke of Zhou's eastern campaign. The geese imagery presents a significant contrast: while Xie Lingyun depicts geese in struggle, Xie Zhan portrays them willingly submitting to Liu Yu's authority. This interesting contrast reveals different attitudes among members of the same Xie clan toward Liu Yu's coming into power.

Unlike his elder cousin, Xie Zhan seems to be lauding the general-turned-duke without reservation. The poem's congratulatory tone culminates in the auspicious imagery found in lines 7 and 8: "Wisps of rosy cloud crown the autumn sun; / a swift west wind flits by the firmament." Liu Yu here is equated with the heaven and the sun, images reserved exclusively for the imperial ruler. Xie Zhan dedicates the final stanza to Kong Jing by alluding to hexagram 15, "Modesty" (Qian), in *The Classic of Changes* to suggest that the old counselor's rejection of the high post was out of humility. Xie Lingyun also alludes to the hexagrams to make meaning, although it is not as clear.[60]

The Classic of Changes is a divination text, which Xie likely used for practical and literary purposes. Deciphering the poet's allusions to the *Changes'* sixty-four hexagrams is sometimes essential for understanding his poetry. Each hexagram consists of two trigrams, which in turn consists of lines that are either solid (yang) or broken (yin). The *Changes* text explains the divinatory significance of individual lines and of the hexagram as a whole. Line 9 of the banquet poem "On the Double Ninth Day" contains an allusion to hexagram 64, "Ferrying Incomplete" (Weiji): "The banquet is hosted to inspire confidence and trust" (Jian yan guang youfu), which it quotes verbatim from the *Changes*.[61] The phrase *youfu* (to have/inspire confidence) is taken from lines fifth yin (6/5) and top yang (9/6) of hexagram 64.[62] The statement for fifth yin reads: "Steadfastness brings good fortune; there is no regret in this. The light of the noble man derives from the confidence he inspires. It brings good fortune."[63] Although this line contains an "auspicious" reading, it needs be considered in conjunction with the statement on the top yang line (9/6), which reads: "One inspires confidence through drinking alcohol; there is no blame; but if he drinks habitually or too much, then he would become remiss in spite of confidence."[64] The top yang line statement should prevail in interpreting line 9 of the poem, because Xie Lingyun, in his use of allusions to the *Changes*, usually foregrounds the commentaries on the yang lines over the yin.[65] One can argue that he intends to caution Liu Yu against hubris. The commentary on the top yang line (9/6) of hexagram 64 reads: "If he drinks habitually or too much, it would be a case of his not knowing and being able to keep to the rules of propriety."[66] Other cautionary messages are found in the commentary on the images of the "Weiji." "Ferrying Incomplete is smooth. The young fox almost gets across. But it still gets its tail wet and in the end there is no good."[67] The commentary on the images represented by the trigrams that make up the top and bottom halves of hexagram 64 reads: "Fire sits above Water: this constitutes the image of Ferrying Incomplete. The noble man should exert caution in discerning circumstances and dwell in their allotted places."[68]

A close look at hexagram 64 suggests that Xie Lingyun's supposed poetic salutation to Liu Yu turns out to be a warning. One may even venture to say that this panegyric poem is a satire wrapped in elaborate intertextual ruses. Liu Yu, not a man of letters, would not have immediately picked up on the messages, nor would this have mattered to him.[69] The poetic intricacy with the intertexts garnered from *The Classic of Poetry* and *The Classic of Changes* would, however, have helped Xie navigate the difficult season of the Jin–Song transition.[70] Peking University Professor Zhang Yinan has pointed out how Xie uses hexagrams to establish correlations between events in real life and their principles as indicated in the image (*xiang*).[71] If *The Classic of Poetry* was used as a handbook of the past, then *The Classic of Changes* was a manual on preparing for an uncertain future. Prognostication is, after all, an extreme form of pragmatism.[72] By the time the Jin had run its course, Xie Lingyun had to seriously consider whether "to serve or not to serve" (*chuchu*), or in the language of the divination text, "whether to advance or withdraw" (*jintui*). The hexagrams, with their images and commentaries, offered reasoned if not always efficacious perspective.

In the penultimate line of "On the Double Ninth Day," Hexagram 22, "Elegance" (Bi), also shows how Xie Lingyun divines the poetic occasion: "That marvelous Way of the Hillside Garden!" Here, "hillside garden" (*qiuyuan*) alludes to the judgment of the fifth yin line (6/5): "Elegance is located in a hillside garden; there are bundles of silk, basketsful and increasing in number. If one is thrifty and careful, in the end, there will be good fortune."[73] The commentary from Wang Bi (226–49) sheds further light on how this may guide a courtier who must ponder whether to stay in or withdraw from a questionable situation:

> Fifth yin is located in the exalted position and constitutes the governing rule of Elegance. It is the culmination of decoration. To decorate something, the natural Way of that thing is injured. To decorate the hillside garden, nothing can bring greater harm than ostentation. Therefore, when Elegance depends on bundles of plain silk, the hillside garden suffers; but when Elegance depends on the hillside garden, bundles of silk proliferate. In decorating things, nothing beats frugality. In the case of greatness, one should be able to economize, which calls necessarily for sparing. In the end, good fortune can be obtained.[74]

The hillside garden in the text signifies moderation. The courtier is advised to disengage, to do away with "decoration" and "adornment" (*shi*), which refers to official trappings. Elegance is read as a sign of the retired noble person. To be rid of gaudy embroidery, one is rewarded with bundles of "plain silk" (*su*). Plain silk refers not only to the moral integrity but also bodily intactness of a gentleman. In the fourth century, there was a renewed interest in practicing self-valuing, the so-called selfishness as propagated by the Warring States Yang-Zhu school of philosophy.[75] Here, the garden that is "sparing" denotes the self and personhood of the courtier. With the "hillside garden" allusion, Xie Lingyun suggests that Kong Jing's retirement is the perfected practice of the Way of the gentleman. In the final line, the poet ceremoniously laments his own "paltry virtue" and "lame pursuits," declaring his inferiority to Kong. But in just a few years, Xie Lingyun would also return to the Guiji mountains to his own hillside garden.

Departure and Return

Xie Lingyun wrote two farewell poems before he left Jiankang in 422. The first is "Neighbors Sending Me Off at Block Hill" (Lin li xiang song Fang-shan 鄰里相送方山).[76]

	祇役出皇邑	For service, I now depart the imperial town;[77]
	相期憩甌越	a date is set for my respite in the Ou and Yue regions.[78]
	解纜及流潮	Untying the cord, I will sail away with the tide;
4	懷舊不能發	thinking of my old friends, I can't bear to leave yet.
	析析就衰林	Soughing and sighing, the desolate forest is my company;
	皎皎明秋月	bright and glistening, the autumn moon shines.
	含情易為盈	Feelings that are held within are now brimming;
8	遇物難可歇	our encounters with the world never cease.
	積痾謝生慮	My sufferings of ill health release me from other concerns in life;
	寡慾罕所闕	lacking desires, I am rarely in want of things.[79]
	資此永幽棲	From now on, I shall forever dwell in obscurity;
12	豈伊年歲別	how can this parting be a matter of months or a year!
	各勉日新志	Let us each strive daily for renewals in virtue;[80]
	音塵慰寂蔑	a message in sound or dust will console my muffled existence.[81]

This is one of Xie Lingyun's poems that relies primarily on direct discourse. The poet is speaking as a friend who is saddened by imminent separation and sees no possibility of future reunion. The choice of unusual words in the opening couplet seems to give the speaker some necessary distance for self-composure. He calls his forced departure "mere service," his exile a "respite" (*qi*). The use of the reduplicative binomes *xixi* and *jiaojiao* in lines 5 and 6 exemplify a classical mode of lyricism that can be traced back to *The Classic of Poetry*. The poem ends with a reference to Lu Ji's "Yearning to Return" (Sigui fu), registering his emotions through an earlier text.[82] The Australian Sinologist J. D. Frodsham notes that Xie Lingyun's exile was the "turning point" in his life, where the "gay roisterer, the dashing man about town died forever."[83] It is tempting to agree with that view, as this poem successfully depicts the sorrowful persona who has been stripped of his identity and is about to be sent off to the edge of the world. The other poem of parting before the poet left the capital provides his exact departure date and more complicated poetic monologue: "On the Sixteenth Day of the Seventh Month of the Third Year of the Yongchu Reign [August 19, 422], I Set Out from the Capital for the Commandery" (Yongchu sannian qiyue shiliu ri zhi jun chu fa du 永初三年七月十六日之郡初發都).[84]

	述職期闌暑	By the end of summer, I have accepted my appointment;
	理棹變金素	when I ready the oars, the season is in its metal phase.[85]
	秋岸澄夕陰	The autumnal shore is lucid in the evening light;
4	火旻團朝露	the Great Fire star shines as the morning dew forms.[86]
	辛苦誰為情	Travails of life, to whom shall I relate the pain?[87]
	遊子值頹暮	A traveler meets his fate in this despondent late season.
	愛似莊念昔	"Loving his own kind," Zhuangzi yearns for his old land;[88]
8	久敬曾存故	"with a long-term admiration," Zengzi cherishes his former friends.[89]
	如何懷土心	What to do with this heart that longs for a place to call home!
	持此謝遠度	Harboring these thoughts, I bid farewell and embark on the far journey.
	李牧愧長袖	Li Mu was ashamed about his dangling sleeves;[90]

12	卻克慙躃步	Xi Ke was embarrassed for his lame gait.[91]
	良時不見遺	Encountering good times, they were not abandoned by the court;
	醜狀不成惡	although unsightly, no evil was contrived.
	曰余亦支離	Alas! Also impaired and broken—this form of mine;[92]
16	依方早有慕	for long I have thought to give myself to the distant land.[93]
	生幸休明世	To be born into the enlightened age has been my good fortune;
	親蒙英達顧	my person has received kind regards from the savants of the day.
	空班趙氏璧	With no merit, I have occupied a place next to "Zhao's jade";[94]
20	徒乖魏王瓠	useless, I am but a misfit like the King of Wei's gourd.
	從來漸二紀	For over two decades, I have joined service;
	始得傍歸路	only now am I able to embark on the road home.
	將窮山海迹	My traces will disappear in the mountains and lakes;
24	永絕賞心晤	now I part with my dear friends whom I shall see no more.

This poem opens with an autumn scene, whose description poses an interesting comparison with that in the "On the Double Ninth Day . . ." Here, nature reveals itself dispassionately. The traditional Chinese calendar divides the year into five seasons according to yin-yang and five-phase (*wu xing*) categorization. All things are connected in the broad scheme of things—yin and yang are forces that support each other with each pushing into the other's existence. In lines 2 through 4, all of nature's five elements make their appearance: wood ("oars"), metal, earth ("shore"), fire, and water ("dew"), with *water* being the connector. Nature's beauty is presented in a poetic order that selectively presents a cultural vision of movement and fate. Line 3 focuses on the progressing and receding shoreline in the evening light, juxtaposing two indices of the mystery of time. The verb "purify" (*cheng*) in this line refers to both what water does to the shore and what the evening light does to the water. This is an example of how the poet uses syntactical ambiguity to expand the poetic vision. Yet what is most curious in this poem and, as far as I am aware, has not been discussed by commentators, is the poet's suggestion in line 15 of his physical impairment, which was preceded by two stories about handicapped ministers who nevertheless achieved great deeds.

In the poems presented thus far in this chapter, the theme of return is constructed along ethical and political lines of reasoning. Another dimension to literati political disengagement in periods such as the Jin–Song transition appears in an account (preserved in the *Wen xuan*) of his visit to the Xie family estate in the Guiji mountains on the way to his Yongjia post: "Passing through the Shining Estate" (Guo Shining shu 過始寧墅).[95]

	束髮懷耿介	Since hair-binding age, I have harbored an uncompromising sense of rectitude;
	逐物遂推遷	driven by worldly matters, I have since followed their transformations.
	違志似如昨	Deviating from my original aim—it happened like yesterday;
4	二紀及茲年	two decades are gone, and here I am.
	緇磷謝清曠	Besmirched and bruised, I am less than pure or unperturbed;
	疲薾慙貞堅	tired and spent, I have not exactly stayed unwavering.
	拙疾相倚薄	Clumsy and ill in health, I have sometimes gone with the current;
8	還得靜者便	upon returning, I hope to find quietude and peace.
	剖竹守滄海	Holding the official tally, I am to guard the glaucous coast;
	枉帆過舊山	bending my sail, I have stopped at the "old mountains";
	山行窮登頓	ascending and descending, the mountain path comes at an end;

12	水陁盡洄沿	whirling and then falling, the river course is exhausted.
	巖峭嶺稠疊	Cliffs pierce the sky; peaks pile on high;
	洲縈渚連綿	sandbars winding, islets extend on and about.
	白雲抱幽石	White clouds embrace a dark rock;[96]
16	綠篠媚清漣	green bamboo leaves frolic over the limpid ripples.[97]
	葺宇臨迴江	A thatched eave overlooks the twirling stream;
	築觀基曾巔	a belvedere is constructed with its foundation on a high peak.
	揮手告鄉曲	Waving goodbye, I part with my townsmen;
20	三載期歸旋	in three years, I will return.
	且為樹枌檟	Make sure to plant some elm and catalpa trees for me;
	無令孤願言	do not let my wish go unfulfilled.

This poem recalls Tao Yuanming's "Return to My Field and Garden" (Gui yuantian ju) in that both speak of the regret at having been caught in the dusty net of the world, and a desire to "return." While Tao Yuanming's return is usually understood as a return to the natural way of life (a utopian agricultural community), Xie Lingyun's return is to the "hillside garden," a place where a person's ethical and natural selves may be preserved.[98] During the Jin–Song transition, this modest wish was often not possible. Xie was not able to return. "Return" (*gui*) in this poem denotes a "natural death," the most consequential or "ultimate return" (*dagui*). "Elm and catalpa" (*fenjia*) in the penultimate line suggest that death was on the mind of the poet, as catalpa wood was used for making coffins.[99]

The poems examined in this chapter are distinguished by their precise documentation of time, with each poem dated to the specific day, month, and year. This meticulous recording reflects Xie's conscious effort to witness pivotal moments in both personal and historical contexts. His poems capture significant events, from Liu Yu's political ascension to Kong Jing's departure from service and his own exile. Beyond mere documentation, Xie interprets these events through the lens of classical texts, particularly *The*

Classic of Poetry and *The Classic of Changes*, offering both evaluative and prognostic perspectives. In doing so, his poetry serves a historiographical purpose. Xie's acute sensitivity to the temporal aspect of events aligns well with early literary traditions where time is always recognized as a basic dimension of nature.

CHAPTER 7

A Life in Natural and Political Times

Seasons, climactic changes, and celestial bodies—the sun, moon, and stars—mark time's passage in Chinese nature writing, evoking emotional responses to these natural rhythms and transformations. Xie Lingyun's poetry is no exception. He conveys his vision of time by blending real-world observations with classical literary imagery. As demonstrated in earlier chapters, he drew motifs from *Songs of Chu*, *The Classic of Poetry*, *The Classic of Changes*, and the *Zhuangzi* to construct a lyric poetry that frames human affairs with omens from nature. For instance, the struggling geese of "On the Double Ninth Day," while alluding to *The Classic of Changes*, are also a commentary on the precarious military ascension of Liu Yu. Xie's detachment in describing momentous events stems from a Daoist worldview, which combines mysticism with acceptance. Behind the visible world lies an invisible law: time itself. This attitude refutes the misconception that Daoism merely advocates inaction. Instead, *The Classic of Changes* guides one to recognize that there is a time for action and a time for restraint. This chapter first examines how natural time binds individual and collective experience in *The Classic of Poetry* and *Songs of Chu*, the two fountainheads of lyric poetry. It then explores Xie's engagement with these traditions, which produced a qualitative shift through his focus on mundane subjects like spring grass, which he uses to unveil the mysterious workings of cosmic time.

Time in Early Chinese Poetry

According to the late Sinologist Chen Shih-Hsiang, the Chinese graph for time, *shi* 時, pictographically represents a foot (on the lower right) stepping alongside the sun (on the left), a signifier of time as a moving and dynamic force. Time constituted a feeling, a cause for existential angst. *Shi*, in denoting its secondary sense of a fixed point in time as found in early texts, does not mean just any moment in time, but, as Chen convincingly demonstrated, a moment that is correct, right, fitting, and good. In other words, *shi*, as used in early poetry, functions as an attribute, suggesting "a sense of omens or auspices for individuals on some occasion, or fortunes of a nation or people."[1] What Chen describes here applies to both *Songs of Chu* and *The Classic of Poetry*, in which the following poem, "The Seventh Month" (Qiyue; Mao 154), illustrates how time constituted a thematic fulcrum in a literary culture, where its interpretative dimensions operate at both individual and collective levels of the human psyche.[2]

1.
In the seventh month, the Fire Star sinks westward;[3]
in the ninth month, we hand out winter coats.
The days of the first month are bitter and biting;
the days of the second are frosty and frigid.
Without a heavy coat,
how can you survive the end of the year?
Days of the third month are for farm tools;
days of the fourth month, toes are raised.[4]
Women and children are gathered
to carry food to the southern fields.
The field-inspector arrives and is delighted.

2.
In the seventh month, the Fire Star sinks westward;
in the ninth month, we hand out winter coats.
Spring days are warm;
orioles are singing.
Our womenfolk, deep baskets in hand,
following that tapering path,[5]
go looking for tender mulberry.[6]
The spring day is lazy and long.
How lush! That wormwood they gather.[7]
In their heart, these girls have worries,
soon they shall "return" with the lord's daughter.[8]

3.

In the seventh month, the Fire Star sinks westward;
in the eighth month, they gather sedges and reeds;
in the silkworm month, they gather mulberry leaves.
They take the ax
to chop off the far boughs
so the young branches may flourish.
In the seventh month, the shrike cries;
in the eighth month, it's time to weave.
There are black and brown silk,
with that red one bright as the sun.
We make an underskirt for the lord's daughter.

4.

In the fourth month, the milkwort is in spike;[9]
in the fifth month, the cicada chirps.
In the eighth month, we harvest.
In the tenth month, leaves are falling.
In the days of the first month, we go hunting.
Taking from the fox, we make a fur coat for the lord.
In the days of the second month, we meet for martial merits;
we keep the one-year-old boar,
and offer the three-year-old boar to the lord.

5.

In the fifth month, the locust rubs its legs;
in the sixth month, the grasshopper shakes its wing.
In the seventh month, they are in the fields;
in the eighth month, they are under the eaves;
in the ninth month, they are in the doorway;
in the tenth month, they are under my bed.
We seal up the holes to smoke out the rats.
We plaster up the crevices in the walls.
Alas! Women and children!
The year is transitioning.
Now come and stay inside.

6.

In the sixth month, we eat wild plums and cherries;
in the seventh month, we cook mallows and beans.
In the eighth month, we harvest the dates.
In the tenth month, we take the rice,
with which to make ale for next spring,
with which we seek longevity.

7.

In the seventh month, we eat melons;
in the eighth month, we cut the gourds.
In the ninth month, we collect hemp seeds.
We gather bitter vegetables, we cut the ailanthus for firewood,
and feed our husbandmen.

8.

In the ninth month, we prepare our threshing floor;
in the tenth month, we store our grains;
the glutinous and the nonglutinous, the early sown and
    the late.[10]
Rice and hemp, beans and wheat.
Alas! Our husbandmen!
Once our crops have been harvested,
they climb high to take charge of constructing the palace.
During the day they thatch;
at night they make ropes.
Rapidly they fix the roofs.
Then it's time to sow the various seeds again.

9.

In the days of second month, they drill ice, *hee-hoe*!
In the days of the third month, they bring it into the cold
    chamber.
On an early morning of the fourth month,
we offer the lamb and sacrifice with garlic.
In the ninth month, the air is cold and frosty;

in the tenth month, we clean the harvesting floor.
Filling up both vessels, we have a feast.[11]
We slaughter a lamb
and bring it to the lord's hall.
Raising the goblets made from buffalo horn, in unison we
    say:
"Myriad years and boundless life!"[12]

This poem tells how the people of Zhou (1045–256 BCE) navigate time by looking at signs of nature, from heavenly stars to earthly worms, especially during the "killing" season of autumn. Their seventh month is the ominous beginning of autumn, hence the title. In the seventh month, the Zhou people anchor their activities. It is the month that begins the poem and is repeated seven times. The significance of seventh month is marked by the "falling" of the Fire Star, the harbinger of the cold season ahead. Omens of death show in the "withering of all grasses." Human life enters the dark *yin* phase that is "bitter and biting," "solemn and killing" (*susha*). To survive nature's timing, humans arrange their time. The year is carved into a carefully designed sequence of work. There is a "right" time for everything. Opportune moments are observed with ritual precision. Good times follow from timeliness. Repetition is the rhythm of continued security.

"The Seventh Month" is a commemorative song, in which the Zhou people are celebrating their good times. The first of the "Bin Airs," which combine personal and collective voices, it constitutes a musical ensemble offered to the Zhou ancestors—King Wen, King Wu, and the Duke of Zhou, praising their epochal creation of an (agri-)cultured way of managing time.[13] *Songs of Chu*, in contrast, famously affords visions of disorder resulting from bad timing and bad times. The songs collected therein often evoke an isolated and embittered voice, revolving around the persona of the loyal yet misunderstood minister Qu Yuan, China's first poet with a name. "Encountering Sorrow" (Lisao), a ninety-three-stanza poem attributed to Qu Yuan, begins with the protagonist speaking in highly stylized terms about his celestial birth—coming down from heaven when the stars are aligned to announce the beginning of a new epoch.[14] Like other heroes in ancient Chinese myths, Qu Yuan's birth starts something correct (*zhen*), resetting the cosmic time.[15] Yet humans, through their evil contrivances, threaten to derail Qu Yuan's efforts to stay true to himself and his adopted fatherland. Condemned to incessantly cultivating virtue and fragrant plants, he is always late, as is his lord-prince, in whose image the poet sees his own decay. As the prince comes under the influence of small-minded slanderers, the poet's garden is overtaken by foul-smelling weeds. The long poem made up of almost four hundred lines degenerates in what can be interpreted as a death note. The self-loving celestial god loses his battle against autumn, a human season that will be visited over and over as a lyrical subject. In the opening lines of the "Nine Changes" (Jiubian), a *sao*-style poem attributed to Song Yu (3rd cent. BCE), the poetic motif known as "lament of autumn" (*beiqiu*) was first established with a timeless image of "trembling leaves."[16]

> Alas! Mournful is the air of autumn!
> Desolate, sad—the grass has withered; the tree is shedding
>   its trembling leaves.
> Shaken and grief-stricken—it is like that person on a distant
>   journey.
> Climbing the mountain, standing over the river, we yearn
>   for his return.[17]

The leaves' precipitous fall translates poetically into the traveler's imminent end, cut off from his kin and land. Leaves are humans; trembling leaves are lives taking their last breath. While "Nine Changes" derives from the autumn motif in "Encountering Sorrow," its description of nature's time far surpasses the latter's allegorical representations of the flora and fauna, amounting to what British Sinologist David Hawkes calls "the first fully developed sense of pathos of natural objects ([Japanese:] *mono no aware*)."[18] In making "autumn's pathos," the poet-speaker impersonates the traveler, envisioning his body as some "withered tree trunk" (*kumu* or *gaomu*) and whose description in the following lines from "Nine Changes" made an indelible impression on later writers.

> August Heaven divides the four seasons evenly;
> I, in particular, feel the pain in this forbidding autumn.

Frosty dew has killed one hundred grasses;
soon the Phoenix tree and catalpa will be bare.
Gone now is the warmth of the sun;
on the way is the long night of darkness.
Years of robust potency and pungent fragrance are behind
    me;
in my weakened state, I feel the pain of autumn.
Autumn forewarns with frosty dew;
winter arrives with grim ice.
Withdrawn is the generous nourishment of summer;
all is now utterly sunken or deeply submerged.
Leaves turn brown and black, losing their color;
branches are in random disarray, crisscrossing.
Overwhelmed and haggard looking, they are spent;
as if dazed and lost, the boughs are sallow and wilted.
Scrawny and skeletal stands the lanky trunk;
looking emaciated, contused, and wounded.
I think of such profuse flourishing—its impending
    fall;
I regret that it has lost the time to have its due.[19]

In this section, the mournful human becomes the tree that has "lost its time," which can be read as a euphemism for premature death. Commentators point out that the "withered tree" stands for the banished courtier whose "talent" (*cai*), a homonym for "timber" (*cai*), is going to waste. The description of the wounded and unsightly appearance of the catalpa calls to mind human's tortured countenance as a reflection of internal afflictions in the lines that followed:

I gather the reins of side-horses to steady the chariot;
for the moment let me roam and relax.
The year hurriedly rushes toward the end;
I fear my time won't keep up.
I lament this life of mine is not properly timed;
meeting a world so troubled and grief-stricken.

To calm myself, I shall linger for a while and have a moment
    to myself;
the crickets are now chirping in the west chamber.
My mind is stirred, the heart startled;
why has sorrow crushed in from all sides?
Looking at the moon, I heave a long sigh.
Pacing with the stars, I stay up till dawn.

The reference to "not meeting one's time" (*bu shi*) emphasizes the importance of observing and minding time's passage. The use of "time" in its dynamic sense here suggests agency—that is, to move along with time and catch up with its pace, turning the ominous to auspicious: to arrive at "that time," "that day," "the correct hour," or "the proper moment."[20] In this passage, the poetic persona "looks up at the moon" and "paces with the stars" to rejoin the rhythm of the celestial time. These poetic gestures suggest the entrenched beliefs about time as the nexus between the heavenly and the human. Lyrical expressions, while intensely subjective and personal, almost always evoke higher power for a restoration of the natural and ethical equilibrium, as is seen in the continued plea in "Nine Changes:"[21]

I alone lament that sweet basil with layered leaves—
soft and supple, such profusion—its scent fills the palatial
    chamber.
Why such heaps of flourishing, yet no substance?
Following wind and rain, it flits and flutters.
I thought that my lord would only wear the basil;
but it is treated just like any other sweet herbs.
Such pity that my ingenious design is not communicated;
I shall leave my lord and soar away.
Pitiful and pathetic, my heart is mourning;
I only wish to see him once and reveal what is on my mind.
Weighing that such alienation is without cause;
afflicting feelings compound in me with more torment.
Alas! My pent-up thoughts about the lord!
Behind that nine-fold gate is my lord!

Ferocious dogs snarl and bark at me.
Doors and bridges are all closed off.
August Heaven is inundated with autumn rain;
when will the Earth be ever dry again?
Despicable! Alone! I guard my lot without benefaction.
Looking up at the clouds floating by! I heave a long sigh!

The image of a lone scholar standing against the "perilous time" was prevalent in the Han literary texts, giving rise to the topos known as "not meeting one's time" (*shi buyu*). Xie Lingyun, familiar with this type of literature, responded to the theme with a twist. Not only did he not write about autumn and decay, Xie reconfigured the poetic mode of time.

The Numinous Pond: Intertextual References

Xie Lingyun's first exile in 422 brought him to Yongjia, where he endured a dark winter after the long river journey had taken a toll on his health. Having bid farewell to his former life and vowing in live in relative obscurity for the remainder of his days, it was in Yongjia that he wrote a poem that would become a timeless work. Probably his first correspondence with friends back in the capital, the poem is titled "Climbing the Tower Overlooking the Pond" (Deng chi shang lou 登池上樓; hereafter, "The Pond").[22]

	潛虬媚幽姿	The submerged dragon entices with its concealed form;[23]
2	飛鴻響遠音	a flying goose calls out from afar.
	薄霄愧雲浮	In reaching the welkin, I am not as good as that cloud-skipper;[24]
4	棲川怍淵沉	as for river-roosting, I am ashamed by that abyss-sinker.[25]
	進德智所拙	Advancement by virtue—I am too clumsy, not clever enough;[26]
6	退耕力不任	withdrawn to plow—I am physically incapacitated.[27]
	徇祿反窮海	Following an emolument, I have turned to this hinterland;[28]

8	臥痾對空林	prostrated in malaise, I face an empty grove.[29]
	衾枕昧節候	Heavy blankets have muffled me from season and climate;
10	褰開暫窺臨	unfurling the portiere, I steal a glance outside.[30]
	傾耳聆波瀾	Turning my ear, I listen to the rippling waves;
12	舉目眺嶇嶔	lifting my eyes, I gaze at the towering cliffs.
	初景革緒風	Tender sunlight begins to repel the northern wind;
14	新陽改故陰	fresh warm air replaces the lingering chill.
	池塘生春草	By the pond, rejuvenated is spring grass;
16	園柳變鳴禽	in the garden, willows have transformed the singing birds.
	祁祁傷豳歌	"How lush!"—that Bin song saddens me;
18	萋萋感楚吟	"What exuberance!"—that Chu tune stirs me.
	索居易永久	Living in solitude, it is easy to feel time's eternity;
20	離羣難處心	away from one's kin, it is hard to settle the mind.[31]
	持操豈獨古	Be persistent and tenacious, as one is never alone!
22	無悶徵在今	"Ridding Melancholy"—that's the sign for now.[32]

The "pond" in the poem, documented in a tenth-century encyclopedia of geography as Duke Xie's Pond or the Numinous Pond, was likely inspired by a literary counterpart.[33] The "Numinous Pond" first appeared in *The Classic of Poetry* (Ling tai; Mao 242), the eighth of a suite of eulogies dedicated to King Wen. The poem describes his construction of a high terrace deemed "numinous" (*ling*), highlighting how his virtue extended to all living beings in his kingdom.

When King Wen built the Numinous Terrace, he planned and oversaw the process;
his people undertook the work, and in less than a day they completed it.

When King Wen built the Numinous Terrace, he said not to rush; his people arrived.
When the king was at the Numinous Park, deer came to prostrate themselves.

> The deer were sleek and well fed; white birds gleamed in
> their shiny plumage.
> When the king was by the Numinous Pond, fish leapt
> joyfully about.
>
> On the posts and cross-beams hung large drums and bells.
> In unison they sounded merry music in the moated hall.
>
> In unison they sounded drums and bells; joyful music came
> from the moated hall.
> The lizard-skin drums rolled thunderous and the blind
> musicians presented their work.[34]

The Mao preface explains the meaning of this poem: "This was when people started to attach themselves to King Wen. When King Wen received Heaven's Charge, common people took delight in his 'numinous virtue,' [*lingde*] which extended to birds, beasts, and insects."[35] The word "numinous," used as a modifier for the terrace, the pond, and the park, marks King Wen's virtue, which ensured enlightened and efficacious government. *Mengzi* (1A.1) cites Mao 242 to remonstrate King Hui of Liang.

> King Hui stood above a pond, seeing deer and geese, and asked: "Did the worthy ancients also take delight in these?" Mencius answered: "Being worthy and then one could delight in these things. For the unworthy, although they were in possession of these, could find no pleasure in them.... King Wen relied on people's work to construct the Terrace and the Pond and the people rejoiced, referring to the terrace as "Numinous Terrace" and the pond as "Numinous Pond." They were happy to see the deer and fish in the park. In antiquity, worthy kings shared their pleasure with the people and therefore they could also take delight in such matters. [On the contrary,] the "Oath of Tang" says: "When will the Sun expire? I shall perish with you." When people wished for the death of Jie, though he had terraces, ponds, birds, and animals, how could he all alone enjoy them?[36]

The pond as constructed in Xie Lingyun's natural scenery calls forth these early traditions to create a layered reading experience for his audience. The poem's "climbing the tower" motif carries particular significance.

In ancient China, "ascending to high places" (*denggao*) served as both a political and literary act—officials would climb towers to "observe" (*guan*) and assess the state of affairs before submitting advice to the throne. Poetry constituted the highest form of this polite and politically charged speech. Sometimes, a line or two from a song from *The Classic of Poetry* was all that was needed to make a poignant point. Poetry was used as both the diagnosis and the cure in the Zhou diplomatic scene.[37] The intertextual references to *The Classic of Poetry* and *Mengzi* set the stage for reading "The Pond."

Nature Rejuvenates: The Symbolism of Spring Grass

The poem's opening couplet contains a pair of images from *The Classic of Changes*: the hidden dragon and the high-flying goose, respectively referring to the courtier who retreats during a perilous time and the one who has met his opportune moment. The second couplet mirrors these textual signs. The use of unusual and convoluted phrasing is striking in the first stanza—for example, "cloud-skipper" for goose and "abyss-sinker" for dragon. Note also that the poet avoids the common word *long* 龍 (dragon) and uses *qiu* 虯 instead to call attention to its contracted and coiled form. He inserts himself into the text with attitudinal verbs of "ashamed" and "chagrined" to express the physical and psychological liminal space in which he finds himself.[38] In couplet 3 this sentiment is made in even clearer terms. From lines 7 through 12, the reader understands that the poet has been sick in bed for much of winter and that he has recently opened the heavy draperies. The season and climate have changed, as seen in lines 13 and 14. The new is replacing the old, as yang pushes out yin. In the next couplet—lines 15 and 16—a vivid scene of nature suddenly emerges after a blanket of difficult words and uncommon vocabulary. A list of simple images—pond, grass, willows, and birds—are strung together with two verbs: *sheng* 生 and *bian* 變. Yet the disarmingly transparent imagery leads to divergent interpretive possibilities as seen in the following English renderings by the most insightful readers of our time.

> Pond and pool grow with grasses of spring,
> garden willows vary the birds that there sing. (Owen)[39]

Upon the pool, spring grass is growing,
the garden willows have changed into singing birds. (Frodsham)[40]

The pond is growing springtime plants,
garden willows have turned to singing birds. (Westbrook)[41]

The pond's banks grow spring grasses,
and garden willows have transformed the singing birds.
(Swartz)[42]

Pond banks sprout spring grasses;
garden willows change [to] singing birds. (Huang)[43]

The pond's banks are putting forth spring grass;
the garden willows have transformed the singing birds.
(Kwong)[44]

Later poets and critics of the Tang-Song period raved about this couplet, especially the "spring-grass" line. Li Bo, a great fan of Xie Lingyun, twice quotes the line verbatim in his own work.[45] Other poets, trying to imitate Xie's imagery, often ended up with disappointing results.[46] Even Bo Juyi lamented his inability to match Xie Lingyun after having composed an "unsatisfactory" poem, titled "Early Summer at the South Pond, Drinking Alone" (Shou xia nan chi du zhuo 首夏南池獨酌):

At the same site as Xie's,
I drink by the pond, listening to the music of wind.
To my chagrin, I don't have a composition of Kangle's caliber;
holding my brush, I murmur meditatively.
A beautiful scene—my talent is shabby;
the poem is finished and yet I am unsatisfied.[47]

In the Song dynasty, Wu Ke 吳可 (*jinshi* in 1109) also laments the difficulty in attempting or matching a perfected line: "Learning to write poetry is like practicing Chan [Zen] meditation; how many perfected couplets are there? *Spring grass by the pond* is the one that has reverberated through heaven and earth to this day."[48] Southern Song critics Hu Zi 胡仔 (1110–70) and Ge Lifang 葛立方 (?–1164) both comment with a mixture of admiration and envy on how the "spring grass" line received such wide acclaim.[49] The iconic status of this line reached new heights in the thirteenth century when the poet Yuan Haowen 元好問 (1190–1257) wrote: "The pond, the grass—a springtime sight of Xie's residence; for thousands of years to come, these five words shall remain as fresh as new."[50]

The recognition and the sensation caused by this single couplet probably began soon after the poem had reached its audience in the capital, according to Zhong Rong's *Gradation of Poets*.

> Whenever Kangle was in the company of Huilian, he was able to compose excellent poetry. One time when he resided in the Western Hall in Yongjia, he spent an entire day contemplating a piece without being able to finish it. He then fell asleep and in a dream he saw Huilian. Immediately the line "by the pond, rejuvenated is spring grass" came to him. Afterward, he would tell others: "This sentence was formed with the help of a divine being. It is not mine."[51]

In the guise of an anecdote, this account expresses sophisticated notions about art and life, and the creative process that links the two. Talent alone is not enough for generating superb art. The artist needs to be inspired. Here Huilian, Xie Lingyun's young cousin, serves as his muse. A gifted poet, Xie Huilian was the mirror image of the older poet and a reminder of Xie Lingyun's youth and unrealized potential. Xie Lingyun's writer's block resulted in turning the literary tradition to a different season: rather than continuing with the "autumn's lament" and "inopportune time," which would have been a befitting poetic occasion, he wrote about the pond with its lush spring grass—a different season, a different time. Nature rejuvenates: in "spring grass" lies the pattern and power of nature. Poetically, Xie Lingyun broke free of the subjective sense of time. The spontaneous "spring grass" captures the law of nature, which operates independently of both inherited cultural understanding and immediate circumstances.

All this recalls how the hexagrams in *The Classic of Changes* encapsulate mysterious forms of cosmic movement. The truth is simple. Here Xie Lingyun, a poet who prides himself for his rare words and contrived structure, emerges with a clear image that cuts through the opaque and impenetrable depths of the universe. "Spring grass" signified Xie's transformation of a lyrical mode from didactic to imagistic, turning away from philosophizing and heading for the spontaneous. When Bao Zhao compared Xie's poetry to a fresh lotus, he likely had this couplet in mind.[52]

Critically speaking, "spring grass" is an example of "naturalness" or "craftiness without trace of craft." This principle of Chinese poetics is spoken of in terms of the notion of *shen* 神, which may variously be rendered as "spirited" or "divinely inspired." When art mimics life so vividly as to create an uncanny resemblance, it is said to evoke the presence of the divine or a force of mysterious origin. One of the earliest stories that best illustrates this aesthetic comes from the *Zhuangzi*.

When carpenter Qing finished carving a bell in the shape of a tiger, those who saw it marveled, [considering] it to be the work of a ghost or spirit. The Marquis of Lu saw it and asked Qing: "What method did you use?" Qing answered: "I am a mere workman. What method can I claim to have? There is just one thing: when I was about to make the bell, I became careful with my breath. I had to fast to quiet the mind. On the third day of fasting, I did not dare to harbor thoughts about felicity, award, title, or emolument; on the fifth day of fasting, I dared not harbor thoughts about artistry or the lack thereof; on the seventh day of fasting, I would suddenly become oblivious of my body. At this point, there were no thoughts of your lord's court. While my ingenuity concentrated, my external bones dissipated. Then I went into mountains and forests to observe nature as endowed by heaven. It was in the wood with form perfected that I saw a bell forming. Then I applied my hands. Otherwise, I would not. Like this, I matched what heaven endowed with the heaven-endowed. Perhaps that's why the bell resembled a divine being."[53]

Perfected art begins with imitation and ends in transcendental representation or the liminal space between art and life. It is where the disembodied artist—the spirit of the artist—meets the heaven-endowed—the naturally existing form. The fourth-century commentator Guo Xiang 郭象 (d. 312) explains *shen* in this passage as: "being unlike what the human makes."[54] Along the same line, Cheng Xuanying 成玄英 (fl. 631–55), the

Tang dynasty Daoist commentator on *Zhuangzi*, offers a more detailed explanation: "Chiseled and carved in such an ingenious and wondrous manner that they are not like the work of man. Those who see the work, startled and suspicious, would claim that ghosts or spirits have made it."[55] *Shen*, or the "divinely inspired," is thus where the natural form meets the essential being of the artist. For centuries, many critics emphasized that "spring grass" evinces qualities of *ziran* 自然 (naturalness), *tianran* 天然 (heavenly endowment), or *hunran* 渾然 (perfection and indivisibleness).[56] As an artist, Xie Lingyun often begins with imitation and adoption of earlier traditions. However, the outcome, as demonstrated with the "spring grass" image, goes beyond those influences. Readers may overlook its textual origins in *The Classic of Poetry* and *Songs of Chu* to see in it the first sign of life and a fundamental form of nature. Contrary to the hermeneutics embedded in the "withering grass," which hints at unrelenting heat from the scorching sun, the "grass" on the pond manifests the influence of water. This is the life-supporting pond in King Wen's park where deer and fish swim and roam free.

In lines 17 and 18, the poet presents his intertextual references to *The Classic of Poetry* and *Songs of Chu*:

	祁祁傷豳歌	"How lush!"—That Bin Song saddens me;
18	萋萋感楚吟	"What exuberance!"—That Chu Tune stirs me.

The "Bin Song" refers to "The Seventh Month" (Qiyue; Mao 154). "How lush!" is taken from the stanza that contains the following lines: "The spring day is lazy and long. / How lush! That wormwood they gather. / In their heart, these girls have worries, / soon they shall 'return' with the lord's daughter."[57] The "Chu Tune" alludes to *Songs of Chu*'s "Summoning the Recluse" (Zhao yinshi): "The prince has gone wandering and not yet returned; spring grass has grown—what exuberance!"[58] What unites the *shi* and *sao* references in this couplet is the theme of return. The lord's daughter soon will "return"—that is, she will be married off to another state. The servant girls who will accompany her on this journey are saddened by the prospect of leaving their homeland of Bin. In contrast, the absence of the wandering prince in springtime leaves something to be desired for the Chu people. The sorrowful tone anchors a chiasmus of "return"—a self-reference to the poet's exile in Yongjia—yet the poetic emotion is restrained.[59]

The poem, from beginning to end, can be understood as an emotional journey from dejection to hope. What begins (the first six couplets) in diminishment and diffidence ends in "no distress" (line 22). In between there are symbolic movements, such as opening the curtains, and signs of life, such as birds and trees. The eye of the poem lies with what I call pivot verbs, in this case *sheng* and *bian* (lines 15 and 16), which function both transitively or intransitively. This ambiguity allows the agency of change to be located in between nature and the awakened human with an eye for the hidden. In writing "The Pond," Xie assumes the stance of a sage who "observes" nature to convey truth. The basic meaning of *guan* is "to examine closely." In political theory, *guan*, the act of observing the law of nature and the ways of people, stands at the center of civil government as well as cultural transformation. *Guan* is also the name of hexagram 20 in *The Classic of Changes*.[60] We read about "contemplative viewing" in the "Appended Explanations" (Xi ci), a general treatise on *The Classic of Changes*.[61]

> The sages designed hexagrams and observed the *images*. They attached explanations to elucidate *good fortune* or *misfortune*. That which is firm and that which is yielding, in their mutual resisting, generate change and transformation. As a result, *good fortune* and *misfortune* are but signs of failure or success, *images* of sorrow or joy. Change and transformation are *images* of advancing or retreating.
>
> Therefore, the gentleman may find security in his place by following the order presented in *The Classic of Changes*; the gentleman may seek delight in his pondering by investigating the explanations of the *lines* of the hexagrams.
>
> Therefore, to remain in his place, the gentleman observes the *images* and mulls over the meanings of the *lines*; to make a move, he observes the movement and mulls over the prognosticated results.
>
> Therefore, since heaven above stands by him, it is *good fortune* and nothing is *inflicting harm*.[62]

The hexagrams of *The Classic of Changes*, down to their shape and lines, are archetypal images of the universe that the sages of antiquity discovered, distilled, and delineated. The scholar-gentleman (*junzi*), through "observing," receives guidance about his moment and his place in the larger scheme of things. In "The Pond," Xie Lingyun, the poet, performs the duties of a sage in contemplatively observing the signs of the cosmos and distilling them into words that convey clear imagistic patterns of nature and the invisible but visualized laws governing the myriad things (*wanwu*), human affairs included.

In both *The Classic of Changes* and *Laozi*, nature denotes more than the objective world that is comprised of things. It is more importantly about the patterns behind the images. *Sheng* and *bian* are the dynamic laws defining nature. The "spring grass" is an image that symbolizes the law of change, movement, and momentum. With this, Xie Lingyun transcends personal time and fate by placing himself into the larger scheme of things and moves with *time*—the most frequent course of action as advised in *The Classic of Changes* hexagrams.[63]

In "The Pond," the poet positions himself as the sage and the gentleman. He solemnly observes signs in the universe by delving deep into the abyss and soaring high above the clouds. He contemplates the meaning of the images of "dragon" and "goose," which leads to acknowledging his personal time—a situation of "not being in the proper place" or "to have lost his place in the world." The "spring grass" image, however, portends change and growth. Guided and informed by the spring grass in *The Classic of Poetry* and *Songs of Chu*, Xie Lingyun's representation of this poetic moment transcends early literary traditions by incorporating the intellectual utility of *The Classic of Changes*, a text that informs how he ends his poem. Often characterized by critics as a "malaise," the final couplet of metaphysical musing is likely a formal play on the "Judgment" lines (lines explaining hexagrams) in *The Classic of Changes*. Xie's poetic creation is, in many aspects, self-consciously modeled on the prognostication text that renders a different notion of time: the personal is always embedded in the universal. Along this line of thinking, there are no good times or bad. There is only change.

CHAPTER 8

Patterning the Dragon

The dragon, a mythical creature prominently featured in *The Book of Changes*, symbolizes artistic perfection. For a talented artist, dotting the eye of a dragon is what brings the creature to life, and it is this defining act that is understood to imbue art with the divine inspiration discussed in chapter 7. In early medieval times, literary writing was widely considered to be like carving a dragon. China's first comprehensive volume of literary criticism, compiled in the sixth century CE by Shen Yue's contemporary Liu Xie, was titled *Literary Mind, Carving the Dragon* (Wen xin diao long). Here, the dragon embodies the elusive goals of various human pursuits, of which literary excellence came to be seen as the most important. The dragon, almost always hidden, waits to be revealed, as already seen in the opening couplet of Xie Lingyun's poem "The Pond."

As an intellectual poet of his time, Xie's greatest contribution was to carve out lyric poetry's form, reviving its representational potential by melding the textual tradition with nature's manifested and mysterious aspects. Regarding Xie's importance in *shi* development, Xiaofei Tian posits: "Xie inspired a series of courtier-poets who came to define *shi* composition before the founding of the Tang: Bao Zhao, Shen Yue, Xie Tiao 謝朓 (464–99), Yu Xin 庾信 (513–81), and the members of the Liang royal family. This explosion of *shi* composition elevated the form to one of the most important literary genres of traditional China."[1] What were Xie's creative steps in this literary revolution? Close examination of the grammar and syntax of the five-syllable-line verse reveals breakthroughs in his use of the pivot verb and parallel couplet.

The Pivot Verb

The sixth-century critic Zhong Rong placed Xie Lingyun in the top rank of his *Gradations of Poets*, providing a general assessment and then an elaboration. The two entries read as follows:

During the Yuanjia era (424–53), there was one Xie Lingyun, whose talent was unmatched. His language was posh, his vocabulary profuse, his style extravagant. His writings were impossible to imitate.[2]

The poetry of Liu-Song's Xie Lingyun, Grand Warden of Linchuan [modern Fuzhou 撫州 in Jiangxi], draws inspiration from Prince Chensi [Cao Zhi] while incorporating Jingyang's [Zhang Xie, d. 307] stylistic elements. His work demonstrates masterful realism, surpassing his predecessors in both audacity and brilliance, though it occasionally suffers from verbosity. In my humble opinion, Xie possessed boundless talent and inspiration, turning his extensive readings and knowledge into original expression. In presenting his inner thoughts, there was never anything left unsaid. In describing external matters, nothing ever seemed to be left out. How opulent indeed! Throughout his works, memorable passages and soaring lines emerge, followed by carefully crafted allusions and innovative prosody in continuous flow. His talent stands out like a towering pine above the brush or white jade shining among pebbles. Even his stylistic flaws cannot diminish the fundamental purity and superiority of his work.[3]

Xie Lingyun was the only poet from the fifth century who was included in Zhong Rong's top rank, which is headed by three Jian'an poets, including Cao Zhi and Wang Can. Tao Yuanming was placed in the middle rank. This recognition by Zhong Rong comes with a paradox: while Zhong acknowledges the density of Xie's poetry as a flaw, he praises its essential purity. Bao Zhao captured this contradiction in his striking metaphor of a lotus blossom—though rooted in mud, it emerges pristine and beautiful. This image perfectly encapsulates the mysterious power of Xie's work. How can such intricate and difficult verses produce moments of crystal clarity? "The Pond" exemplifies Xie's ability to transform complexity into transcendent insight.

In the previous chapter, we examined how the couplet featuring "spring grass" and "garden willows" evoked centuries of enthusiastic responses from poets and critics. In line 15—which can be translated word-for-word as "pond banks grow spring grass"—the intransitive verb *sheng* (grow) is placed before the noun, making it formally transitive. The resultant indeterminacy calls attention to the identity of the agent. Where does the force of change lie?

Does it come from an external source or is it self-generated? These are the kinds of metaphysical questions Xie Lingyun's contemporaries were interested in exploring. While the philosopher concludes these are unanswerable, as the ultimate truth is ineffable, the poet relies on the suggestive in-between space where the answer can be pointed to without being named. Language is no match for image in conveying paradoxes and ambivalences. The reader, piqued by the curious verbal positioning of *sheng*, may linger in the indeterminacy where the relation between the spring grass and the pond signifies the workings of nature. Similarly, in line 16, the verb *bian* can be read as both transitive and intransitive. As a transitive verb, the line reads "garden willows transform the singing birds," demonstrating aspects of the "transformation" with regard to its fluid agent-recipient relation, which allows the images of the line to evoke a richly sustained and variable vision. In other words, the picture in the reader's mind is not only multidimensional, but also dynamic. The mosaic of change and variegation of life is activated with a few simple phrases strung together in an inverted verb-object structure. The birds may be changing in their types, their looks, their sounds, or even their "attitudes."[4] This change is part of a natural cycle, seemingly caused by the growth of willows that are turning green. In this couplet, spring emerges as a result of gradual advancement in the guise of sudden revelation.

It is worth noting that the images in this couplet—the springtime garden, ponds and pools, willow trees, and homing birds—are intertextual signs and symbols of a harmonious community blessed with a generous and fair-minded patron-prince. Xie Lingyun's springtime garden harkens back to Cao Cao's West Garden, which he used to entertain the Jian'an scholars. The birds in this poetry are invariably projected images of the scholars themselves. Sometimes there is one proud bird standing alone. Other times, a flock of birds gathers in a tall and welcoming tree, which stands for a generous patron. Xie Lingyun, in exile and isolation, expresses his hope about a harmonious court where talented people like himself may find home and shelter. Indeed, the message embedded in the bird imagery of line 16 is "all are welcome."

Xie Lingyun is acutely aware of the poetic traditions in which he is writing. His indebtedness to Jian'an poetry is particularly worth noting in his use of pivot verbs, as in the cases featuring *sheng* and *bian* demonstrated earlier. In Cai Zong-qi's study of five-syllable line poetry, he recounts his observation about the genre:

> Before the rise of pentasyllabic poetry, disyllabic compounds were the basic metrical unit in Chinese poetry. A tetrasyllabic line is normally made up of two disyllabic compounds and consequently a 2+2 beat constitutes the standard semantic rhythm in tetrasyllabic poetry from the *Book of Poetry* onwards. With the addition of one monosyllabic word, pentasyllabic poetry creates a semantic rhythm less monotonous than the even beat of tetrasyllabic poetry. In a pentasyllabic line, . . . a 2+3 semantic rhythm becomes a distinct trait of pentasyllabic poetry. This semantic rhythm can be further divided because there is a secondary caesura between the monosyllabic word and disyllabic compound in the final unit. . . . In short, the imbalance of the disyllabic and trisyllabic units, together with shifting of the secondary caesura, creates a varied, fluid rhythm hitherto unseen in Chinese poetry.[5]

The five-syllable line allows for more rhythmic variation, particularly through Xie Lingyun's careful attention to its central syllable. By emphasizing this middle position, he creates dynamic patterns that enrich the line's rhythm, syntax, and meaning while avoiding monotony.

Evolution of the Five-Syllable Line

How to maximize the semantic and syntactic function of the extra syllable depends on its position. An examination of five-syllable lines produced during and after Jian'an that have counterparts in *The Classic of Poetry* reveals how the five-syllable line evolved:

Mao 129, line 8: 道阻且長   The road is rugged and far.

"Nineteen Old Poems" 1, line 5:   The road-path is rugged and far.
    道路阻且長

In this example, a monosyllabic noun is changed into a disyllabic compound, creating the five-syllable line, whose meaning remains largely unchanged. The improvement lies not in meaning but in euphony. The new five-syllable line contains a "balanced foot" (bisyllable phrase) and an "unbalanced foot" (trisyllable phrase), enhancing musicality and rhythm.[6] Nevertheless, in this example, the connective particle *qie* (and) in the "unbalanced foot" functions largely to strike a rhythmic and syntactic balance, with a modicum addition to sentential meaning. The topic-comment grammatical form is commonly found in early specimens of the five-syllable line. More examples follow. They are collected from three sets of data: the "Nineteen Old Poems" (Gushi; hereafter, GS), Lu Ji's "Imitations of Old Poems" (Nigushi; hereafter, LJNG); Lu Ji's "Music Bureau Poems" (Yuefushi; hereafter, LJYF); and some additional examples from the corpus of the eighth-century poet Liu Fu (fl. 770s), who excelled in the ancient-style poetry (hereafter, LF). The first number denotes the piece in the set and the second denotes the line number.

道路阻且長 (GS 1:5)	The road-path is rugged *and* far.
河漢清且淺 (GS 7:7)	The He River and the Han River are clear *and* passable.
惠音清且悲 (LJNG 9:14)	The gentle tone is clear *but* sad.
纖手清且閑 (LJNG 10:6)	Her slender hands are fair *and* pleasing.
天道夷且簡 (LJYF 2:1)	Heaven's path is smooth *and* easy.
涼風嚴且苛 (LJYF 3:10)	The cold wind is biting *and* severe.
營生奧且博 (LJYF 8:12)	Preserving life, it is profound *and* broad.
沃野爽且平 (LJYF 9:2)	The fertile land spreads far *and* wide.
惠心清且閑 (LJYF 10:6)	The gentle heart is pure *and* kind.
土風清且嘉 (LJYF 14:13)	The local customs are pure *and* laudable.
結根奧且堅 (LJYF 15:7)	The joined roots are deep *and* strong.
玉質清且柔 (LF 1:12)	His jade-like substance is pure *and* gentle.
衣巾清且涼 (LF 2:2)	His robe and kerchief are cool *and* pleasant.
日沒路且長 (LF 4:1)	The sun is setting, yet the road is [*and*] far.
士卒勇且仁 (LF 5:16)	Officers and soldiers are brave *and* good.
萬山修且阻 (LF 8:8)	The endless mountain roads are long *and* rugged.
紗窗深且閒 (LF 14:1)	Behind the screen lies a deep *and* spacious chamber.

A close look at the examples here reveals something fascinating about the early stages of making the five-syllable line. In the two-syllable balanced foot, we see primarily noun phrases in which the first or second element describes or completes the syllable without adding necessary or new meaning. In other words, they can be called "place-holders" or padding units that keep the syllabic count consistently five. However, due to the lack of semantic substance, these elements are artificial, if not empty of real meaning. Similarly, we see similar inefficiency in the use of the connective particle *qie* (and) in the unbalanced foot. The formulaic "an X thing is of a Y quality" poetically speaking is not sophisticated or generative due to the mechanic pairing of synonyms, some of which seem to have lost any sort of specific meaning. For example, the use of the descriptive word *qing* 清 (which appears repeatedly in the list here, and is translated as "clear," "pure," etc.) to describe disparate nouns—such as music, climate, heart, and local customs—shows it was a popular term adopted ubiquitously to describe aesthetically and ethically pleasant things. When overused though, *qing* was turned into a cliché at best, a meaningless syllabic filler at worst. A syntactically more complex construction involved the insertion of a negative word such as *nan* or *bu* in the pivot position of the five-syllable line. The following examples all include *nan* 難, meaning "can't be."

空床難獨守 (GS 2:10)   The empty bed *can't* be kept by oneself.

歡樂難具陳 (GS 4:2)   The joy and pleasure *can't* be fully related.

歸雲難寄音 (LJNG 1:12)   Clouds *can't* send my words home.

離思難獨守 (LJNG 6:10)   Thoughts in separation *can't* be kept to oneself.

亮節難為音 (LJNG 1:16)   The shining virtue *can't* be expressed in words.

淑美難窮紀 (LJYF 14:33)   The fine goodness *can't* be completely recounted.

繁華難久鮮 (LJYF 15:10)   Flourishing splendor *can't* be sustained for long.

輕舟難載月 (LF 13:7)   The light skiff *can't* carry the moon.

Similarly, note that in the following examples, the particle *bu* 不 in the middle position negates a verbal phrase.

遊子不顧返 GS 1:12   The traveling man *doesn't* look back.

聊厚不為薄 GS 3:6   Be generous! *Don't* be cheap.

牽牛不負軛 GS 7:14　　The Ox star [Altair] *doesn't* carry its yoke.

終日不成章 GS 10:5　　All day, she *doesn't* complete a piece.

脈脈不得語 GS 10:10　　Eyeing affectionately, she *doesn't* say a word.

焉得不速老 GS 11:6　　Impossible–this *doesn't* cause aging.

生年不滿百 GS 15:1　　Years in this life *don't* reach a hundred.

既來不須臾 GS 16:13　　Though he has come, he *doesn't* stay long.

懼君不識察 GS 17:14　　I fear that you *don't* recognize.

憂愁不能寐 GS 19:19　　Sad and worried, I *can't* sleep.

還期不可尋 LJNG 1:10　　The date to return *doesn't* come.

循形不盈襟 LJNG 1:16　　Stroking this body—it *doesn't* fill the robe.

羽觴不可算 LJNG 2:8　　Winged-cups *can't* be counted.

睆焉不得度 LJNG 3:10　　Gazing over the distance—it *can't* be crossed.

采采不盈掬 LJNG 4:3　　Gathering, it *doesn't* fill my palm.

攬之不盈手 LJNG 6:4　　Plucking, it *doesn't* fill my hand.

歲寒不敢雕 LJNG 7:4　　In cold weather, it *doesn't* wither.

大樑不架楹 LJNG 12:14　　A great timber *doesn't* stand as the pillar.

朝餐不免冑 LJYF 3:17　　During a meal, he *doesn't* take off the helmet.

攬衣不及裳 LJYF 7:6　　Gathering the robe, he *doesn't* reach for the garment.

酖毒不可恪 LJYF 8:18　　Poisoned alcohol *can't* be indulged.

冶容不足詠 LJYF 10:39　　Seductive appearance *isn't* worthy of praise.

守一不足矜 LJYF 11:13　　Guarding the one truth *isn't* worthy of bragging.

四時不必循 LJYF 11:18　　Four seasons—one *doesn't* have to follow.

微芳不足宣 LJYF 15:2　　Minor virtue *isn't* worthy of proclaiming.

日月不能周 LF 1:18　　The sun and the moon *can't* be followed.

一水不可渡 LF 8:7　　A single river *can't* be ferried.

白日不與我 LF 9:3　　The bright sun *doesn't* agree with me.

辛勤不得意 LF 9:6　　Diligent, yet I *can't* achieve what I am after.

重關不能守 LF 9:12　　Layered gates *can't* be guarded.

嬌多不肯別 LF 11:7　　When love is deep, one *isn't* willing to part.

The high frequency in the use of *bu* in the middle position reveals a limitation in early five-syllable line poetry. The mechanical repetition of the colloquial negation word, although wasteful of the poetic space, does highlight the middle position as central to a five-syllable line. In other examples, the verb *duo* 多 (to abound in, to have in abundance, for the most part) is seen used in the middle position as either the main verb or an adjunct to the main verb.

王侯多第宅 GS 3:12	Kings and lords *held in abundance* mansions and houses.
蘭澤多芳草 GS 6:2	The thoroughwort marsh *has in abundance* fragrant herbs.
燕趙多佳人 GS 12:11	Yan and Zhao *have in abundance* glamorous beauties.
白楊多悲風 GS 14:7	In the white poplar trees *there is abundant* sad wind.
戚戚多滯念 LJNG 8:5	When moved in heart, one *has abundant* pent-up thoughts.
京洛多妖麗 LJNG 9:11	In the capital Luoyang, *there are in abundance* bewitching beauties.
志士多苦心 LJYF 1:4	Ambitious souls *abound in* inner turmoil.
涼野多險艱 LJYF 5:2	In the desolate fields *there are in abundance* difficulties and hardship.
親友多零落 LJYF 7:11	Of kin and friends, *there are many* who are lost or deceased.
高臺多妖麗 LJYF 10:3	On the high terraces, *there are many* bewitching beauties.
窈窕多容儀 LJYF 10:11	Winsome and charming, she *has much* appeal in countenance and deportment.
豪彥多舊親 LJYF 11:10	Among the stalwarts and scholars, *there are many* old friends.
山澤多藏育 LJYF 14:13	In mountains and marshlands, *there are abundant* resources.
時鳥多好音 LJYF 16:6	Seasonable birds *for the most part* sing good tunes.
寤寐多遠念 LJYF 16:17	In dream and in sleep, I *have many* concerns for the distant one.

In addition to the examples of monosyllabic markers and particles, there are a few bisyllabic idioms such as *yihe* 一何 (how very . . .), which are used in the middle of a sentence as a marker for tone or mood.

音響一何悲 GS 5:6	The sound and tone—*how very* sad!
歲暮一何速 GS 12:6	The year is now ending—*how very* fast!
音響一何悲 GS 12:15	The sound and tone—*how very* sad!
高談一何綺 LJNG 2:9	High-minded conversations—*how very* gorgeous!
故鄉一何曠 LJNG 4:5	Homeland—*how very* far away!
名都一何綺 LJNG 8:9	The famous towns—*how very* gorgeous!
東城一何高 LJNG 7:8	The east city wall—*how very* high!
高樓一何峻 LJNG 9:1	The high tower—*how very* impressive!
廛里一何盛 LJYF 8:3	Houses and residences—*how very* prosperous!
鮮膚一何潤 LJYF 10:9	Delicate skin—*how very* smooth!
佳人一何繁 LJYF 10:20	Beautiful women—*how very* many!
憂思一何深 LJYF 16:19	Pensive thoughts—*how very* deep!

When a binomial descriptive occupies the "unbalanced foot," the bisyllable *yihe* is always replaced with *he* 何 (how).

洛中何鬱鬱 GS 3:9	In Luoyang, *how* lush and luxurious!
四顧何茫茫 GS 11:4	Looking around, *how* vast and distant!

These examples demonstrate how, in the initial transition from four-syllable to five-syllable verse, modal, emphatic, and qualitative markers, including *he*, perform a double function: as prosodic fillers and extralinear modal indices. Other examples, including exhortative phrases, indicate the performative and vernacular origins of early five-syllable line-verse. Below are a few examples: *hebu* 何不 (why not), *buru* 不如 (better yet), and *dang* 當 (should).

何不策高足 GS 4:11	*Why not* whip a high-hoofed horse?
何不秉燭遊 GS 15:4	*Why not* roam all night with a candle in hand?

不如飲美酒 GS 13:17　　*Better yet* drink fine brew.
不如早旋歸 GS 19:6　　*Better yet* return early.
不如學神仙 LF 4:17　　*Better yet* practice the art of immortality.

為樂當及時 GS 15:5　　To make merry, one *should* grasp the moment.
揚聲當及旦 LJNG 2:14　　To spread a reputation, one *should* start early.
欲鳴當及晨 LJYF 11:12　　If you wish to be heard, you *should* begin early.

Also notable are formulaic constructs of rhetorical questions that use particles of interrogation, negation, lament, and exclamation, as well as other modes of expression in the form of adjuncts or modifying adverbials, some of which reveal a colloquialism that would later disappear. The overall impression of being addressed directly by a dear friend through these grammatical elements arguably contributes to the appealing impression that critics such as Zhong Rong characterized as "lived," "experienced," "remembered," or "ancient" (*gu*).[7]

焉得不速老 GS 11:6　　*How* can one not hasten to old age?
焉能凌風飛 GS 14:16　　*How* can one ride with the wind?

棄友焉足歎 LJYF 2:12　　An alienated friend, *how* is it worth lamenting?

愁思當告誰 GS 19:8　　Sad thoughts, to *whom should* I recount?
人生當幾時 LJNG 8:3　　This life, *how long should it be*?

會面安可知 GS 1:6　　Our next meeting, *how could it* be known?
人生安得長 LJYF 7:18　　This life, *how could I extend it*?
吾子安得停 LJYF 9:18　　People like us, *how could we stop and rest*?
吾壽安得延 LJYF 13:12　　My lifespan, *how could I extend it*?
尺素安可論 LF 7:10　　A message on the foot-long-silk, *what more to say*?

安用知吾道 LF 1:19　　*Why* practice my way?
安可以比方 LF 3:16　　*What could I* compare this to?

惡木豈無枝 LJYF 1:3	*What* tree doesn't have branches?
履冰豈惡寒 LJYF 2:8	Walking on ice, *how* could it *not* be cold?
朗鑒豈遠假 LJYF 2:17	The shining mirror, *how* is it far?
悼別豈獨今 LJYF 4:8	Mournfully we part, *how* is it just us?
征人豈徒旋 LJYF 6:12	Men on the campaign, *how* could they return in vain?
鳴玉豈樸儒 LJYF 11:5	Jingling jade, *how* are they coarse scholars?
矩步豈逮人 LJYF 11:16	Squarely pacing, *how* am I to catch others?
豈得常顧群 LF 7:6	*How* could I always care about my peer?
豈能長壽考 GS 11:10	*How* can one live a long life?

The expanded space in the five-syllable line reveals interesting patterns in early usage. Rather than strong verbs or actions, poets typically filled this middle position with grammatical particles or caesuras. While they used colloquial markers, questions, and modifiers to create an intimate speaking voice—giving their poetry a conversational directness and vitality—they left much of the position's syntactic potential unexplored. Further, these early experiments with the form, focused on creating direct emotional connection with readers, achieved less in terms of imagery and meaning than what would follow. It was Xie's poetry that fully realized the potential of the middle position in a five-syllable line. In presenting nature, rather than relying on direct address, Xie's work let imagery convey meaning through the verbal element in the middle position. This is what I argue is the crucial move to complete the evolution from the four- to five-syllable line, elevating the latter to new artistic heights, which became crucial in presenting not only nature but its invisible law.

Xie Lingyun's Innovative Five-Syllable Line

The contribution Xie Lingyun made in the genre transition from the four-syllable to the five-syllable line has to do with how and where to position the extra syllable. The key development found in Xie Lingyun's poetry is his tendency (1) to place the monosyllabic unit in the middle of a sentence; and (2) to allow the unit to assume a verbal sense by virtue of its positioning. Therefore, Xie Lingyun's five-syllable line is more often a 2+1+2 structure than the 2+2+1. When a monosyllabic extra syllable functions as a verb in the middle of a five-syllable line, the poetic line gains a dynamic element.[8]

In "The Pond," the poetic center is given to verbs or words that can be used as verbs. The syntactic pattern is uniformly 2+1+2, putting the focus on the middle syllable where the reader's attention is directed. In the poem's eleven couplets, eleven pairs of middle-position words are key to understanding the poet's feeling, which morphs like a dragon. These verbs both represent nature's movement and trace human feelings. Beginning and ending with *The Classic of Changes*, the poem perceives both inner and outer worlds through time's rhythmic patterns, like a divination reading nature's immanent order. The middle syllables of the lines seem to be conducting the emotional meditation the poet goes through. The following examples from "The Pond" demonstrate the dynamic actions and conflicting moods that the poem conveys.

> *mei* 媚 "to entice" / *xiang* 響 "to call out" (lines 1–2)
> *kui* 愧 "to be humbled ("not as good as") / *zuo* 怍 "to be
>   ashamed" (lines 3–4)
> *ling* 聆 "to listen" / *tiao* 眺 "to gaze" (lines 11–12)
> *ge* 革 "to repel" / *gai* 改 "to replace" (lines 13–14)
> *sheng* 生 "to emerge" / *bian* 變 "to change" (lines 15–16)
> *shang* 傷 "to sadden" / *gan* 感 "to stir" (lines 17–18)
> *yi* 易 "to be easy" / *nan* 難 "to be hard" (lines 19–20)

These pairs of third syllables form a map of the poet's internal struggles. As pivot verbs, they bridge the "balanced foot" and "unbalanced foot" in each line in a way that resemble the twists and turns of the inner vision and voice of the poet. The wide space between the "submerged dragon" and the "soaring geese" is traveled. The poet's final understanding of his situation derives from the wisdom imparted from *The Classic of Changes* as well as the natural scenery outside, which Xie associated with the divinatory signs. When nature meets the text, order is restored. The poet may now see his exile to Yongjia as a "return." In the returning birds, he finds assurance and renewed hope. In sum, the inter- and intralinear connections generated through syntax culminates with the pivot verbs *sheng* and *bian*—things happen and life changes.[9] In novelty, transparency, and intertextuality, "The Pond" measures well against the standards of regulated verse from the High Tang.[10] Xie Lingyun was a poet ahead of his time, as the Australian Sinologist J. D. Frodsham explains:

> The development of nature verse is undoubtedly bound up with the development of the five-word line. This not only took the poet out of the restrictive confines of earlier verse, but enabled him to write flowing descriptive passages, since he was no longer forced to chop them up into the short and relatively clumsy lengths of the four-word line. . . . The four-word poems are greatly inferior to the five-word poems treating the same subject.[11]

The pivot verbs provide a grammatically concrete frame, in which the extra syllable in the pentasyllabic line expands the poet's expressive space.

Parallelism Recalibrated

Parallel phrasing is another element of the five-syllable line that benefitted from Xie Lingyun's innovations.[12] The thirteenth-century critic Yan Yu 嚴 羽 (ca. 1180–1230) remarked: "Lingyun, in his poems, already utilized parallel couplets throughout. This was why he did not match up to the Jian'an writers."[13] Yan Yu considered parallelism, if used excessively, a detraction from poetic value, but he failed to recognize that it was through this experimentation that a breakthrough could be achieved.

The distinguished scholar Kang-i Sun Chang, in her study of poetry from the Six Dynasties, characterized Xie Lingyun's crowning achievements: "For the first time the aesthetic appreciation of mountains and waters and the ecstasy of viewing nature so typical of the Six Dynasties attitude is fully expressed in [Xie Lingyun's] poetry."[14] She further notes that it was Xie's "superb mastery of parallelism" and "painstaking workmanship" that made him stand out as a poet.[15] Hong Kong poet and scholar Charles Kwong argued similarly in his study of the aesthetics of parallelism in Chinese poetry, characterizing Xie's way of "writing about Nature" as "meticulously 'man-made'"[16]:

> Water and land, sky and fields, cataract and blossoms: these systematic actions, high and low objects, panoramic and close scenes, all crystalize into graphic descriptions through the lens of a poet with the aesthetic touch and verbal facility to express his ordering act. Within each couplet, Nature is neatly framed and painstakingly hammered into a set of corresponding elements—as parallelism.[17]

Like Chang, Kwong noted the realism and dynamism of Xie's poetic description.[18] Kwong, however, differed in attributing the "real scenery" not so much to the poet's dependence on the external world, but instead to his art. Xie's parallelism, according to Kwong, was enriched by "internal parallelism within each line" and "intra-linear parallelism," in addition to the expected interlinear patterning. Kwong also observed: "If one puts aside the fourth character in each line, there is even an internal parallelism within each line."[19]

Examination of the intralinear structure of the five-syllable lines sheds light on the workings of what Kwong called the "strict architecture" and "precise verbal engineering" in Xie Lingyun's poetry.[20] The first two syllables make up a bisyllabic unit, referred to in this analysis as Unit X, and the remaining three syllables form a trisyllabic unit, or Unit Y, which can be further divided into a monosyllabic and a bisyllabic unit, represented as {2 1} or {1 2}.[21] The monosyllabic unit, as demonstrated earlier, is poetically most effective when placed in the middle of the line, assuming the function of a verb. The bisyllabic unit, grammatically, falls into three syntactic patterns: VO=Verb Object; AH=Adjunct Head; and SP=Subject Predicate.[22] The bisyllable phrases, important building blocks of the five-syllable line, form two possible sequential constructs, with the monosyllable either at the end or in the middle. We have seen examples from the early "ancient poems" in the five-syllable line style of the 2-1-2 structure with the middle adverbial phrase. Gradually these adverbs such as "how," "so," "such," and "how very," came to be replaced with verbs in a poetic transition from the emotive to the descriptive. Examples of parallelism (outlined in table 1) can be seen in the following excerpt from Xie Lingyun's "Upon First Leaving the Commandery," first discussed in chapter 5.[23]

	遡溪終水涉	Sailing upstream, we arrive at the end of the waterway;
24	登嶺始山行	ascending the ridges, the trek in the mountains is about to start.
	野曠沙岸淨	Fields in the distance are laced with neat sandbars;
	天高秋月明	the sky is remote, with an autumn moon shining bright.
	憩石挹飛泉	Resting on the rock, I draw water from a flying spring;
28	攀林搴落英	trudging in the forest, I gather fallen blossoms.

This example demonstrates a parallelism of concentrated verbal phrases as bases for multilayered syntactic interactions. The level of complexity was unprecedented, although Xie Lingyun drew his inspiration from the Jian'an poets.[24] Another shaping force was Xie Hun, Xie Lingyun's talented uncle whose sole surviving poem shows its own homage to the art as well the convivial spirit of the Jian'an era.[25]

TABLE 1. Parallelism in "Upon First Leaving the Commandery"

Lines 23–28, "Departing"	Bisyllabic + Trisyllabic	VO=Verb Object AH=Adjunct Head SP=Subject Predicate	Literal translation
溯溪終水涉	2 {1 2}	VO {V AH} >> VO VO	Coursing upstream, finish, water wading
登嶺始山行	2 {1 2}	VO {V AH} >> VO VO	Climbing the peak, begin, mountain trekking
野曠沙岸淨	2 {2 1}	SP {AH V} >> SP SP	Fields vast, sandy shore, unstirred
天高秋月明	2 {2 1}	SP {AH V} >> SP SP	Sky high, autumn moon, bright
憩石挹飛泉	2 {1 2}	VO {V AH} >> VO VO	Resting on a stone, cup, flying stream
攀林搴落英	2 {1 2}	VO {V AH} >> VO VO	Pulling a tree branch, grab, falling petals

	悟彼蟋蟀唱	Awakened, I am, at the song of the cricket![27]
	信此勞者歌	How aptly it sings of the human toils!
	有來豈不疾	Years come and go—never dally;
4	良游常蹉跎	those good parties—are no more.[28]
	逍遙越城肆	Once we freely roamed about the marketplace;
	愿言屢經過	full of yearning, we frequented our visits.
	回阡被陵闕	Over winding paths, crossing hills, we arrived at the watchtower;
8	高台眺飛霞	from the high terrace, we gazed on the flying aurora.
	惠風蕩繁囿	A gentle wind rushed through the lush gardens;
	白雲屯曾阿	white clouds amassed above the layered peaks.
	景昃鳴禽集	At sunset, singing birds flocked together;
12	水木湛清華	the pond, the trees, limpid, fresh with blossoms.
	褰裳順蘭沚	With my robe girt up I followed the thoroughwort bank;
	徙倚引芳柯	waiting, pacing back and forth, I pulled scented boughs.
	美人愆歲月	The fair one lost his season and time;
16	遲暮獨如何	in the dusk of his years, what would I do?
	無為牽所思	Let it not tug at your mind and heart;
	南榮誡其多	Nanrong warned against obsessive yearning.[29]

This poem, composed of nine couplets, is a lament for lost friends. The "excursion" mentioned in the title seems to refer to a past gathering. Intertextual references to *The Classic of Poetry* and *Songs of Chu* contribute to the theme of nostalgia. It opens with a reference to "The Cricket" (Mao 114), a poem about lost friendship. In the main part, parallel couplets describe the site of gathering. Lines 7 through 14 (couplets 4 through 7) culminate in an imagistic line.[30] In terms of syntactic structure, Xie Hun's descriptive section is consistently 2 {1 2}, with one exception in line 11. In poetic technique as well as thematic resonance, Xie Hun's piece is demonstrably influenced by Cao Zhi's "Lord's Feast" discussed in chapter 6. A commissioned piece, it praises Cao Pi as the benefactor of scholars.[31] The imagery of a pond with fish and a garden with birds, as discussed earlier, symbolizes sociopolitical harmony. The qualities of clarity and transparency are emphasized in the repeated use of the word *qing* 清 (purity) in lines 3, 5, and 9 as the modifier to "night," "scene," and "waves." "Purity," the antithesis of *zhuo* 濁 (dirty, muddy, and corrupt), rose to a prevalent aesthetic-ethical value in poetic discourses of the Wei-Jin period.[32] In Cao Zhi's poem, *qing*'s broad semantic range extends from the natural to the social. Birds and fish are guests themselves, who freely frolic and roam in the domains of their generous host—the long slope, the limpid pool, and the high branch. The rapport between the host and his guests shines particularly through the smooth movements of the chariots, portrayed as lightly galloping and swiftly soaring. The dynamic and vibrant scenery emerges out of a string of verbs used in the pivot position in lines 3, 5, 7, 8, 9, 10, 11, and 13, generating the 2-1-2 syntactical patterning that both Xie Hun and Xie Lingyun came to adopt and improve. The poetic energy arrives at the pinnacle of the last couplet where the subject's mood becomes so elated that the final line comes out as an exclamation, as if made on behalf of the guests, to wish eternity to this ephemeral moment. Cao Zhi's eulogy of his brother culminates in the image of the moon whose pure aura is compared to the appeal of Cao Pi who was the fair and just patron, surrounded by guests orderly arrayed like stars in the night sky.

In addition to *qing*, purity and cleanness are also conveyed with the verb *cheng* 澄 (to cleanse). In Cao Zhi's piece, line 5 reads: 明月澄清景 (Bright moon/cleanse/pure light) where *cheng* functions as a pivot verb in a syntactic 2-1-2 construct. The unusual doubling up of *cheng* with *qing* results in a semantically reinforcing reading of the imagery. Line 12 of Xie Hun's poem reads: 水木湛清華 (water/trees/limpid/pure blossoms) where *cheng* is replaced with *zhan* 湛, which is another word, albeit less familiar, for "pure" or "clear." Xie Hun's defamiliarizing choice of word highlights "purity" as the valued principle governing human relationships even two hundred years after Jian'an. Xie Hun's couplets 7 and 8 allude to the *Songs of Chu* motif of the "fair one," connoting the patronage of a prince-patron or a like-minded friend. Xie Hun's poem ends on a pensive and melancholic tone, lamenting the absence of a noble benefactor and the harmony he brings to a community in crisis. At the time of the composition, Xie Hun was barely thirty years old, but he played the role of a family elder for his nephews, including Xie Lingyun, who received praise and pointed criticism at the poetry club. The social, political, and most importantly, artistic and humanistic bonding of the surviving members of the Xie clan resembled the ideal as represented in Jian'an literature.

Yet, the good days were few and memorable moments were like the beautiful reflection of trees and flowers in the water, at the same time clear and yet easily disturbed by political storms. The disturbance of peace and the loss of harmony during the three hundred years of disunion led to explorations of other worlds in literary expression. The loss of the classical "numinous garden" of King Wen, along with real and imagined locales of peace and harmony all found their way into poetry and prose in the two hundred years after Jian'an. The Bamboo Grove, for example, originally the place where the Buddha had preached, became a favorite Chinese motif in art and literature. The Peach Blossom Spring, another literary sanctuary, was made famous by Tao Yuanming. Rising most prominently during the fourth century were the so-called famous mountains, which émigré communities explored and called home. Earlier poetic accounts of the imagined beauty of the wilderness, such as Lu Ji's "Summoning the Recluse" (Zhaoyin), furnished a literary roadmap for the discovery of "ultimate joy" (*zhile*).[33]

	明發心不夷	Till daybreak, my heart remained unsettled;
	振衣聊躑躅	gathering my robe, I pace to and fro.
	躑躅欲安之	Pacing to and fro, where should I go?
4	幽人在浚谷	A secluded person lives in the deep ravine.
	朝采南澗藻	At dawn, he gathers cress in the southern stream;
	夕息西山足	at dusk, he reclines by the foot of West Hill.
	輕條象雲構	Soft twigs resembles eaves with cloud carvings;
8	密葉成翠幄	dense foliage forms curtains in halcyon-green.
	激楚佇蘭林	The agitated sounds of the Chu tune linger in the thoroughwort grove;[34]
	回芳薄秀木	swirling fragrance spreads through the edge of the forest.
	山溜何泠泠	Mountain brooks—hear how they murmur;

12 飛泉漱鳴玉　flying waterfalls scrub jade-like stones, ringing along.

哀音附靈波　Lamenting tones dash off with the numinous waves;[35]

頹響赴曾曲　listless echoes depart into the mountain nooks.

至樂非有假　The ultimate pleasure—it doesn't depend on falsehood;

16 安事澆淳樸　why serve to mar the simple and pure?

富貴苟難圖　If honor and wealth are hard to devise,

稅駕從所欲　let me unhitch the horse to follow my heart's desire.

Far from Xie Lingyun's description of real mountain dwelling, this poem follows the imagination of the possibilities of a simpler and purer way of life. The sound and sight of nature call out to the speaker, who questions the utility of service when it takes away from what is truly valued. Another third-century poet, Zuo Si (ca. 250–305), expanded on this vision and spells out in even clearer terms what was desired and preferred to political engagement.[36]

杖策招隱士　Grasping my staff, I set out to call on the recluse;

荒塗橫古今　the deserted path has been like this since time immemorial.

巖穴無結構　Cliffs and caverns have no human construction;

4 丘中有鳴琴　from the middle of the hillock—a sounding zither.

白雪停陰岡　A white snow lingers on the shadowed ridge;

丹葩曜陽林　crimson petals gleam in sunlit groves.

石泉漱瓊瑤　Stony streams rush over agates and jades;

8 纖鱗亦浮沈　fine fins swim to the surface and then sink.

非必絲與竹　There are no harps or flutes;

山水有清音　mountains and waters have their own clear notes.

何事待嘯歌　What need is there for whistling and singing,

12 灌木自悲吟　when trees and bushes on their own make mournful tones?

秋菊兼餱糧　　Autumn chrysanthemums are mixed in with
　　　　　　　　　dried grains;
幽蘭間重襟　　secluded thoroughworts are inserted in folds of
　　　　　　　　　gowns.
躊躇足力煩　　Pacing and pausing, my feet grow weary;
16　聊欲投吾簪　　I would cast away the pins of my official cap.

The fifth couplet contains the most quoted line from the *Wen xuan*: "Mountains and waters have their own clear notes" 山水有清音. Here, "mountains and waters" stand for the unadorned and unaffected substance of a person, while "clear notes" refer to the messages he conveys through literary expressions. Again, the quality of *qing* (purity or clarity) is the highlighted aesthetical and ethical principle around which thinker-writers such as Xie wished to establish not only in their sociopolitical life but also in personal cultivation. Mountains, as they are often portrayed in Jin and Song literature, are the epitome of nature; they exhibit the natural order that is missing from the power center.

Xie Lingyun's poetic vision of nature's law certainly shows influence from the works of Lu Ji and Zuo Si. Yet his textual knowledge and his decision to purposefully opt for more difficult, esoteric phrasing and imagery from *The Classic of Changes* constituted his unique style, as is seen in the utilization of the "dragon" image.[37] His choice of the rare word *qiu* for "dragon," rather than the common *long*, calls attention to the central role *The Classic of Changes* played in his creative process. "Hidden dragon" is the recluse who retreats from the world. In this line, the poet invites us to see the coiling and writhing dragon as inviting and charming, albeit concealed and hidden in the depth of a pool. It is a self-reference: his exile as a phase of incubation before a breakthrough. The use of the pivot verb *mei* 媚 as found in the second line of the poem is worth noting. Scholars have rendered the line differently, largely due to differences in understanding the syntactic function of *mei*.

> The hidden dragon displays a mysterious beauty. (Frodsham, 1967)[38]
> Submerged dragons make enticing their mysterious forms.
> 　　(Westbrook, 1980)[39]

A dragon, submerged, enhances sequestered charms.
> (Owen, 1996)[40]

A submerged dragon entices with mysterious charms.
> (Swartz, 2007)[41]

The submerged dragon attracts with its cloistered manner.
> (Huang, 2010)[42]

The hidden dragon charms with its obscure form. (Kwong,
> 2011)[43]

Its hidden form lends charm to the sunken kraken. (Tian, 2011)[44]

All of the translations treat *mei* as a verb, but disagree on how it functions grammatically.[45] *Mei* is an example of the critical middle-positioning of a word that assumes a verbal sense. Grammatically, *mei* interacts with both the subject—dragon (*qiu*)—and "its form" (*zi*)—a potential object or compliment. In the middle position, *mei* can function grammatically as both transitive and intransitive: (1) to charm; or (2) to be charming. Therefore, grammatically, *mei* is ergative.[46] The sentence thus contains two clauses: (1) the hidden dragon charms; and (2) the dragon's form charms. Therefore, the line can be paraphrased as: "The hidden dragon, in its sequestered form, charms [those who recognize it]." The object could be left undefined, or, as the modern scholar Ye Xiaoxue has suggested, it could refer back to the "dragon."[47] In other words, the intricately designed poetic image of the hidden dragon is a summation of the wisdom on reclusion in *The Classic of Changes*, as explained in the following commentary:

> In terms of human affairs, this symbolizes a great man who is still un-recognized. Nonetheless he remains true to himself. He does not allow himself to be influenced by outward success or failure, but confident in his strength, he bides his time. Hence it is wise for the man who consults the oracle and draws this line to wait in calm strength of patience. The time will fulfill itself.[48]

The "hidden dragon" line in Xie's poem has a matching image: that of the "flying goose" (*feihong*) in the second line, which is variously rendered as follows:

The flying goose has a cry that sounds from afar. (Frodsham,
    1967)[49]
Flying geese echo their distant cries. (Westbrook, 1973)[50]
The swan in flight sends its voice echoing far. (Owen, 1996)[51]
The flying goose echoes its far-off cries. (Swartz, 2007)[52]
The soaring goose sounds out far-reaching tones. (Huang, 2010)[53]
The flying goose sounds its far-reaching cry. (Kwong, 2011)[54]
The soaring swan sounds off its far cries. (Tian, 2011)[55]

Once again, how to read the syntax of the line depends on the ergative verb *xiang* (to sound), which is found in the middle of the sentence. Westbrook, Owen, and Swartz read *xiang* as a transitive verb, while others render it as intransitive. However, these two functions, transitive and intransitive, are not necessarily mutually exclusive in the Chinese text. Instead, they lend to layered configurations in image- and meaning-making. It seems impossible to render this line in English without losing the richness of the original and sounding disjointed. The central image here, "flying goose," forms an antithesis with the "hidden dragon." It takes us back to *The Classic of Changes*. Hexagram 53, "Development" (Jian), is the *locus classicus* for the image of a wild goose in the canonical explication and exegesis for difficult situations and how to overcome them. As explained in the commentary to hexagram 53, the yang or unbroken line at the top reads: "The wild goose gradually draws near the cloud heights. Its feathers can be used for the sacred dance."[56] Goose feathers are used in ritual ornaments and ceremonies, so they symbolize, for the scholar-gentleman, service or even sacrifice to the court. In other words, the flying goose, although rising high, is about to be sacrificed. As such, it constitutes the perfect antithesis to the hidden dragon.

Textual images such as these are integrated with representation of natural sceneries in Xie Lingyun's landscape description. On more than one occasion, however, the line between the two is blurred. The "spring grass" is both textual and natural. Poetic movements hinged on pivot verbs do not always go in predictable directions. The crisscrossing, ambiguation, and liminal spaces are where and how Xie Lingyun as a poet worked most effectively. The careful reader may glimpse the poet behind the poetic images. He beckons, but always hides.[57] If we pay attention to the verbs in the middle of the line, we can see that Xie's nature always has a compassionate and often playful person hidden in plain sight. Consider the following couplets and their pivot verbs:

白雲抱幽石　　White clouds hug the darkly secluded boulder;
綠筱媚清漣　　green bamboo charms the limpid ripples.[58]

海鷗戲春岸　　Seagulls frolic by the springtime beach;
天雞弄和風　　heavenly pheasants skip along the gentle breeze.[59]

長林羅戶穴　　Tall trees line up by the caved gates;
積石擁基階　　piling rocks cluster about the stairways.[60]

In these examples, not only do birds such as seagulls and pheasants behave like humans, but inanimate things such as clouds, rocks, and plants display human emotions and act according to a natural order. Personification is a universal and common literary device. In Xie Lingyun's application, the boundary between nature and human consciousness dissolves. The mind's eye of the poet becomes the "eye" of nature in the following example: "Birds chirping [nature knows or lets it be known that the birds] are roosting for the night; / leaves falling [nature senses or lets it be sensed that] cold wind/weather commences" 鳥鳴識夜棲，木落知風發.[61]

Symmetrical matching and pairing, as recognized features in a parallel structure, are more readily visible than antitheses and chiasmata or crossovers. Through his play with syntax and structure, Xie transformed the five-syllable line-verse, allowing it to arrive at a place free from the rigid boundaries of language.[62] His labor paid off, albeit unbeknownst to the poet himself.

CHAPTER 9

A Buddhist End

In the first half of the fifth century, robust Buddhist activities spread across China. The capital of the Eastern Jin, Jiankang, became a center for monks and scholars, who explored Buddhism from both religious and intellectual angles.[1] Xie Lingyun's passionate contributions to the development of the religion is a well-studied topic.[2] His writings that reflected both directly and indirectly his involvement with the Buddhist communities in Jiankang and Guiji suggest that his conception of nature and his representation of its mysticism were also part of the religious outlook of his time.

A Disciple of Buddhist Master Huiyuan

According to *Biographies of Eminent Monks* (Gaoseng zhuan), Xie Lingyun visited the Buddhist retreat at Mount Lu (in present day Jiangxi) and had an audience with the eminent monk Huiyuan (334–416) before his passing.[3] The retreat, whose construction was finished in 412, was famous for its otherworldly aesthetics:

> The retreat Huiyuan had constructed thoroughly exhausted the beauty
> of mountains. Carrying the Incense Burner Peak on its back, it was
> belted on the side by ravines teeming with springs. Stairways continued
> up from the rock; beams were placed among the pines. Clear rivulets
> veiled the steps; white clouds filled the chambers. In addition, there were
> meditation glades separated from the temple. Dense woods, where mists
> gather; stone mats, which lichen cover. In general, all that meets the eye
> and all the places one can set foot on evince an atmosphere in which
> one's spirit is cleansed and energy is condensed.[4]

The retreat at Mount Lu housed a painting on silk of the Buddha's shadow, which might have been partly inspired by Faxian's (337–422) report of a gigantic Buddha image found in a stone cave south of Nagarahāra (modern

Jelālābād) in northern Afghanistan.[5] The Buddha image was reported to be gloriously visible in every detail from a distance, and yet blurry and indistinct when an onlooker approached.[6] Like the Way as expounded in *Laozi*, the Buddha's wisdom is distant and mysterious. When Faxian returned to China and reported on his fourteen-year pilgrimage to India, bearing his eyewitness account as well as a treasure trove of Buddhist scriptures, Xie Lingyun was among his audience in Jiankang.[7] Word of Faxian's pilgrimage spread far and wide, including to Mount Lu where Huiyuan had resided with his followers. In this circle was Buddhabhadra (359–429), a master of meditation from Kapilavastu in northern India and the translator of the *Sutra of the Oceanic Samādhi of Visualizing the Buddha* (Guanfo sanmei hai jing) and the *Avatamsaka Sutra* (Huayan jing) from Sanskrit into Chinese.[8] Buddhabhadra, proffering a translation of an Indian meditation manual, advocated the principle of Samādhi (meditative concentration), which Huiyuan endorsed. To facilitate this meditation practice, Huiyuan had the retreat constructed, commissioned the painting of the Buddha's shadow, personally composed an inaugural inscription, and invited additional commemorative inscriptions to be established on site.[9] Xie Lingyun, among those commissioned, produced a solemn reflection on Buddhist teachings in the tetrasyllabic verse form, prefaced with an account of the literary-religious occasion.

> Buddha's Shadow, with preface
> (Foying ming bingxu 佛影銘並序[10])
>
> The great compassionate Buddha raises all beings, coming into contact with them through sympathy. The causation for each contact has different beginnings and paths. It is difficult to register through outer forms, but approachable through the underlying principle. These have been exhaustively documented and discussed in scriptures and commentaries. Although "the boat hidden in the gully" has come and gone,[11] the Symbolic Teaching endures.[12] Lamenting the way of the world, our reverence toward the Buddha's teachings has increased and deepened by the day.
>
> Monk Faxian's trip to Jetavana has brought back a detailed account of the Buddha's shadow, which is most marvelous and magnificent. There, on the rugged surface of the secluded cave, the Buddha has re-

portedly lodged his form. His countenance and deportment [are said to]
be stately and majestic; his distinguishing features are completely preserved. No one knows the beginning and end of how he got there, but
the image itself has always been clear.

When the Dharma-master of Mount Lu heard of the Buddha's
shadow, he became delighted. Since then, he has visited a secluded cave
and examined the empty chamber. To the north, it pillows on a high
peak; to the south it looks over a deep gully. He traced the portions provided to him and committed the image to green paint. Not only is this
image vivid in presenting the Buddha's form, it also is extremely effective
in conveying his mind.

The monk Daobing traveled far to make known Huiyuan's intent
[and] ordered me to compose an inscriptive text to be carved into the
stone. The function of the inscription is to spread merit, yet there has
never been merit as grand as that of the Buddhist founder. Considered
in this light, how could I, someone whose intellect is shallow and whose
learning scratches only the surface, propagate and relate this great merit?

The Buddha's deeds and traces are now in the distant past; forever we
shall yearn [for him] in vain. For this reason, I have exhaustively chimed
out what my meager talent allows in order to pledge my heartfelt sincerity. Not even an iota of his grand scheme, in its mystery and profundity,
is presented below. I could only hope that I have expressed my earnest
mind enough to touch the sentient beings. Even the flying owls have
time to change their cry, and the *icchantikas* [those destined to never
attain enlightenment] can find a path to extricate themselves. They shall
seek the Pure Land and relieve their weary countenances at the site of
worship. The Buddha does not deceive us, and all uttermost efforts will
be rewarded. Grasping the brush, I initiate the following words. Myriad
emotions arising, I cannot but heave a deep sigh.

夫大慈弘物。因感而接。接物之緣。端緒不一。難以形撿，易以理
測。故已備載經傳。具著記論矣。雖舟壑緬謝，像法猶在。感運欽
風日月彌深。

　法顯道人至自祇洹。具說佛影偏為靈奇。幽巖嶄壁若有存形。
容儀端莊相好具足。莫知始終常自湛然。

廬山法師聞風而悅。於是隨喜幽室即考空巖。北枕峻嶺南映彪
澗。摹擬遺量寄託青采。豈唯象形也篤。故亦傳心者極矣。

道秉道人遠宣意旨命余制銘。以充刊刻。古銘所始寔由功被。
未有道宗崇大。若此之比豈淺思膚學所能宣述。事經徂謝永眷罔
已。輒磬竭劣薄以諧心許。徽猷祕奧萬不寫一。庶推誠心頗感群
物。飛鴞有革音之期。闡提獲自拔之路。當相尋於淨土解顏於道
場。聖不我欺致果必報。援筆興言，情百其慨。

	群生因染	All sentient beings are karmically defiled;[13]
	六趣牽纏	to the Six Paths they are tethered.[14]
	七識迭用	The Seven Consciousnesses function [through us] in alteration;[15]
4	九居屢遷	through the Nine Abodes, they transmigrate incessantly.[16]
	劇哉五陰	How severe and poisonous—the Five Aggregates![17]
	倦矣四緣	How tiresome—the Four Causal Conditions![18]
	遍使輪轉	Everywhere [these] cause the wheel of living to turn;
8	苦根迍邅	due to the roots of suffering, they trudge along.
	迍邅未已	Trudging along—there is no end to it.
	輪轉在己	Yet the turning of the wheel resides within oneself.
	四緣雲薄	The Four Causal Conditions pile on like clouds;
12	五陰火起	the Five Aggregates flare up like fire.
	亹亹正覺	[Yet], steady and firm is Perfect Enlightenment.
	是極是理	Ultimate, this true principle!
	動不傷寂	Moving—yet it does not injure tranquility;
16	行不乖止	progressing—yet it does not deviate from stillness.
	曉爾長夢	It awakens you from your long dream;
	貞爾沈詖	it corrects your entrenched deviations;
	以我神明	to use my divine intelligence;
20	成爾靈智	to accomplish your numinous wisdom.
	我無自我	"I" lacks "coming from me";
	實承其義	surely it follows the same principle;
	爾無自爾	"You" lacks "coming from you";
24	必祛其偽	falsehood must be done away with.
	偽既殊塗	The paths of falsehood are multiple;

	義故多端	its meaning has many roots;
	因聲成韻	relying on sound, it becomes rhymes;
28	即色開顏	reaching form, it breaks into a visage;
	望影知易	viewing the shadow image, knowing is made easy;
	尋響非難	tracing its echo, it is no longer hard;
	形聲之外	beyond its form and sound,
32	復有可觀	there is more to be contemplated.
	觀遠表相	Looking afar, the image is manifest;
	就近曖景	going near, the sight turns blurry;
	匪質匪空	neither substance nor void,
36	莫測莫領	no one can grasp or fathom it.
	倚巖輝林	Leaning against the cliff, it brightens the forest;
	傍潭鑒井	lounging by the side of the pool, it is mirrored in a well;
	借空傳翠	availing itself of the sky, it conveys its kingfisher blue;
40	激光發囧	agitating in the daylight, it emits shining light.
	金好冥漠	His golden eminence comes out of the dim obscurity;[19]
	白毫幽暖	his white tuft of hair shines from the secluded darkness;[20]
	日月居諸	Oh sun, oh moon!
44	胡寧斯慨	Why do I have this eulogy?
	曾是望僧	It is all because of this eminent monk.[21]
	擁誠俟對	He in sincerity waits on the image.
	承風遺則	He has received the word and passed on the principle
48	曠若有概	that is all-encompassing and yet succinct.
	敬圖遺蹤	To revere the painting of the lingering trace,
	疏鑿峻峰	he has dug the mountain and channeled the peak.
	周流步櫺	Connecting all around are walking corridors;
52	窈窕房櫳	here and there hidden are the meditation cells.
	激波映墀	Splashing ripples veil the steps;
	引月入窗	the moon is graspable from the windowpane.
	雲往拂山	When clouds depart, they brush against the mountains;
56	風來過松	when the wind descends, it blows over the pines.
	地勢既美	The topography is majestic;

	像形亦篤	the image and form are vivid.
	采淡浮色	The color is subtle, its hue lightly floating;
60	詳視沈覺	one shall focus his beholding and concentrate on envisaging.
	若滅若無	It now fades away as if never existing;
	在摹在學	one shall ever trace, ever study.
	由其潔精	Following its pure essence,
64	能感靈獨	one can resonate with the Buddha's singularity.
	誠之云孚	Utter sincerity and confidence
	惠亦孔續	bring forth bounty beneficence.
	嗟爾懷道	Alas! To embrace the way,
68	慎勿中惕	be vigilant and never give in to
	弱喪之推	pushes of feebleness and bereavements;
	闡提之役	or the drags of the nonbelievers.[22]
	反路今覯	The path to return is now in sight;
72	發蒙茲覿	the way out of ignorance can now be seen.
	式厲厥心	Do steel your hearts,
	時逝流易	as time flows away easily.
	敢銘靈宇	Reverently, I present this inscription for the numinous eaves.
	敬告振錫	Respectfully, I report Buddha's bestowment of salvation.

These words came from Xie Lingyun in the 410s while he was still an active participant in the capital's intellectual circle, which was frequented by Buddhist monks. For Huiyan's commissioned piece, Xie chosen the appropriate four-syllable line, traditionally reserved for formal genres such as eulogies, encomiums, epitaphs, and, of course, inscriptions. Throughout the 76-line text, he expounds on important Buddhist concepts, saying that he is convinced of the Buddhist wisdom that separates form and sound from eternal truth. He praises Huiyuan for building the retreat, comments on the blending of architectural ingenuity with the natural environment, and admires the efficacy of the painting of the Buddha's shadow. This elegant inscription marked the beginning of Huiyuan's lifelong devotion to Buddhist communities, which reciprocated Xie's friendship. This meeting with Huiyuan, according to Xie's modern biographer J. D. Frodsham, was a turning point for the young poet: "Out of this chance visit grew a religious conviction which was to influence his whole life."[23] When Huiyuan passed away in 416, Xie composed a dirge, also a four-syllable line verse, to honor the religious master, professing therein that since age fifteen he had hoped to become Huiyuan's disciple.[24] Xie's interest in Buddhism is seen in his investigation into the "most important theological problem of the day," the merits of instantaneous enlightenment (*dunwu*) as opposed to gradual enlightenment (*jianwu*).[25] The debate centered on whether truth can be achieved gradually through the accumulation of learning or in an instantaneous moment of insight. The two methods would determine the conditions and kinds of truth achieved. Xie embraced the innovative if not iconoclastic idea of sudden enlightenment as proposed by Zhu Daosheng (355–434), whom Xie met in Jiankang in 409.[26] As a celebrity intellect in the capital, Xie was entitled to comment on the new theory, whose inclusiveness appealed to the underprivileged and undervalued. Frodsham posits: "As a Buddhist layman, he [Xie Lingyun] was unique for his time in his understanding of the scriptures. His grasp of the subtler points of Buddhist theology is remarkable in an age when very few of the Chinese clerics themselves displayed any real insight into this essentially foreign doctrine. . . . He made no mean contribution to the development of Mahāyāna Buddhism in China."[27]

Xie Lingyun's Buddhist Friends

Xie Lingyun's theories on sudden enlightenment can be found in his correspondences with his longtime friend Monk Tanlong (?–425?) and his former rival Wang Hong (370–432), which are included in *Dissertation on Distinguishing the Fundamentals* (Bianzong lun), a well-studied text that shows how Xie served as a spokesperson for his monk friends and helped propagate their ideas.[28] His approach to the Buddhist doctrines is tinted with a calm philosophical musing rather than religious fervor, often displaying a syncretism that reconciled Buddhism and Confucianism.

Xie's scholastic pursuits and collaborations with eminent monks resumed after his return to the capital in 426. He associated with Monk Huirui

(d. after 424), a celebrated master at Emperor Wen's court who compiled a Chinese dictionary of Buddhist terms. Xie may have even lent a hand in Huirui's dictionary project, as is reported in the latter's biography:

> Xie Lingyun of the Chen Commandery was fond of Buddhist principles and for the most part understood the non-Chinese words. He consulted Rui concerning various words in the sutras together with their numerous pronunciations and different meanings, whereupon Rui compiled *Glossary [Arranged According to] the Fourteen [Vowel-] Sounds [of the Sanskrit Alphabet]* [Shisi yin xun xu], listing the Sanskrit and Chinese item by item so that they could be clearly understood, and giving the words of the texts a basis in the glossary.[29]

Xie Lingyun, together with his friend Fan Tai, advised Emperor Wen on the transformative function of Buddhism as a religion and how it complemented the moral teachings afforded in the six Confucian Classics: *Poetry, Documents, Rites, Music, Changes,* and *Spring and Autumn Annals.* "When it comes to seeking the numinous, the fundamental, the true, and the profound," Xie wrote, "how could one not take Buddhist sutras as guidance?"[30] In other words, Confucian wisdom assisted with the governance and education of the people, while Buddhism provided spiritual enrichment. After Fan Tai passed away in 428, Xie Lingyun left Jiankang, returning once again to Guiji, where he continued with land-development projects, including building Buddhist retreats for his monk friends. In his "*Fu* on Dwelling in the Mountains" (Shan ju fu 山居賦), Xie professes to use his mountain villa as a home for the "remote and reclusive" (*youren*), an apparent reference to Buddhist monks, judging from the following excerpt from the *fu*, the expository and epideictic form usually reserved for weighty topics.[31]

	敬承聖誥	Reverently, I receive the sage's proclamation.
	恭窺前經	Respectfully, I peek into the canons of previous age.
	山野昭曠	Mountains and fields are bright and capacious.
320	聚落羶腥	Cities and towns are fetid and filthy.

	故大慈之弘誓	Thereupon the Great Compassion vows to universally
324	拯羣物之淪傾	raise the sunken and fallen among the myriad things.
	豈寓地而空言	How could one sojourn in the world yet release empty promises?
324	必有貸以善成	One must avail his goodness to accomplish good.
	欽鹿野之華苑	I honor Gautama's Deer Park where the Four Noble Truths were explicated;
	羨靈鷲之名山	I yearn for the famed Magic Vulture Peak where the *Lotus Sutra* was explained;
	企堅固之貞林	I long for the correct and firm grove where the *Nirvana Sutra* was construed;
328	希菴羅之芳園	I desire the fragrant Mango Garden where he preached the *Vimalakirti Sutra*.
	雖綷容之緬邈	Although his lucid countenance is now distant,
	謂哀音之恒存	his compassionate tone is preserved forever.
	建招提於幽峯	I construct retreats by secluded peaks,
332	冀振錫之息肩	hoping to offer respite to those on long pilgrimages.
	庶鐙王之贈席	Might this emulate Mount Sumera Buddha's offering of a couch to Vimalakirti,
	想香積之惠餐	or remind one of the beneficent meals at the Incense Accumulation Temple?
	事在微而思通	Circumstances, subtle as they are, need to be penetrated through thinking;
336	理匪絕而可溫	the order of things, never diminishing, should be reviewed.[32]

In constructing the Buddhist retreats, Xie vowed to follow an ascetic principle of "manifesting the plain" (*xiansu*) and "embracing the un-adorned" (*baopu*):

| | 面南嶺 | Facing the southern peaks, |
| | 建經臺 | I had a scripture terrace erected. |

	倚北阜	Couched against the northern mound,
356	築講堂	a lecture hall was constructed.
	傍危峰	To commune with the solitary peak,
	立禪室	I had a meditation chamber constructed next to it.
	臨浚流	Overlooking a deep ravine
360	列僧房	are living quarters for monks.
	對百年之高木	Facing the tall trees that are over one hundred years old,
	納萬代之芬芳	we could smell their fragrance spreading for myriad ages.
	抱終古之泉源	Embracing the sweet spring from antiquity,
364	美膏液之清長	we savored the lingering purity of its unctuous nectar.
	謝麗塔於郊郭	I bid farewell to the gorgeous pagodas by the suburbs;
	殊世間於城傍	I left the world behind at the city walls.
	欣見素以抱樸	Delighted, I saw the guileless and embraced the unadorned;
368	果甘露於道場	verily, I relished the sweet dew at the Buddhist court.[33]

In the commentary on this passage, Xie introduces his two Buddhist friends—Tanlong and Faliu—in an affectionate tone that reminds the reader of Xie's Jian'an writing style.

These two masters chose spiritual devotion over family ties, leaving behind wives and children to enter the mountains. They cut all worldly connections, abstaining from meat and fish and clothing themselves in discarded rags. Even when confronted with marvelous things, they remained unmoved. I, a mere poet, similarly sought this path from the west and have yet to find the way. Our aims and situations were similar. While traveling to the waterfall at Stone Gate Mountain, I encountered these noble recluses. When it was time to bid farewell, we shared an aspiration: to pursue a quiet life on the eastern mountain and face death in

the west. Our meeting brought such joy that a single day felt like a thousand years. If only we had met sooner![34]

In the main text of the *fu*, Xie speaks of the monks's pursuit of *ling* (meaning
"immortality" in Daoist terminology), citing legendary immortals such as
Foqiu and Anqi.

	賤物重己	Taking external things lightly, they valued their person;
	棄世希靈	casting aside the world, they yearned for the noumenal.
	駭彼促年	Seeing time slip away,
388	愛是長生	they devoted themselves to the art of longevity.
	冀浮丘之誘接	They waited to be delivered by Foqiu;
	望安期之招迎	they anticipated the summoning from Anqi.[35]

In Xie's eclectic religious and philosophical beliefs system, Buddhism functions to reaffirm rather than replace Daoism.

In 431, Xie's land development and construction projects brought him
into conflict with the local authorities, which had repercussions; he returned to the capital to plead with Emperor Wen.[36] While there, he again
occupied himself with Buddhist activities by working on collating and
improving the translation of the *Mahaparinirvana Sutra*. This northern
version promised the evidence that nonbelievers (*icchantikas*) possessed
Buddha nature, and its arrival in the capital around 430 gave Zhu Daosheng's concept of *dunwu* more credence. Xie transformed the rather crude
Chinese version by Dharmaksema (385–433) into a polished Chinese text.
He also wrote commentaries on the *Diamond Sutra* that are now unfortunately lost.

The Last Journey and a Revised Death

Xie Lingyun's pursuits involving both Buddhism and Daoism remained
at an intellectual level. He appeared most interested in the ideas, and he
seemed to practice neither religion. Time after time, the choices he made

in life demonstrated that he was more philosophical than religious, more eccentric than conformist. In that sense, he was a poet and an aristocrat to the end.[37] The last episode of Xie's life echoed his exile a decade earlier. Once again, he was sent away to the south, although this time he would not be passing through or returning to his home estate in Guiji. This became the regret of his life, as he would write upon leaving the capital, in the poem "Departing Fort Rock" (Chu fa Shishou cheng 初發石首城).[38]

	白圭尚可磨	A blemished jade may still be polished;
	斯言易為緇	the slander has permanently tarnished my reputation.[39]
	雖抱中孚爻	Although I hold tight to the "Inner Truth,"
4	猶勞貝錦詩	still I have been harassed due to the "woven tales."[40]
	寸心若不亮	I fear my innermost feelings remain unknown;
	微命察如絲	this inconsequential life truly is dangling by a thread.[41]
	日月垂光景	The sun and the moon bequeath light and shine;
8	成貸遂兼茲	for such bestowal, I now have an assigned post.
	出宿薄京畿	I have set out and spent the night just outside the capital;
	晨裝搏增颸	at dawn, the luggage is readied, the wind growing stronger.
	重經平生別	Once again, I bid farewell to my dear friends;
12	再與明知辭	for the second time, I will take leave of my kin.
	故山日已遠	My old mountain home grows more distant by the day;
	風波豈還時	amidst the wind and waves, will there be return?
	迢迢萬里帆	Long and far, the ten-thousand-*li* sail;
16	茫茫終何之	vast and hazy, where will I end?
	遊當羅浮行	For roaming, I shall visit Mount Luofu;[42]
	息必廬霍期	for resting, I shall go to Mount Lu or Mount Huo.[43]
	越海陵三山	I shall cross the oceans and scale the three mountains,

20	遊湘歷九嶷	leave my footprints on Mount Jiuyi and by the River Xiang.[44]
	欽聖若旦暮	Yearning for the sage king, I shall meet Shun one day;
	懷賢亦悽其	commiserating with the worthy, I am saddened by Qu Yuan.
	皎皎明發心	Bright and pure is my heart, like the sky at dawn;[45]
24	不為歲寒欺	it shall not grow timid in face of the bitter cold.

Probably written in January of 432, this poem showcases Xie Lingyun's mature writing style. It can be neatly divided into three parts, each of which comprises four couplets. The first section accounts for the reason that has set him on this journey. The middle section succinctly compares his current farewell with the one ten years prior on the other side of the capital. He could see himself living in isolation then, but this time the certainty is absent. Sensing his own end, the poet seeks companionship in ancient worthies such as Shun and Qu Yuan, both famous for their wandering and dying away from home. Xie, following in their footsteps, embarks on his last journey into the southern wilderness. It is worth noting that the literal sense of Mount Jiuyi is "nine doubts." There are relatively few abstruse allusions in this composition. The rather direct tone is unusual, perhaps suggestive of Xie's resignation. Also palpable is his reluctance conveyed through the use of two reduplicative binomes in lines 15 and 16, as the poet looks back on his life.

The sense of nostalgia is also strong in the following poem, "On the Way, Thinking of the Old Days in My Mountain Home" (Daolu yi shanzhong 道路憶山中), written in the spring of 432.[46]

	采菱調易急	The "Collecting Caltrop" has a tune that rushes along;
	江南歌不緩	the "Southland" is a song of agitated pace.
	楚人心昔絕	The man from ancient Chu became disenchanted;
4	越客腸今斷	now this traveler of Yue is torn inside.[47]
	斷絕雖殊念	Disenchanted or torn, each has different thoughts;

	俱為歸慮歎[48]	yet it is the same wish to return that causes our lament.
	存鄉爾思積	Still cherishing his state, worries overcame him;
8	憶山我憤懣	recalling my mountain living, I become indignant.
	追尋棲息時	I look back on the time when I lived in reclusion;
	偃臥任縱誕	sprawling or reclining, I absurdly followed my whims.
	得性非外求	Keeping with my natural disposition, I had no wishes of the world;
12	自己為誰纂	self-sufficient, I bothered no one.
	不怨秋夕長	I didn't complain about the long nights of autumn;
	常苦夏日短	I only thought that the summer days were too short.
	濯流激浮湍	I bathed in the currents and splashed among the whirling tides;
16	息陰倚密竿	leaning against the bamboo, I took shade in the dense grove.
	懷故叵新歡	Thinking of the past, I find no joy in the present;
	含悲忘春暖	harboring sadness, I am oblivious of the spring warmth.
	悽悽明月吹	A melancholy tune on the pipe is "Bright Moon";
20	惻惻廣陵散[49]	a heart-wrenching song is "Guangling."
	殷勤訴危柱	Vigorously, sadness pours from the tall pegs;
	慷慨命促管	overwhelmed, I order a shrill piece on the flute.

The churning emotions within the poet are expressed through his response to different music pieces mentioned throughout the poem. The agitated tones of southern music finds a subtle resonance in the poem's rhymes, which is uniformly constructed in the deflected (*ze*) tone, traditionally reserved for feelings of distress.[50] Still, the poet finds a companion. As a sojourner in Yue, he is in the land of Chu, Qu Yuan's place of exile. The poet laments that happy days are now distant memories. He'd rather live in past agony than recognize springtime in the present. Sadness dominates the poems written during the last journey of Xie Lingyun's life, as seen here again in "Entering Pengli Lake" (Ru Pengli Hukou 入彭蠡湖口).[51]

	客遊倦水宿	The traveler has grown tired of living in a boat;
	風潮難具論	winds and waves—such hardship cannot be fully retold.
	洲島驟迴合	Isles and sandbars suddenly appear and then disappear;
4	坼岸屢崩奔	embankments often crash and collapse.
	承月聽哀狖	On moonlit nights, I listen to gibbons' mournful cries;
	浥露馥芳蓀	on mornings soaked in dew, I smell the iris's fragrance.
	春晚綠野秀	Now in late spring, green meadows are luxuriant;
8	巖高白雲屯	over the lofty peaks, white clouds arrive to stay.
	千念集日夜	A thousand thoughts gather day and night;
	萬感盈朝昏	myriad feelings overflow at dawn and dusk.
	攀崖照石鏡	I climb the cliff to see my reflection in the Stone Mirror;
12	牽葉入松門	clutching vines, I enter the Pine Gate.
	三江事多往	There, many legends of the past in the Three Rivers;
	九派理空存	the truth exists in its own accord in the Nine Tributaries.
	靈物吝珍怪	Numinous things withhold their marvelous wonder;
16	異人秘精魂	an otherworldly being conceals its spirit and soul.
	金膏滅明光	The yellow metal balm no longer glimmers in the dark;[52]
	水碧綴流溫	water chalcedony ceases to flow in a warm stream.
	徒作千里曲	In vain, I play the Thousand-League tune;[53]
20	絃絕念彌敦	strings snapped, my thoughts weigh me down even more.

In these last poems, one striking development in Xie Lingyun's style is the lack of a metaphysical closure. The poems, like this one, are not put in emotional order. "Weary" and "despairing," the poet writes in an unprecedented self-revelatory fashion, as his life felt like a long boat journey going through "winds and waves." Experiences and encounters, governed by chance and fate, elude one the same way that scenery unfolds before the eye of the river traveler. The outside world the poet sees and describes mirrors his inner landscape—thoughts pile up and weigh on him heavily like the gathering clouds. To escape his own mind, the poet stops at the legendary sites where the lore of immortality abounds. The excursion, unfortunately, ends in disenchantment as well, as he finds no "glimmer" or "stream" of life-giving elements.

The despairing tone follows Xie into the poetic space of arguably the last travel or sightseeing piece concerning the plausibility and veracity of immortality, something that understandably surfaces frequently as he considers his own end. "Arriving at the Third Valley of Mayuan Huazi Ridge" (Ru Huazigang shi mayuan disangu 入華子岡是麻源第三谷) was composed shortly after Xie assumed his post in Linchuan in 432. The opening of the poem suggests that the Huazi mountain excursion took place during winter.[54] If so, this was the last winter of Xie's life.

<table>
<tr><td></td><td>南州實炎德</td><td>The Southern State verifies its fiery merit;</td></tr>
<tr><td></td><td>桂樹陵寒山</td><td>osmanthus trees stand tall in the cold mountains.</td></tr>
<tr><td></td><td>銅陵映碧澗</td><td>The Copper Hill is reflected in the emerald stream;</td></tr>
<tr><td>4</td><td>石磴瀉紅泉</td><td>over those rocky steps a crimson spring rushes forth.</td></tr>
<tr><td></td><td>既枉隱淪客</td><td>Recluses have made their way here;</td></tr>
<tr><td></td><td>亦棲肥遯賢</td><td>so have worthy men who escaped the time.</td></tr>
<tr><td></td><td>險徑無測度</td><td>The narrow tracks cannot be scaled;</td></tr>
<tr><td>8</td><td>天路非術阡</td><td>paths leading to heaven have no directions or marks.</td></tr>
<tr><td></td><td>遂登群峰首</td><td>I ascend the highest peak of the entire range;</td></tr>
<tr><td></td><td>邈若升雲煙</td><td>so remote, I feel like hovering over the hazy mists.</td></tr>
<tr><td></td><td>羽人絕髣髴</td><td>Feathered men of the past departed into this "nebulous obscurity";</td></tr>
<tr><td>12</td><td>丹丘徒空筌</td><td>the Cinnabar Hill uselessly exists as nothing but an empty trap.</td></tr>
<tr><td></td><td>圖牒復磨滅</td><td>Charts and registers are also blotted out and obliterated;</td></tr>
</table>

	碑版誰聞傳	inscriptions and carvings are not transmitted.
	莫辨百代後	A hundred generations later, nobody can distinguish
16	安知千載前	things that happened a thousand years earlier.
	且申獨往意	Here I make known my intention to leave the world,
	承月弄潺湲	to receive the moon and dally in the murmuring stream.
	恒充俄頃用	Let this be of use in an instant,
20	豈為古今然	not the state that transcends the past or present.

This is a poem about disillusionment with life itself and the vacant promises of the art of longevity. Huazi Ridge is a famous locale for Daoist practitioners, who concocted elixirs using cinnabar, of which there were rich deposits in the area. This mountain attracted many who aspired for immortality and it is recorded by Xie as such. However, the second part of the poem seems to question the existence of these immortals and efficacy of the mountain. Standing in the hazy mists overlooking the world at his feet, the poet seems to realize the nihilism of the phenomenal world. The sights, messages, and lore are all traps left behind after the truth has been temporarily encountered. The poet then captures a moment with the moon and the murmuring stream. In the penultimate line, Xie seems to be saying that he accepts the usefulness of the momentary pleasure. A visit to the mountain leads to the understanding that recalls Tao Yuanming's famous line: "There is true meaning in this, yet the moment when I try to say something about it, words have failed."

J. D. Frodsham writes of the last stage of Xie Lingyun's life and poetic production: "He composed a series of magnificently conceived poems recording his journey. The prevailing mood in these verses is one of nostalgia."[55] Frodsham also speculates on the forces that would eventually drive Xie to erratically suicidal behavior: "It is not difficult to understand why he chose to behave so mutinously. He had been unjustly slandered by an inferior, kept virtual prisoner in the capital for a year and then sent packing into the wilds of Jiangxi like a criminal. His arrogant spirit could brook so much but no more. How could he have brought himself to settle down to the dull routine of the magistrate's office, like a whipped child doing penance?"[56] Indeed before long, Xie would run afoul of local authority and an arrest warrant would arrive at his doorstep. What happened next was historical drama, laconically captured in a few words in *The Liu-Song History* (Song shu): "Lingyun captured his captor. He raised an army to facilitate his rebellious flight. Subsequently he set his mind on sedition."[57] It seemed that, "at this final indignity," he "lost his last shred of self-control."[58] *The Liu-Song History* records a quatrain, presenting it as evidence of Xie's treasonous intent:

韓亡子房奮	When Han perished, Zifang rose up;[59]
秦帝魯連恥	when Qin claimed the throne, Lu Lian was ashamed.[60]
本自江海人	I originally was a man of the rivers and seas;[61]
忠義感君子	loyal and righteous, these gentlemen moved me deeply.[62]

This poem is not recorded anywhere else. It may even have been a fabricated piece of evidence. If this was indeed written by Xie, he aligns himself with two anti-Qin heroes and calls himself a "man of the rivers and seas," a euphemism for an outlaw. When Xie was finally captured, Emperor Wen again resorted to leniency. Still, Xie could not go without punishment, and so was exiled further south to Guangzhou. The journey took place in November or early December of 432. Stripped of all his titles and positions, Xie must have sensed the end of his life. Shortly after his arrival, he was arrested and sentenced to execution for having plotted a rebellion in order to revoke his exile. As Frodsham points out, *The Liu-Song History* account of the "plot" is "pitifully thin" and "flimsy."[63] It further reports that Xie left a final word prior to his execution.[64]

	龔勝無餘生	Gong Sheng could not live out his life;[65]
	李業有終盡	Li Ye also plunged to his end.[66]
	嵇公理既迫	Lord Xi was hard-pressed because of his principle;
4	霍子命亦殞	Master Huo, for his part, lost his life.[67]
	淒淒陵霜葉	Solemn are the frostbitten autumn leaves;
	納納衝風菌	soaking wet are the storm-braving day mushrooms.

	邂逅竟幾時	How much time does one have for this "chance meeting?"[68]
8	修短非所慘	Such brevity is not what I grieve.
	送心自覺前	Now I deliver my heart before the self's awakening,
	斯痛久已忍	such pain has been endured for a long time.
	恨我君子志	I most resent that my gentlemanly wish
12	不獲巖上泯	to "expire on the cliff" is not to be attained.

The earliest source of this poem is Xie Lingyun's biography in *The Liu-Song History*. It is composed of six couplets (twelve lines), which can be divided into three parts made up of two couplets. Each line of the first part contains an allusion to a historical figure whose life-and-death story reflects how Xie has come to terms with his final moments. Through Gong Sheng and Li Ye—two Han loyalists who chose death during the era of Wang Mang's (r. 9–23) usurpation—Xie sees his impending death as a martyrdom. "Lord Xi" in line three has been identified as Xi Kang (223–62) or Xi Kang's son Xi Shao (253–304). Frodsham surmises: "Lingyun could not but have felt the analogy between his own case and Xi Kang's very keenly. Xi Kang too had been unjustly put to death on the flimsiest of evidence. One has only to compare Xi Kang's valedictory poem 'Mysterious Sadness' with our poem to see the resemblance."[69] Sinologist Tim Chan agrees with this identification and points out that Xi Kang's tragic death constitutes a feature of the genre he terms "*ante-mortem* poetry."[70]

The modern annotator of Xie Lingyun's collected works, Gu Shaobo, however, believes it is Xi Kang's son Xi Shao whom Xie is thinking of. Xi Shao died trying to protect Emperor Hui of Jin in a battle. His attendant had warned Xi Shao to prepare a thoroughbred horse, which would facilitate his escape. Xi Shao declined and reasoned that there was no need for such a horse:

The emperor is leading a rectification campaign in person to cut down the rebels. In principle [*li*] there should be a campaign, but not an actual battle [meaning that the usurper or rebel should submit himself in the presence of the emperor]. If the imperial carriage [a euphemism for the emperor] were under attack, I—the humble servant of the emperor— would still preserve a minister's integrity, so what use is there for a thoroughbred horse [implying that he would die protecting the emperor]?

大駕親征，以正伐逆，理必有征無戰。若使皇輿失守，臣節有在，駿馬何為?[71]

Here Xi Shao uses "double persuasion"—a technique commonly employed among the Warring States rhetoricians—to explain his reasoning (*li*), which puts him in the position of a martyr. The phrase *li ji po* (under the force of principle) in the poetic line gives credence to Gu Shaobo's annotation.[72]

Three considerations support the Xi Shao theory. First, the presence of the word "principle" (*li*) in Xie Lingyun's line associates the reference more closely with Xi Shao's death than with that of his father Xi Kang. Second, the contextual reading of the first four lines makes Xi Shao's story more relevant and consistent with the other allusions, where there is emphasis on the character trait of loyalty. All the historical precedents died protesting a usurper, and the circumstances of Xi Shao's death fit with this overarching theme. Third, the reference to a "lord" (*gong*) is appropriate for Xi Shao, not his father Xi Kang, since Xi Shao was conferred that honorable title after his death.[73] However, the compelling presence of Xi Kang's antemortem example is difficult to rule out, as Xie's poem was written under similar circumstances, especially considering that Xie expressed the same regret of not being able to live out his life in the mountains as a recluse.[74] What we have here is an intriguing case where the poet's evocation of a lesser-known allusion maximizes the poetic space. Both Xi Kang and Xi Shao lost their lives because of a political struggle—one died a rebel and the other a loyalist. The irony is salient. In a time of rampant political injustice, trying to live out one's natural lifespan is impossible. This seems to be the poignant message that Xie Lingyun encapsulates in a short poetic line. He had already witnessed plenty of untimely deaths in his own clan and class, and could find solace only by making sense of his life through historical precedents.

A profound sadness is expressed in part two of the poem, first through a pair of natural images and then in a philosophical statement on death. Frostbitten autumn leaves and storm-braving young mushrooms symbolize vulnerability in a harsh environment. Still, Xie says, however brief one's life is, no one should bemoan this "chance meeting" (*xiehou*) — that is, life is an improbable event.[75] Such imagery evokes familiar Daoist views of life's transience. However, the final section invites an alternative Buddhist interpretation, particularly in line 9: "Now I deliver my heart before the self's awakening."[76] This line exists in two significant variants. While the *Wen xuan* version preserves "self's awakening" (*zijue*), Buddhist texts like the *Expanded Collection on the Propagation of the Light* (Guang Hongming ji) and *The Jeweled Forest of the Garden of Dharma* (Fayuan zhulin) preserve "correct awakening" (*zhengjue* 正覺; Sanskrit *sambodhi*).[77] It is possible that this textual variation reflects Buddhist communities' attempt to claim Xie as one of their own, even though the poem's themes are open also to Daoist reading.[78] What is certain is that Xie expresses regret for not having been able to "die on the cliff," meaning to live out his natural life in the mountains. Like many others, he was unable to extricate himself from the entanglements of court politics and completely lost control over his life's circumstances. The ideal of a pure, wise gentleman who is at the same time worldly and unworldly had proven to be elusive after all.

Conclusion

Despite being plagued by social unrest, political upheaval, and internecine strife, the three centuries following the end of Han empire were a period of significant cultural transformation. In literature, one of the era's monumental achievements was the establishment of five-syllable-line *shi* poetry as the most prized vehicle for literati self-expression. *Shi* as a category occupied an important place in the *Wen xuan*, which was widely memorized and studied in the ensuing centuries. Of all the poets included in this important anthology, Xie Lingyun's five-syllable-line works were most prominently represented both in number and type (see appendix 2). This was hardly surprising, because Xie was recognized as a watershed figure in the development and transformation of a literary genre. Critics and poets from the fifth century onward never ceased reading and appreciating Xie's works. Tang poet Bo Juyi (772–846) composed the following poem about "Duke Xie" as a critical response.

	吾聞達士道	Thus I have heard: the Way of those with penetrating vision—
	窮通順冥數	in good fortune or bad, they complied with unknowable fate.
	通乃朝廷來	When the path was unobstructed, they went into service;
4	窮即江湖去	when the road was blocked, they wandered off to rivers and lakes.
	謝公才廓落	Duke Xie—his talent was vast and uncommon;
	與世不相遇	yet he was born in a disconsonant time.
	壯志鬱不用	Despite his aspiration, he wasn't retained, much to his dismay.
8	須有所洩處	Necessarily, there had to be a way to release his pent-up energy.
	洩為山水詩	Releasing, it became poems of "mountains and waters";

	逸韻諧奇趣	their resonance is out of this world; so were his unusual proclivities.
	大必籠天海	In broad strokes, he covered heaven and ocean;
12	細不遺草樹	in details, he didn't neglect a blade of grass or a tree branch.
	豈惟玩景物	He surely was not just engaging with the appearance of things.
	亦欲攄心素	Also was he unfurling the unadorned threads emanating from the heart.
	往往即事中	In recording events of past and present,
16	未能忘興諭	he never overlooked drawing analogies and references.
	因知康樂作	As such, I understand the works of Kangle,
	不獨在章句	to be more than just stanzas and sentences.

Bai's evaluation of Xie covered the form, content, and purpose of lyric poetry. He also inadvertently created a category for Xie's poetry. Appearing for the first time in line 9, the term *shanshui shi* (mountains and waters poetry) would turn into a convenient and consistent handle for understanding Chinese nature writing; Xie's body of work stood as the most important early influence. The chapters in this volume have demonstrated that Xie's poetic innovations resided not only in content. In his poems, "mountains and waters," among other phenomena of the natural world, also assumed symbolic and abstract dimensions.

By attending to the development of the lyric (*shi*) form in Chinese poetry, this book has highlighted the lyrical, linguistic, ethical, and aesthetic structures of Xie Lingyun's work. The lyric voice in his poetry is not that of an individual, but of collective frustrated literati represented by personages of earlier times. Xie seldom saw himself as an exception, but always as a historical reflection. Nor did he believe in social isolation. His lyrical yearnings were often mapped out as psychological journeys with patterns of human relationships performed poetically through images of nature. A contemplative thinker, he was drawn to balance and symmetry, while sensitive to the momentum of change. Movement, linguistically realized through the pivot verb in five-syllable lines, set his poetry apart from earlier works.

"Mountains and waters," through Xie's poetic design, became reified images of cosmic law and the energy behind it. Similar to yin and yang, mountains and waters transform, to the discerning eye, cosmic mystery into patterned words, syntax, and stories. Xie was not the only or the first poet to write about nature or think about the world at large, but his writing yielded an elegant poetic pattern that could be reproduced in myriad ways. Xie inspired a new way of writing based on a new way of seeing "mountains and waters" as potent signs of the cosmic law. For the first time, *shanshui* manifested the pure and clear world. Such was Xie's nature, standing in opposition to the opacity in other aspects of his life whose details faded with time.

Nature, in Xie's poetry, was reconfigured in poetic form. Through parallelism, pivot verbs, and a penetrating vision, Xie presented nature's dynamic movement as well as its innumerable miens and phenomenal facades. Xie's contemplation of nature through poetry has inspired many to follow in the past millennium and half. The following poem by Bo Juyi features a spiritual approach through literary communion with nature that is akin to that of Xie Lingyun.

IN THE MOUNTAINS, ALL ALONE, I RECITE A POEM
(SHANZHONG DU YIN 山中獨吟)

人各有一癖	Others have their respective addictions;
我癖在章句	my addiction lies in stanzas and lines.
萬緣皆已消	Myriad affinities have all dissipated;
此病獨未去	this addiction [of writing poetry] alone is yet to leave me.
每逢美風景	Whenever there is a lovely climate and sight,
或對好親故	or when I meet my dear kin and old friends—
高聲詠一篇	excited, I chant a poem loudly,
恍若與神遇	as if I have come across the divine spirit.
自為江上客	By myself I have sojourned on the river;
半在山中住	half of the time, I spend dwelling in the mountains.
有時新詩成	Occasionally, when I finish a new poem,
獨上東巖路	alone I embark on the path leading up the east cliff.

身倚白石崖	My body clings to the white boulder bluff.
手攀青桂樹	My hand grabs onto the branches of the black osmanthus.
狂吟驚林壑	Madly chanting, I bring fright to forests and ravines;
猿鳥皆窺覷	gibbons and birds, in unison, peer at me.
恐為世所嗤	My fear is that I am the laughing stock of the world,
故就無人處	so I come to this place where no others live.

The theme of nature and the melodic cadence that we now associate with Chinese lyric poetry is thus a legacy of the dramatic life and times of Xie Lingyun.

Notes on Roaming Famous Mountains

XIE LINGYUN

Food and clothing are what humans need for living; mountains and waters are what humans naturally gravitate toward. Now we are entangled in the necessities of life, which block the path of our natural inclinations. It is commonly believed that joy and fulfillment can be found only in the Grand Hall [i.e., public service] and that those who sleep on the cliff [i.e., dwell in the mountains] and drink from a stream lack great ambition and, therefore, can only care for their mortal selves. I disagree with this. If a gentleman is inclined to care for the world and also endowed with the ability to save the world, then, in times of turmoil and disorder that call for someone with special talent, he should go against his natural disposition, but only out of expediency, to ferry across those in need. Surely the arena of fame and profit is inferior to nature's sphere, which is chaste and boundless. I can speak of a ruler of myriad chariots [i.e., a large state] who let go of his reins and ascended to heaven [i.e., became an immortal] from Tripod Lake. I can also name an heir apparent who found freedom on Mount Song. Additionally, there was one Tao Zhu who declined to serve as the minister to the king of Yue; the Marquis of Liu resigned as preceptor to the Han emperor. Judging from these examples, it is evident [that the chaste and free realm of nature is superior to the arena of fame and profit].

A. Yongjia Commandery
  1. In the mountains of Hengyang, varnish-plant is commonly found.[1]
  2. On Mount Loushi [Tower Boulder], gardenia is commonly seen.[2]
     So is camphor, which is usually three, four, or five arm-spans in circumference.[3]

3. Mount Shishi [Stone Chamber].

a. Following Nan Creek for 130 *li* [forty miles], one comes upon a stone chamber. To its north is a clear spring. Inside, it is seven *zhang* [seventy-five feet] tall, thirteen *zhang* [140 feet] wide, and sixty *bu* [six hundred feet] deep. It can seat one thousand people. Its shape resembles a turtle back. The stone is a yellowish white. Upon tapping, it makes the sound of a drum. The cliff along the mountain stands at twelve *zhang* [130 feet] tall. Local old people call this Stone Chamber Corridor.

b. This famous (stone) chamber abounds in yellow rhizoma [wild ginger] among other herbs.[4]

c. Stone Chamber has purple asters.[5]

4. Geyser Mountain

a. On top of Geyser Mountain there is a big lake, from which a giant solitary boulder emerges. On all sides, it is covered in beehives. According to *The History of the Han*, Zhu Maichen once submitted a memorial saying: "The King of Yue resides in Geyser Mountain. With one person guarding a defile, a thousand men won't be able to pass."

b. Zhuji and Jinzhou abound in black leek.[6]

c. Geyser Mountain abounds in peony.[7]

5. Corridor Mountain

a. When seen from afar, the mountain seems like eaves of a roof. Hence its name.

b. In Corridor Mountain, there is a tree that resembles fagara [*Zanthozylum*], but it smells like basil [*Ocimum basilicum*].[8] Local people call it mountain basil.

6. Broken Boulder Mountain · Boulder Sail Mountain

a. Two hundred *li* [sixty-two miles] south of Broken Boulder Creek is Boulder Sail whose width and length are about the same as Broken Boulder. The texture and color are similar. It is said that some ancient man broke a boulder to make a sail. This is the origin of the names broken boulder and boulder sail.

7. Balcony Mountain

a. On Balcony Mountain, there are tall paulownia trees that are over one hundred arm-spans in circumference. Compared to them, those special paulownia south of Mount Yi are inferior.

8. Crimson Rock Mountain

    a. Southeast equidistant from the two counties of Yongning and Angu lies Crimson Rock, which also rests against the ocean.

    b. On Crimson Cliff Mountain, amidst spring water and boulders, is a banana grove that reaches a height of ten *zhang* [108 feet].

9. New Creek

    a. Oysters from New Creek taste sweet and are better than those from Purple Creek.

10. Earth's Vein Mountain

    a. Wang Yan's *Record of Mountains* calls it Muliu Mountain; it is also called Earth's Vein.

11. Lotus Mountain

    a. Lotus Islet has protruding rocks that resemble young lotus blossoms. Their color is often blue and white.

    b. Lotus Mountain has marvelous birds that love their own form. Looking at their own shadows, they let down their guard and are often caught by hunters. People call them "home birds" or "prison birds."

B. Dongyang Commandery

1. Pink Cloud Mountain

    a. Everywhere on this mountain is a lot of Dragon Whisker Grass.[9] It is said that [in the past, someone] tried to clamber on a dragon's whiskers. When he fell, the whiskers turned into this grass. There is also a solitary boulder that stands, directly from the ground, three hundred *zhang* [3,280 feet] tall. The mountain stands above the water, several thousand peaks stretching on, some of which resemble the shape of ram's horn.

    b. Next to Pink Cloud Mountain, there is a lone pinnacle, standing resolutely and piercing into the clouds for two hundred *zhang* [2,187 feet], looking down on the water on three sides, with a circumference of 160 *zhang* [1,750 feet]. On the top, there is a lake where lotus flowers bloom. Nearby is a cliff known as

Treading Void. Gazing at the pinnacle from afar, it is lower than
Treading Void. Seeing it up close, Treading Void is beneath it.

C. Guiji Commandery

1. Stone Cliff Mountain

a. There is a lake surrounded on three sides by high mountains.
The Stone Cliff Mountain nestles up against the sandbars in the
water. There are five ravines. The first ravine on the south is now
the location of the Stone Cliff Vihāra.

2. Yangzi Gallery [Riverside Tower]

a. From the Yangzi Gallery, one walks south for two *li* [two-thirds
of a mile] or so, and the lake can be seen on the left; on the right
is the Yangzi.

3. Southern Gate Gallery

a. Turning north from Shining, there is an islet seven *li* [two miles]
long, pointing directly toward the Southern Gate Gallery in the
Retreat. Over one hundred *bu* [656 feet] from the Southern Gallery, one comes upon Mount Heng.

4. Stone Gate Mountain

a. The two cliffs on Stone Cliff Mountain form the approximate
shape of a gate, hence the name. Waterfalls rush downward,
shining crimson and shimmering halcyon. (Based on fascicle 8
of *YWLJ*.)

b. Stone Cliff has six gullies. One travels upstream from Stone Gate
and enters the gap between the two mountains. On two sides are
stone cliffs. The one on the right faces the gully river. (Based on
the Li Shan commentary of Lingyun's "Ascending the Summit of
Stone Gate," fascicle 22 of *WX*.)

5. Fuyu Mountain

a. *The Classic of Mountains and Seas* records: "Gazing north from
Fuyu Mountain, one sees Juqu Lake." Nowadays from He Mountain, which is to the north of Birdway in Yuyao, one can gaze
upon Juqu Lake. It is Fuyu Mountain.

6. In Heng Mountain, among the low shrubs, one often finds parsley
roots.[10]

7. Divine Lad Creek, cutting open Southern Mountain and Qili Mountain, is several *li* from Jinzhu Gully.

8. Following the cliff of Stone Crate Mountain, one climbs up for over one hundred *zhang* [1,092 feet]. It is all green lichen, with no other vegetation.

9. From the top of Guilin Mountain, one gazes into the distance and sees the tip of Sheng Mountain and Qiangzhong Creek.

10. Tianmu Mountain

    a. On Tianmu Mountain, there are maple trees that are over ten *zhang* [ninety-eight feet] tall; they make a soughing and whispering sound.

    b. On Maple Ridge, Stone Depth, and Osmanthus Ridge, shade is cast in bright daylight; ice forms in mid-summer. A nearby mountain seems far; a distant mountain seems close; everything seems covered by silky gauze, shaded among cliffs. Looking down, one sees the tips of the tress. Looking up, one sees stars and constellations.

D. Linchuan Commandery: Huazi Ridge

1. Huazi Ridge

    a. Huazi Ridge is in the third valley of Ma Mountain. According to old folks, Hua Ziqi was a disciple of Master Luli. They used to gather on top of this mountain and that is why the mountain is called Huazi.

    b. On Huazi Ridge, there are eight thousand feet of spruce that cover the face of the cliff.

2. On the west side of Jinzhou Mountain, the spruce is sparse, yet it is the favored home of gibbons. They mournfully cry all through the night. Travelers dread this.

3. One can see gibbons reach down for water by linking themselves [in a chain] that extends for one hundred *zhang* [1,093 feet].

遊名山志

夫衣食，生之所資；山水，性之所適。今滯所資之累，擁其所適之性耳。俗議多云：歡足本在華堂，枕巖嗽流者乏於大志，故保其枯槁。余謂

不然，君子有愛物之情，有救物之能，橫流之弊，非才不治，故有屈己以
濟彼。豈以名利之場，賢於清曠之域耶！語萬乘則鼎湖有縱巒，論儲貳則
嵩山有絕控。又陶朱高揖越相，留侯願辭漢傅。推此而言，可以明矣。

A. 永嘉郡

1. 橫陽諸山、草多恆山。[11]

2. 樓石山多梔子也。樓石山多章（木尤），皆三、四、五圍。[12]

3. 石室山

   a. 楠溪入一百三十里有石室，北對清泉，高七丈，廣十三
      丈，深六十步，可坐千人。狀如龜背，石色黃白。扣之聲
      如鼓。沿山石壁，高十二丈，故老傳云，是石室步廊。
      （太平寰宇記卷99）

   b. 名（石）室藥多黃精。[13]

   c. 石室紫苑。[14]

4. 泉山

   a. 泉山頂有大湖，中有孤岩獨立，皆露密房。《漢史（書）
      》朱買臣上書云：越王居泉山，一人守險，千人不得
      上。[15]（太平寰宇記卷99）

   b. 竹際及金州多麥（麦）門冬。[16]

   c. 泉山多牡丹。[17]

5. 步廊山

   a. 遠望如有屋宇之形，因而名之。（太平寰宇記卷99）

   b. 步廊山有一樹如椒，而氣是羅勒，土人謂為"山羅勒"
      也。[18]

6. 破石山・石帆山　破石溪南二百餘里，又有石帆，脩廣與破石
   等度。質色亦同。傳云，古有人以破石之半為石帆，故名彼
   為石帆，此名破石。[19]

7. 吹臺有高桐、皆百圍。嶧陽孤桐、方此為劣。[20]

8. 赤石山

   a. 永寧、安固二縣，中路東南便是赤石，又枕海。[21]

   b. 赤巖山水石之間唯有甘蕉林高者十丈。[22]

9. 新溪　　新溪蠣味偏甘，有過紫溪者。[23]

10. 地肺山　地肺山者，王演山記謂之木榴山。一名地肺。[24]

11. 芙蓉山

a. 芙蓉渚有聳石頭，如初生芙蓉，色皆青白。[25]

b. 芙蓉山有異鳥，愛形顧影不自藏，故為羅者所得。人謂宅鳥牢鳥。[26]

B. 東陽郡

1. 縉雲山

a. 凡此諸山多龍須草。以為攀龍而墜，化為此草。又有孤石、從地特起、高三百丈。以臨水、綿連數千峰、或似羊角之狀。（太平寰宇記99）

b. [謝靈運名山記云：] 縉雲山旁有孤石，屹然干雲，高二百丈，三面臨水，周圍一百六十丈，頂有湖、生蓮花，有巖相近，名步虛山。遠而望之，低於步虛；迫而視之，步虛居其下。

C. 會稽郡

1. 石壁山　湖三面悉高山，枕水渚。山溪澗凡有五處。南第一谷，今在所謂石壁精舍。[27]

2. 臨江樓　從臨江樓步路南上二里於，左望湖中，右傍長江也。[28]

3. 南門樓　始寧又北轉一汀七里，直指舍下園南門樓，自南樓百許步，對橫山。[29]

4. 石門山

a. 石門山，兩巖間微有門形，故以為稱。瀑布飛瀉，丹翠交曜。[30]

b. 石門澗六處，石門溯水上，入兩山口，兩邊石壁，右邊石巖，下臨澗水。[31]

5. 浮玉山　山海經有浮玉山，北望具區。今余姚鳥道北禾山於具區相望，即浮玉也。[32]

6. 橫山諸小草多苐蓀。[33]

7. 神子溪，南山與七里山分流，去斤竹澗數里。[34]

8. 石簣山緣崖而上，高百許丈，里悉青苔，無別草木。[35]

9. 桂林頂，遠則嵊尖疆中。[36]

10. 天姥山

a. 天姥山上有楓十餘丈，蕭蕭然。（太平寰宇記96）

b. 楓林嶺石潭溪桂林嶺，白晝結陰，盛夏凝冰，近山之遠，
遠山之近，有若羅縠，映於岩間，俯觀木末，仰視羅星。

D. 臨川郡：華子岡

  1. 華子岡

    a. 麻山第三谷。故老相傳，華子期者，祿里弟子，翔集此
頂，故華子為稱也。[37]

    b. 華子岡上杉千仞，被在崖側。[38]

  2. 金州山西面杉疏，偏為白遠所棲，竟夕哀鳴，行人所惡。

  3. 觀掛猿下飲，百丈相連。

Appendix 2

Xie Lingyun's Poems in the Wen xuan

	Title and *Wen xuan* Location	*Wen xuan* Category	Date
1	Recounting Ancestral Virtues 述祖德詩 (19.912–15)	Recounting Ancestral Virtues 述德	423–26
2	On the Double Ninth Day, Attending the Farewell Assembly Hosted by the Duke of Song at the Cavalry Terrace in Honor of Secretariat Director Kong 九日從宋公戲馬臺集送孔令詩 (20.960–61)	Lord's Feast 公宴	Ninth month, 418
3	Neighbors Sending Me Off at Block Hill 鄰里相送方山 (20.980–81)	Farewell Ritual 祖餞	Autumn 422
4	Attending the Emperor, Journeying to the Northern Fortress outside Jingkou 從游京口北固應詔 (22.1037–38)	Excursions and Sightseeing 遊覽	Spring 427
5	An Evening Outing at Western Archery Hall 晚出西射堂 (22.1038–39)	Excursions and Sightseeing	422–23
6	Climbing the Tower Overlooking the Pond 登池上樓 (22.1039–40)	Excursions and Sightseeing	422–23

7	An Excursion to the Southern Pavilion 游南亭 (22.1041–42)	Excursions and Sightseeing	422–23
8	Traveling to Auburn Rocks, Advancing to the Ocean of Sails 游赤石進帆海 (22.1042–43)	Excursions and Sightseeing	422–23
9	Returning from the Stone Cliff Retreat: Composed on the Lake 石壁精舍還湖中作 (22.1044–45)	Excursions and Sightseeing	Summer 424
10	Ascending the Summit of Stone Gate 登石門最高頂 (22.1045–46)	Excursions and Sightseeing	430
11	Gazing from Lake Shaman while I Traveled from the Southern Mountain to the Northern Mountain 於南山往北山經湖中瞻眺 (22.1046–47)	Excursions and Sightseeing	Spring 425
12	Following Jinzhu Gully, I Cross the Mountain and Travel along a Brook 從斤竹澗越嶺溪行 (22.1048–49)	Excursions and Sightseeing	Summer 425
13	Composed Reverently at the Prince of Luling's Tomb 廬陵王墓下作 (23.1093–96)	Sorrow and Lament 哀傷	Spring or summer 426
14	Composed upon Returning to My Old Residence: Presented to Secretariats Yan and Fan 還舊園作見顏范二中書 (25.1195–97)	Presentation and Reply 贈答	Sometime between April 1 and September 21, 428, according to Huang Jie and Frodsham

15	Composed upon Ascending the Scarp at the Oceanside after Departing from Qiangzhong: For My Young Cousin Huilian, Presented also to Yang Xuanzhi and He Zhangyu, Who Wrote Matching Pieces 登臨海嶠初發彊中作與從弟惠連見羊何共和之 (25.1198–99)	Presentation and Reply	Autumn 429
16	Presented to My Cousin Huilian 贈從弟惠連 (25.1199–200)	Presentation and Reply	Spring 428
17	On the Sixteenth Day of the Seventh Month of the Third Year of the Yongchu Reign, I Set Out from the Capital for the Commandery 初發都 [永初三年七月十六日之郡初發都] (26.1236–38)	Traveling 行旅	Autumn 422
18	Passing through My Family Villa in Shining 過始寧墅 (26.1238–39)	Traveling	Autumn 422
19	Fuchun Islet 富春渚 (26.1239–41)	Traveling	Autumn 422
20	Seven-League Rapids 七里瀨 (26.1241–42)	Traveling	Autumn 422
21	Ascending the Lone Islet in the Ou River 登江中孤嶼 (26.1242–43)	Traveling	Early summer 423
22	Upon First Leaving the Commandery 初去郡 (26.1243–45)	Traveling	Autumn 424
23	Departing Fort Rock 初發石首城 (26.1245–47)	Traveling	Winter 431–32

24	On the Way, Thinking of the Old Days in My Mountain Home 道路憶山中 (26.1247–48)	Traveling	Spring 432
25	Entering Pengli Lake 入彭蠡湖口 (26.1248–49)	Traveling	Spring 432
26	Arriving at the Third Valley of Mayuan Huazi Ridge 入華子崗是麻源第三谷 (26.1250–51)	Traveling	Winter 432
27	The Ballad of Guiji 會吟行 (28.1316–19)	Music Bureau 樂府	423 (?)
28	From the Southern Tower I Gaze for My Belated Guest 南樓中望所遲客 (30.1395–96)	Miscellaneous 雜詩	Summer 424
29	South of the Fields, I Had a Garden Planted, the Stream Dammed, and a Hedge Built 田南樹園激流植援 (30.1397)	Miscellaneous	424
30	Reading in My Study 齋中讀書 (30.1397–98)	Miscellaneous	423
31	On Stone Gate—A Newly Constructed Lodge—There Are High Mountains on All Sides, Winding Streams, Rocky Shallows, Slender Bamboo, and a Thick Grove 石門新營所住四面高山迴溪石瀨修竹茂林 (30.1399–1400)	Miscellaneous	Spring 430
32	Eight Poems Reconstructing the Wei Crown Prince's Gathering in Ye 擬鄴中詩八首 (30.1433–39)	Miscellaneous	426–28

Chinese Character Glossary

A'lian 阿連
ai shanshui 愛山水
Aishang 哀傷

Ban Gu 班固
Bao Si 褒姒
Bao Zhao 鮑照
baopu 抱樸
beiqiu 悲秋
bu shi 不時
Buxu 步虛

"Cai qi" 采芑
"Cai wei" 采薇
Cai Yong 蔡邕
Cao Zhi 曹植 (Zijian 子建)
Chang'an 長安
chaoyin 朝隱
Chen Commandery 陳郡
cheng 澄
cheng riju 乘日車
Chengguo 成國
Chu ci 楚辭
"Chu ju" 出車
chuchu 出處
Chuxue ji 初學記
Cui Yin 崔駰

"Da Xie zhongshu shu" 答謝中書書
Daoyong 道雍
denggao 登高
Dharmakṣema 曇無讖
"Di du" 杕杜
dili ji 地理記

Ding Yi 丁儀
Donghai 東海
"Dongshan" 東山
Du Fu 杜甫
dunwu 頓悟

Eastern Jin 東晉
erbao 二寶

Fayuan zhulin 法苑珠林
Former Qin 前秦
fu 賦
fuyang 俯仰

gaomu 槁木
Gaoseng zhuan 高僧傳
Gaozu 高祖
gong 宮
Gong Sheng 龔勝
gongyan 公讌
"Gu feng" 谷風
guan 觀
"Guanfo sanmei hai jing" 觀佛三昧海
    經
Guang Hongming ji 廣弘明集
gui 歸
Guiji 會稽
Gushu 姑熟

Han 漢
Hangzhou 杭州
"He cao bu huang" 何草不黃
He Changyu 何長瑜
He Xu 何勗

Huayan jing 華嚴經
Huirui, Monk 釋慧叡
Huizhong 回踵

Jia Yi 賈誼
"Jian" 漸
Jiangling 江陵
Jiankang 建康
jianwu 漸悟
Jin 晉
Jin-Song 晉宋
Jingling 竟陵
jintui 進退
"Jiubian" 九辯
"Ju gong" 車攻

Kangle 康樂
Ke 客
kelian 可憐
Kong Chunzhi 孔淳之
kumu 枯木

Langye 琅邪（琊）
Laozi 老子
li 理
Li Bo 李白
Li Ye 李業
Liang 梁
Liang shu 梁書
Linchuan 臨川
ling 靈
lingde 靈德
lingyu 零雨
Linhai 臨海
Liu Che 劉徹
Liu Dan 劉誕
Liu Daolian 劉道憐
Liu Shao 劉紹
Liu Wu 劉武

Liu Yi 劉毅
Liu Yifu 劉義府
Liu Yikang 劉義康
Liu Yilong 劉義隆
Liu Yiqing 劉義慶
Liu Yizhen 劉義真
Liu Yu 劉裕
"Liu yue" 六月
liuyi 六義
Lu Ji 陸機
Lu Xun 魯迅
Lu Zhan 陸展
Lu Zhonglian 魯仲連
luanli 亂離
Lulian 魯連
Luling 廬陵

mei (pleasing) 美
mei (alluring) 媚
Meng Yi 孟顗

Nan shi 南史

Pan Yue 潘岳
Peihuang 岯崲
Pengcheng 彭城
Pingtai 平台

qi 奇
"Qi'ai" 七哀
"Qi yue" 七月
"Qian" 謙
Qian Mu 錢穆
qifu 棄婦
qing 清
qingyin 清音
qingyun ti 青雲梯
qiuyuan 丘園
Quan Liang wen 全梁文

Sanjiangkou 三江口
Sanxuan 三玄
shang 賞
Shangyu 上虞
shanshui shi 山水詩
Shanyang 山陽
Shanyin 山陰
shen 神
shenli 神理
Shen Yue 沈約
"Shengmin" 生民
shi (poetry) 詩
shi (adornment) 飾
shi buyu 時不遇
Shi pin 詩品
Shijing 詩經
Shining 始寧
Shisi yin xun xu 十四音訓敘
sifu 思婦
sigui 思歸
"Sigui fu" 思歸賦
Sima Dewen 司馬德文
Sima Xiangru 司馬相如
sishi 四始
siyou 四友
"Siyue" 四月
Song shu 宋書
Song Yu 宋玉
su 素
Sun Chu 孫楚 (Zijing 子荊)
Sun Chuo 孫綽
susha 肅殺

Taiping huanyu ji 太平寰宇記
Taiping yulan 太平御覽
Taishan 泰山
Taiyuan 太元
Taizhou 台州
Taizu 太祖

Tang 唐
Tanlong, Monk 釋曇隆
Tao Hongjing 陶弘景
tonghuai ke 同懷客
tuan 彖
Tukou 涂口

Wang Bao 王褒
Wang Bi 王弼
Wang Can 王粲
Wang Hua 王華
Wang Hong 王弘
Wang Hongzhi 王弘之
Wang Mang 王莽
Wang Tanshou 王曇首
Wang Xianzhi 王獻之
Wang Xiu 王琇
Wang Xizhi 王羲之
Wang Zan 王瓚
wanwu 萬物
Wei 魏
"Weiji" 未濟
Wen xuan 文選

"Xi ci" 繫辭
Xi Kang 嵇康
Xi Shao 嵇紹
xiangcao meiren 香草美人
xiangzhuan 象傳
xiansu 見素
Xianyun 獫狁
Xiao Gang 蕭綱
Xie An 謝安
Xie Fangming 謝方明
Xie Hongwei 謝弘微
Xie Huan 謝瑍
Xie Hui 謝晦
Xie Huilian 謝惠連
Xie Jingren 謝景仁

Xie Lingyun 謝靈運
Xie Ke 謝客
Xie Wei 謝微
Xie Xuan 謝玄
Xie Yao 謝曜
Xie Zhan 謝瞻
xiehou 邂逅
xing (evocative imagery) 興
xing (form) 形
xinglü 行旅
xinglu nan 行路難
Xu Xianzhi 徐羨之
Xu Xun 許詢
xuan 玄
Xuan, King of Zhou 周宣王
xuanyan 玄言
Xuanyuan 宣遠
Xue Daoshuang 薛道雙
Xun Yong 荀雍
Xunyang 潯陽

Yan Yanzhi 顏延之 (Yannian 延年)
Yang Xiong 揚雄
Yang Xuanzhi 陽璿之
Yangjia 陽夏
yanshangmin 巖上泯
Yaofan 曜璠
Yijing 易經
Yin Jingren 殷景仁
Yin Zhongwen 殷仲文
Yingchuan 潁川
Yiwen leiju 藝文類聚
Yongjia 永嘉
you 幽

You, King of Zhou 周幽王
You mingshan zhi 遊名山志
"You Tiantai shan fu" 遊天台山賦
youfu 有孚
youren 幽人
youxian 遊仙
yu 羽
yuan 遠
Yuan Shu 袁淑
Yuanjia 元嘉
Yuankang 元康
"Yuanyou" 遠遊

Zengcheng 曾城
Zhang Heng 張衡
Zhang Liang 張良
zhangce 扙策
Zhao Qin 趙欽
zhao yinshi 招隱士
"Zhaoyin" 招隱
Zheng Wangsheng 鄭望生
zhengfu 征夫
zhile 至樂
zhili 至理
Zhong Rong 鍾嶸
Zhongxuan 仲宣
Zhu Daosheng 竺道生
Zhuangzi 莊子
Zifang 子房
zijue 自覺
Zong Qishou 宗齊受
Zuo Si 左思
Zuozhuan 左傳

Notes

ABBREVIATIONS

AM   *Asia Major*

AS   *Asiatic Studies*

BMFEA   *Bulletin of the Museum of Far Eastern Antiquities*

CLEAR   *Chinese Literature: Essays, Articles, Reviews*

EMC   *Early Medieval China*

HJAS   *Harvard Journal of Asiatic Studies*

JAOS   *Journal of the American Oriental Society*

JAS   *Journal of Asian Studies*

MS   *Monumenta Serica*

TP   *T'oung Pao*

SBBY   *Sibu beiyao* 四部備要

SBCK   *Sibu congkan* 四部叢刊

SKQS   *Wenyuan ge siku quanshu* 文淵閣四庫全書

T   *Taishō shinshū daizōkyō* 大正新修大藏經

XXSKQS *Xu xiu siku quanshu* 續修四庫全書

INTRODUCTION

1. After northern China fell under the control of the non-Han peoples of the steppe, the noble clans who had lived in the central and northern plains abandoned the Chinese heartland and fled south to establish a court in Jiankang (modern Nanjing, also known as the Southern Capital).

2. Owen, *An Anthology of Chinese Literature*, 319.

3. Swartz, *Reading Philosophy, Writing Poetry*, 236–72.

4. Frodsham, *The Murmuring Stream*.

5. Westbrook, "Landscape Description in the Lyric Poetry and 'Fuh on Dwelling in the Mountains' of Shieh Ling-yunn," (PhD diss., Yale, 1973). See also Westbrook, "Landscape Transformation in the Poetry of Hsieh Ling-yün," 237–54.

CHAPTER 1. XIE LINGYUN IN PLACE AND TIME

1. Li Yanshou, comp., *Nan shi* 19.539.

2. See Ledderose, "Some Taoist Elements in the Calligraphy of the Six Dynasties," 246–78.

3. Calligraphy and painting were part of the Daoist education Xie Lingyun received at the home of Du Mingshi. Du was a master from the sect of the Way of the Heavenly Master. See Frodsham, *Murmuring Stream* 1:58–59; see also Chen Yinke, "Tianshi dao yu Binhai diyu zhi guanxi," 462–66.

4. Shen Yue, comp., *Song shu* 67.1754.

5. *Song shu* 58.1590–91.

6. *Song shu* 58.1591; *Nan shi* 19.538–39.

7. See Li Wenchu, *Zhongguo shanshui shi shi* [History of Chinese landscape poetry], "Introduction."

8. *Nan shi* 34.881.

9. *Chenwu* 塵物. See Xie Lingyun's "Shu zude shi," *Wen xuan* 19.914.

10. Cao Xu, *Shi pin jizhu*, 28.

11. Ke or "sojourner" was a nickname of Xie Lingyun's. It is imbued with the Daoist view of life as a sojourn.

12. *Nan shi* 50.1247.

13. *Nan shi* 50.1247.

14. The large size is in no small part due to the inclusion of several of Xie Lingyun's literary works such as the "Rhapsody on the Northern Punitive Campaign" (Zhuan zheng fu), which is around five thousand characters (*Song shu* 67.1744–54), and "Rhapsody on Dwelling in the Mountains" (Shanju fu; *Song shu* 67.1754–71), which is even longer. For a translation and discussion of "Rhapsody on the Northern Punitive Campaign," see Xiaofei Tian, *Visionary Journeys*, 287–340. For translations and studies of "Rhapsody on Dwelling in the Mountains," see Francis Westbrook, "Landscape Description in the Lyric Poetry and 'Fu on Dwelling in the Mountains,'" 177–337; Mark Elvin, *The Retreat of the Elephants*, 338–68; David R. Knechtges, "How to View a Mountain in Medieval China," 1–56, and Wendy Swartz, "There's No Place Like Home," 21–37.

15. This is Sima Dewen (386–421), who later became Emperor Gong of Jin (r. 419–20), the last ruler of the Eastern Jin.

16. This took place shortly after Liu Yi's (?–412) triumphant campaign to eradicate Huan Xuan (369–404). See Frodsham, *Murmuring Stream*, 1:11–12.

17. The term Exalted Ancestor (Gaozu) refers to the founding emperor of a dynasty. In this case, it refers to Liu Yu who founded the Liu-Song in 420.

18. The date was April 16, 413.

19. This likely took place toward the end of 415, according to Frodsham's estimation

based on a reference (1.14) in Xie Zhan's (387–421) "Answering Lingyun from Ancheng." See Frodsham, *Murmuring Stream*, 1:20.

20. Liu Yu's northern campaign took place in the eighth month of 416. See Sima Guang, *Zizhi tongjian*, 3689.

21. Liu Daolian (368–422) was the less prominent brother of Liu Yu, by the same father. Daolian fathered Liu Yiqing (403–44), the compiler of *Shishuo xinyu*. Daolian had formerly served under Xie Yan (?–400) and associated with Xie Fangming (380–426). For Liu Daolian's biography, see *Song shu* 51.1461–64.

22. Liu Yu arrived at Pengcheng after his campaign on March 18, 418. See *Song shu* 67.1744–53 for the full text of this *fu*.

23. This took place sometime after February 11, 419. See Frodsham, *Murmuring Stream*, 2:24n212.

24. Liu Yu ascended the throne in July 420.

25. This two-thousand-bushel post was reserved for members of the "highest gates." So were the posts in the Imperial Library.

26. This passage reads like a character evaluation by the compiler Shen Yue, who could have written this himself or inherited the official-sounding account from a pre-existing document, such as the record of a court case.

27. Liu Yizhen was second son of Liu Yu. His wife was a daughter of Xie Jingren (370–416).

28. These terms are likely the official charges that formed the basis for demoting and exiling Lingyun in 422.

29. The Xie family estate lay fifty *li* (fifteen miles) west of modern Shangyu on the Eastern Mountain (Dongshan). Dongshan, also called Beifu or North Peak, was well known, as it had been established by Lingyun's great-great-uncle Xie An (320–85), where he had lived as a recluse. Lingyun's grandfather Xie Xuan (343–88) developed the family estate when he served as governor of Guiji from 387 to 388. When Lingyun came in 423, he built his villa on South Peak. The estate, according to Frodsham, was "virtually a large island, ringed by two rivers and encircled by hills, and was large enough to contain two lakes, several landscape gardens, fields where cereals and vegetables grew, fishponds and plantations of trees and bamboos." See Frodsham, *Murmuring Stream*, 1:33; 2:34n48.

30. Grand Ancestor (Taizu) refers to Liu Yilong, Emperor Wen of Liu-Song.

31. Frodsham argued, based on the different versions of this sentence in *Song shu* and *Nan shi*, that the work was given imperial approval, yet never recognized as a complete history of the Jin. See Frodsham, 2:57n17.

32. This section is likely an interpolation by those who held a different and apparently more charitable view of Lingyun, especially regarding his relationship with Emperor Wen. This information was not incorporated into the Shen Yue account until the

Qing dynasty. The source of this eighty-nine-character paragraph was first included in the *Nan shi*. Its logic is somewhat at odds with the rest of Shen Yue's account.

33. One *li* is about 0.311 miles.

34. For Fu Long's biography, see *Song shu* 55.1550–53.

35. Note that this passage covers similar content as the previous one, but with more details, showing the different sources utilized in the compilation of this biography.

36. This name alludes to the four favorite disciples of Confucius or the four companions of King Wen. See Frodsham, *Murmuring Stream*, 1:62; 2:6254.

37. *Zi* (style name) is a secondary or polite name taken by a male upon reaching marriageable age, which often had a semantic similarity with the personal name given at birth. Paul Kroll et al., *Student's Dictionary*, 629.

38. Liu Dan (433–59) was the sixth son of Liu Yilong, Emperor Wen of Liu-Song.

39. Liu Shao was the fifth son of Liu Yilong.

40. Zifang refers to Zhang Liang (250–186 BCE), a famous Han minister who earlier in his life had risen up against the Qin. For his biography, see *Shiji* 55.2033–49.

41. Lulian refers to Lu Zhonglian (ca. 305–245 BCE) who thwarted the invasion of Qin on behalf of the state of Zhao, but refused to be rewarded afterward. See *Shiji* 83.2459–69.

42. The term "rivers and oceans" (*jianghai*), or more commonly "rivers and lakes" (*jianghu*), refers to the real and imagined world outside conventional society and political authority. This notion can be traced all the way back to the *Zhuangzi*.

43. "Gentlemen principled in *loyalty and righteousness*" refers to those who dissent with or disapprove of the central court, usually on the grounds of ritual propriety or humane government.

44. Liu Yikang was the fourth son of Liu Yu, the younger brother of Liu Yilong. Yikang harbored imperial ambitions, and he dominated Emperor Wen's decision making at court. In 451, Yikang suspected of an insurrection and put to death. For his biography, see *Song shu* 68.1789–95.

45. Gong Sheng (68 BCE–11 CE) was a Han dynasty martyr, who starved himself to death to protest Wang Mang's (45 BCE–23 CE; r. 9–23) usurpation of the Han throne. For Gong Sheng's biography, see *Han shu* 72.3080–83.

46. Li Ye (d. 25), like Gong Sheng, protested Wang Mang's usurpation. He left court to live in retirement. After Wang Mang died, another usurper, Gongsun Shu, called on Li Ye to serve in his regime. After Li Ye refused, a jar of poisoned ale was placed on his doorstep. He drank it and died. See *Han shu* 81.2668–70.

47. "Lord Xi" in line three has been identified as either Xi Kang (223–62) or Xi Kang's son Xi Shao (253–304). Xi Kang was put to death on a charge of treason. His son Xi Shao, in contrast, died as a loyalist.

48. Master Huo refers to Huo Yuan (fl. 290), a Western Jin (266–316) man who lost his life for refusing to serve in the government of a usurper. See *Jin shu* 94.2435–36.

49. "Chance meeting" (*xiehou*) here refers to human life.

50. "Self-awakening" is the Daoist notion of death.

51. "To expire on the cliffs" (*yanshangmin*) is to "live out one's life in the mountains."

52. *Song shu* 67. 1777.

53. For a discussion of the background and context, see Su Jui-lung 蘇瑞隆, "Lun Xie Lingyun de 'Zhuan zheng fu'" 論謝靈運的《撰征賦》, *Wen shi zhe*, no. 5 (1990): 48–52.

54. In the fifth century and later, eccentricity and unrestrained behavior were regarded as admirable personal traits. That Xie Lingyun was emulated by great Tang poets such as Li Bo and Du Fu speaks volumes about the fluidity of the character evaluation found in official accounts. What the Confucian or orthodox historian may regard as an incriminating personal flaw could be worn with pride by a countercultural avant-garde writer, whose sophistication was almost always rooted in dissenting from the political power. Xie Lingyun's "disgraceful" end in the marketplace, along the same line of reasoning, could be interpreted as no less than a badge of honor for sympathetic readers or like-minded poets such as Li Bo.

55. The two descriptors of Xie Lingyun's character in Shen Yue's account are *bianji* (headstrong and incautious) and *shehao* (extravagant and unrestrained), which should be considered as gestures of excess and impracticality common among the aristocrats of the time. As Frodsham posits: "Fastidiousness and eccentricity, both qualities conspicuous in Lingyun, were carefully cultivated by the aristocracy of the Six Dynasties." *Murmuring Stream*, 1:9. Xie Lingyun was made an example of in an anecdote that describes him as being unable to move by himself without the help of a team of attendants due to his penchant for sartorial splendor. See *Song shu* 30.884.

56. Xie Lingyun's violent and untimely death was but one of many that the Xie clan sustained. For other early deaths by capital punishment among members of the Xie clan, see Cynthia Chennault, "Lofty Gates or Solitary Impoverishment," 298–99.

57. For a study of Shen Yue's life and works, see Richard B. Mather, *The Poet Shen Yüeh*.

58. The meaning of *fenpi* is likely comparable to its use in Wang Bao's "Dongxiao fu": 其仁聲則若飈風紛披，容與而施惠.

59. Pingtai or Level Terrace refers to the literary court of Liu Wu, King of Liang (fl. 168–144 BCE).

60. This refers to the currents and trends of literary productions.

61. The "supreme virtue" is the philosophy of *Laozi*. The dark pearl is the philosophy of *Zhuangzi*.

62. *Gong* is the name of the first or lead musical note in the pentatonic scale. *Yu* is the fifth note in the pentatonic scale.

63. "Drizzling rain" (*lingyu*) is from Sun Chu's poem "A Parting Poem Written at Zhiyang Precinct on Behalf of the Staff of the General Chastening the West." See *Wen xuan* 20.975–76.

64. See *Song shu* 67.1778–79; cf. Mather, *The Poet Shen Yüeh*, 40–44.

65. It is worth noting that the dormant period in the fourth century coincided with the time when the Chinese court came to be established south of the Yangzi following a large-scale exodus. Daoist cannons such as the *Laozi* and *Zhuangzi* dominated intellectual debates, turning poetry into paraphrases of *Lao-Zhuang* ideas. Referred to as "abstruse learning" (*xuanxue*), the philosophical discourses of the time brought about a kind of poetry known as the "poetry of the arcane" (*xuanyan shi*). For a study, see Wendy Swartz, "Revisiting the Scene of the Party: A Study of the Lanting Collection," *JAOS* 132, no. 2 (2012): 275–300.

66. Yan Yanzhi, although often named together with Xie Lingyun, is a lesser figure. This practice of pairing of poets and writers is not uncommon in the construction of literary and art history. In the *Wen xuan*, there are twenty-one poems by Yan and forty poems by Xie Lingyun. Critics have also pointed out Yan may have been more at ease with prose than poetry. See *Nan shi* 34.881; Frodsham, *Murmuring Stream*, 1:82.

67. Innovation in prosodic patterning (*shenglü*) was influenced and inspired by Buddhist chanting. Conscious construction of euphony in the five-syllable line was the missing piece that gave regulated verse the patterning in sound and syntax.

68. See Cao Xu, *Shi pin jizhu*, 160.

69. A *dou* (peck) is equivalent to ten pints.

70. See Liang Zhangju 梁章鉅 (1775–1849), *Langji congtan* 浪跡叢談 (Beijing: Zhonghua Shuju, 1981), 3:444. Liang points out that this saying as frequently quoted by commentators has its origin in the *Nan shi*. It is not locatable. See also Frodsham's note on this, *Murmuring Stream*, 2:78n103; Ye Xiaoxue, *Xie Lingyun shi xuan*, 184.

CHAPTER 2. PERFORMING LITERARY FRIENDSHIP

1. Qian Mu 錢穆, "Du *Wen xuan*" 讀文選, in *Zhongguo xueshu sixiangshi luncong* 中國學術思想史論叢 (Taipei: Dongda Tushu, 1976–80), 3:97–133. Lu Xun 魯迅, "Wei Jin fengdu ji wenzhang yu yao ji jiu zhi guanxi" 魏晉風度及文章與藥及酒之關係, in *Lu Xun quanji* 魯迅全集 (Beijing: Renmin Wenxue Chubanshe, 1981), 3:501–19.

2. See Michael Nylan, "Confucian Piety and Individualism in Han China," 1–27. On page 24, she posits: "It is clear by late Eastern Han times that the *shi* 士 [scholar-class], in response to the 'Proscribed Factions' legislation, had come to define their own iden-

tity largely by their pronounced opposition to other powerful groups (mainly the *waiqi* [distaff members], eunuchs, and military men above, as well as the despised commoners below, called the 'cold people'). The need by the *shi* to maintain their separate group identity, and also to celebrate it, led to the writing of 'exemplary lives' and to the coining of those in-group witticisms called *qingyi* ('pure critiques'). Hence, the greater emphasis on character evaluation found in the late Han and Wei-Jin periods, far from being a sign of rampant individualism, may well have portended a strong desire for greater group cohesion."

3. For a discussion, see Ping Wang, "Making Friends with the Men of the Past," 89–97.

4. For a study on reform and restoration of Wei court music, see Howard Goodman, "A History of Court Lyrics in China during Wei-Chi Times," *AM* 19, nos. 1/2: 57–109.

5. See Ping Wang, "Making Friends with the Men of the Past," 89–97.

6. For the Chinese text, see *Wen xuan* 30.1432–39. For previous studies, see Brigitta Lee, "The Rhetoric of Poetic Style: Imitation as a Form of Literary Criticism," in "Imitation, Remembrance and the Formation of the Poetic Past in Early Medieval China" (PhD diss., Princeton University, 2007), 156–230; Nicholas Williams, "Community and Individual at the Jian'an Court," in "The Brocade of Words: Imitation Poetry and Poetics in the Six Dynasties" (PhD diss., University of Washington, 2010), 210–26; and Rebecca Doran, "Perspective and Appreciation in Xie Lingyun's 'Imitations of the Crown Prince of Wei's Gatherings in Ye,'" *EMC* 17 (2011): 51–73. See also Frodsham, *The Murmuring Stream*, 2:79n117. Ye is a city in present-day Linzhang County, Hebei.

7. Xie Lingyun's list of writers excludes Kong Rong 孔融 (153–208) from Cao Pi's list of the Seven Masters, but adds Cao Zhi to the group. For studies of the "Seven Masters of Jian'an," see for example Zhang Keli, *Jian'an wenxue lungao*; Han Geping, *Jian'an qizi zonglun*; Itō Masafumi, *Kenan shijin to sono dentō*; Wang Pengting 王鵬廷, *Jian'an qizi yanjiu* 建安七子研究 (Beijing: Beijing Daxue Chubanshe, 2004); Wang Mei, *Jian'an wenxue jieshou shi lun*. The most recent important study of Jian'an is Tian Xiaofei's *The Halberd at Red Cliff: Jian'an and the Three Kingdoms* (Cambridge, MA: Harvard University Asia Center, 2018).

8. Song Yu (3rd cent. BCE), Tang Le, and Jing Cuo are names mentioned at the end of Qu Yuan's biography in *Shiji* 84.2491. They are referred to as disciples and followers of Qu Yuan.

9. Zou Yang (ca. 206–129 BCE), Mei Sheng (?–140 BCE), Zhuang Ji [also Yan Ji] (ca. 188–105 BCE), and Sima Xiangru served at the court of Liu Wu or King Xiao of Liang (?–144 BCE), who was brother of Emperor Jing of Han (157–41 BCE). For additional information on these literary figures of the Western Han, see Knechtges and Chang, *Ancient and Early Medieval Chinese Literature*, 1:663–67, 4:2310–12, and 4:2361–63.

See also Michael Loewe, *A Biographical Dictionary of the Qin, Former Han and Xin Periods, 221 BC–AD 24* (Leiden: Brill, 2000), 753–54.

10. Xu Yue (fl. 141–87 BCE), Zhuang An (fl. 141–87 BCE), and Zhufu Yan (fl. 141–87 BCE) all served as Gentlemen of the Palace (*Langzhong*) at Emperor Wu of Han's court. See *Shiji*, 112.2953–65. See also, Knechtges and Chang, *Ancient and Early Medieval Chinese Literature*, 3:1727–28, 4:2309, 4:2324–26; and Loewe, *A Biographical Dictionary*, 624.

11. *Wen xuan* 31.1432.

12. For the text, see *Wen xuan* 42.1894–96.

13. See Zhu Xiaohai 朱曉海, "Du *Wenxuan* zhi 'Yu Zhaoge ling Wu Zhi shi' deng san pian shu hou" 讀《文選》之「與朝歌令吳質書」等三篇書後, *Guangxi shifan daxue xuebao* (*Zhexue shehui kexue ban*) 40, no. 1 (2004): 70–75.

14. Assmann, *Cultural Memory and Early Civilization: Writing, Remembrance, and Political Imagination* (Cambridge: Cambridge University Press, 2011), 113–14.

15. *Wen xuan* 52.2271.

16. For a tabulation of the deaths of office-holding members of the Xie clan, see Cynthia Chennault's "Lofty Gates or Solitary Impoverishment? Xie Family Members of the Southern Dynasties," *TP* 85 (1999): 249–327.

17. See *Jin shu* 79.2079. Liu Yu was said to have regretted the killing of Xie Hun, saying on the day of his inauguration: "I truly regret [killing Xie Hun] and that the younger generations won't be witnessing his refinement and elegance."

18. *Wen xuan* 42.1895.

19. *Wen xuan* 42.1897.

20. *Wei shu* 2.88.

21. *Wen xuan* 30.1433.

22. Cf. a similar line in the "Changge xing" (Long song ballad): "All streams travel east to join the ocean." *Wen xuan* 27.1280.

23. This line alludes to *Analects* 2/1: "He who conducts government by means of moral power is like the North Star. It stays in its place, while all other stars come to support it."

24. "Empyrean Han" is double entendre for the Han imperial house and the heavens. For an example, see *Hou Han shu* 49.1644.

25. "Long Ford" refers to the Milky Way as well as the Han court.

26. "Between heaven and earth" here refers to the entire world. "Traverse flows" denotes floodwaters as well as social upheaval and political chaos. See *Mengzi*, "Teng Wengong" 3A.4: "In the time of King Yao, the world was not yet peaceful. Floodwater traversed the land." The "traverse flows" here may refer to the havoc wreaked by Dong Zhuo (d. 192).

27. "The King of the Cao Clan" refers to Cao Cao. See Li Shan's gloss in *Wen xuan* 30.1433.

28. "Areas under the Eaves" refers to north China and the Central Plains.

29. As heir apparent of Cao Cao, Cao Pi sees himself as the rightful successor, inheriting the reverence and respect accorded to men of talent and worth.

30. The *locus classicus* of "cherishing the principle of benevolence" (*huairen*) is *Mengzi* 6B/4.

31. "These many gentlemen" refers to those who pledged loyalty to Cao Cao's court, including the "Seven Masters."

32. "Daily renewing" is a kenning for "virtue." See the Commentary on the Judgments of *The Classic of Changes*, Hexagram 26 "Daxu" [The Taming Power of the Great]: "On a daily basis one renews their virtue," in Richard John Lynn, trans., *The Classic of Changes*, 26.

33. Here the "principle" refers to the grand law of the universe. See the "Tianxia" chapter of *Zhuangzi*: "In discerning the beauty of Heaven and Earth, we perceive the principle governing all matters." *Zhuangzi jishi* 10B.1069.

34. For the allusion to "dust on the beams," see *Wen xuan* 30.1427.

35. For "Shu zude shi" 述祖德詩, see *Wen xuan* 19.912–14.

36. For information on Wang Can as a writer, see Knechtges and Chang, *Ancient and Early Medieval Chinese Literature*, 2:1144–49.

37. *Wen xuan* 30.1433–34.

38. These two lines form an opening that compares the fall of the Han to that of the Western Zhou under the rule of King You (d. 771 BCE) and King Li (d. 828 BCE). During the reigns of Emperor Huan (132–67) and Emperor Ling (156–89), the Han court was plagued with power struggles between the consort families and the eunuchs. Note the phrase *bandang* 板蕩 is composed of two *Shijing* poems, Mao 254 and 255, with respective topics on King You and King Li.

39. The area between the Yi and Luo rivers refers to Luoyang, the Eastern Capital, which was sacked by Dong Zhuo. *Hanyao* refers to Hangu Pass and Mount Yao, two landmarks east of Chang'an, the Western Capital, which was also pillaged. Cf. Cao Zhi's "Two Poems to Ying Yang" (Song Yingshi shi 送應氏詩), in *Wen xuan* 20.974–75 and Wang Can's "Seven Sorrows I," in *Wen xuan* 23.1087. It is noteworthy that Xie Lingyun adopts Wang Can's famous phrase, *luan wu xiang* 亂無象 (unsightly chaos), with minor modifications.

40. Xie Lingyun assumes Wang Can's voice, narrating his departure from the heartland. Cf. the third line of Wang Can's "Seven Sorrows I," in *Wen xuan* 23.1087.

41. Cf. the fourth line of Wang Can's "Seven Sorrows I," *Wen xuan* 23.1087.

42. Cf. Wang Can's "*Fu* on Ascending the Tower" (Denglou fu), especially lines 5–6 and 13–14. In this famous piece, Wang Can gives a moving account of his emotions while surveying the land of Chu, a place Wang Can had lived in exile for a decade. See *Wen xuan* 11.489–90.

43. "Shi wei" 式微 is the title of Mao 36.

44. Supreme Chancellor refers to Cao Cao. August Divinity refers to Han Emperor Xian (181–234), who Cao Cao held in protection.

45. This means that the noblemen of the entire realm lent their support to Cao Cao.

46. Lines 11–18 recount Cao Cao's military campaign to Jingzhou. When Liu Biao died in 208, Cao Cao took over Jingzhou. Wang Can joined Cao Cao's court. Both "Splendorous Luminescence" and "Lucid Brilliance" are honorific references to Cao Cao—the regent of the Han royal house.

47. Lines 19–20 offer praise to Cao Pi, the designated heir, who was considered a benevolent patron of talented writers.

48. *Xijian* 息肩 literally means "resting shoulders." See Knechtges, *Wen xuan*, 1:245, lines 48–49.

49. *Mingliang* 明兩 or "Double Brightness" is a kenning for crown prince.

50. Lines 21–26 recall the excursions and banquets at Yecheng.

51. See *Wen xuan* 30.1434. For an account of Chen Lin as a writer, see Knechtges and Chang, *Ancient and Early Medieval Chinese Literature*, 1:109–12.

52. *Fen* (miasma) refers to the widespread chaos.

53. Yuan Shao (154–202) raised an army and occupied the region north of the Yellow River.

54. *Dan* 單 could also be read as *dan* 癉 (exhausted). See the following line in Mao 254: "The people below are completely exhausted" 下民卒癉.

55. This refers to Chen Lin's service under Yuan Shao.

56. *Xianggong* 相公 (prime minister) refers to Cao Cao.

57. The Eastern Capital is Luoyang.

58. His Luminous Virtue refers to Cao Pi.

59. Similar lines are found in the "Lord's Feast" poems by Cao Zhi and Ying Yang. See *Wen xuan* 20.943 and *Wen xuan* 20.947.

60. *Youmo* (*locus classicus* in the *Chu ci*) means "quiet silence."

61. For a study, see John Makeham, *Name and Actuality in Early Chinese Thought* (Albany: State University of New York Press, 1994). There is a translation of the text, in Makeham, *Balanced Discourses* (Beijing: Foreign Languages Press; New Haven: Yale University Press, 2002). For an account of Xu Gan as a writer, see Knechtges and Chang, *Ancient and Early Medieval Chinese Literature*, 3:1684–89.

62. See Yu Shaochu 俞紹初, "Jian'an qizi nianpu" 建安七子年譜, in *Jian'an qizi ji* 建安七子集 (Beijing: Zhonghua Shuju, 2005), 406.

63. For the text, see *Quan Sanguo wen* 55.1360b.

64. *Wei shu* 1.26, 1.53.

65. Such aloofness was considered a trait for the pure-minded gentleman who preferred private cultivation to worldly gain.

66. These locations are associated with lofty-minded recluses such as Xu You and Chao Fu, who lived during the reign of the legendary sage-king Yao. Xu You refused the offer of the throne and retired to Mount Ji and lived on the northern side of the River Ying. This action demonstrated his purity of character. See Huangfu Mi 皇甫謐 (215–82), *Gao shi zhuan* 高士傳, SBBY (Taipei: Taiwan Zhonghua, 1965), 1.2a–3a. See also *Wen xuan* 55.2386; 30.1435.

67. In this context, "unadorned words" refers to discourses about pure virtue in a life lived free of the trappings brought about by worldly success.

68. *Tixie* 提攜, literally "holding someone by the hand," also means "associating and assisting each other, oftentimes a like-minded friend." See *Liji zhengyi*, "Qu li shang" 曲禮上, 15.1234.

69. Jiaodong in the Latter Han was part of the coastal kingdom of Beihai 北海, east of modern Pingdu 平度, Shandong. See Tan Qixiang 譚其驤, *Zhongguo lishi dituji* 中國歷史地圖集 (Shanghai: Ditu Chubanshe, 1982), 2:45.

70. Gaomi 高密 was also located in Beihai.

71. Ji-Pu is short for Mount Ji and the Pu River. They allude to the reclusive moral cultivation as pursued by sages such as Xu You and Zhuangzi.

72. Blessed Illumination, with a literal sense denoting just and orderly rule, is a complimentary reference to Cao Cao.

73. For a study of Liu Zhen's poetry, see Wu Fusheng, "'I Rambled and Roamed Together with You': Liu Zhen's (d. 217) Four Poems to Cao Pi." *JAOS* 129, no. 4 (2009): 619–33. For an account of Liu Zhen as a writer, see Knechtges and Chang, *Ancient and Early Medieval Chinese Literature*, 1:595–97.

74. *Wen xuan* 30.1436: 卓犖偏人而文最有氣所得頗經奇.

75. *Shi pin jizhu*, 110: 其源出於古詩，仗氣愛奇。。。但氣過其文，雕潤恨少.

76. *Wen xuan* 52.2271: 文以氣為主.

77. Yanzi (ca. 578–500 BCE) was a capable minister of Qi who famously defended his honor when the King of Chu insulted his short stature. For Yanzi's biography, see *Shiji*, 62.2134–37.

78. Liu Zhen's native place was Ningyang in Dongping (in Shandong). See *Wei shu* 21.599.

79. Xu is Xuchang (in modern Henan), where Cao Cao held his court.

80. The broad stream here stands for Cao Cao's generous protection of the scholars.

81. Liyang (in modern Henan) was a garrison for Cao Cao's military troops. Situated on the northern bank of the Yellow River, this was the site for a major battle against the army of Yuan Shao.

82. Jiying (modern Yingxian, Hubei) was a city on the Yangzi. Cao Cao stationed his troops here and fought Liu Biao, the governor of Jingzhou.

83. "Enlightened One" refers to Cao Cao.

84. These two lines allude to Mao 66, "Gentleman Away on Service" 君子于役: "The roosters are perching in their coop; / the sun is setting. / The goats and cows have come back; / but the gentleman is away on service. / How could I not think of him?" 雞棲于塒，日之夕矣，羊牛下來，君子于役，如之何勿思.

85. For an account of Ying Yang as a writer, see Knechtges and Chang, *Ancient and Early Medieval Chinese Literature*, 3:1941–43.

86. *Wen xuan* 30.1437: 汝穎之士，流離世故，頗有飄薄之歎.

87. For a study of the "birds" trope, see Qian Zhixi, "Wei Jin shige zhong de feixiang yixiang" 魏晉詩歌中的飛翔意象, *Wenxue yichan*, no. 5 (1989): 38–45.

88. "Geese in the Clouds" alludes to "Great Geese" (Mao 181), which contains these lines: "The great geese are in flight; / sorrowful is their cawing and crying" 鴻雁于飛，哀鳴嗷嗷. The Mao preface explains that the piece was written in praise of King Xuan 宣王, who provided a home to those who had been scattered about.

89. "Tucked Wings" is a mountain north of Yanmen 雁門, where the mythical Torch Dragon 燭龍 lays in hiding. See *Huainanzi* 淮南子 (Beijing: Zhonghua Shuju, 1989), 2.150.

90. Weak Water is the name of a river that lies east of Mount Kunlun. The name denotes that the water is not strong enough to bear the weight of a feather. See Knechtges, *Wen xuan*, 2:32.

91. Liangchuan refers to Daliang 大梁 (modern Kaifeng, Henan).

92. Ying and Xu are towns in Henan, referring respectively to Yingchuan 穎川 and Xuchang 許昌.

93. Guandu 官渡 (modern Henan) was the site where Cao Cao defeated Yuan Shao.

94. Wulin 烏林 (modern Hebei) was where Cao Cao was defeated by Zhou Yu 周瑜 (175–210).

95. "Heaven's Canopy" refers to Cao Cao's court.

96. Yanlu 延露 also reads 延路 (Endless Road). It is the title of a popular song. "Receiving Dew" is likely an embellished and revised version. See *Huainanzi* 18.619; *Wen xuan* 5.231; 13.602.

97. For an account of Ruan Yu as a writer, see Knechtges and Chang, *Ancient and Early Medieval Chinese Literature*, 1:775–77.

98. *Wen xuan* 30.1438: 管書記之任，故有優渥之言.

99. The term *duoshi* (various officers) is found in the *Shijing* and *Shujing*. Cf. "Wen wang" (Mao 235) and "Qing miao" (Mao 266), where the term is used to refer to supporters and followers of King Wen.

100. Bohai is in modern Hebei.

101. Nanpi is a county in Bohai. See Cao Pi's "Letter to the Magistrate of Zhaoge, Wu Zhi," which contains the famous reference to the so-called sojourns in Nanpi: "Ev-

ery so often I would look back on our excursions in Nanpi, which were unforgettable"
每念昔日南皮之游，誠不可忘. See *Wen xuan* 42.1895.

102. The reference to the "bend of the Yellow River" recalls Cao Pi's letter, which has the following lines: "Then we yoked our chariots and went on excursions. Heading north we followed the bend of the Yellow River" 時駕而遊，北遵河曲. See *Wen xuan* 42.1896.

103. "Eating duckweed" or "feeding on duckweed" alludes to Mao 161. It refers here to the time when Ruan Yu received the patronage of Cao Cao.

104. For an account of Cao Zhi as a writer, see Knechtges and Chang, *Ancient and Early Medieval Chinese Literature*, 1:90–106.

105. *Wen xuan* 30.1438: 公子不及世事但美遨遊然頗有憂生之嗟.

106. The Heir Apparent refers to Cao Pi.

107. The self is constructed through social interactions rather than having an existence separate from it. See George Mead, *Mind, Self & Society from the Standpoint of a Social Behaviorist* (Chicago: University of Chicago Press, 1934).

CHAPTER 3. THE UNTRAMMELED HERO

1. "Prominent families" is a rough translation of a number of Chinese terms that are used to refer to influential clans variously called *daxing* 大姓 (major surnames), *gaomen* 高門 (tall gates), *shengmen* 盛門 (prosperous gates), *shijia* 勢家 (influential families), and *shizu* 勢族 (influential clans). For historical background, see Tang Zhangru's (1911–94), "Shizu de xingcheng he shengjiang," in *Wei Jin Nanbeichao shilun shiyi*, 53–63.

2. For a comprehensive study of this work, see Qian Nanxiu, *Spirit and Self in Medieval China*. Jack Chen, in *Anecdote, Network, Gossip, Performance*, shows through a person-person network graph (p. 71) that Xie An possessed the highest degree of centrality in the network of the *Shishuo*—the text that retrospectively meted out praise and blame through anecdotal tales. Its function was similar to that of an official history. For a complete translation, see Richard Mather, *Shih-shuo hsin-yü*. For Mather's comment on Xie An, see "Introduction," xviii.

3. For the Battle of Fei River, see Fang Xuanling et al., comps., *Jin shu* 114.2917–18, 79.2074–75, 2081–83. See also Tian Yuqing, "Chenjun Xie shi yu Feishui zhi zhan," in *Dong Jin menfa zhengzhi*, 189–243; Wang Zhongluo, "Feishui zhi zhan yu Fu Jian de baiwang," 淝水之戰與苻堅的敗亡 in *Wei Jin Nanbeichao shi*, 1:254–68; Ding Fulin, *Dong Jin Nanchao Xie shi wenxue jituan yanjiu*, 22–27; Michael C. Rogers, "The Myth of the Battle of the Fei River," *TP* 54 (1968): 50–72.

4. Xie An's growing influence was a source of concern for Emperor Xiaowu. His merit was not rewarded until after his death. *Jin shu* 9.232–35. Tian Yuqing, *Dong Jin menfa zhengzhi*, 215–16.

5. Xie Lingyun was born a few weeks later.

6. See Mao 156.

7. Rogers, "The Myth of the Battle of the Fei River," 71, 72.

8. For text, see *Wen xuan* 19.912–15. See also Dunhuang manuscript fragments of the *Wen xuan*, Φ242, acquired by Russian Indologist Sergei F. Oldenbourg and held at the Institute of Oriental Studies at the Russian Academy of Sciences in St. Petersburg. Modern scholar Gu Shaobo dates this piece to 423, during Xie Lingyun's first exile in Yongjia. See Gu Shaobo, *Xie Lingyun ji jiaozhu*, 105.

9. Scholar Yue refers to Yue Yi 樂毅 (fl. 280s BCE), a capable statesman and general who served the state of Yan. For his biography, see Sima Qian, *Shiji* 80.2427–37. Fan Li 范蠡 (536–448 BCE) was a strategist for the state of Yue. See *Shiji* 41.1739–56.

10. Cf. "Fu on Communicating with the Hidden" (You tong fu): "Mu rested at ease and yet protected the state of Wei." See *Wen xuan* 14.644.

11. "Pure dust" here means influence.

12. The "perspicacious and sagacious one" refers to Xie An.

13. Worthy Minister refers to Xie An.

14. For a discussion of "Recounting Virtues" as a category in the *Wen xuan*, see Hu Dalei, *Wen xuan shi yanjiu*, 25–32.

15. See *Yiwen leiju* 20.373.

16. *Yiwen leiju* 20.373.

17. "Numinous Dazzle," referring to the sun, is also a kenning for heaven.

18. "Nine Virtues" or "Ninth Virtue" means the ultimate or complete virtue.

19. Lord Liu refers to Liu Bei (161–223). To avenge the death of Guan Yu (?–220) at the hands of the Wu State, Liu Bei launched an attack on Wu in the summer of 221, shortly after declaring himself emperor in Shu. Lu Xun, as the Wu general, successfully adopted a strategy that was initially thought of as passive, but which eventually led to the exhaustion of the Shu army. In the final confrontation between Wu and Shu at Yiling (in modern Yichang, Hubei) in summer of 222, Lu Xun's army dealt a heavy blow to Shu. Liu Bei passed away in the following spring.

20. "Bird set loose" is a derogatory reference to Liu Bei.

21. This couplet mentions the two advantages upon which Liu Bei based himself, namely the favorable geographical condition of Shu and his claim to be an offspring of the Han imperial clan.

22. This victory refers to Lu Xun's battle over Liu Bei in Yiling, also known as Xiling.

23. Western Xia refers to Shu, which, following the death of Liu Bei in spring of 222, became a pacified state. Without threats in the west, Wu was secured.

24. "Bow reverently" could mean two things: (1) it describes the ritual posture of a civil official upon accepting a position; (2) it describes the gesture of leaving court service. Here, it perhaps refers to Lu Xun's acceptance of a civil position. In year 244,

over two decades after Lu Xun's military triumph over Liu Bei, Lu Xun was appointed as minister of Wu.

25. Also mentioned are Yue Yi and Fan Li.

26. See *Shiji* 44.1839.

27. See *Analects* 16/14, 19/2, 19/8; Alan Berkowitz, *Patterns of Disengagement*, 39n85.

28. See *Zuozhuan*, Xi gong 26. Duke Xiao of Qi 齊孝公 (r. 642–33 BCE) set out to invade the northern border of Lu. The Duke of Lu sent Zhan Xi to reward the Qi army with food and drink. Zhan Xi was able to dissuade the Duke of Qi to withdraw his troops.

29. Xie adopted poetic license here in using Jin instead of Qin. Although the attack came from Qin, the reward ceremony took place in Jin. This "error" has caught the attention of scholars. The historical event itself was first recorded in the *Zuozhuan*. In 627 BCE, Qin launched a surprise attack on Zheng. Xiangao was en route to Zhou when he met the Qin army at Hua [alt. pron. Gu] 滑 (administrative seat Fei or Bi 費, southeast of modern Yanshi, Henan). Claiming to speak for the ruler of Zheng, he conducted a reward ceremony for the Qin army. Concerned that Zheng had already prepared itself, the Qin army turned back, but not before destroying Hua. See *Zuozhuan*, Xi gong 26. Li Shan refers to the account in *Lüshi chunqiu*: "Qin launched a surprise attack on Zheng, whose merchant Xiangao saw it. He then feigned to act on behalf of the lord of Zheng to reward the soldiers. The three Qin commanders excused their action: Our lord has sent his three vassals Bing, Shu, and Shi to the border to examine the roads of Jin. We have become lost and have fallen into the territory of your great state," *Wen xuan* 19.913. The Qing dynasty *Wen xuan* scholar Zhu Jian (1769–1850) suggests that Li Shan cited *Lüshi chunqiu* rather than the *Zuozhuan* because it contained a various graph [晉 with 耳 radical to the left]. See Zhu Jian, *Wen xuan jishi*, 16.2b. Gu Yanwu 顧炎武 (1613–1682) suggested that Xie Lingyun used Jin to avoid Qin in the same couplet, *Ri zhi lu* 日知錄 (Taipei: Wen Shi Zhe, 1979), 22.607. Huang Jie (1873–1935) rejected Gu Yanwu and argued that Hua belonged to the territory of Jin. Hence the army of "Jin." *Xie Kangle shizhu*, 2.2b.

30. During the reign of King Xiaocheng of Zhao 趙孝成王 (r. 265–45 BCE), Qin sent Bo Qi 白起 (332–257 BCE) to lay siege to the Zhao capital of Handan 邯鄲. The King of Wei 衛 sent the Liang general Xinyuan Yan 新垣衍 (?–?) to honor King Zhao of Qin 秦昭王 (325–251 BCE) as emperor. Lu Zhonglian happened to be traveling through Zhao. He dissuaded Lord Pingyuan 平原君 (?–251 BCE) on the matter and therefore deterred Qin's invasion of Zhao. See *Shiji* 83.2460–65.

31. Stephen Owen renders *da-ren* as "the Perfected Man," *An Anthology of Chinese Literature*, 112; David Knechtges renders it as "the Perspicacious Man," *Wen xuan or Selections of Refined Literature*, 3:47.

32. *Analects* 12/20.

33. *Analects* 6/30.

34. Xu Shen, *Shuowen jiezi*, 2.5b. See also Duan Yucai, *Shuowen jiezi zhu*, 2.8b.

35. For examples of the use of *qiong-da* in Han and Wei-Jin texts, see *Quan Han wen* 26.4b-5a, 19.8a-11a; *Quan Hou Han wen* 23.6a, 23.8b-11a; *Wen xuan* 14.636, 11.491, 10.440.

36. *Zuozhuan*, Duke Zhao 7, 1296.

37. In oracle-bone script, *sheng* is written with two elements representing an ear and a mouth, or sometimes an ear and two mouths, and this form was used as late as the sixth century CE in the "stone classics" of the Northern Wei dynasty. Another variant oracle-bone form adds the symbol for "human being" to the ear and the mouth, and this form has always been recognized as the source of the current form. See Jao Tsung-i, "Speaking of 'Sages': The Bronze Figures of San-hsing-tui," in *Sages and Filial Sons: Mythology and Archaeology in Ancient China*, ed. Julia Ching and R. W. L. Guisso (Hong Kong: Chinese University Press, 1991), xiii; see also Julia Ching, "Who Were the Ancient Sages?" in *Sages and Filial Sons*, 1–22.

38. *Shang shu*, in *Shisanjing zhushu*, 2.20a: 月正元日，舜格于文祖，詢于四岳，闢四門，明四目，達四聰.

39. Charles Holcombe, in his discussion of the moral and cultural ideals of the Eastern Jin, adopts the term "super-person." See *In the Shadow of the Han*, chap. 6.

40. Ge Hong (284–364), *Baopu zi waipian*, 22.535: 順通塞而一情，任性命而不滯者，達人也.

41. The most notable example is certainly the *sao*-style poem "Far Roaming" (*Yuan you*), as collected in the *Chu ci*. It ushered in a whole sub-genre of poetry that came to be known as the *youxian* or "roaming immortals." For a study, see Paul Kroll, "On 'Far Roaming,'" *JAOS* 116, no. 4: 653–69.

42. See the final stanza of "Far Roaming," in Kroll, "On 'Far Roaming,'" 663.

43. For the photographic reprints of the Dunhuang *Wen xuan* manuscript held in the Russian Academy of Sciences in St. Petersburg, see Mengliefu 孟列夫 (L. N. Menshikov) and Qian Bocheng 錢伯城, ed., *E cang Dunhuang wenxian* 俄藏敦煌文獻 (Shanghai: Shanghai Guji Chubanshe, 1992–2000), 4:338–58. See also Jao Tsung-i, ed., *Dunhuang Tulufan ben Wen xuan* 敦煌吐魯番本文選 (Beijing: Zhonghua Shuju, 2000), 35–46; and Luo Guowei 羅國威, *Dunhuang ben 'Zhaoming wenxuan' yanjiu* 敦煌本《昭明文選》研究 (Harbin: Heilongjiang Jiaoyu Chubanshe, 1999), 125. The commentary in the Dunhuang manuscript reads: "Mo Di, in valuing himself, disregarded the world. Hence it read 'to value oneself.' It is the better reading. 'To abandon' is 'to cast away.'" 墨翟貴己不肯留意天下，故貴自我，作貴勝，遺，棄.

44. See *Zhuangzi*, chap. 2: "Qiwulun."

45. For a study of the origins and changing meaning of the term, see Ogawa Tamaki 小川環樹, *Lun Zhongguo shi* 論中國詩 (Beijing: Zhonghua Shuju, 2017), 49–66.

46. For Jia Yi's biography, see *Shiji* 84.2491–92; for Chinese texts of "The Owl," see *Shiji* 84.2496–2504; *Han shu* 48.2227–29; *Wen xuan* 13.604–08. Jia Yi wrote this piece in 173 BCE during his exile in Changsha. For translations, see James Robert Hightower, "Chia Yi's 'Owl Fu,'" *AM*, n.s. 8 (1959): 125–30; Burton Watson, trans., *Records of the Grand Historian* (New York: Columbia University Press, 1993) 1:512–15; David R. Knechtges, *Wen xuan or Selections of Refined Literature*, 3:41–49; Owen, *An Anthology of Chinese Literature*, 110–13.

47. Here, "time" refers to the "opportune time," the "destined time," or the "right time."

48. This is an oxymoron.

49. The First Emperor of Qin preferred to call himself *zhenren*, i.e., an otherworldly immortal. See Yu Yingshi, "Life and Immortality in Han China," 94.

50. This passage contains the earliest employment of the phrase *da-ren* in a literary text.

51. See Hightower, "Chia Yi's 'Owl Fu,'" 125.

52. *Zhuangzi jishi* 6B.614–15.

53. Cf. "Humans come from the gathering of life-breath; when life-breath gathers, there is life; when life-breath dissipates, there is death," *Zhuangzi jishi* 7B.733. "Simply because it's in the human form, we especially take delight in it; and yet we don't realize that even the human form has myriad shapes and endless transformations and permutations," *Zhuangzi jishi* 3B.244.

54. *Zhuangzi jishi* 4A.323.

55. *Zhuangzi jishi* 3A.229.

56. *Zhuangzi jishi* 5A.428: 忘乎物，忘乎天，其名為忘己。忘己之人，是之謂入於天.

57. See Paul Kroll, "Between Something and Nothing," *JAOS* 127, no. 4 (2007): 403–13.

58. In the famous "Letter in Reply to Ren An," attributed to Sima Qian, the author investigated the problem with noble suicide. For a recent study, see Stephen W. Durrant, Li Wai-yee, Michael Nylan, and Hans van Ess, *The Letter to Ren An & Sima Qian's Legacy* (Seattle: University of Washington Press, 2016).

59. *Li sao* is the title of the long autobiographical lament attributed to Qu Yuan.

60. See *Shiji* 84.2481–86.

61. See *Han shu* 87A.3521.

62. *Zhuangzi jishi* 1A.28.

63. Tian Yuqing, *Dong Jin menfa zhengzhi*, 202.

64. *Nan shi* 19.546: "Since the Eastern Jin, the Xie clan transmitted the 'lofty way.'" 謝氏自晉以降，雅道相傳.

65. Wang Yongping, *Dong Jin Nanchao jiazu wenhua shi luncong*, 11.

66. See Wang Yongping's discussion of the Xies as *mingshi* 名士 (men of repute). Wang, *Dong Jin Nanchao jiazu wenhua shi luncong*, 11.

CHAPTER 4. A HOME IN THE MOUNTAINS

1. Written by the Liang dynasty Daoist master Tao Hongjing (456–536) and titled "Da Xie zhongshu shu" (In reply to Secretary Xie), the letter was addressed to Xie Wei (ca. 500–536), a great-great-grandson of Xie Jingren and cousin of Xie Lingyun. Xie Wei served in the Liang Imperial Secretariat. See Yao Silian, comp., *Liang shu* 50.717-18, and Li Yanshou, comp., *Nan shi* 19.529–30.

2. See *Quan Liang wen* 46.3215b–3216a.

3. This work was lost after the Song dynasty. Remnants of the text were found scattered in several Tang and Song sources: the two early Tang miscellanies *Yiwen leiju* and *Chuxue ji*, the Song miscellany *Taiping yulan* and its contemporary geographical encyclopedia *Taiping huanyu ji*, and Li Shan's (630–89) commentary to the *Wen xuan*. See Zhao Shugong's 趙樹功 "Xie Lingyun *You mingshan zhi* bianming ji yiwen" 謝靈運 《遊名山志》 辨名及佚文, *Wenxian* 文獻, no. 2 (2009): 175–77. The reconstructed text of the *You mingshan zhi* includes thirty-two entries, covering four administrative commanderies: Yongjia (modern Wenzhou), Dongyang (modern Jinhua), Guiji (modern Shaoxing), and Linchuan (modern Fuzhou, Jiangxi).

4. See *Han shi wai zhuan* 1/9, 1/27. Famous examples of men who died for uncompromising principle include Bo Yi, Shu Qi, Bao Jiao, and Jie Zitui.

5. The chamber in the lone rock alludes to the story of a recalcitrant Eastern Yue king who put up a desperate resistance against Emperor Wu of Han's punitive hunt. Ban Gu, comp., *Han shu* 64A.2791.

6. Gu, *Xie Lingyun ji jiaozhu*, 275.

7. This refers to the Yellow Emperor. See *Shiji* 12.468.

8. This refers to Prince Qiao, a son of King Ling of Zhou (?–545 BCE) whose biography is included in the *Lie xian zhuan* (Collected traditions of immortals). See *Lie xian zhuan jian zhu*, 65–68.

9. Tao Zhu refers to Fan Li. Marquis of Liu refers to Zhang Liang.

10. See Zhao Shugong, "Xie Lingyun *You mingshan zhi* bianming ji yiwen," 176; *Xian du zhi* 仙都志, *Zhengtong daozang*, 18.498b.

11. The ancient sage-king Yao lost his worldly ambition on a visit to Mount Guye; see *Shiji* 28.1394. Huangdi rode away on a dragon to Mount Jing; see *Han shu* 25A.1227–28. The luminary vassals Zhang Liang and Fan Li both refused rewards after having established meritorious deeds. Fan Li helped establish Yue; see *Shiji* 41.1745. Zhang Liang assisted with the founding of Han; see *Shiji* 55.2048.

12. For the text of the "Shanju *fu*," see *Song shu* 67.1754; Gu, *Xie Lingyun ji jiao zhu*,

318. For an analysis, see Mark Elvin, "Nature as Revelation," 321–68; Wendy Swartz, "There's No Place Like Home," *Early Medieval China* 21 (2015) 12: 21–37. See also Mather, "Landscape Buddhism," 74; David Knechtges, "Zhongguo gudai de wenren shanyue youguan," 1–63.

13. See Swartz, "There's No Place Like Home," 30.

14. *Song shu* 67.1754.

15. *Song shu* 67.1754: 判身名之有辨，權榮素其無留.

16. Richard B. Mather, "The Controversy Over Conformity and Naturalness During the Six Dynasties," in *History of Religions* 9, nos. 2/3 (1969): 169–70.

17. For a study of the notion of *shen*, see Zong-qi Cai, "The Conceptual Origins and Aesthetic Significance of 'Shen' in Six Dynasties Texts on Literature and Painting," in *Chinese Aesthetics*, 310–42. See also Nanxiu Qian, *Spirit and Self*, 179.

18. Before Li Si was executed, he recalled fondly the carefree days of hunting with his greyhounds by his side. *Shiji* 87.2562. Lu Ji, after suffering a waterloo in Shu, yearned to hear again the calling of cranes on his family estate, Fang Xuanling et al., comps., *Jin shu* 54.1480.

19. *Jin shu* 67.1756: 幽人憩止之鄉; *Jin shu* 67.1756: 隨地勢所遇耳.

20. *Jin shu* 67.1756: 謂經始此山，遺訓於後也·性情各有所便，山居是其宜也.

21. For text, see *Wen xuan* 22.1045–46. Stone Gate is the name of a mountain.

22. See *Chu ci buzhu* 12.232–34.

23. *Chu ci buzhu* 12.234: 王孫兮歸來！山中兮不可以久留.

24. *Chu ci buzhu* 1.67.

25. For Lu Zhonglian's biography, see *Shiji* 83.2459–69. For a study, see Qian Mu 錢穆, "Lu Zhonglian kao" 魯仲連攷, in *Xian Qin zhuzi xinian* 先秦諸子繫年 (Hong Kong: Hong Kong University Press, 1956), 2:472–77.

26. *Shiji* 83.2465.

27. *Wen xuan* 22.1027. "Bamboo nodes" (*jie*) puns with "integrity."

28. As a member from the prominent Xie clan, Xie Lingyun was always accompanied by large entourage. See *Song shu* 67.1775.

29. *Meiren* is sometimes translated as the Fair One, denoting an enlightened and sympathetic prince-patron or friend whose noble character is likened to the pungent aroma of a medicinal herb.

30. For the text, see *Wen xuan* 30.1399–1400.

31. Cf. "Gently blowing is the autumn breeze" 嫋嫋兮秋風 in "Lady of the Xiang River" 湘夫人. Frodsham's rendering of *niaoniao* as "howl" (1:136) or "gustily" (2:152) neglects the metonymy of wind that associates with the gentle and willowy figure of Lady Xiang.

32. Cf. "王孫遊兮不歸，春草生兮萋萋" in "Summoning of the Recluse" 招隱士.

33. My reading of *dun* 敦 as "to gather, to come together" follows Zheng Xuan's gloss of Mao 246, Line 1: 敦彼行葦. Cf. also Mao 156, Line 11: 敦彼獨宿 and Line 33: 有敦瓜苦. In both case, *dun* is glossed as *tuan* 團 (round); when used as a verb, it means "to gather."

34. The reversed spatial-temporal order is reportedly experienced from the famed immortal land beyond the height of heavens, where the sun, the moon, and other celestial bodies are seen as coming from below. This phenomenon, known as "inverted light" (*daoying*), is mentioned in various Han and Six Dynasties poetic writings. See *Shiji* 117.2062; *Wen xuan* 15.675, 22.1063, 35.1600.

35. The term *zhizhe* 智者 (the wise) may refer to the those intellectual friends and associates with whom Xie Lingyun discusses metaphysics and religion.

36. The title comprises nine *bi*-syllable phrases, eight of which are grammatical adjunct-heads: "stone-gate," "newly-constructed," "four-sides," "high-mountains," "winding-streams," "rocky shallows," "slender bamboos," and "thick-groves." The order of "mountains," "streams," "shallows" follows from high to low. The embedded image of "bamboo grove" (*zhulin*) evokes the group of eccentric figures known as the "Seven Worthies of the Bamboo Grove" 竹林七賢. Scholars have argued that the group was likely a construction in the fifth century by none other than members of the Xie clan and their prodigies and disciples. For book-length studies, see He Qimin, *Wei Jin sixiang yu tanfeng*, 1967; Spiro, *Contemplating the Ancient*, 1990. See also Mather, *Shih-shuo hsin-yü*, "Introduction."

37. The lines allude to Sun Chuo's 孫綽 (314–71, alt. 310–71) "You Tiantai shan fu" 游天台山賦 (*Wen xuan* 11.497): "treading on the slippery moss-covered rocks . . . holding on to the dangling twigs of kudzu" 踐莓苔之滑石 . . . 援葛藟之飛莖. Xie seems to interrogate the earlier poet by turning the lines into questions. For a translation of Sun Chuo's *fu*, see Knechtges, *Wen xuan*, 2:243–53.

38. *Chu ci buzhu* 2.92: 嫋嫋兮秋風.

39. *Chu ci buzhu* 12.373: 春草生兮萋萋.

40. *Chu ci buzhu* 2.93: 與佳期兮夕張.

41. *Chu ci buzhu* 2.79: 瑤席兮玉瑱.

42. *Chu ci buzhu* 9.330–31: 瑤漿蜜勺，實羽觴些；挫糟凍飲，酎清涼些；華酌既陳，有瓊漿些.

43. *Chu ci buzhu* 2.65: 洞庭波兮木葉下.

44. *Chu ci buzhu* 12.376: 攀援桂枝.

45. *Chu ci buzhu* 7.279.

46. Gu Shaobo, *Xie Lingyun ji jiaozhu*, 176.

47. Yang Shen 楊慎 (1488–1599), *Sheng'an shihua jian zheng* 升庵詩話箋證, annotated by Wang Zhongyong 王仲鏞 (1915–97) (Shanghai: Shanghai Guji Chubanshe, 1987), 59.

48. See *Zhuangzi jishi* 8B.832. Guo Xiang's commentary reads: "As the sun rises, one roams; as the sun sets, one rests."

49. See Huo Guigao, "Jin-Song 'wenyi' yu Xie shi 'xuanxue weiba' chengyin" 晉宋 "文義" 與謝詩 "玄學尾巴" 成因. *Baoding xueyuan xuebao* 保定學院學報25, no. 6 (2012): 1–11.

50. In explaining the multivalent *li*, Leon Hurvitz posits: "The semantic Odyssey of *li* would be about as follows: arrangement of fields—arrangement of things in general—arrangement of affairs—the natural order, in which affairs are arranged—the adaptation of oneself to this natural order, in which every individual controls his passions—a rational socio-political order." See "Chih Tun's Notions of *Prajñā*," *JAOS* 88, no. 2 (1968): 243–61.

51. See *Wen xuan* 22.1044–45.

52. This alludes to "Lord of the East"; see *Chu ci buzhu*, 2.107.

53. Tim Chan's reading of these images as obstruction to enlightenment. See *Considering the End* (Leiden: Brill, 2012), 133.

54. Gu Shaobo, *Xie Lingyun ji jiao zhu*, 112.

55. See *Wen xuan* 22.1031–65.

56. Yin Zhongwen 殷仲文, a talented poet, was killed by Liu Yu for having sided with Huan Xuan—the "usurper of the Jin throne." For Yin's biography, see *Jin shu* 99.1343. Frodsham considered Yin as one of the early "nature poets." See J. D. Frodsham, "The Origins of Chinese Nature Poetry," *Asia Major*, n.s. 8 (1960): 68–103.

57. See *Wen xuan* 20.969, 23.1071, 25.1162; Lu Qinli, *Xian Qin Han Wei Jin Nanbeichao shi*, 297, 499, 576, 607, 608, 699, 715.

58. For text, see *Wen xuan* 22.1046–47. This poem is dated to the year 425 in Gu Shaobo, *Xie Lingyun ji jiao zhu*, 118–19. It is an account of a boat journey on Lake Shaman, located in the Xie estate. Xie Lingyun departed from the Southern Mountains (Mount Tu 嶀山 and Mount Stone Gate, modern Sheng County 嵊縣, Zhejiang). The Northern Mountains were where Lingyun's grandfather Xie Xuan constructed the Xie family villa.

59. The sunlit cliff refers to the southern mountains.

60. The shaded peaks refer to the northern mountains.

61. Based on the larger context, I have chosen to read 迴 for 逈 or "distant."

62. This line alludes to *The Classic of Changes*, hexagram 40, "Release" (Xie 解). See Richard Lynn, *The Classic of Changes*, 381–86.

63. This line alludes to *The Classic of Changes*, hexagram 46, "Rising" (Sheng 升). See Richard Lynn, *The Classic of Changes*, 423–27.

64. Swartz, "Naturalness in Xie Lingyun's Poetic Works," 371–72.

65. Westbrook, "Landscape Transformation in the Poetry of Hsieh Ling-yun," 239.

66. Richard Lynn, *The Classic of Changes*, 381.

67. Richard Lynn, *The Classic of Changes*, 424.

68. Richard Lynn, *The Classic of Changes*, 424.

CHAPTER 5. POETIC LONELINESS

1. See *Chu ci buzhu*: 紛吾乘兮玄雲 (2.99), 登九天兮撫彗星 (2.105), 青雲衣兮白霓裳 (2.109), etc.

2. See Kroll, "Far Roaming." For a study of "*Fu* on the Great One" and its implications of the religious and political context at the Han court, see Fukunaga Mitsuji 福永光司. "Taijin fu no shisōteki keifu: Jifu no bungaku to Rō Sō no tetsugaku" 大人賦の思想的係譜: 辭賦の文學と老莊の哲學, *Tōhōgaku hō* 41 (1970): 97–126.

3. The Cao family wrote poetry in the Han "roaming immortals" theme. See Funatsu Tomihiko 船津富彥, "Sō Shoku no yūsenshi ron" 曹植の遊仙詩論, *Tōyō bungaku kenkyū* 13 (1965): 49–65; "Gi no Butei no yūsen bungaku ni tsuite" 魏の武帝の遊仙文學について in *Yoshioka hakase kanreki kinen Dōkyō kenkyū ronshū* 吉岡博士環曆記念道教研究論集 (Tokyo: Tosho Kankōkai, 1977), 165–92. See also Wang Jing 王璟, "Jiuzhou buzu bu, yuan de ling yun xiang: Cao Zhi youxian shi tan xi" 九州不足步，願得凌雲翔: 曹植遊仙詩探析, *Gujin yiwen* 31, no. 2 (2005): 42–53.

4. For the Chinese text, see *Wen xuan* 11.493–501. For studies, see Richard Mather, "The Mystical Ascent of the T'ien-t'ai Mountains: Sun Ch'o's *Yu T'ien-t'ai-shan fu*," *MS* 20 (1961): 226–45; Chen Wancheng 陳萬成, "Sun Chuo 'Tiantai shan fu' yu daojiao" 孫綽《天台山賦》與道教, *Dalu zazhi* 86, no. 4 (1993): 43–48.

5. For the text, see *Wen xuan* 21.1018–25.

6. The phrase derives from the second line of "Summoning the Recluse: A Countering Piece" by the otherwise unknown Wang Kangju 王康琚: "A greater hermit hides in the court" 大隱隱朝市. See *Wen xuan* 22.1030.

7. For the text, see *Wen xuan* 26.1242–43; see also Gu Shaobo, *Xie Lingyun ji jiaozhu* 83–85. Gu dates the piece to 423 when Xie Lingyun was in Yongjia. The island in the Ou River remains a popular tourist site today in Wenzhou. On the island there is a rock garden and a museum-temple dedicated to Xie Lingyun.

8. I follow Gu Shaobo in reading 新 for 雜, an emendation adopted in the Song and later editions of the *Wen xuan. Xie Lingyun ji jiaozhu*, 84.

9. *Zhen* may be construed as either "immortals" or "truth principle."

10. Mount Kunlun is the famed mythic mountain where the Queen Mother of the West lives.

11. See *Wen xuan* 20.1042–43. See also *Xie Lingyun ji jiaozhu*, 78–80. Gu Shaobo dates this poem to summer of 423 during Xie's exile in Yongjia. Auburn Rocks (Chishi 赤石) was an ocean-side mountain south of Yongjia. Ocean of Sails (Fanhai 帆海),

also located south of modern Wenzhou and north of Rui'an 瑞安, was a traffic hub busy with sailboats passing through.

12. For the use of *qiongfa* to refer to ocean, see *Zhuangzi jishi* 1A.14.

13. Cf. Cao Zhi's "Luoshen *fu*" (*Fu* on the goddess of the Luo River), *Wen xuan* 19.899: 川后靜波.

14. Tianwu is the lord of water. See Yuan Ke 袁珂, *Shan hai jing jiaozhu* (Shanghai: Shanghai Guji, 1980), 4:256.

15. Rock blossom, according to Li Shan, is a type of shellfish that grows on rocks. See *Wen xuan* 22.1043.

16. The ocean moon is another type of shellfish, also known as window shells. Li Shan says it is as big as a mirror and the whitish transparent shell is shaped in a perfect circle. *Wen xuan* 22.1043.

17. "Empty boat" alludes to the *Zhuangzi*, "Shan mu" 山木: "People can, in roaming the world, become empty of themselves, and then no one can harm them" 人能虛己以遊世，其孰能害. See *Zhuangzi jishi* 7A.675. An empty boat here is used as a pun, referring both to the poet and his conveyance.

18. Zhonglian is Lu Zhonglian.

19. In the "Yielding the Throne" (Rangwang 讓王) chapter of *Zhuangzi*, there is an account that discusses the Prince of Wei (魏公子, aka Zimou of Zhongshan 中山子牟) who is quoted as saying: "my body is above the river and ocean, but my heart yearns for the tower of Wei. What do I do?" See *Zhuangzi jishi* 9B.979.

20. This is a reference to the *Zhuangzi*. Master Ren, also known as Taigong Ren 太公任, is cited for criticizing Confucius's regard for service and offers the following warning: "A straight tree is hacked down first and sweet springs run dry first" 直木先伐甘泉先竭; "the one whose deed is done shall fall; the one whose fame is achieved will wane" 功成者墮, 名成者虧. See *Zhuangzi jishi* 9B.979.

21. See *Zhuangzi jishi* 1A.14.

22. For the text, see *Wen xuan* 26.1241-42, *Xie Lingyun ji jiaozhu* 51-53.

23. Yanzi is Yan Guang 嚴光 (d. 41 CE), an Eastern Han recluse who left court and retired to fish and farm in the mountains of Guiji. For his biography, see Fan Ye, comp., *Hou Han shu* 83.2763-2764.

24. Master Ren is a legendary fisherman from Guiji. See *Zhuangzi jishi* 9A.925.

25. Gu Shaobo gives a detailed account of this place. See *Xie Lingyun ji jiaozhu*, 51-52.

26. Line 10 is constructed from two quotations from the *Laozi*: "Pure and still—it looks as if it would ever so continue" 湛兮似或存 and "Such is what is known as essential and wondrous" 是謂要妙. What is described in both statements is the Way.

27. See *Wen xuan* 22.1048-49; *Xie Lingyun ji jiaozhu*, 121-23.

28. More will be said on this critical term in chap. 8.

29. Lines 15, 16, 17, and 18 together make a lyrical performance of the "fragrant plants and fair ones" (香草美人) theme from the *Chu ci*.

30. The opening lines of *Chu ci*'s "Mountain Spirit" read: "That figure by the nook of the mountain, / draped in fig-leaves and girded with dodder. / Her eyes inviting, her smiles charming. / I love you and your secluded beauty." See *Chu ci buzhu* 2.113.

31. See Gu Shaobo, *Xie Lingyun ji jiaozhu*, 121–22, 123.

32. For the text, see *Wen xuan* 23.1093–96, *Xie Lingyun ji jiaozhu*, 131–34. The word *xia* 下 in the title suggests an offering with respect. Hence my choice to render the title with "reverently."

33. Yunyang is in modern Danyang, Jiangsu.

34. Zhufang is modern Zhenjiang, Jiangsu.

35. Here, the broad river refers to the Yangzi.

36. This refers to Emperor Wen's reign.

37. Yanzhou (modern Changzhou, Jiangsu) was where the Wu prince Jizha had been enfeoffed. The prince was on good terms with Lord Xu who passed away before Jizha could gift him the precious sword. See Gu Shaobo's note. *Xie Lingyun ji jiaozhu*, 133.

38. Gong Sheng was a young talent who starved himself to death following Wang Mang's forced recruitment. The old man of Chu was an anonymous admirer who came to mourn Gong Sheng's demise. See Li Shan commentary, *Wen xuan* 23.1095.

39. When Jizha returned, Lord Xu had passed away. See *Wen xuan* 25.1094.

40. I read 疑 as 擬 in this line.

41. For an account and analysis of the series of events and their implications surrounding the murder of Liu Yizhen, see Wang Yongping 王永平, "Luling wang Liu Yizhen zhi si yu Liu Song chuqi zhi zhengju: Cong yige cemian toushi Jin Song zhi ji shizu yu hanmen de douzheng" 廬陵王劉義真之死與劉宋初期之政局: 從一個側面透視晉宋之際士族與寒門 的鬥爭, *Jiangsu shehui kexue*, no. 4 (2009): 209–16. See also Gu, *Xie Lingyun ji jiaozhu*, 131–32;, *Murmuring Stream*, 1:29–31, 48–49.

42. *Song shu* 67.1743.

43. *Wen xuan* 23.1093–94.

44. Xie Lingyun's detractors used his return to accuse him of being a turncoat. His moral integrity was believed to have been compromised. In their view, Xie Lingyun should not have answered the court summons and stayed in reclusion. This view is problematic, as Shen Yucheng has convincingly shown it to be an anachronistic value judgment. The concept of loyalty to one's dynasty didn't shape into a strong literati moral code until the twelfth century. To impose this retrospectively on Xie Lingyun was an erroneous although popular interpretative approach. Xie's sense of loyalty was placed with his clan rather than the dynasty, as Shen argues. See Shen Yucheng, "Xie Lingyun de zhengzhi taidu he sixiang xingge," 262.

45. Yan-Zhou 延州 is formed from the names of two fiefdoms of Ji Zha: Yanling

延陵 (modern Changzhou 常州, Jiangsu) and Zhoulai 州來 (modern Fengtai 鳳台, Anhui). For accounts on Ji Zha, see *Zuozhuan* (Xiang 29 and 31), *Shiji* 31.1449–65.

46. See *Wen xuan* 23.1094.

47. Gong Sheng appears a few times in Xie's poetry. For the story of an anonymous Chu elder paying homage at Gong Sheng's tomb, see *Han shu* 72.3057.

48. Xie Huilian's father was Xie Fangming 謝方明 (381–427); he served as governor of Guiji from 422 to 426. See *Nan shi* 19.535–37; *Song shu* 53.1522–24.

49. See *Song shu* 67.1774–75. For a study, see Williams, "A Conversation in Poems," 491–506.

50. For the Chinese text, see *Wen xuan* 25.1193–94. For an English translation, see Williams, "A Conversation in Poems," 495–97.

51. Earlier, Xie Huilian had been stripped of his rank and banned from holding office for writing poetry to his homosexual lover. See *Song shu* 51.1468, 53.1524–25. For the text of the poem, see *Wen xuan* 25.1199–200; *Xie Lingyun ji jiaozhu*, 170–73.

52. Xie Lingyun referred to his ill health in another poem written in early 423.

53. This mountain abode is likely the lodge on the Stone Gate.

54. Several scholars read the friend (*huan'ai* 歡愛) referred to in these lines as Liu Yizhen, who passed away in 424. See Huang Jie, *Xie Kangle shi zhu*, 136; Li Yunfu, *Xie Lingyun ji*, 92n3; Gu Shaobo, *Xie Lingyun ji jiaozhu*, 171n6.

55. This phrase refers to his old age. Xie Lingyun was almost forty years old when he met Xie Huilian.

56. Xie Lingyun seems to urge his young cousin to continue and persist in adversity.

57. For the text, see *Wen xuan* 24.1123–25. For a study of the work, see Zong-qi Cai, *The Matrix of Lyric Transformation*, 119–25.

58. See *Yiwen leiju* 29.518: 懷人行千里，我勞盈十旬。別時花灼灼，別後葉蓁蓁.

59. Williams, "A Conversation in Poetry," 500.

60. Xie Lingyun used this word to refer to the early death of Prince Luling in line 21 of the poem.

61. The cause of Xie Huilian's death is not explained in his official biography. *Song shu* 53.1525.

62. *Song shu* 53.1525: 其文甚美。又為雪賦凶亦以高麗見奇.

63. For the text, see *Wen xuan* 23.1078–79.

64. *Cheng* in this line means to prevail or overcome.

65. The Chinese literary tradition had established autumn as the killing season beginning with the *Chu ci*.

66. This notion can be traced back to Confucius whose "sad but not injurious" 哀而不傷 became a motto for lyrical expression.

67. See *Wen xuan* 26.1243–45; Gu, *Xie Lingyun ji jiaozhu*, 97–102.

68. Peng is Peng Xuan 彭宣 (d. 4 CE), a Western Han scholar who specialized in the studies of the *Yijing*. He hailed from Xie Lingyun's ancestral hometown Yangjia. During Emperor Ai's reign (6 BCE–1 CE), he served as the great minister of public works and was enfeoffed as Marquis of Changping. When Wang Mang rebelled, he left court service. See *Han shu* 71.3051–53. Xue refers to Xue Guangde 薛廣德, a *Shijing* scholar who served as grandee secretary in the beginning of the Western Han. He also retired from court service. See *Han shu* 71.3046–48, 110B.4260.

69. Duke Gong refers to Gong Yu 貢禹 (124–43 BCE), a top Han official known for his elucidation of the classics and his lofty character. He lived during Emperor Yuan's reign (48–33 BCE) and submitted memorials promoting frugality and modesty in court life. See *Han shu* 72.3069–80.

70. This line alludes to *Li sao*: "All others press forward in greed and gluttony" 眾皆競進以貪婪兮. See *Chu ci buzhu* 1.15.

71. This alludes to the *Zhuangzi*: "He who understands the conditions of life does not strive after what is no use to life" 達生之情者不務生之所無以為. See *Zhuangzi jishi* 7A.630.

72. Zhou Ren was a scribe of the Zhou dynasty. His attitude toward service was that one should strive yet also know when to stop. See *Analects* 16/1. Xie Lingyun says that he knows enough to stop when needed.

73. Zhangqing refers to Sima Xiangru. See *Han shu* 57B.2589.

74. Master Shang refers to Shang Zhang 尚長 or Xiang Zhang 向長, who was recommended to serve Wang Mang but refused. Having married off his sons and daughters, he went into the mountains and roamed with his friends. He told his family to think of him as if "he had passed on." See *Hou Han shu* 83.2758–59.

75. Master Bing refers to Bing Manrong 邴曼容. See *Han shu* 72.3083.

76. Yuanxing was a reign period (402–4) of the Eastern Jin. Xie Lingyun entered court service in year 405. See *Wen xuan* 26.1244; *Xie Lingyun ji jiaozhu*, 100.

77. Jingping was a reign period (423–24) of the Liu-Song. Xie Lingyun resigned from his post in Yongjia in 423. See Gu, *Xie Lingyun ji jiaozhu*, 100.

78. *Jiangying* refers to, by synecdoche, ritual and official duties, including appointments and dismissals.

79. The "battle" refers to making a choice between serving in court or leading a private life. To win the inner battle means deciding to leave office. See *Han Feizi* 韓非子, annot., Chen Qiyou 陳奇猷 (1917–2006), (Beijing: Zhonghua Shuju, 1958), 7.216.

80. This alludes to *Zhuangzi*, where Confucius is quoted as saying that one can only see their reflection in still water, not in flowing water, implying that stillness and stopping are necessary in order to achieve a clear view of things. See *Zhuangzi jishi* 2.193.

81. Sage kings from high antiquity.

82. "Jirang" is the name of a song transmitted from high antiquity. There are two

explanations for *jirang*: (1) it's a game of aiming and tossing, or (2) it refers to playing music on an earthen pot. In either case, it is a reference to finding contentment in a simple life and a harmonious society that is free of greed. See Gu Shaobo, *Xie Lingyun ji jiaozhu*, 101–2; Huang Hui 黃暉, *Lunheng jiaoshi* 論衡校釋 (Beijing: Zhonghua Shuju, 1982), 5.253.

83. See Li Shan's commentary in the *Wen xuan* 16.1245.

84. See *Zhuangzi jishi* 28.966.

CHAPTER 6. THE HILLSIDE GARDEN

1. *Quan Tang shi* 226.2443: 焉得思如陶謝手.

2. For the Chinese text of the *fu*, see Shen Yue, comp., *Song shu* 67.1744–53. For a study, see Su Jui-lung 蘇瑞隆, "Lun Xie Lingyun de Zhuan zheng fu" 論謝靈運的《撰征賦》, *Wen shi zhe* 5 (1990): 48–52. For a translation, see Xiaofei Tian, *Visionary Journeys*, 287–340.

3. *Song shu* 67.1753.

4. For the text, see *Wen xuan* 20.960–61. For a translation, see Wu Fusheng, *Written at Imperial Command: Panegyric Poetry in Early Medieval China* (Albany: State University of New York Press, 2008), 79–80. In reading this poem, I benefited from discussions with David R. Knechtges, who translated this poem for his *Wen xuan* project (to be published by Brill). We both found some parts of the text impenetrable. Through many drafts, the translation presented here may still not be free of some debatable points.

5. The last month of autumn is the ninth lunar month. The northern border refers to Pengcheng, which was located at the northern frontier of Eastern Jin's territory, a little over two hundred miles northwest of Jiankang.

6. This line alludes to "The Fourth Month" 四月(Mao 204/2): "The autumn days were bitterly cold; / a hundred kinds of grass were withering. Turmoil and troubles made me sick; / where could we return" 秋日淒淒，百卉具腓。亂離瘼矣，爰其適歸? "The Fourth Month" here constitutes an interpretive index, hinting at human troubles in the natural season of deterioration and death. My translation of the line takes into consideration Satō Masamitsu's observation ("Xie Zhan, Xie Lingyun de wenxue," 359) that Xie Lingyun makes up the phrase *yanghui* 陽卉 to create the image of withering grass under the scorching sun.

7. *Hantan* 寒潭 or "frigid pool" refers to the contemplative mind, reflecting like a mirror without dust. Cf. the phrase *tansi* 覃思 or 潭思, *Han shu* 87B.3575. *Tan* is a Chu dialect word for a deep pool. See Kroll et al., *Dictionary*, 442.

8. *Shengxin* 聖心, "Sagacious Mind," refers to the mind of a ruler, in this case Liu Yu. *Sheng* is a word usually reserved for the emperor, which Liu Yu was not yet at the

time. His intention to take the throne, however, had already been clear to those around him. See *Liuchen zhu Wen xuan* 20.29a.

9. *Yunqi* 雲旗 or "cloud-pennants" are flags decorated with cloud patterns. See *Liuchen zhu Wen xuan* 20.29a.

10. *Zhugong* 朱宮, "vermilion palace," refers to Liu Yu's lodge at Pengcheng. See *Liuchen zhu Wen xuan* 20.29a.

11. *Lanzhi* 蘭厄, "fragrant ale," is an alcoholic drink scented with powdered thoroughwort (*lan cao* 蘭草). See *Han shu* 22.1064. *Shizhe* 時哲, "savant of our day," refers to Kong Jing in whose honor the banquet was held.

12. This line alludes to *The Classic of Changes*, hexagram 64, "Weiji" 未濟, 6/5 (fifth yin) and 9/6 (top yang). For a translation of hexagram 64, see Lynn, *The Classic of Changes*, 549–50.

13. This line alludes to Mao 161, "Lu ming" 鹿鳴 (Deer Cry), which is a banquet song praising comity and loyalty between lords and vassals. The phrase *hele* 和樂 comes from the line that reads, "In harmonious conviviality we indulge ourselves" 和樂且湛. The term is seen also in the "Lesser Preface" to "The Sixth Month" (Liu yue 六月; Mao 177): "When 'Lu ming' [i.e., the social mores as reflected in the poem] was abandoned," harmonious conviviality disappeared." Mao 177 is, according to the "Lesser Preface," about King Xuan of Zhou's (?–782 BCE) northern campaign against the Xianyun tribe. See *Mao shi zhengyi*, 12–2.1a.

14. This line alludes to *Zhuangzi*, chapter 11, "Zai you" 在宥 (Letting be), the opening lines of which read: "I have heard of letting the empire be instead of governing." See *Zhuangzi jishi* 11.364.

15. This line alludes to *Zhuangzi*, chapter 2, "Qiwu lun" 齊物論 (A discourse on making all things equal)—the *locus classicus* of *chuiwan* 吹萬, "Breezing on the Myriad," which compares a benevolent ruler to the gentle breeze, spreading grace and influence to nurture his people without harsh measures. See *Zhuangzi jishi* 1B.50. The third-century commentator Sima Biao 司馬彪 (240–306) explains the concept in the following terms: "The climate is gentle and breezy; myriad beings are being nourished and supplicated; the phenomenal world exhibits an unusual sight. [The sage king] allows each living being to have their natural way and that is it. He would stop and do no further." See *Wen xuan* 20.960. The two *Zhuangzi* references summarily present the ideal of noninterfering rulership.

16. A search of the phrase *guike* 歸客 (returning sojourner) in the Scripta Sinica database yields this poem as its *locus classicus*. Although Xie Lingyun may not have been the first to use the term given the low preservation rate of early and medieval texts, his poetry perhaps helps to popularize the term to become one of the most frequently used idioms and poetic concepts in modern Mandarin. *Sui* 遂 (watercourse) in this line is used as a verb. I have emended *yu* 嵎 (mountain nook) to *yu* 隅 (corner,

outlying place, border) following the *Liuchen zhu Wen xuan* 20.29b. This reading is accepted in most of the *Wen xuan* editions except the Li Shan version. See Gu Shaobo, *Xie Lingyun ji jiaozhu*, 25.

17. *Tuoguan* 脫冠, "taking off the cap," means to resign or retire from an official post. This is another possible neologism, unattested in extant texts before Xie Lingyun's time.

18. This line uses the language of the *Chu ci*. For example, the phrase *mizhao* 弭棹 (curbing/resting the oars) recalls *Chu ci*'s *mijie* 弭節 (curbing/slacking the pace). Xie Lingyun replaces "pace" with "oars" to highlight the traveling by boat. *Wangzhu* 枉陼 (渚) (winding sandbars) is another dialectal word of Chu. Cf. *Chu ci*, "She jiang" 涉江, 4.130; "Xiang ju" 湘君: "At dusk, we curb the pace and moor at the northern sandbar" 夕弭節兮北渚. See *Chu ci buzhu* 2.63.

19. See *Liuchen zhu Wen xuan* 20.29b.

20. The *fucan* 浮驂 (roving chariot) line refers Liu Yu's entourage. Lines 17 and 18 describe the scene where the councilman Kong Jing parts ways with Liu Yu. *Fu* 浮 is glossed as *xing* 行, see *Liuchen zhu Wen xuan* 20.29b.

21. This line borrows the *Shijing* colloquialism, i.e., the use of numerous grammatical particles to show the mood and tone of the speaker. *Qi* 豈, an adverb, is a rhetorical question marker. *Yi* 伊 is a prosodic filler used in the *Shijing*. Cf. "The First Lunar Month" (Zheng yue 正月; Mao 192): "Is there someone whom you could blame 伊誰云憎?" See also Mao 225: "It is not that it was made to dangle; / but that the sash had much length to spare" 匪伊垂之，帶則有餘. The rhetoric structure, "it is not this, but that . . . ," is applied often to manifest the true but hidden conditions of things. Xie Lingyun here seems to say that he shares Kong Jing's desire to leave court but is unable to. The second half of the line has an inverted syntax. *Chuantu* 川途 (river journey) functions as a prepositional object to *nian* 念.

22. Li Shan paraphrases this difficult line as: "Kong Jing retires to 'cultivate simplicity' [*yangsu* 養素] and yet I [Xie Lingyun] am ashamed for staying at the court." *Suxin* 宿心, the "long cherished aim," refers to the desire to "embrace simplicity." See *Wen xuan* 20.960.

23. *Qiuyuan dao* 丘園道 "Way of the Hillside Garden" alludes to *The Classic of Changes*, hexagram 22 ("Bi" 賁), 6/5, "This is Elegance from a hillside garden, so bundles of silk increase to great number. If one is sparing, in the end, there will be good fortune." See Lynn, *The Classic of Changes*, 276–77.

24. *Bolie* 薄劣 alludes to Pan Yue's 潘岳 (247–300) "Xianju fu" 閒居賦, the coda of which contains the line: "Surely my use is paltry and my talent is meagre" 信用薄而才劣. See *Wen xuan* 16.706.

25. Kong Jing, a native of Shanyin of Guiji (modern Shaoxing, Zhejiang), backed Liu Yu with military and financial support in order to put down the coastal rebellions in

401 and eradicate the usurper Huan Xuan in 404. For Kong Jing's biography, see *Song shu* 54.1531–1532.

26. *Song shu* 54.1532.

27. Located in Pengcheng (modern Xuzhou, Jiangsu), this terrace was associated with Xiang Yu 項羽, the famous Chu general who challenged and lost to the Han founder Liu Bang 劉邦. Kong Jing's biography in the *Song shu* mentions his mystical prowess in subduing the malevolent spirit of Xiang Yu, which speaks to the extent of the role Kong Jing played in Liu Yu's military exploits. See *Song shu* 54.1532.

28. For a detailed discussion of the background of this occasion and a list of attendees to the banquet, see Satō Masamitsu, "Xie Zhan, Xie Lingyun de wenxue," 349–53; see also Wu Fusheng, *Written at the Imperial Command*, 75–77.

29. Wu Fusheng, *Written at the Imperial Command*, 75–77. The pronoun *qi* 其 in this statement refers to the phrase *ci shi dong gui* 辭事東歸, i.e., Kong Jing's decision to decline service and return east.

30. The "Lord's Feast" 公讌 follows a poetic convention of offering flattering remarks to the lord or host of a banquet. There are four poems in the section that celebrate a banquet hosted by Cao Pi upon his promotion to General of the Gentlemen-of-the-Household of All Purposes 五官中郎將. These Jian'an compositions are early models of poetry written at imperial command. See *Wen xuan* 20.943–73.

31. See Ma Ruichen, *Mao shi zhuan jian tongshi*, 21.683. When the full bloom of summer is over, decline and deterioration begin, followed by chaos.

32. The *Lesser Preface* is part of the Mao commentary that provides historically specific and highly moralistic interpretations of individual pieces in the *Shijing*.

33. For a discussion of the thematic signification and structuring through imagistic analogy in *The Classic of Poetry*, see C. H. Wang, "The Theme," *The Bell and the Drum: Shih Ching as Formulaic Poetry in an Oral Tradition* (Berkeley: University of California Press, 1974), 98–125.

34. For a grammatical and philological discussion of the line 爰其適歸, see Ma Ruichen, *Mao shi zhuan jian tongshi*, 21.685.

35. *Shijing quanshi*, 271.

36. Bracken fern was a medicinal herb to treat indigestion and headaches. Its young fiddlehead is edible and considered a delicacy in East Asia.

37. In the *Shijing*, there are two songs by this title, *Mao shi* 119 and 169. Number 119 is a lament of being without brothers. The red pear tree, although leafy and gorgeous, yields tart instead of sweet fruit.

38. Mao glosses *qi* as a kind of bitter vegetable, such as sowthistle. Lu Ji, as cited in *Maoshi Zhengyi* 10.2, gives a detailed description: "*Qi*, similar to the bitter vegetable, has stems that are green with a white sheen. Pluck its leaves and white fluid flows out.

Fresh and robust leaves can be eaten raw. It can also be steamed. People from Qing-zhou call it *qi*. The *qi* from regions west of the Yellow River and the Gansu corridor is especially delicious. Foreign people from the west never left the pass because of *qi*."

39. The following list is compiled from the *Maoshi zhengyi*; Qu Wanli's *Shijing quan-shi* was also consulted.

40. Of these, Mao 167, 168, and 169 are considered a suite of antiwar poems that chastise military actions, commiserate the lamentable fate of soldiers, and urge "return."

41. For a discussion of "valley wind" as "wife's complaint," see C. H. Wang, *The Bell and the Drum*, 103–6.

42. See *Mao shi zhengyi* 13–1.1a. Although modern scholars have done away with this reading, the fifth-century audience would associate this with the last depraved king of the Western Zhou. See C. H. Wang, *The Bell and the Drum*, 104.

43. *Wen xuan* 20.943.

44. See Gu Shaobo, *Xie Lingyun ji jiaozhu*, 24.

45. For Xie Zhan's biography, see *Song shu* 56.1557–59. See also Knechtges and Chang, *Ancient and Early Medieval Chinese Literature*, 3:1636–39; Frodsham, *The Murmuring Stream*, 1:8.

46. For the text, see *Wen xuan* 20.956–57.

47. This line alludes to Mao 154/1, "The Seventh Month" 七月: "In the seventh month, the fire star flows west; in the ninth month, cold-season clothes are distributed" 七月流火，九月授衣. Qu Wanli reads 154 as a song about Bin customs by Bin soldiers who had followed Duke of Zhou on the eastern campaign. *Shijing quanshi*, 271.

48. Lü Yanji 呂延濟 (fl. 718) comments: "With the arrival of the first frost, adhesives and paints become hardened and they can't be used to work on tools or vessels." See *Liu chen zhu Wen xuan* 20.25b.

49. This line alludes to the *Zuozhuan*, Xiang 29, in which *chaomu* 巢幕 (a nest built on the tent) describes the precarious position an official finds himself in when serving an illegitimate regime. Here it refers to the northern groups that Liu Yu had vanquished.

50. This line alludes to Mao 159/2, "Minnow Net" 九罭: "The wild geese fly along the sandbars" 鴻飛遵渚. This is a song in which the residents of the east express sadness upon the Duke of Zhou's departure at the end of the campaign.

51. *Xunshang* 迅商, according to Li Shan, refers to the swift autumn wind arriving from the west. See *Wen xuan* 20.957.

52. *Yangluan* 揚鑾 literally means "raising high the chariot bells." It is derived from *yangbiao* 揚鑣 (raising high the horse's cheek-bar). Cf. the phrase *yangbiao feimo* 揚鑣飛沫, *Wen xuan* 17.508.

53. *Siyan* 四筵 (four sitting mats) can be read as metonymy for all guests sitting at the banquet. Note that in this period, sitting mats and drinking wares would have been placed on the ground.

54. *Sitong* 絲桐 (string and paulownia) indicates the zither and other string instruments.

55. *Fuguan* 扶光 is "light of Fu(-sang)" 扶桑, which is the legendary tree from which the sun rises every day. *Si* 汜 is short for Mengsi 濛(蒙)汜 or "Murky Shore," into which the sun sets every day. See *Chu ci* 3.88: 出自湯谷，次于蒙汜.

56. *Yangsu* 養素 derives from the *Laozi* line "exemplify simplicity, embrace the uncarved block" 見素抱樸. See Lynn, *The Classic of the Way and Virtue*, 82. *Zhong* 終 means "to end or die." Here it implies a "good end" (善終) and a "death that fulfills the heavenly ordained terms" (終天年). The English word *culminate*—with senses of "exalted," "summit," and "reaching a point of highest development"—is an appropriate equivalent for *zhong*. This alludes to *The Classic of Changes*, hexagram 15, "Modesty" (Qian 謙), 9/3, "Diligent about his Modesty, the noble man has the capacity to maintain his position to the end, and this means good fortune" 勞謙，君子有終，吉. See Lynn, *The Classic of Changes*, 231.

57. *Linliu* 臨流 alludes to *Chu ci*, "Chou si" 抽思, 4.139, "Facing the stream, I heave a long sigh" 臨流水而太息. In early medieval poetry, *linliu* is a trope of "homesickness," "yearning and longing for friends and relatives." Cf. Tao Yuanming's line "Facing the stream, I bid farewell with friends" 臨流別友生, *Wen xuan* 26.1235.

58. Li Zhouhan 李周翰 (fl. 718) reads the line as Xie Zhan expressing regret for not being able to travel with Kong Jing and that their respective unpredictable journeys that lie ahead are like tumbleweeds. Within a few years, Xie Zhan, Kong Jing, and Liu Yu would all pass.

59. See *Mao shi zhengyi* 8-1.7a: "This is a poem that lays out the Zhou king's enterprise. When Duke of Zhou met with rebellions, he [in this song] gave account of their ancestors such as Lord Millet so as to make known where the Zhou customs and morals had originated and how arduous the king's work had been" 陳王業也。周公遭變，故陳后稷先公風化之所由致，王業艱難也.

60. Li Shan, quoting the *Song shu*, reports that Zhan's composition was ranked the better of the two poems composed among the invited guests. See *Wen xuan* 20.956.

61. See *Zhou yi jijie* 12.387.

62. A hexagram is composed of six solid and broken lines that are determined in the process of divining. A solid line "⚊" is referred to as yang 陽 or "nine" (九), and a broken line "⚋" is a yin 陰 or "six" (六). Each hexagram is formed by combining two three-line figures or trigrams. There are eight trigrams and sixty-four hexagrams. In reading a hexagram, one begins from the bottom. Thus, the bottom line is designated "first" (*chu* 初), and the rest are respectively "second," "third," "fourth," "fifth," and

"top" (*shang* 上). To indicate the nature of the line (that is, whether it is yang or yin), the numbers nine or six are used. For example, the top line of hexagram 22 (Bi 賁) is called "Nine at the top" (*shangjiu* 上九).

63. 貞吉，无悔，君子之光，有孚，吉. See *Zhou yi jijie* 12.387; see also Lynn, *The Classic of Changes*, 549.

64. 有孚于飲酒，无咎，濡其首，有孚，失是. See *Zhou yi jijie* 12.388; see also Lynn, *The Classic of Changes*, 549–50.

65. See Zhang Yinan's study of the pattern and style of Xie Lingyun's use of hexagrams in poetry, "Xie Lingyun shiwen huayong *I* dian fangshi yanjiu," 99.

66. 飲酒濡首，亦不知節也. See *Zhou yi jijie* 12.388; see also Lynn, *The Classic of Changes*, 550.

67. 未濟，亨。小狐汔濟。濡其尾，無攸利. See *Zhou yi jijie* 12.383–84; Lynn, *The Classic of Changes*, 545.

68. 火在水上，未濟，君子以慎辯物居方. The upper trigram is Li 離, signifying Fire; the lower trigram is Kan 坎, signifying water. See *Zhou yi jijie* 12.385; Lynn, *The Classic of Changes*, 550.

69. Wu Fusheng is of the opinion that there were proven cases where Liu Yu had shown tolerance, affected or not, of open criticism. See *Written at Imperial Command*, 76.

70. For a study on Xie Lingyun use of the *Yi jing*, see Zhang Yinan, "Xie Lingyun shiwen huayong yi dian fangshi yanjiu," *Yunnan daxue xuebao* 11, no. 2 (2011): 94–101.

71. Zhang Yinan, "Xie Lingyun shiwen huayong yi dian fangshi yanjiu," 99.

72. Chennault, "Lofty Gates or Solitary Impoverishment?" 261: "Generally speaking, it was through an ability to adapt to changes in the court's power structure that Xie males of the Southern Dynasties reached the upper ranks. Those whose careers were both accomplished and long-lasting possessed, among other practical talents, a political acumen that helped them surface on the victor's side after contests for leadership, and the well-spoken wit to extricate themselves from compromising situations."

73. 賁于丘園，束帛戔戔，吝，終吉。See *Zhou yi jijie* 5.153; see also Lynn, *The Classic of Changes*, 276.

74. 處得尊位，為飾之主，飾之盛者也。施飾於物，其道害也。施飾丘園，盛莫大焉，故賁于束帛，丘園乃落，賁于丘園，帛乃戔戔。用莫過儉，泰而能約，故必吝焉，乃得終吉也. See *Zhou yi zhengyi* 3.63a; see also Lynn, *The Classic of Changes*, 276–77.

75. For a discussion, see A. C. Graham, "The Right to Selfishness."

76. *Wen xuan* 20.980–81. Block Hill was located fifty *li* (sixteen miles) east of the capital. One of the four major fords in the vicinity of Jiankang, Block Hill was named for its shape, which resembled a square seal. Protruding from the river, it was also known as Mount Tianyin or Heavenly Seal Mountain.

77. The use of *zhi* 衹, an uncommon word, seems to distance the poet from the occasion.

78. Ou and Yue are ancient names for modern southern Zhejiang and parts of Fujian.

79. *Laozi jiaoshi*, 75.

80. *Rixin* 日新 alludes to *The Classic of Changes*, hexagram 26, "Great Domestication" (Daxu 大畜). The Commentary on the Judgment of "Daxu" reads: "In *Daxu*, we find the hard and strong and the sincere and substantial gloriously renewing their virtue with each new day." See *Zhou yi zhengyi*, 3.67b.

81. *Yinchen* alludes to a line from Lu Ji's 陸機 "Yearning to Return": 思歸賦: 絕音塵於江介. See *Wen xuan* 13.602, 20.981.

82. See Li Shan's commentary in *Wen xuan* 20.981.

83. Frodsham, *The Murmuring Stream*, 1:32.

84. See *Wen xuan* 26.1236–38.

85. "Metal phase" refers to autumn.

86. The fire star is Antares, which is considered the harbinger of autumn. Also known as the "heart star" 心宿, it is the brightest star in the constellation of Scorpius.

87. This line alludes to a lament by Lu Ji upon leaving his hometown to take up an office in the northern capital Luoyang: "such bitterness and hardship, no one understands." See *Wen xuan* 24.1147, 26.1229.

88. This alludes to a story in the *Zhuangzi* about an exile from the state of Yue who grows ever more homesick. See *Zhuangzi jishi* 8B.821.

89. See Li Shan's commentary. *Wen xuan* 26.1236

90. Li Mu (?–229 BCE), a famous general from the state of Zhao, had short arms, but it did not prevent him from achieving military victories against both the Xiongnu and the state of Qin. See *Zhanguo ce* 戰國策, Qin 5 (Shanghai: Shanghai Guji, 1978), 289.

91. Xi Ke (?–587 BCE), a grandee of the state of Jin, walked lamely and was jeered by members of the Qi household. See *Wen xuan* 26.1237.

92. Zhili is the name of a recluse whose body was deformed but who nevertheless was able to live out his heavenly ordained years. *Zhuangzi jishi* 2B.180.

93. *Fang* 方 is a place that is not in the center of the world, namely the court.

94. This alludes to Lin Xiangru, the resourceful and courageous minister of Zhao who secured the return of the priceless jade disc known as Mr. He's Jade. See *Shiji* 81.2439–41.

95. For text, see Gu Shaobo, *Xie Lingyun ji jiaozhu*, 41–44; *Wen xuan* 26.1238–39. For translations, see Frodsham, *Murmuring Stream*, 1:118; Owen, "Librarian in Exile," 214–15.

96. This line alludes to Zuo Si's 左思 "Zhaoyin" (Summoning the Recluse): "White snow lingers on a dark ridge" 白雲停陰岡, *Wen xuan* 22.1027. Unlike Zuo Si, Xie Lingyun personifies nature with the use a transitive verb.

97. Regarding Xie Lingyun's use of the word *mei* 媚, Yang Rur-Bin posits that *mei* was aesthetically preferred among the cultured elite in fifth-century Jiangnan. Xie Lingyun was a leading member of this group. Yang reads *mei* as representing "facial features; the radiance of face and eye(brows) that are lovely and fresh." Yang concludes that *mei* signifies "radiant outward beauty" that "manifests the Way." Yang Rur-Bin, "Shanshui shi ye shi gongfu lun," 17–20.

98. Stephen Owen posits that this poem is not about a "return." Instead, it is about a "passing through." See "Librarian in Exile," 212.

99. See Gu Shaobo, *Xie Lingyun ji jiaozhu*, 44.

CHAPTER 7. A LIFE IN NATURAL AND POLITICAL TIMES

1. Chen, Shih-Hsiang, "The Genesis of Poetic Time: The Greatness of Ch'ü Yuan, Studied with a New Critical Approach," *Tsing Hua Journal of Chinese Studies* 10 (1973): 1–44; 12.

2. For the Chinese text, see *Shijing quanshi* 263–70.

3. The seventh month of the Xia dynasty calendar is the ninth month in the Zhou. The Fire Star (α Scorpii; aka Antares), with its prominent movement through the sky, marks seasonal transitions. Its sinking (*liu* 流) marks the arrival of autumn. It is a red supergiant star in the Milky Way galaxy and the fifteenth brightest star of the night sky. Antares is visible in the sky throughout the night around May 31 of each year, when the star is in opposition to the sun. At this time at the equator, Antares rises at dusk and sets at dawn. For approximately two to three weeks on either side of November 30, Antares is not visible in the night sky because it is in near conjunction with the sun; this period of invisibility is longer in the northern hemisphere than in the southern hemisphere, since the star's declination is significantly south of the celestial equator.

4. *Juzhi* 舉趾 (raising toes) refers to setting foot in the fields and preparing the soil for spring planting.

5. *Weihang* 微行 is also glossed as 牆下徑 (the path by the wall).

6. The tender mulberry leaves are used to raise silkworms.

7. This is the Chinese mugwort (*aihao* 艾蒿).

8. The young servant girls will follow the lord's daughter to her husband's home. When a girl marries, she is "returning."

9. *Yao* 蔘 is Chinese senega (*Polygala tenuifolia*) or *yuanzhi* 遠志. It has purple to blue flowers and its root is used as an anti-inflammatory medicine.

10. The glutinous is pinnacled millet, used for brewing; the nonglutinous is foxtail millet, used for cooking.

11. One for the dead and one for the living.

12. *Shijing quanshi*, 263–70.

13. See *Mao shi zhengyi* 8–1.14: "There is never one piece that has all the three modes of *feng*, *ya*, and *song*. Yet this piece, as an exception, means to say that the teachings of the lord of Bin were reasons that led to the king's accomplishments" 諸詩未有一篇之內備有風、雅、頌，而此篇獨有三體者。。。言此豳公之教，能使王業成功故也.

14. For the Chinese text, see *Chu ci buzhu* 1.47. For a complete translation, see David Hawkes, *The Songs of the South*, 67–95; see also Owen, *Anthology*, 162–75.

15. *Zhen* 貞.

16. Sima Qian mentions Song Yu as a disciple of Qu Yuan. Although a number of *sao* and *fu* pieces were attributed to him, Song Yu's historical existence remains a mystery. The "Nine Changes," often divided into eleven sections, is written in apparent imitation of the *Lisao* whose prosodic pattern and themes are borrowed with unrivaled treatment. For the text, see *Chu ci buzhu* 8.182–96. For a translation, see David Hawkes, *The Songs of the South*, 207–19.

17. See *Chu ci buzhu* 8.282.

18. David Hawkes, *The Songs of the South*, 208.

19. See *Chu ci buzhu* 8.185–87.

20. Chen Shih-Hsiang, "The Genesis of Poetic Time," 11–20.

21. Chen Shih-Hsiang, "The Genesis of Poetic Time," 24.

22. For the text, see *Wen xuan* 3.1039–40.

23. There are a number of possible explanations for 虯 *qiu*, with early textual appearances in the *Chu ci*. Wang Yi's gloss of *qiu* as a hornless dragon has been dismissed as wrong in the new Kroll Classical Chinese dictionary, whose editors posit that *qiu* is essentially a kind of dragon distinctive for its coiling, contracted, and convoluted form. The submerged or hidden dragon is apparently an allusion to *Yijing*'s hexagram "Qian" 乾: "Hidden dragon; do not act" 潛龍勿用.

24. To reflect Xie Lingyun's typical choice of unusual vocabulary, I use "welkin" instead of the common word "sky." The "cloud-skipper" refers to the goose in the previous line.

25. The "abyss-sinker" refers to the dragon in the first line. Cf. Tao Yuanming: "Gazing at the clouds, one is shamed by the soaring birds, / looking down at the river, I am chagrined by the swimming fish" 望雲慚高鳥，臨水愧游魚. *Jin shi* 16.982.

26. *Jinde* 進德 means to serve the court. It is an *Yijing* term: "A gentleman, in his advancement through virtue and cultivation of career, should accord with time. Only then there would be no blame" 君子進德修業，欲及時也，故無咎. *Zhouyi zhengyi* 1.20.

27. Lines 5 and 6 compare two courses of action available to someone like Xie Lingyun: *jin* versus *tui* or "to serve the court or to withdraw to a private life." Cf.

Zhouyi zhengyi 7.308: "That which transforms contains images of advancing or retreating" 變化者，進退之象也.

28. The verb *fan* 反 probably also has a sense of "return," since Yongjia is also on the east coast of China, where Xie Lingyun had been before moving to the capital in the year 400.

29. Here, the choice of *ke* or *e* 痾 for illness is typical of Xie Lingyun's penchant for using rare words.

30. In Li Shan's *Wen xuan*, the fifth couplet is missing. For a discussion of the variant version, see Hu Kejia 胡克家, *Wen xuan kaoyi* 文選考異, *juan* 4.

31. This is an allusion to *Liji zhushu* 禮記註疏: "I have been separated from the crowd and lived by myself. It has been a long time" 吾離群而索居，亦已久矣!

32. *Wumen* 無悶, literally "no distress," alludes to the "Wen yan" of the *Yijing*: 遯世無悶，不見是而無悶.

33. See *Taiping huanyu ji* 99: "Duke Xie's Pond is located about three leagues northwest of Wenzhou, east of the Mount Grain Storehouse" 謝公池，在溫州西北三里，其池在積谷山東. When I visited the pond in May 2012, it was part of a reconstructed replica of Xie Lingyun's residence.

34. For the Chinese text, see *Shijing quanshi*, 476–77.

35. *Mao shi zhengyi* 16.5.

36. *Mencius* 1A.1.

37. This tradition is seen as early as the Spring and Autumn era. The Wu prince Ji Zha, for example, was able to "observe" the customs and mores of each of the fifteen Zhou states when he was presented with a musical performance of their songs. Wang Can's "Deng lou fu" is another example where the poet observed and commented on social dissipation at the end of the Han.

38. These self-deprecating lines may be a common mode in first-person narration, and yet the imagery and the vocabulary are so fresh that the reader is drawn into the language without a sense of affectedness. They effectively connect the reader to the poet's professed quandary of not belonging.

39. Owen, *Anthology*, 321.

40. Frodsham, *Murmuring Stream*, 1:121.

41. Westbrook, "Landscape Transformation in the Poetry of Hsieh Ling-yun," 242–44.

42. Swartz, "Pentasyllabic *Shi* Poetry: Landscape and Farmstead Poems," in Cai Zong-qi, ed., *How to Read Chinese Poetry: A Guided Anthology* (New York: Columbia University Press, 2008), 137.

43. Huang, "Excursion, Estates, and the Kingly Gaze," 121.

44. Kwong, "The Aesthetics of Parallelism," 211.

45. See *Quan Tang shi* 170.1755; 177.1805.

46. See *Quan Tang shi* 272.3062; 745.8477.

47. *Quan Tang shi* 459.5219.

48. Gu Shaobo, *Xie Lingyun ji jiaozhu*, 484: 驚天動地至今傳.

49. Gu Shaobo, *Xie Lingyun ji jiaozhu*, 486–87.

50. *Yuan Haowen quanji* 元好問全集, ed. Yao Dianzhong 姚奠中 (Taiyuan: Shanxi Renmin Chubanshe, 1990), 11.339. 池塘春草謝家春，萬古千秋五字新.

51. Cao Xu, *Shi pin jizhu*, 284: 康樂每對惠連輒得佳語。後在永嘉西堂，思詩竟日不就，寤寐間忽見惠連，即成池塘生春草。故嘗云：此語有神助，非我語也.

52. *Nan shi* 34.881: 謝五言如初發芙蓉，自然可愛。君詩若鋪錦列繡，亦雕繢滿眼. Bao Zhao's evaluation sets apart Xie Lingyun from Yan Yanzhi, whose art is in the second part of the statement: "Your [Yan Yanzhi] poetry is like brocade spread and arrays of embroidery; what meets the eye are ornate decorations." Zhong Rong also compared the two in the following terms: "Xie, the Sojourner, was the leading poet of the Yuanjia era; Yan Yannian [Yanzhi] was the runner-up. Both produced works that were crown jewels in the five-syllable line form and they commanded the attention of their time through their embellished words." *Shi pin ji zhu*, 28: 謝客為元嘉之雄，顏延年為輔。斯皆五言之冠冕，文詞之命世也. Shen Yue ranked Xie and Yan as equals, *Song shu* 73.1904: 延之與陳郡謝靈運俱以詞彩齊名. See the informative study on this topic by Wendy Swartz, "Naturalness in Xie Lingyun's Poetic Works," 355–86.

53. *Zhuangzi jishi* 7A.658–59.

54. *Zhuangzi jishi* 7A.658: 不似人所作也.

55. *Zhuangzi jishi* 7A.658: 彫削巧妙，不類人工，見者驚疑，謂鬼神所作也.

56. See Gu Shaobo, *Xie Lingyun ji jiaozhu*, 487, 490, 491.

57. 春日遲遲，采蘩祁祁，女心傷悲，殆及公子同歸.

58. See *Chu ci buzhu* 12.233: 王孫遊兮不歸，春草生兮萋萋. Cf. David Hawkes, *The Songs of the South*, 244.

59. The balanced emotional tone of the poem may remind the reader of the critical notion as expressed in the phrase "sorrowful yet without injury" (*ai er bushang* 哀而不傷)—a comment from Confucius praising "Osprey Singing" (Guan ju 關雎; Mao 1): "'Guan ju' expresses a delight that is not wanton; a grief that is not injurious" 關雎，樂而不淫，哀而不傷. See *Analects* 3/20.

60. Wilhelm, *The I Ching*, 82.

61. The "Xi ci," also called the "Xi ci zhuan" (Commentary on the appended explanations) or "Da zhuan" 大傳 (Great treatise), presents a general discussion of the purpose and meaning of the *Yijing*. For a study of the "Xi ci," see Willard J. Peterson, "Making Connections," 67–116.

62. *Yijing jijie* 13.393–96. I have italicized the Yijing terminology, such as *jixiong* 吉

凶, *xiang* 象, etc. 聖人設卦觀象，繫辭焉而明吉凶，剛柔相推而生變化。是故，吉凶者，失得之象也。悔吝者，憂虞之象也。變化者，進退之象也。。。是故，君子所居而安者，易之序也。所樂而玩者，爻之辭也。是故，君子居則觀其象，而玩其辭；動則觀其變，而玩其占。是以自天祐之，吉无不利.

63. As Wilhelm posits, the situation represented by the hexagram as a whole is called time; it has to do with movement, meaning the decrease or growth, the emptiness or fullness, and so on. See "The Time" in Wilhelm, *The I Ching*, 359.

CHAPTER 8. PATTERNING THE DRAGON

1. Denecke et al., *Handbook of Classical Chinese Literature*, 244.

2. Cao Xu, *Shi pin jizhu*, 28: 元嘉中，有謝靈運，才高詞盛，富艷難蹤.

3. *Shi pin jizhu*, 160–61: 宋臨川太守謝靈運詩。 其源出於陳思。雜有景陽之體。故尚巧似。而逸蕩過之。頗以繁蕪為累。嶸謂若人與多才高。寓目輒書。內無乏思。外無遺物。其繁富宜哉。然名章迥句。處處閒起。麗典新聲。絡繹奔會。譬猶青松之拔灌木。白玉之映塵沙。未足貶其高潔也。

4. Wendy Swartz reads the transformation as depicting the "attitude of the birds," *How to Read Chinese Poetry*, 137. Owen's translation of this line implies the kinds of birds change: "garden willows vary the birds that there sing," *An Anthology of Chinese Literature*, 321.

5. Zong-qi Cai, *The Matrix of Lyric Transformation*, 10.

6. See Zhao Minli and Benjamin Ridgway, "A Discussion of the Principles for the Combination of 'Feet' in the Pentasyllabic *Shi* Genre," *Journal of Chinese Literature and Culture* 2, no. 2 (2015): 286–323.

7. Note that *gu* 古 is a cognate of *gu* 故, which means "lived and experienced." Thus, the aesthetic appeal of "ancientness" is paradoxically its immediacy and presence, familiarity and universality. Timelessness is sometimes a mere sense of déjà vu.

8. Early usage can be seen in the "Round Fan" and the "Woman in the Tower" poems where the meaning of both pieces hinges on the axial effect of the pivot verbs.

9. The fifth couplet also poses some interesting reading. "Quilts and pillows have covered me from seasonal transitions; / opening the curtains, I, for a brief moment, steal a glance out" (衾枕昧節候 / 褰開暫窺臨). Aside from the apparent pairing of "quilts and pillows" and "curtains," the rest of the couplet does not contain a recognizable parallelism until we look at the third syllables or pivots: *mei* 昧, which means "darkness, the time before the sun is out," and *zan* 暫, "a sudden and brief segment in time." They hold the lines together by constituting subsemantically an antithesis in that the former is a long and suppressive darkness and the latter a sudden break from it. It is

important to note that this couplet signals the transition in the poem from a dark and depressive introspection to a bright and hopeful looking out. This break, coming at the middle of the poem, is both seasonal and psychological, both of which ripen to usher in a change from the dark period after a long dormancy. The world outside undergoes a seasonal transformation that beckons the bedridden person into his rejuvenation.

10. Stephen Owen pinpoints the seventh century as a turning point for the *shi* art. Xie Lingyun, considered in this light, was a forerunner. See Owen, *The Poetry of the Early T'ang*, 12–13: "During this period [the seventh century] the poetic language was refined into the condensed and flexible medium used by the great poets of the eighth and ninth centuries. From their search for novelty of expression evolved the syntactic freedom and ability to shift word classes found in later Chinese poetry. . . . And from their attention to the surprising use of individual words in lines evolved a particular concentration on style and diction which characterizes later poets from Tu Fu to Wang Shih-chen. Yet their contributions were collective rather than individual, and, with the partial exception of Yu Hsin, it would be difficult to point out a single poet who towers above the rest."

11. Frodsham, *Murmuring Streaming*, 1:92.

12. In Xie's poetry, there are around one hundred couplets that contain descriptive landscape elements.

13. See Guo Shaoyu 郭紹虞, *Canglang shihua jiaoshi* 滄浪詩話校釋 (Taipei: Liren Shuju, 1983), 158: 靈運之詩，已是徹首尾成對句矣，是以不及建安也.

14. Kang-i Sun Chang, *Six Dynasties Poetry*, 78.

15. Kang-i Sun Chang, *Six Dynasties Poetry*, 67.

16. Charles Yim-tze Kwong, "The Aesthetics of Parallelism in Chinese Poetry: The Case of Xie Lingyun," in *The Yields of Transition*, 203–23; 205.

17. Kwong, "The Aesthetics of Parallelism in Chinese Poetry," 206.

18. Kwong, "The Aesthetics of Parallelism in Chinese Poetry," 206.

19. Kwong, "The Aesthetics of Parallelism in Chinese Poetry," 206.

20. Kwong, "The Aesthetics of Parallelism in Chinese Poetry," 206.

21. The brackets indicate a syntactic hierarchy. The second bisyllabic phrase cannot operate at the same grammatical plane as the first bisyllabic unit, because it is subjugated to the trisyllabic unit.

22. Refer to Ge Xiaoyin's study of the surging of bisyllabic phrases during the Han.

23. *Wen xuan* 26.1244.

24. According to Zhong Rong, Cao Zhi and Zhang Xie 張協 (ca. 255–ca. 310) were two important influences. For an account on Zhang Xie as a literary figure and his works, see Knechtges and Chang, *Ancient and Early Medieval Chinese Literature*, 4:2180–82.

25. Xie Hun reportedly called out Lingyun's slack in practice and predicted that,

with Lingyun's natural talent, he had the potential to excel in the art. Shen Yue, *Song shu* 58.1591.

26. *Wen xuan* 22.1034–35. The West Pond was an artificial moat excavated during the reign of Emperor Ming of Jin (Sima Shao 司馬紹, r. 323–26). See *Shishuo xinyu jianshu*, 598. See also Mather, *Shih-shuo hsin-yü*, 302.

27. The phrase "song of the cricket" alludes to Mao 144, a poem urging good men to seize the day. The chirping of crickets signals the arrival of autumn and that the *yang* (surging) phase has come to an end.

28. This couplet is missing from the Wuchen 五臣 edition.

29. Nanrong is a Zhuangzi allusion, in which one is advised not to indulge in pensive thinking: "Keep intact your person, make secure your life, and do not allow your pensive thoughts linger on and on" 全汝形抱汝生無使汝思慮營營. See *Zhuangzi jishi*, 23.777.

30. The phrase *qinghua* 清華 in this line was used to name a Ming imperial garden; Qinghua University later adopted the name.

31. Li Shan identified the "lord" as Cao Pi. For a discussion and translation of the piece, see Cutter, "Cao Zhi's (192–232) Symposium Poems," *CLEAR* 6, nos. 1/2 (1984): 1–32, 6–11. Cao Pi hosted parties of celebration upon being named the General of the Gentlemen-of-the-Household for All Purposes.

32. For *qing* as a key aesthetic paradigm, see Jiang Yin, "Qing: Gudian shi meixue de hexin fanchou," 32–77.

33. *Wen xuan* 22.1029–30.

34. *Jichu* 激楚 is a music known for expressing strong emotions.

35. On the medieval aesthetics of "sad tones," see Ronald Egan, "The Controversy over Music and 'Sadness' and Changing Conceptions of the *Qin* in Middle Period China," *HJAS* 57 (1997): 5–66.

36. *Wen xuan* 22.1027–28.

37. Hexagram "Qian" 乾: "The submerged dragon does not act. See Richard Lynn, *The Classic of Changes*, 123. The phrase "hidden dragon" is used to explain the bottom line—"nine at the beginning" (初九)—of the hexagram "Qian." See also Wilhelm, *The I Ching*, 7–8.

38. Frodsham, *Murmuring Stream*, 1:121.

39. Westbrook, "Landscape Transformation in the Poetry of Hsieh Ling-yun," 242.

40. Owen, *Anthology of Chinese Literature*, 321.

41. Swartz, "Pentasyllabic *Shi* Poetry," 137.

42. Huang, "Excursion, Estates, and the Kingly Gaze," 121.

43. Kwong, "The Aesthetics of Parallelism," 211.

44. Xiaofei Tian, *Visionary Journeys*, 124.

45. Frodsham's "display" treats *mei* as transitive verb. The renderings of Westbrook,

Swartz, Huang, and Kwong show an agreement on *mei* being an intransitive verb. Tian's "lends charm to" reads *mei* as intransitive and translates it in a transitive sense. Owen's "enhance" inventively sidesteps the question of *mei*'s verbal function.

46. An ergative verb can be either transitive or intransitive, with the same word used as the object of the transitive form and as the subject of the intransitive form.

47. *Xie Lingyun shi xuan*, 44.

48. Wilhelm, *The I Ching*, 7–8.

49. Frodsham, *Murmuring Stream*, 1:121.

50. Westbrook, "Landscape Transformation in the Poetry of Hsieh Ling-yun," 242.

51. Owen, *Anthology of Chinese Literature*, 321.

52. Swartz, "Pentasyllabic *Shi* Poetry," 137.

53. Huang, "Excursion, Estates, and the Kingly Gaze," 121.

54. Kwong, "The Aesthetics of Parallelism," 211.

55. Xiaofei Tian, *Visionary Journeys*, 124.

56. Wilhelm, *The I Ching*, 208.

57. An apt example is found in the second couplet of the "Climb the Tower by the Pond," where the middle-positioned verbs *kui* 愧 (ashamed) and *zuo* 怍 (chagrined) could be interpreted as self-effacement and self-conceitedness.

58. *Wen xuan* 26.1239.

59. *Wen xuan* 22.1047.

60. *Wen xuan* 22.1045.

61. Lu Qinli, *Xian Qin Han Wei Jin Nanbeichao shi* 2.1167.

62. See Ye Jiaying, *Han Wei Liuchao shi jiang lu*, 456–58. Ye posits that Xie's parallelism has many layers and surpassed Cao Zhi in complexity and richness. Furthermore, she argues that Xie inspired some of Du Fu's most celebrated couplets.

CHAPTER 9. A BUDDHIST END

1. See Tang Yongtong, *Han Wei Liang Jin Nanbeichao fojiao shi*, 297–99, 317–25.

2. For Xie Lingyun as a Buddhist, see Tang Yongtong, "Xie Lingyun," *Han Wei Liang Jin Nanbeichao fojiao shi*, 436–40; Frodsham, "Hsieh Ling-yün's Contribution to Medieval Chinese Buddhism," 27–55; and Richard Mather, "The Landscape Buddhism of the Fifth-Century Poetry Hsieh Ling-yun," 67–79. For a concise list of Xie Lingyun's Buddhist interests, see Zürcher, *Buddhist Conquest*, 412n125.

3. *Gaoseng zhuan*, T 6.361a. For Huiyuan's biography, see *Gaoseng zhuan*, T 6.357c–361b. For studies of Huiyuan, see Walter Liebenthal, "Shih Hui-yüan's Buddhism as Set Forth in His Writings," *JAOS* 70 (1950): 243–59; Tang Yongtong, *Han Wei Liang Jin Nanbeichao fojiao shi*, 341–73, 437; Zürcher, *Buddhist Conquest*, 204–53.

4. *Gaoseng zhuan*, T 6.358b.

5. Around 412, Faxian 法顯, after fourteen years of traveling in the western regions, returned to Jiankang with a trove of Buddhist lore. The exact date of Faxian's return is controversial and undetermined. There would be two more reports of a significant sighting of the Buddha's shadow in 520 and 630. See Frodsham, *Murmuring Stream*, 2:19n162. For Faxian's biography, see *Gaoseng zhuan* 3.337b–338b. See also Zürcher, *Buddhist Conquest*, 224.

6. For a translation of the descriptive passage from Faxian's report, see Frodsham, *Murmuring Stream*, 1:19.

7. See Tang Yongtong, *Han Wei Liang Jin Nanbeichao fojiao shi*, 274.

8. *T* 15:654–79.

9. *Gaoseng zhuan, T* 6.358b.

10. For text, see *Guang Hongming ji* 廣弘明集, *T* 15.199b-c. For a study and translation, see Eugene Wang, "The Shadow Image in the Cave," 419–21. See also Frodsham, *Murmuring Stream*, 1:178–83; and Mather, "Landscape Buddhism," 76–78.

11. "The boat hidden in the gully" is an allusion from *Zhuangzi*, but here refers to "the historical Buddha." See Mather, "Landscape Buddhism," 77. See *Zhuangzi jishi* 3A.243: "Someone hid his boat in the gully; a mountain is hidden in the marshland; these can be called secure indeed. Yet in the middle of the night, someone of Herculean strength carried them and ran away. The benighted one would have no knowledge of it" 夫藏舟於壑，藏山於澤，謂之固矣。然而夜半有力者負之而走，昧者不知也.

12. The Symbolic Teaching 像法 refers to what comes between True Teaching 正法 and Degenerate Teaching 末法, respectively falling into three consecutive periods. See *Saddharma-pundarika T* 2.11c–12a: "For thirty-two *kalpas* he offered broad salvation to myriad beings; the True teaching now came to be exhausted and the Symbolic teaching followed in another thirty-two *kalpas*" 三十二小劫，廣度諸眾生。正法滅盡已，像法三十二.

13. "Karmically defiled" for *yinran* 因染 is a suggestion from Ross Henderson. Frodsham has "tainted by Causation."

14. The Six Paths refer to the six directions of reincarnation, also called the six ways 六道: (1) 地獄趣 *naraka-gati*, or that of the hells; (2) 餓鬼趣 *preta-gati*, of hungry ghosts; (3) 畜生趣 *tiryagyoni-gati*, of animals; (4) 阿修羅趣 *asura-gati*, of malevolent nature spirits; (5) 人趣 *manusya-gati*, of human existence; (6) 天趣 *deva-gati*, of deva existence. The 六趣輪迴經 is attributed to Aśvaghoṣa.

15. The Seven Consciousnesses are the base consciousness, the thinking consciousness, and the five consciousnesses associated with the sense organs: eyes, ears, nose, tongue, and skin.

16. The Nine Abodes are the nine realms of existence for sentient beings.

17. The Five Aggregates (Skt. *skandhas*; Ch. *wuyin* 五陰 or *wuyun* 五蘊) are the

five aspects of human intelligence: form, perception, conception, volition, and consciousness.

18. The four causal conditions 因緣 (*hetu-pratyaya*) or the "four worldly senses" 四塵 are form, odor, taste, and touch.

19. The golden color is one of the distinguishing marks 好相 of the Buddha.

20. *Baihao* 白毫 refers to the white tuft of hair between the Buddha's eyebrows, from which beams of radiance shine forth. See Frodsham, *Murmuring Stream*, 1:183.

21. This refers to Huiyuan.

22. *Chanti* 闡提, or *icchantika*, is an incorrigible unbeliever who lacks faith in Buddhism and has no prospect of attaining enlightenment.

23. Frodsham, *The Murmuring Stream*, 1:14.

24. "I, at the aims-establishing age, hoped to trail among your disciples" 予志學之年希門人之末. For the text of "A Dirge for Master Huiyuan" (Huiyuan fashi lei 慧遠法師誄), see *Guang hong ming ji* 廣弘明集 (comp. in 664 by Daoxuan 道宣, 596–667), *T* 23.267a-b. Frodsham, *The Murmuring Stream*, 1:13–20.

25. See Tang Yongtong, "*Dunwu jianwu* zhi zheng" 頓悟漸悟之爭, *Han Wei Liang Jin Nanbeichao fojiao shi*, 625–29; see also Frodsham, "Hsieh Ling-yun's Contribution to Medieval Chinese Buddhism," 34.

26. Zhu Daosheng arrived in Jiankang in 409 and Frodsham convincingly argues for a meeting between him and Lingyun at the time. Frodsham, *Murmuring Stream*, 2:35n57. In the "Bianzong lun," Zhu Daosheng was referred to not by name but as the "Buddhist with the new doctrine" 新論道士.

27. See Frodsham, "Hsieh Ling-yun's Contribution to Medieval Chinese Buddhism," 28.

28. Wang Hong was the one who censored Xie in 418. Frodsham suggests this was a politically motivated attack on Xie Lingyun. See Frodsham, *Murmuring Stream*, 1:24–25. That Xie Lingyun corresponded with Wang Hong on the matter of "sudden enlightenment" was remarkable. For studies of the *Dissertation* and Xie Lingyun's expositions on *dunwu*, see Tang Yongtong, "Xie Lingyun shu Daosheng dunwu yi" 謝靈運述道生頓悟義, *Han Wei Liang Jin Nanbeichao fojiao shi*, 663–69; Qian Zhixi 錢志熙, "Xie Lingyun 'Bian zong lun' he shanshui shi" 謝靈運《辯宗論》和山水詩, *Beijing daxue xuebao* (*Zhexue shehui kexue ban*) (1989:5): 39–46; Koga Hidehiko 古賀英彥, "Tongo no kōsatsu Ben sō ron" 頓悟の考察弁宗論, *Zengaku kenkyū* 74 (1996): 1–35; Morino Shigeo 森野繁夫, "Sha Reiun 'Ben sō ron' ni tsuite" 謝靈運＜弁宗論＞について, *Chūgokugaku ronshū* 21 (1998): 1–18; 23 (1999): 1–13; 24 (1999): 32–48; 27 (2000): 57–74; 28 (2001): 1–27; and Ji Zhichang 紀志昌, "Xie Lingyun 'Bian zong lun' 'dunwu' yi 'zhezhong Kong Shi' de xuanxue quanshi chutan" 謝靈運《辯宗論》 "頓悟" 義 "折衷孔釋" 的玄學詮釋初探, *Taida zhongwen xuebao* 32 (2010): 167–208.

29. *Gaoseng zhuan*, T 7.367a-b. 陳郡謝靈運篤好佛理。殊俗之音多所達解。迺諧叡以經中諸字并眾音異旨。於是著十四音訓敘。條列梵漢昭然可了。使文字有據焉. Mather, "The Landscape Buddhism of the Fifth-Century Poetry Hsieh Ling-yun," 72.

30. *Gaoseng zhuan* T 7.367c. See Monk Huiyan's 慧嚴 (363-443) biography: 六經典文本在濟俗為治。必求靈性真奧。豈得不以佛經為指南耶。

31. Shen Yue, comp., *Song shu* 67.1756: 幽人懟止之鄉.

32. Shen Yue, *Song shu* 67.1764.

33. Shen Yue, *Song shu* 67.1765.

34. Shen Yue, *Song shu* 67.1765.

35. Shen Yue, *Song shu* 67.1765.

36. How disruptive Xie Lingyun's land reclamation practice actually was a question that is beyond the scope of this study. Mark Elvin, based on his reading of Xie Lingyun's nature writing, posits that it reveals a "subtle concept of the 'environment' as an interrelated complex of different but mutually interdependent forms of life in varying habitats, even if he did not have a general term for it," and that in his mind, "there was no conflict between the excitement of what we now call 'development,' that is, the practical mastering of nature, and the spiritual inspiration to be drawn from contemplating nature, that is, grasping that it is immeasurably greater than we are, and driven by processes that we can only partly intuit or discover." Elvin further estimates Xie Lingyun's action from a convincingly refreshing angle: "He delighted in having his serfs fell ancient trees and open new roadways through the wilderness. Anyone who has ever owned a substantial expanse of relatively untouched land—a disappearing minority, it is true—can probably feel a certain empathy with this inner urge. It would be unreasonable of us to think him unreasonable in this regard. Only in millennial hindsight has it become apparent with what imperceptible subtlety improvement can transform itself into its contrary: destruction." Mark Elvin, *The Retreat of the Elephants*, 336.

37. See Frodsham, *Murmuring Stream*, 1:79.

38. Gu Shaobo, *Xie Lingyun ji jiaozhu*, 186-89; *Wen xuan* 26.1245-47. For a translation, see Frodsham, *Murmuring Stream*, 1:152; 2:175. According to traditional account, this poem was written in 432 after Xie's quarrel with Meng Yi. He was leaving the capital where he had come to defend himself and was subsequently dispatched to Linchuan (modern Jiangxi) as its governor. The season described in the poem seems to point to springtime. For Ford Rock, see Frodsham, *Murmuring Stream*, 2:175.

39. This alludes to Mao 256.

40. "Inner Truth" is hexagram 61 in *The Classic of Changes*.

41. This alludes to Mao 200.

42. Mount Luofu is in modern Guangdong. Ge Hong is said to have practiced his Daoist art of living there. Xie Lingyun wrote a *fu* piece on Mount Luofu.

43. Mount Lu is in modern Jiangxi; Mount Huo is in modern Anhui and is also known as Mount Tianzhu.

44. Mount Jiuyi and River Xiang are in modern Hunan. Jiuyi is where the sage king Shun died. Xiang is where Qu Yuan was exiled and committed suicide.

45. Cf. Mao 116. 明發不寐，有懷二人.

46. Gu, *Xie Lingyun ji jiaozhu*, 189–91; *Wen xuan* 26.1247–48. Frodsham, *Murmuring Stream*, 1:153; 2:179–80.

47. This self-reference as a native of Yue is significance, since it denotes a voluntary change of identity on Lingyun's part. Shining Commandery, the burial site for both his grandfather and father, replaced Chen Commandery in the north as Lingyun's ancestral home.

48. *Wen xuan* has 款, which I emended to 歎.

49. "Guangling san" was the song Xi Kang 嵇康 played before his execution.

50. Frodsham, *Murmuring Stream*, 2:180.

51. For the text of "Entering the Pengli Lake" 入彭蠡湖口, see *Wen xuan* 26.1248–49 and Gu Shaobai, *Xie Lingyun ji jiaozhu*, 191–94; Frodsham, *Murmuring Stream*, 1:154; 2:181–82. The modern name for Lake Pengli is Lake Poyang. See also Westbrook's translation in Liu Wu-chi and Irving Yucheng Lo, eds., *Sunflower Splendor*, 66–67.

52. A type of life-enhancing element.

53. A song about separation.

54. Huazi Ridge was where Master Hua allegedly turned into an immortal. Master Hua was the most accomplished and famous disciple of Luli 祿里 (or 甪里), one of the worthies of the group known as the "Four Hoary Heads" from the third century BCE. This was also where the Daoist goddess Magu practiced her art.

55. Frodsham, *Murmuring Stream*, 1:75.

56. Frodsham, *Murmuring Stream*, 1:75.

57. *Song shu* 67.1777.

58. See Frodsham, *Murmuring Stream*, 1:76.

59. Zifang is the style name of Zhang Liang 張良 (d. 187 BCE), one of the five founding ministers of the Han.

60. Lu Zhonglian 魯仲連 (ca. 3rd cent. BCE) was a native of Qi. He went to Zhao to form an allegiance against Qin.

61. The term "rivers and seas" 江海 or, in later martial arts fiction, "rivers and lakes" 江湖, refers to a wild place where outlaws live.

62. *Song shu* 67.1777.

63. Frodsham, *Murmuring Stream*, 1:78. Ye Xiaoxue, in his analysis of Xie Lingyun's death, is of the opinion that even the seemingly sympathetic Liu Yilong was a knowing participant in bringing down this last important member of the Xie clan. See Xie, *Xie Lingyun shi xuan*, 179–80.

64. For a translation and analysis of this piece, see Chan, *Considering the End*, 179–84.

65. Gong Sheng (68 BCE–11 CE) was a Han dynasty martyr who starved himself to death to protest Wang Mang's (r. 9–23) usurpation of the Han throne. For Gong Sheng's biography, see *Han shu* 72.3080–83.

66. Li Ye (d. 25 CE), like Gong Sheng, protested Wang Mang's usurpation. He left court to live in retirement. After Wang Mang died, another usurper, Gongsun Shu, called on Li Ye to serve in his regime. When Li Ye rejected him, a jar of poison ale was delivered to his doorstep, which he drank and died. See Ban Gu, comp., *Han shu* 81.2668–70.

67. Master Huo refers to Huo Yuan 霍原 (fl. 290) who lost his life refusing to serve a potential usurper. See Fang Xuanling et al., comps., *Jin shu* 94.2435–36.

68. *Xiehou* here refers to the brief human life.

69. Frodsham, *Murmuring Stream*, 2:75n82.

70. Chan, *Considering the End*, 177, 182.

71. Gu, *Xie Lingyun ji jiaozhu*, 205. *Jin shu* 89.2300.

72. As Tim Chan points out, scholars' opinions are split regarding the identification of Lord Xi. See *Considering the End*, 18285.

73. *Jin shu* 89.2300.

74. For Xi Kang's "Youfen" 幽憤, see *Wen xuan* 23.1081–85. See also Chan, *Considering the End*, 177–78.

75. For the *locus classicus* of *xiehou*, see Mao 94, "Ye you mancao" 野有蔓草.

76. See Chan, *Considering the End*, 180n76.

77. See Chan's discussion on this variant, *Considering the End*, 183–86.

78. Chan, *Considering the End*, 183–86.

APPENDIX 1

1. Hengyang (modern Pingyang in Zhejiang) is in Yongjia. Hengshan (*Orixa japonica*) is also known as *changshan* 常山, *shuqi* 蜀漆 (Szechuan varnish), or *hucao* 互草. Smith, *Chinese Medicinal Herbs*, 292.

2. Gardenia refers to both the flower and fruit of a shrub common in south China. The flower is white or yellowish, with pleasant scent. The fruit, called yellow berry, is smooth, oblong, orange-brown, or yellowish, two-celled berry. See Smith, *Chinese Medicinal Herbs*, 183–85. See also Read, *Chinese Medicinal Plants*, 21, S 82.

3. For the medicinal and daily uses of camphor, see Smith, *Chinese Medicinal Herbs*, 87–88.

4. *Huangjing, Polygonatum falcatum*, is also called 黃芝，鹿竹，仙人餘糧，救窮草，野生薑. Read, *Chinese Medicinal Plants*, 223, S 687. See also Smith, *Chinese*

Medicinal Herbs, 339–40:"The root, leaves, flowers, and fruit are all eaten. For medicinal use, the root is steeped in wine, or administered in powder. The Taoists make much of this plant and call it the food of the immortals . . . it is also regarded as demulcent, arthritic, lenitive, and prophylactic. It is also administered in confirmed leprosy."

5. *Ziyuan*, a lung-soothing cough suppressant, is also called 紫菀，青菀，紫蒨，返魂草，夜牽牛. Read, *Chinese Medicinal Plants*, 3, S 12. See also Smith, *Chinese Medicinal Herbs*, 56–57: "The root . . . is used in the treatment of pulmonary affectious, in haemoptysis, hematuria, puerperal hemorrhage, and dysuria. It is also considered to be quieting to the nervous system, and is therefore used in the restless crying of children."

6. *Maimendong, Liriope spicata*, is also called 烏韭，羊韭，馬韭，不死草，階前草. Read, *Chinese Medicinal Plants*, 222, S 684. See also Smith, *Chinese Medicinal Herbs*, 291: "The root is the part used in medicine . . . it is supposed to benefit the dual principles, and is therefore tonic and aphrodisiac, promoting fertility. It assists the memory and promotes the secretion of milk."

7. *Mudan, Paeonia moutan*, is also known in Chinese as 花王, 百兩金. See Read, *Chinese Medicinal Plants*,171, S 537. See also Smith, *Chinese Medicinal Herbs*, 300–301. "The bark of the root is the part used in medicine. . . . It is prescribed in fevers, colds, nervous disorders, hemorrhages, headaches, and menstrual difficulties. Its prolonged use is supposed to give vigor to the body and to lengthen life."

8. This fragrant plant is valued for its scent and medicinal efficacy as an anti-inflammatory. It seeds are used in the treatment of the opacity of the cornea and are said to remove films and opacities. Smith, *Chinese Medicinal Herbs*, 289.

9. *Longxu, Juncus balticus* or bulrush, is a kind of alpine soft rush. Its other Chinese names are 燈心草, 虎鬚草. Read, *Chinese Medicinal Plants*, 225, S 695. See also Smith, *Chinese Medicinal Herbs*, 224: "It is said to be antilithic, diuretic, pectoral, lenitive, sedative, derivative, and discutient. The ashes of a lamp wick are placed upon a mother's nipples, and thus administered to a nursing child for the relief of night crying."

10. *Xiongqiong, Conioselinum univittatum*, is also called 川芎, 胡藭, 香果. It refers to the root of the plant; the leaf is called *jiangli* 江籬, which resembles angelica. When the plant is still young, before any roots have formed, it is called *miwu* 蘪蕪, which is often dried and added to scent pouches. According to Smith, *Chinese Medicinal Herbs*, 123–24, the root of *xiongqiong* is used for "colds, headache, anemia, menorrhagia, retained placenta, sterility, pains and aches of all kinds, including toothaches, hemoptysis, phthisis, strumous difficulties, rheumatism, and fluxes. The leaves are said to be anthelmintic, and are also used in the treatment of diarrhea and dysentery. The flowers of the plant are used in the preparation of facial cosmetics." See also Read, *Chinese Medicinal Plants*, 56, S 216.

11. *TPYL* 959.4390a.

12. *TPYL* 960.4392b.

13. *TPYL* 989.4509a.

14. *TPYL* 993.4529a.

15. The line 越王居泉山 is missing in Gu Shaobo.

16. *TPYL* 989.4507a.

17. *TPYL* 992.4524b.

18. This entry is not collected in *TPYL*. *Qimin yaoshu* 齊民要術 10.625.

19. *YWLJ* 8.143.

20. *CXJ* 28.690.

21. *WX* 22.1042.

22. *TPYL* 975.4425a.

23. *TPYL* 942.4316b.

24. *CXJ* 5.92.

25. *TPYL* 52.381a.

26. *TPYL* 928.4256a.

27. *WX* 22.1044.

28. *WX* 25.1198.

29. *WX* 30.1395.

30. *YWLJ* 8.144.

31. *WX* 22.1045.

32. 乾隆紹興府志卷4.

33. *TPYL* 990.4514b.

34. *WX* 22.1048.

35. *TPYL* 1000.4556a.

36. *WX* 25.1198.

37. *WX* 26.1250.

38. *TPYL* 957.4382a.

Selected Bibliography

PREMODERN CHINESE SOURCES

Ban Gu 班固 (32–92), comp. *Han shu* 漢書. Beijing: Zhonghua Shuju, 1962.

Cao Xu 曹旭, ed. and comm. *Shi pin jizhu* 詩品集注. Shanghai: Shanghai Guji Chubanshe, 1994.

Chen Shou 陳壽 (233–297), comp. *Sanguo zhi* 三國志. Beijing: Zhonghua Shuju, 1962.

Chunqiu Zuozhuan zhengyi 春秋左傳正義. In *Shisanjing zhushu*.

Daoxuan 道宣 (596–667). *Guang hongming ji* 廣弘明集. *T* 52, no. 2103.

———. *Xu gaoseng zhuan* 續高僧傳. *T* 50, no. 2060.

Duan Yucai 段玉裁 (1735–1815). *Shuowen jiezi zhu* 說文解字注. Shanghai: Shanghai Guji Chubanshe, 1981.

Fan Ye 范曄 (398–445), comp. *Hou Han shu* 後漢書. Beijing: Zhonghua Shuju, 1965.

Fang Xuanling 房玄齡 (579–648) et al., comps. *Jin shu* 晉書. Beijing: Zhonghua Shuju, 1965.

Ge Hong 葛洪 (283–343). *Baopuzi* 抱朴子. In *SBCK*.

———. *Baopuzi neipian jiaoshi* 抱朴子內篇校釋. Annotated by Wang Ming 王明. Beijing: Zhonghua Shuju, 1991.

———. *Baopuzi waipian jiaojian* 抱朴子外篇校箋. Annotated by Yang Mingzhao 楊明照. Beijing: Zhonghua Shuju, 1991.

———. *Shenxian zhuan jiaoshi* 神仙傳校釋. Annotated by Hu Shouwei 胡守為. Beijing: Zhonghua Shuju, 2010.

Guo Qingfan 郭慶藩 (1844–1896), comp. *Zhuangzi jishi* 莊子集釋. Beijing: Zhonghua Shuju, 1961.

Han Ying 韓嬰 (fl. 200–130 BCE). *Han shi waizhuan ji shi* 韓詩外傳集釋. Annotated by Xu Weiyu 許維遹. Beijing: Zhonghua Shuju, 1980.

Hong Xingzu 洪興祖 (1090–1155), comp. *Chu ci buzhu* 楚辭補註. Beijing: Zhonghua Shuju, 1983.

Huainanzi 淮南子 (2nd cent. BCE). *Xinbian zhuzi jicheng* 新編諸子集成. Beijing: Zhonghua Shuju, 1989.

Huijiao 慧皎 (497–554). *Gaoseng zhuan* 高僧傳. *T* 50, no. 2059.

Li Dingzuo 李鼎祚 (fl. 750s), comp. *Zhou yi jijie* 周易集解. Beijing: Zhonghua Shuju, 2016.

Li Fang 李昉 (925–996) et al., comps. *Taiping yulan* 太平御覽. Beijing: Zhonghua Shuju, 1960.

Li Yanshou 李延壽 (fl. 650s), comp. *Nan shi* 南史. Beijing: Zhonghua Shuju, 1975.

Liji zhengyi 禮記正義. In *Shisanjing zhushu*.

Liu Yiqing 劉義慶 (403–444). *Shishuo xinyu jianshu* 世說新語箋疏. Annotated by Yu Jiaxi 余嘉錫. Shanghai: Shanghai Guji Chubanshe, 1993.

Lunyu zhushu 論語注疏. In *Shisanjing zhushu*.

Ma Ruichen 馬瑞辰 (1782–1853), comp. *Mao shi zhuan jian tongshi* 毛詩傳箋通釋. Beijing: Zhonghua Shuju, 1989.

Mao shi zhushu 毛詩註疏. In *Shisanjing zhushu*.

Mengzi zhushu 孟子注疏. In *Shisanjing zhushu*.

Ouyang Xun 歐陽詢 (557–641) et al., comps. *Yiwen leiju* 藝文類聚. Beijing: Zhonghua Shuju, 1965.

Quan Sanguo wen 全三國文. See Yan Kejun.

Quan Tang shi 全唐詩. Beijing: Zhonghua Shuju, 1960.

Shangshu zhengyi 尚書正義. In *Shisanjing zhushu*.

Shen Yue 沈約 (441–513), comp. *Song shu* 宋書. Beijing: Zhonghua Shuju, 1974.

Shi Daoshi 釋道世 (fl. 7th cent.), Zhou Shujia 周叔迦, and Su Jinren 蘇晉仁, comps. *Fayuan zhulin jiaozhu* 法苑珠林校注. Beijing: Zhonghua Shuju, 2003.

Shisanjing zhushu 十三經註疏. Beijing: Zhonghua Shuju, 1980. Photomechanically reduced reproduction of a woodblock edition by Ruan Yuan 阮元 (1764–1849).

Sibu beiyao 四部備要. 2,500 vols. Shanghai: Zhonghua Shuju, 1920–36.

Sibu congkan chubian 四部叢刊初編. 2,100 vols. Shanghai: Shangwu Yinshuguan, 1919–22.

Sima Guang 司馬光 (1019–1086). *Zizhi tongjian* 資治通鑑. Beijing: Zhonghua Shuju, 1956.

Sima Qian 司馬遷 (145–86 BCE), comp. *Shiji* 史記. Beijing: Zhonghua Shuju, 1959.

Taishō shinshū daizōkyō 大正新修大藏經. Edited by Takakusu Junjirō 高楠順次郎 and Watanabe Kaigyoku 渡邊海旭. Tokyo: Taishō Issaikyō Kankōkai, 1924–32.

Wei Shou 魏收 (507–572), comp. *Wei shu* 魏書. Beijing: Zhonghua Shuju, 1974.

Xia Chuancai 夏傳才, comp. *Cao Cao ji zhu* 曹操集注. Zhengzhou: Zhongzhou Guji, 1986.

Xiao Tong 蕭統 (501–531), comp. *Liuchen zhu Wen xuan* 六臣注文選. Beijing: Zhonghua Shuju, 1987.

———. *Wen xuan* 文選. Shanghai: Shanghai Guji Chubanshe, 1986.

Xie Lingyun 謝靈運. *Sha Kōraku bunshū* 謝康樂文集. Annotated by Morino Shigeo 森野繁夫. Tokyo: Hakuteisha 白帝社, 2003.

———. *Sha Kōraku shishū* 謝康樂詩集. Annotated by Morino Shigeo. 2 vols. Tokyo: Hakuteisha, 1993–94.

———. *Xie Kangle shi zhu* 謝康樂詩注. Annotated by Huang Jie 黃節. Beijing: 1925.

———. *Xie Lingyun ji* 謝靈運集. Annotated by Li Yunfu 李運富. Changsha: Yuelu Shushe, 1999.

———. *Xie Lingyun shixuan* 謝靈運詩選. Annotated by Ye Xiaoxue 葉笑雪. Shanghai: Gudian Wenxue Chubanshe, 1957.

Xu Jian 徐堅 (659–729) et al., comps. *Chuxue ji* 初學記. Beijing: Zhonghua Shuju, 1962.

Xu Shen 許慎 (58–148). *Shuowen jiezi* 說文解字. Beijing: Zhonghua Shuju, 1963.

Yan Kejun 嚴可均 (1762–1843), comp. *Quan shanggu Sandai Qin Han Sanguo Liuchao wen* 全上古三代秦漢三國六朝文. Beijing: Zhonghua Shuju, 1991.

Yue Shi 樂史 (930–1007) et al., comps. *Taiping huanyu ji* 太平寰宇記. Beijing: Zhonghua Shuju, 2007.

Zhong Rong 鍾嶸 (468–518). *Shi pin jizhu* 詩品集注. Annotated by Cao Xu 曹旭. Shanghai: Shanghai Guji Chubanshe, 1994.

Zhou li zhushu 周禮註疏. In *Shisanjing zhushu*. Annotated by Zheng Xuan 鄭玄 (127–200); commentary by Jia Gongyan 賈公彥 (fl. 650s).

Zhu Jian 朱珔 (1769–1850), comp. *Wen xuan jishi* 文選集釋, 1836; rpt. in *Xuan xue congshu* 選學叢書. Taipei: Guangwen Shuju, 1966.

Zhu Xi 朱熹 (1130–1200). *Shiji zhuan* 詩集傳. In *SBCK*.

MODERN SOURCES

Ami Yūji 綱祐次. *Chūgoku chūsei bungaku kenkyū* 中國中世文學研究. Tokyo: Shinjusha, 1960.

Ashmore, Robert. *The Transport of Reading: Text and Understanding in the World of Tao Qian*. Cambridge, MA: Harvard University Press, 2010.

Bate, Jonathan. *The Song of the Earth*. Cambridge, MA: Harvard University Press, 2000.

Berkowitz, Alan. "Courting Disengagement: 'Beckoning the Recluse' Poems of the Western Jin." In *Studies in Early Medieval Chinese Literature and Cultural History*, edited by Paul W. Kroll and David R. Knechtges, 88–96. Provo, UT: The T'ang Studies Society, 2003.

———. *Patterns of Disengagement: The Practice and Portrayal of Reclusion in Early Medieval China*. Stanford: Stanford University Press, 2000.

Cai Zhongxiang 蔡鍾翔. "'Dian lun Lun wen' yu wenxue de zijue" 《典論·論文》 與文學的自覺. *Wenxue pinglun*, no. 5 (1983): 19–25, 56.

Cai, Zong-Qi. *Chinese Aesthetics: The Ordering of Literature, the Arts, and the Universe in the Six Dynasties*. Honolulu: University of Hawai'i Press, 2004.

———. *The Matrix of Lyric Transformation: Poetic Modes and Self-Presentation in Early Chinese Pentasyllabic Poetry*. Ann Arbor: University of Michigan, 1996.

Campany, Robert Ford. *Making Transcendents: Ascetics and Social Memoriy in Early Medieval China.* Honolulu: University of Hawai'i Press, 2009.

———. *To Live as Long as Heaven and Earth: A Translation and Study of Ge Hong's Traditions of Divine Transcendents.* Berkeley: University of California Press, 2002.

Cao Daoheng 曹道衡. *Nanbeichao wenxue biannian shi* 南北朝文學編年史. Beijing: Renmin Wenxue Chubanshe, 2000.

———. *Zhonggu wenxue shi lunwen ji* 中古文學史論文集. Beijing: Zhonghua Shuju, 1986.

Cao Xu 曹旭, comp. *Shi pin jizhu* 詩品集註. Shanghai: Shanghai Guji Chubanshe, 1994.

Chan, Alan K. L., and Yuet-keung Lo, eds. *Interpretation and Literature in Early Medieval China.* Albany: State University of New York Press, 2010.

———. *Philosophy and Religion in Early Medieval China.* Albany, NY: State University of New York Press, 2010.

Chan, Timothy Wai Keung. *Considering the End: Mortality in Early Medieval Chinese Poetic Representation.* Leiden: Brill, 2012.

———. "Ruan Ji's and Xi Kang's Visits to Two 'Immortals.'" *MS* 44 (1996): 141–65.

Chang, Kang-i Sun 孫康宜. *Six Dynasties Poetry.* Princeton: Princeton University Press, 1986.

Chen Changming 陳昌明. *Chenmi yu chaoyue: Liuchao wenxue zhi ganguan bianzheng* 沈迷與超越 – 六朝文學之感觀辯證. Taipei: Liren Shuju, 2005.

Chen Chuanxi 陳傳習. *Zhongguo shanshui hua shi* 中國山水畫史. Nanjing: Jiangsu Meishu Chubanshe, 1988.

Chen, Jack. *Anecdote, Network, Gossip, Performance. Essays on the Shishuo Xinyu.* Cambridge, MA: Harvard University Asia Center, 2021.

Chen Jinfeng 陳金鳳. *Wei Jin Nanbeichao zhongjian didai yanjiu* 魏晉南北朝中間地帶研究. Tianjin: Tianjin Guji, 2005.

Chen Meizu 陳美足. *Nan chao Yan Xie shi yanjiu* 南朝顏謝詩研究. Taipei: Wenshizhe Chubanshe, 1989.

Chen Yinke 陳寅恪. "Tianshi dao yu Binhai diyu zhi guanxi" 天師道與濱海地域之關係. *Bulletin of the National Research Institute of History and Philology* 3, no. 4 (1933): 439–66.

Chen Zhongfan 陳鍾凡. *Han Wei Liuchao wenxue* 漢魏六朝文學. 1935; rpt. Shanghai: Shangwu Yinshuguan, 1964; Taipei: Shangwu Yinshuguan, 1967.

Cheng Shude 程樹德 et al., comps. *Lun yu jishi* 論語集釋. Beijing: Zhonghua Shuju, 1990.

Cheng, Yu-yu 鄭毓瑜. "Bodily Movement and Geographic Categories: Xie Lingyun's 'Rhapsody on Mountain Dwelling' and the Jin-Song Discourse on Mountains and Rivers." *American Journal of Semiotics* 23, nos. 1–4 (2007): 193–219, 376–77.

———. "Guifan de huiyin: Han Jin xinglü fu de dili lunshu" 歸反的回音：漢晉行旅賦的地理論述. In *Shibian yu chuanghua: Han Tang, Tang Song zhuanhuan qi zhi wenyi xianxiang* 世變與創化： 漢唐、唐宋轉換期之文藝現象, edited by Yi Ruofen 衣若芬 and Liu Yuanru 劉苑如, 135–92. Taipei: Zhongyang Yanjiuyuan, 2000.

———. "Shenti xingdong yu dili zhonglei: Xie Lingyun shanjufu yu Jin Song shiqi shanchuan shanshui lunshu" 身體行動與地理種類：謝靈運山居賦與晉宋時期山川山水論述. In *Youguan: Zuowei shenti jiyide zhonggu wenxue yu zong-jiao* 遊觀：作為身體技藝的中古文學與宗教, edited by Liu Yuanru 劉苑如, 64–99. Taipei: Zhongyanyuan Wenzhesuo, 2009.

Cheng Zhangcan 程章粲. *Shizu yu Liuchao wenxue* 世族與六朝文學. Harbin: Heilongjiang Jiaoyu Chubanshe, 1998.

———. *Wei Jin Nanbeichao fu shi* 魏晉南北朝賦史. Nanjing: Jiangsu Guji Chubanshe, 1992.

Chennault, Cynthia. "Lofty Gates or Solitary Impoverishment? Xie Family Members of the Southern Dynasties," *TP* 85 (1999): 249–327.

Cutter, Robert Joe. "Cao Zhi's (192–232) Symposium Poems." *CLEAR* 6, nos. 1 & 2 (1984): 1–32.

De Crespigny, Rafe. *Imperial Warlord: A Biography of Cao Cao 155–220 AD*. Leiden: Brill, 2010.

Declercq, Dominik. *Writing Against the State: Political Rhetorics in Third and Fourth Century China*. Leiden: Brill, 1998.

Denecke, Wiebke, Wai-yee Li, and Xiaofei Tian, eds. *The Oxford Handbook of Classical Chinese Literature (1000 BCE–900 CE)*. New York, NY: Oxford University Press, 2017.

Deng Shiliang 鄧仕良. *Liang Jin shi lun* 兩晉詩論. Hong Kong: Zhongwen Daxue, 1972.

Derrida, Jacques, and Avital Ronell. "The Law of Genre." *Critical Inquiry* 7, no. 1 (1980): 55–81.

Diény, Jean-Pierre. *Portrait anecdotique d'un gentilhomme chinois: Xie An (320–385) d'après le Shishuo xinyu*. Paris: Collège de France, Institut des Hautes Études Chinoises, 1993.

Ding Chengquan 丁成泉. *Zhongguo shanshui shi shi* 中国山水诗史. Wuchang: Huazhong Shifan Daxue Chubanshe, 1990.

Ding Fulin 丁福林. *Dong Jin Nanchao Xie shi wenxue jituan yanjiu* 東晉南朝謝氏文學研究. Xi'an: Shijie Tushu Chuban Xi'an Youxian Gongsi, 2014.

———. "Xie Hun he tade shanshui shi" 謝混和他的山水詩. *Gudian wenxue zhishi*, no. 4 (2004): 63–69.

Du Xiaoqin 杜曉勤. *Qi Liang shige xiang sheng Tang shige de shanbian* 齊梁詩歌嚮盛唐詩歌的嬗變. Taipei: Shangding Wenhua Chubanshe, 1996.

Elvin, Mark. *The Retreat of the Elephants: An Environmental History of China*. New Haven: Yale University Press, 2004.

Fang Zushen 方祖燊. *Han shi yanjiu* 漢詩研究. Taipei: Zhengzhong Shuju, 1967.

———. *Wei Jin shi dai shi ren yu shi ge* 魏晉時代詩人與詩歌. Taipei: Lantai Shuju, 1973.

Field, Stephen. "Hexagram Landscapes in Six Dynasties Poetry." *Tamkang Review* 28, no. 4 (1998): 118–41.

Frodsham, J. D. "Hsieh Ling-yun's Contribution to Medieval Chinese Buddhism." *International Association of Historians of Asia Conference Proceedings* 2 (Taipei, 1962): 27–55.

———. *The Murmuring Stream: The Life and Works of the Chinese Nature Poet Hsieh Ling-yün (385–433), Duke of K'ang-Lo*. 2 vols. Kuala Lumpur: University of Malaya Press, 1967.

———. "The Origins of Chinese Nature Poetry." *AM* 7, no. 1 (1960): 68–104.

Fu Gang 傅剛. *Wei Jin Nanbeichao shige shi lun*. 魏晉南北朝詩歌史論. Changchun: Jilin Jiaoyu Chubanshe, 1995.

Funazu (Funatsu) Tomihiko 船津富彥. *Sha Reiun* 謝靈運. Tokyo: Shūeisha, 1983.

Gao Huaping 高華平. "Xie Lingyun Fojiao zhushu yanjiu" 謝靈運佛教著述研究. *Zhongguo wenhua yanjiu* 中國文化研究 4 (2006): 156–65.

Gao Jianjun 高建軍. "Qianxi Xie Lingyun de 'kuang'ao'" 淺析謝靈運的 "狂傲". *Gudian wenxue zhishi* 古典文學知識 1 (2007): 42–47.

Gao Jing 高靜. "Qing xin ji shanshui, ri mu si Nanrong: Du Xie Hun 'You Xichi'" 情新寄山水, 日暮思南榮：讀謝混 《游西池》. *Gudian wenxue zhishi*, no. 1 (2010): 22–25.

Ge Xiaoyin 葛曉音. *Badai shi shi* 八代詩史. Xi'an: Shaanxi Renmin Chubanshe, 1989.

———. "Lun Nanbeichao Sui Tang wenren dui Jian'an qianhou wenfeng jianbian de butong pingjia" 論南北朝隋唐文人對建安前後文風演變的不同評價. *Wen xue pinglun congkan* 30 (1988): 1–19.

———. *Shanshui tianyuan shipai yanjiu* 山水田園詩派研究. Shenyang: Liaoning Daxue Chubanshe, 1993.

———. *Xian Qin Han Wei Liuchao shige tishi yanjiu* 先秦漢魏六朝詩歌體式研究. Beijing: Beijing Daxue Chubanshe, 2012.

———. *Xie Lingyun yanjiu lunji* 謝靈運研究論集. Guilin: Guangxi Shifan Daxue Chubanshe, 2001.

Goh, Meow Hui. *Sound and Sight: Poetry and Courtier Culture in the Yongming Era (483–493)*. Stanford: Stanford University Press, 2010.

Graham, A. C. *Disputers of the Tao: Philosophical Argument in Ancient China*. La Salle, IL: Open Court, 1989.

————. "The Right to Selfishness: Yangism, Late Mohism, Chuang Tzu." In *Individual-ism and Holism: Studies in Confucian and Taoist Values*, edited by Donald J. Munro, 73–84. Ann Arbor: Center for Chinese Studies, University of Michigan, 1984.

Gu Nong 顧農. "Guizu shiren Xie Lingyun de jieju" 貴族詩人謝靈運的結局. *Wenshi zhishi* 文史知識 5 (2003): 60–65.

————. "Xie Lingyun *Lu ling wang mu xia zuo* jiedu" 謝靈運《廬陵王墓下作》解讀. *Gudian wenxue zhishi* 古典文學知識 2 (2006): 12–16.

Gu Shaobo 顧紹柏, ed. and commentator. *Xie Lingyun ji jiaozhu* 謝靈運集校注. Zhengzhou: Zhongzhou Guji Chubanshe, 1987.

————. *Xie Lingyun ji jiaozhu* 謝靈運集校注. Taipei: Liren, 2004.

Gu Yanwu 顧炎武 (1613–1682). *Ri zhi lu jiaozhu* 日知錄校注. Edited by Chen Yuan 陳垣 (1880–1971). Hefei: Anhui Daxue Chubanshe, 2007.

Guo Li 郭麗. "Wei Jin Nan Bei chao shiqi wenxue jiazu de xingsheng ji shige chuang-zuo tedian: Yi Chen jun Xie shi jiazu wei zhongxin" 魏晉南北朝時期文學家族的興盛及詩歌創作特點：以陳郡謝氏家族為中心. *Zhongguo yunwen xuekan* 中國韵文學刊 25, no. 2 (2011): 13–21.

Guo Shaoyu 郭紹虞. *Canglang shihua jiaoshi* 滄浪詩話校釋. Taipei: Liren Shuju, 1983.

Han Geping 韓格平. *Jian'an qizi zonglun* 建安七子綜論. Changchun: Dongbei Shifan Daxue Chubanshe, 1998.

Hawkes, David. *The Songs of the South: An Anthology of Ancient Chinese Poems by Qu Yuan and Other Poets*. Harmondsworth, UK: Penguin, 1985.

He Chengbang (Ho Shing-bon) 何成邦. *Lu Ji shige de yuyan fengge yanjiu* 陸機詩歌的語言風格研究. Hong Kong: Hong Kong University Press, 2012.

He Qimin 何啓民. *Wei Jin sixiang yu tanfeng* 魏晉思想與談風. Taipei: Shangwu Yinshuguan, 1967.

Hightower, James Robert. *Han shih wai chuan: Han Ying's Illustrations of the Didactic Application of the* Classic of Songs. Cambridge, MA.: Harvard University Press, 1952.

Holcombe, Charles. *In the Shadow of the Han: Literati Thought and Society at the Be-ginning of the Southern Dynasties*. Honolulu: University of Hawai'i Press, 1994.

Holzman, Donald. *Chinese Literature in Transition from Antiquity to the Middle Ages*. Variorum Collected Studies Series. Aldershot, UK: Ashgate, 1998.

Hong Shunlong 洪順隆. *Liuchao shi lun* 六朝詩論. Taipei: Wenjin Chubanshe, 1978.

————. *You yinyi dao gongti* 由隱逸到宮體. Taipei: Wenshizhe Chubanshe, 1984.

Hsu Cho-yun 許倬雲. *Ancient China in Transition: An Analysis of Social Mobility, 722–222 B.C.* Stanford: Stanford University Press, 1965.

Hu A'xiang 胡阿祥. *Liuchao jiangyu yu zhengqu yanjiu* 六朝疆域與政區研究. Beijing: Xueyuan Chubanshe, 2005.

Hu Dalei 胡大雷. "*Bian zong lun* yu Xie Lingyun dui xuanyan shi de gaizhi" 《辨宗論》與謝靈運對玄言詩的改制. *Wenzhou shifan xueyuan xuebao (Zhexue shehui kexue ban)* 溫州師範學院學報 (哲學社會科學版) 25, no. 1 (2004): 34-38.

———. *Wen xuan shi yanjiu* 文選詩研究. Guilin: Guangxi Shifan Daxue Chubanshe, 2000.

———. *Zhonggu wenxue jituan* 中古文學集團. Guilin: Guangxi Shifan Daxue Chubanshe, 1996.

Hu Guorui 胡國瑞. *Wei Jin Nanbeichao wenxue shi* 魏晉南北朝文學史. Shanghai: Wenyi Chubanshe, 1980.

Hu Miao 胡淼. *Shijing de kexue jiedu* 詩經的科學解讀. Shanghai: Shanghai Renmin Chubanshe, 2007.

Huang, Tse-chang Harrison. "Excursion, Estates, and the Kingly Gaze: The Landscape Poetry of Xie Lingyun." PhD diss., University of California, Berkeley, 2010.

Huang Yazhuo 黃亞卓. *Han Wei Liuchao gongyan shi yanjiu* 漢魏六朝公宴詩研究. Shanghai: Huadong Shifan Daxue Chubanshe, 2007.

Huo Guigao 霍貴高 and Jiang Jianyun 姜劍雲. "Xie Lingyun Ruxue renge lunxi" 謝靈運儒學人格論析. *Wuling xuekan* 武陵學刊 36, no. 6 (2011): 1-5.

———. "Xie Lingyun xuanyan fu de dute gexing" 謝靈運玄言賦的獨特個性. *Mingzuo xinshang* 名作欣賞 4 (2010): 113-14.

———. "'Yuanjia zhi xiong' lishi yiyun jiedu: Dui Xie Lingyun lishi diwei de zai renshi" 元嘉之雄" 歷史意蘊解讀：對謝靈運歷史地位的再認識. *Wenzhou daxue xuebao (Shehui kexue ban)* 溫州大學學報 (社會科學版) 21, no. 4 (2008): 38-43.

Huo Jianbo 霍建波. *Song qian yinyi shi yanjiu* 宋前隱逸诗研究. Beijing: Renmin Chubanshe, 2006.

Itō Masafumi 伊藤正文. *Ken'an shijin to sono dentō* 建安詩人とその伝統. Tokyo: Sōbunsha, 2002.

———. "Ryū Tei den ron" 劉楨傳論. In *Yoshikawa hakushi taikyū kinen Chūgoku bungaku ronshū* 吉川博士退休紀念中國文學論集. Tokyo: Chikuma Shobō, 1968. Reprinted in *Ken'an shijin to sono dentō* 建安詩人とその伝統. Tokyo: Sōbunsha, 2002.

Jiang Jianyun 姜劍雲. "Xie Lingyun fanyi *Jingang jing* xiaokao" 謝靈運翻譯 《金剛經》 小考. *Wenxue yichan* 6 (2005): 32.

———. "Xie Lingyun rungai *Huayan jing* de yi ze ziliao" 謝靈運潤改 《華嚴經》 的一則資料. *Wenxian jikan* 文獻季刊 4 (2007): 132.

———. "Xie Lingyun yu 'heiyi zaixiang' Huilin" 謝靈運與 "黑衣宰相" 慧琳. *Zongjiaoxue yanjiu* 宗教學研究 2 (2007): 83-87.

———. "Xie Lingyun yu Huiyan, Huiguan" 謝靈運與慧嚴、慧觀 . *Hebei daxue xuebao (Zhexue shehui kexue ban)* 河北大學學報 (哲學社會科學版) 30, no. 6 (2005): 80-85.

———. "Xie Lingyun yu Huiyuan jiaoyou kaolun" 謝靈運與慧遠交遊考論. *Taiyuan shifan xueyuan xuebao (Shehui kexue ban)* 太原師範學院學報 (社會科學版) 4, no. 2 (2005): 63–73.

———. "Xie Lingyun yu 'niepan sheng' Zhu Daosheng" 謝靈運與 "涅槃聖" 竺道生. *Guangzhou daxue xuebao (Shehui kexue ban)* 廣州大學學報 (社會科學版) 4, no. 9 (2005): 13–18.

———. "Xie Lingyun yu Qiantang duming shi" 謝靈運與錢塘杜明師. *Zhongguo daojiao* 中國道教 3 (2005): 45–47.

———. "Xie Lingyun yu 'toutuo seng' Tanlong jiaoyou kao" 謝靈運與 "頭陀僧" 壜隆交遊考. *Jiangxi shifan daxue xuebao (Zhexue shehui kexue ban)* 江西師範大學學報(哲學社會科學版) 40, no. 1 (2007): 3–6.

Jiang Jianyun and Huo Guigao. "Jin Song 'wenyi' yu Xie shi 'xuanxue weiba' chengyin" 晉宋 "文義" 與謝詩 "玄學尾巴" 成因. *Baoding xueyuan xuebao* 保定學院學報 25, no. 6 (2012): 1–11.

———. "Lun Xie Lingyun de wenxue sixiang" 論謝靈運的文學思想. *Qinzhou xueyuan xuebao* 欽州學院學報 23, no. 2 (2008): 59–63.

———. "Lun Xie Lingyun shi qing, jing, li zhi yuanrong" 論謝靈運詩情、景、理之園融. *Hebei daxue xuebao (Zhexue shehui kexue ban)* 河北大學學報 (哲學社會科學版) 35, no. 1 (2010): 28–32.

Jiang Jianyun and Wang Yanjun 王岩峻. "'Qiaosi' yihuo 'ziran'? Xie Lingyun shanshui shi yishu tezheng bianshuo" "巧似" 抑或 "自然"? 謝靈運山水詩藝術特徵辯說. *Shanxi daxue xuebao (Zhexue shehui kexue ban)* 山西大學學報 (哲學社會科學版) 32, no. 2 (2009): 39–42.

———. "Xie Lingyun dui niepan foxing de renshi yu shiwen chuangzuo" 謝靈運對涅槃佛性的認識與詩文創作. *Zhongguo shige yanjiu dongtai* 中國詩歌研究動態 1 (2008): 66–74.

———. "Xie Lingyun yu *Daban niepan jing* de gai zhi" 謝靈運與《大般涅槃經》的改治. *Jinyang xuekan* 晉陽學刊 4 (2009): 100–103.

Jiang Jianyun and Xu Haiyan 許海岩. "Lun Xie Lingyun dui banruo xingkong de renshi yu shiwen chuangzuo" 論謝靈運對般若性空的認識與詩文創作. *Baoding xueyuan xuebao* 保定學院學報 25, no. 3 (2012): 85–105.

Jiang Jianyun and Zhang Runping 張潤平. "Xie Lingyun shanshui shi Daoxue yiyun jiedu" 謝靈運山水詩道學意蘊解讀. *Mingzuo xinshang* 名作欣賞 4 (2009): 90–93.

Jiang Yin 蔣寅. "Chaoyue zhi chang: Shanshui duiyu Xie Lingyun de yiyi" 超越之場：山水對於謝靈運的意義. *Wenxue pinglun* 文學評論, no. 2 (2010): 90–97.

———. "Qing: Gudian shi meixue de hexin fanchou" 清：古典詩美學的核心範疇. In *Gudian shixue de xiandai quanshi* 古典詩學的現代詮釋, 32–77. Beijing: Zhonghua Shuju, 2023.

Jiao Xun 焦循, comp. *Mengzi zhengyi* 孟子正義. Beijing: Zhonghua Shuju, 1987.

Knechtges, David R. "Culling the Weeds and Selecting Fine Blossoms: The Anthology in Early Medieval China." In *Culture and Power in the Reconstitution of the Chinese Realm, 200-600*, edited by Scott Pearce, Audrey Spiro, and Patricia Buckley Ebrey. Cambridge, MA: Harvard University Asia Center, 2001.

———. "How to View a Mountain in Medieval China." *Hsiang Lectures on Chinese Poetry*. Montreal: Centre for East Asian Research, McGill University, 2012.

———. "Liu Kun, Lu Chen, and Their Writings in the Transition to the Eastern Jin." *CLEAR* 28 (2006): 1-66.

———. *Wen xuan or Selections of Refined Literature*. Vol. 1, *Rhapsodies on Metropolises and Capitals*. Princeton: Princeton University Press, 1982.

———. *Wen xuan or Selections of Refined Literature*. Vol. 2, *Rhapsodies on Sacrifices, Hunting, Travel, Sightseeing, Palaces and Halls, Rivers and Seas*. Princeton: Princeton University Press, 1987.

———. *Wen xuan or Selections of Refined Literature*. Vol. 3, *Rhapsodies on Natural Phenomena, Birds and Animals, Aspirations and Feelings, Literature, Music, and Passions*. Princeton: Princeton University Press, 1996.

———. "Zhongguo gudai de wenren shanyue youguan: Yi Xie Lingyun 'Shan ju fu' wei zhu de taolun" 中國古代的文人山嶽遊觀：以謝靈運「山居賦」為主的討論. In *Youguan: Zuo wei shenti jiyi de zhonggu wenxue yu zongjiao* 遊觀：作為身體技藝的中古文學與宗教, edited by Liu Yuan-ju 劉苑如, 1-63. Taipei: Zhongyang Yanjiuyuan Zhongguo Wenzhe Yanjiu Suo, 2009.

Knechtges, David R., and Taiping Chang, eds. *Ancient and Early Medieval Chinese Literature: A Reference Guide*. Leiden: Brill, 2012-14.

Kroll, Paul W. "Between Something and Nothing." *JAOS* 127 (2007): 403-13.

———. "Lexical Landscapes and Textual Mountains in the High T'ang." *TP* 84 (1998): 62-101.

———. "On 'Far Roaming.'" *JAOS* 116, no. 4 (1996): 653-69.

———. "Portraits of Ts'ao Ts'ao: Literary Studies on the Man and the Myth." PhD diss., University of Michigan, 1976.

Kroll, Paul W., and David R. Knechtges, eds. *Studies in Early Medieval Chinese Literature and Cultural History: In Honor of Richard B. Mather and Donald Holzman*. Provo, UT: T'ang Studies Society, 2003.

Kroll, Paul W., William Hubbard Baxter, William G. Boltz, David R. Knechtges, Y. Edmund Lien, Antje Richter, Matthias L. Richter, and Ding Xiang Warner. *A Student's Dictionary of Classical and Medieval Chinese*. Rev. ed. Boston: Brill, 2017.

Kwong, Charles 鄺龑子. "The Aesthetics of Parallelism in Chinese Poetry: The Case of Xie Lingyun." In *The Yields of Transition: Literature, Art, and Philosophy in Early*

Medieval China, edited by Jana S. Rošker and Nataša Vampelj Suhadolnik, 203–23. Newcastle, UK: Cambridge Scholars Publishers, 2011.

Lai Yanyuan 賴炎元. *Han shi waizhuan jin zhu jin yi* 韓詩外傳今註今譯. Taipei: Taiwan Shangwu Yinshuguan, 1972.

Lakoff, George, and Mark Johnson. *Metaphors We Live By*. Chicago: University of Chicago Press, 1980.

Ledderose, Lothar. "Some Taoist Elements in the Calligraphy of the Six Dynasties." *TP* 70 (1984): 246–78.

Lee, Brigitta. "Commemorating Literary Perfection: Xie Lingyun's 謝靈運 Imitative Remembrances of Ying Yang 應瑒 (d. 217)." *Tang Studies* 26 (2009): 39–63.

Lee Fong-mao 李豐楙. *Liuchao Sui Tang youxianshi lun ji* 六朝隋唐遊仙詩論集. Taipei: Taiwan Xuesheng Shuju, 1996.

——. *You yu you: Lichao Sui Tang youxian shi lunji* 憂與遊：六朝隋唐游仙詩與論集. Taipei: Xuesheng Shuju, 1996.

Li Sennan 李森南. *Shanshui shiren Xie Lingyun* 山水詩人謝靈運. Taipei: Wen Shi Zhe Chubanshe, 1989.

Li Wenchu 李文初. *Zhongguo shanshui shi shi* 中國山水詩史. Guangdong: Gao-deng Jiaoyu Chubanshe, 1991.

Lin Jing 林靜. "Xie Lingyun shanshui shi dui ju yishu tanwei" 謝靈運山水詩對句藝術探微. *Beijing daxue xuebao (Zhexue shehui kexue ban)* 48, no. 1 (2011): 80–86.

Lin Wenyue 林文月. *Chenghui ji* 澄輝集. Taipei: Hongfan Shudian, 1983.

——. *Shanshui yu gudian* 山水與古典. Taipei: Chunwenxue Congshu, 1976.

——. *Xie Lingyun* 謝靈運. Taipei: Heluo Tushu Chubanshe, 1977.

——. *Xie Lingyun ji qi shi* 謝靈運及其詩. Taipei: Taiwan Daxue Wenxue Yuan, 1966.

——. "Xie Lingyun Linzhong shi kaolun" 謝靈運臨終詩考論. In *Zhonggu wenxue luncong*, 223–52.

——. *Zhonggu wenxue luncong* 中古文學論叢. Taipei: Da'an Chubanshe, 1989.

Liu Ming-ch'ang 劉明昌. *Xie Lingyun shanshi yishu mei tanwei* 謝靈運山水藝術美探微. Taipei: Wenjin, 2007.

Liu, Wu-chi, and Irving Yucheng Lo, eds. *Sunflower Splendor: Three Thousand Years of Chinese Poetry*. Bloomington: Indiana University Press, 1975.

Liu Zeming 劉則鳴. "Xie Lingyun 'Ni Yezhong ji bashou' kaolun" 謝靈運《擬鄴中集八首》考論. *Shanghai shifan daxue xuebao (Shehui kexue ban)* 29, no. 1 (2000): 66–73.

Loewe, Michael. *A Biographical Dictionary of the Qin, Former Han and Xin Periods, 221 BC—AD 24*. Leiden: Brill, 2000.

——. *Early Chinese Texts: A Bibliographical Guide*. Berkeley, Calif: Society for the Study of Early China, 1993.

Lu Kanru 陸侃如 and Feng Yuanjun 馮沅君. *Zhongguo shishi* 中國詩史. Jinan: Shandong Daxue, 1996.

Lu Qinli 逯欽立. *Han Wei Liuchao wenxue lunji* 漢魏六朝文學論集. Xi'an: Shaanxi Renmin, 1984.

———. *Xian Qin Han Wei Jin Nanbeichao shi* 先秦漢魏晉南北朝詩. Beijing: Zhonghua Shuju, 1983.

Lu Xun 魯迅. "Wei Jin fengdu ji wenzhang yu yao ji jiu zhi guanxi" 魏晉風度及文章與藥及酒之關係. In *Lu Xun quanji* 魯迅全集, 3:501–19. Beijing: Renmin Wenxue Chubanshe.

Luo Guowei 羅國威. "Xin faxian de Xie Lingyun yiwen ji 'Shu zu de shi' yizhu" 新發現的謝靈運佚文及《述祖德詩》佚注. *Liaoning daxue xuebao*, no. 3 (1996): 84–87.

Lynn, Richard John, trans. *The Classic of Changes: A New Translation of the* I Ching *as Interpreted by Wang Bi*. New York: Columbia University Press, 1994.

———. *The Classic of the Way and Virtue*. New York: Columbia University Press, 1999.

Mather, Richard B. "The Landscape Buddhism of the Fifth-Century Poetry Hsieh Lingyun." *JAS* 18, no. 1 (1958): 67–79.

———. *The Poet Shen Yüeh (441–513): The Reticent Marquis*. Princeton: Princeton University Press, 1988.

———, trans. *Shih-shuo hsin-yü: A New Account of Tales of the World*. 2nd ed. Ann Arbor: Center for Chinese Studies, University of Michigan, 2002.

Mei Chia-ling 梅家玲. "Lun Xie Lingyun 'Ni Wei taizi Yezhong ji shi bashou bing xu' de meixue tezhi jianlun Han Jin shifu zhong de nizuo, daiyan xianxiang ji qi xiangguan wenti" 論謝靈運〈擬魏太子鄴中集詩八首并序〉的美學特質兼論漢晉詩賦中的擬作、代言現象及其相關問題. *Taida Zhongwen xuebao* 7 (1995): 155–215.

Morino Shigeo 森野繁夫. *Rikuchō shi no kenkyū* 六朝詩の研究. Tokyo: Dai'ichi Gakushūsha, 1976.

———. *Sha Reiun ronshū* 謝靈運論集. Tokyo: Hakuteisha, 2007.

———. "Sha Reiun shi chū" 謝靈運詩注. *Chūgoku chūsei bungaku kenkyū* 20 (1991): 112–16.

Nylan, Michael. "Confucian Piety and Individualism in Han China." *JAOS* 116, no. 1 (1996): 1–27.

Obi Kōichi 小尾郊一. *Sha Reiun: Kodoku no sansui shijin* 謝靈運：孤独の山水詩人. Tokyo: Kyūko Shoin 汲古書院, 1983.

———. *Shinjitsu to Kyokō: Rikuchō Bungaku* 真実と虚構：六朝文学. Tokyo: Kyūko Shoin, 1994.

Okamura Shigeru 岡村繁. "Sō Hi no Tenron Ronbun ni tsuite" 曹丕の《典論論文》について. *Shinagaku kenkyū* 24/25 (1960): 75–85.

Owen, Stephen. *An Anthology of Chinese Literature: Beginnings to 1911*. New York: Norton, 1996.

———. "The Librarian in Exile: Xie Lingyun's Bookish Landscapes." *EMC* 10–11, no. 1 (2004): 203–26.

———. *The Making of Early Chinese Classical Poetry*. Cambridge, MA: Harvard University Asia Center, 2006.

———. *The Poetry of the Early T'ang*. New Haven: Yale University Press, 1977.

Owen, Stephen, and Shuen-fu Lin, eds. *The Vitality of the Lyric Voice: 'Shih' Poetry from the Late Han to the T'ang*. Princeton: Princeton University Press, 1986.

Pearce, Scott, Audrey Spiro, and Patricia Ebrey, eds. *Culture and Power in the Reconstitution of the Chinese Realm, 200–600*. Cambridge, MA: Harvard University Asia Center, 2001.

Peterson, Willard. "Making Connections: 'Commentary on the Attached Verbalizations' of the *Book of Change*." *HJAS* 42, no. 1 (1982): 67–112.

Puett, Michael. *The Ambivalence of Creation: Debates Concerning Innovation and Artifice*. Stanford: Stanford University Press, 2001.

Qian Mu 錢穆. *Zhongguo wenhuashi daolun* 中國文化史導論. Beijing: Shangwu Yinshuguan, 1994.

Qian, Nanxiu 錢南秀. *Spirit and Self in Medieval China: The Shih-Shuo Hsin-yü and Its Legacy*. Honolulu: University of Hawai'i Press, 2001.

Qian Zhixi 錢志熙. *Wei Jin Nanbeichao shige shishu* 魏晉南北朝詩歌史述. Beijing: Beijing Daxue Chubanshe, 2005.

———. *Wei Jin shige yishu yuanlun* 魏晉詩歌藝術原論. Beijing: Beida Chubanshe, 1993.

Qian Zhongshu 錢钟書. *Guanzhui bian* 管錐篇. 4 vols. Beijing: Zhonghua Shuju, 1979.

Qu Wanli 屈萬里. *Shijing quanshi* 詩經詮釋. Taipei: Lianjing, 1999.

Read, Bernard E. *Chinese Medicinal Plants from the Pen Ts'ao Kang Mu, AD 1596*. Beiping: French Bookstore, 1936. Rpt. Taipei: Southern Materials Center, 1977.

Rošker, Jana S., and Nataša Vampelj Suhadolnik, eds. *The Yields of Transition*. Newcastle, UK: Cambridge Scholars Publishing, 2011.

Satō Masamitsu 佐藤正光. "Xie Zhan Xie Lingyun de wenxue yu tamen de zhouwei: Dui Pengcheng Xima tai zhi yanyou ji zuopin kaocha" 謝瞻、謝靈運的文學與他們的周圍：對彭城戲馬臺之宴遊及作品考察. In *Wei Jin Nanbeichao wenxue lunji*, edited by Xianggang Zhongwen Daxue Zhongguo Yuyan Wenxue Xi 香港中文大學中國語言文學系, 349–60. Taipei: Wen Shi Zhe Chubanshe, 1994.

Shen Yucheng 沈玉成. "Xie Lingyun de zhengzhi taidu he sixiang xingge" 謝靈運的政治態度和思想性格. *Shehui kexue zhanxian* 2 (1987): 259–70.

Smith, F. Porter. *Chinese Medicinal Herbs*. Edited by Beatrice Bliss. San Francisco: Georgetown Press, 1973.

Spiro, Audrey G. *Contemplating the Ancients: Aesthetic and Social Issues in Early Chinese Portraiture*. Berkeley: University of California Press, 1990.

Sun Changwu 孫昌武. "'Ju zhong you yan' yu 'shiyan'" 「句中有眼」與「詩眼」. In *Youxue jilu: Sun Changwu zi xuan ji* 遊學集錄: 孫昌武自選集, 206–20. Tianjin: Nankai Daxue Chubanshe, 2004.

———. "Zaoqi Zhongguo Fofa yu wenxue li de 'zhenshi' guannian" 早期中國佛法與文學里的「真實」觀念. *Wenxue yichan*, no. 4 (2011): 4–15.

Sun Chong 孫翀. "Xie Lingyun jiju Qiantang Duzhi yu jiazu xinyang de zhongduan" 謝靈運寄居錢塘杜治與家族信仰的中斷. *Shijie zongjiao yanjiu*, no. 2 (2010): 113–19.

Sun Mingjun 孫明君. "Xie Lingyun de zhuangyuan shanshui shi" 謝靈運的莊園山水詩. *Beijing daxue xuebao (Zhexue shehui kexue ban)* 43, no. 4 (2006): 68–74.

———. "Xie Lingyun 'Ni Wei taizi Yezhong ji shi bashou' zhong de Yexia zhi you" 謝靈運《擬魏太子鄴中集詩八首》中的鄴下之遊. *Shaanxi shifan daxue xuebao (Zhexue shehui kexue ban)* 35, no. 1 (2006): 24–28.

———. "Xie Lingyun 'Ni Wei taizi Yezhong shi bashou' erti" 謝靈運《擬魏太子鄴中詩八首》二題. *Wenxue yanjiu* 105 (2008): 83–97.

———. "Zhuang Lao gaotui, shanshui fang zi: Dong Jin shizu wenxue de tezheng ji qi liubian" 莊老告退 山水方滋：東晉士族文學的特徵及其流辨. *Beijing daxue xuebao (Zhexue shehui kexue ban)* 46, no. 5 (2009): 55–62.

Sun Shangyong 孫尚勇. "Xie Lingyun 'Shu zu de shi ershou' de chuangzuo zongzhi he niandai" 謝靈運《述祖德詩二首》的創作宗旨和年代. *Du Fu yanjiu xuekan* 139, no. 1 (2019): 103–10.

Swartz, Wendy. "Naturalness in Xie Lingyun's Poetic Works." *HJAS* 70, no. 2 (2010): 355–86.

———. *Reading Philosophy, Writing Poetry: Intertextual Modes of Making Meaning in Early Medieval China*. Cambridge, MA: Harvard University Asia Center, 2018.

———. *Reading Tao Yuanming: Shifting Paradigms of Reception History (427–1900)*. Cambridge, MA: Harvard University Asia Center, 2008.

———. "There's No Place Like Home: Xie Lingyun's Representation of His Estate in 'Rhapsody on Dwelling in the Mountains.'" *EMC* 21 (2015): 21–37.

Swartz, Wendy, and Robert Ford Campany, eds. *Memory in Medieval China: Text, Ritual, and Community*. Leiden: Brill, 2018.

Swartz, Wendy, Robert Ford Campany, Yang Lu, and Jessey J. C. Choo, eds. *Early Medieval China: A Sourcebook*. New York: Columbia University Press, 2014.

Tang Yongtong 湯用彤. *Han Wei Liang Jin Nanbeichao fojiao shi* 漢魏兩晉南北朝佛教史. Beijing: Zhonghua Shuju, 1955.

———. *Wei Jin xuanxue lungao* 魏晉玄學論稿. Shanghai: Shanghai Guji Chubanshe, 2001.

Tang Zhangru 唐長孺. "Jiupin zhongzheng zhidu shishi" 九品中正制度試釋. In *Tang Zhangru wencun*, 92–132.

———. "Shizu de xingcheng he shengjiang" 士族的形成和升降. In *Wei Jin Nanbeichao shi lun shiyi*, 53–63.

———. *Tang Zhangru wencun* 唐長孺文存. Shanghai: Shanghai Guji Chubanshe, 2006.

———. *Wei Jin Nanbeichao shi lun shiyi* 魏晉南北朝史論拾遺. Beijing: Zhonghua Shuju, 1983.

———. *Wei Jin Nanbeichao Sui Tang shi luncong* 魏晉南北朝史論叢. Beijing: Sanlian, 1955.

———. *Wei Jin Nanbeichao Sui Tang shi luncong xubian* 魏晉南北朝史論叢續編. Beijing: Sanlian, 1959.

———. *Wei Jin Nanbeichao Sui Tang shi sanlun* 魏晉南北朝隋唐史三論. Wuhan: Wuhan Daxue Chubanshe, 1993.

Tian, Xiaofei. *Tao Yuanming and Manuscript Culture: The Record of a Dusty Table.* Seattle: University of Washington Press, 2004.

———. *Visionary Journeys: Travel Writings from Early Medieval and Nineteenth-Century China.* Cambridge, MA: Harvard University Asia Center, 2011.

Tian Yuqing 田餘慶. *Dong Jin menfa zhengzhi* 東晉門閥政治. Beijing: Beijing Daxue Chubanshe, 2012.

Wagner, Rudolf G. *Language, Ontology, and Political Philosophy in China: Wang Bi's Scholarly Exploration of the Dark (Xuanxue).* Albany: State University of New York Press, 2003.

Wang, Eugene. "The Shadow Image in the Cave: Discourse on Icons." In *Early Medieval China: A Sourcebook*, edited by Wendy Swartz et al., 405–27. New York: Columbia University Press, 2014.

Wang Kuo-ying 王國瓔. *Zhongguo shanshui shi yanjiu* 中國山水詩研究. Taipei: Lianjing Chuban, 1986.

Wang Lijian 王力堅. *You shanshui dao gongti: Nanchao de weimei shifeng* 由山水到宮體：南朝的唯美詩風. Taipei: Taiwan Shangwu Yinshuguan, 1997.

Wang Mei 王玫. *Jian'an wenxue jieshou shi lun* 建安文學接受史論. Shanghai: Shanghai Guji Chubanshe, 2005.

———. *Liuchao shanshui shi shi* 六朝山水詩史. Tianjin: Tianjin Renmin, 1996.

Wang, Ping. *The Age of Courtly Writing: Wen xuan Compiler Xiao Tong (501–31) and His Circle.* Leiden: Brill, 2012.

———. "Contemplating 'Return' (*gui* 歸): Xie Lingyun's 謝靈運 (385–433) 'Hillside Garden' (*qiuyuan* 丘園)." *Journal of Chinese Humanities* 7 (2021): 286–309.

————. "Fengliu yiwu Xie Kangle: Shanshui, shanju, dili shuxie yihuo zhengzhi biaoshu" 风流遗物谢康乐—山水、山居、地理书写抑或政治表述. In *Zhonggu wenxue Zhong de shi yu shi* 中古文学中的诗与史 [History and poetry in early medieval Chinese studies], 189–207. Shanghai: Fudan Daxue Chubanshe, 2020.

————. "Jiazu, ziwuo, yu daren lixiang: Xie Lingyun 'Shu zude shi' beijing jiedu" 家族、自我、與達人理想: 謝靈運之《述祖德詩》背景解讀. In *Haiwai Hanxue yanjiu yicong* 海外漢學研究譯叢 [Translations of overseas sinological studies], 29–44. Nanjing: Fenghuang Chubanshe, 2020.

————. "Making Friends with the Men of the Past (*shangyou*): Literati Identity and Literary Remembering in Early Medieval China." In *Memory in Medieval China: Text, Ritual, and Community*, edited by Wendy Swartz and Robert Ford Campany, 82–123. Brill: Leiden, 2018.

————. "Plaint, Lyricism, and the South." In *Southern Identity and Southern Estrangement in Medieval Chinese Poetry*, edited by Ping Wang and Nicholas Morrow Williams, 79–107. Hong Kong: Hong Kong University Press, 2015.

Wang Shumin 王叔岷, comp. *Lie xian zhuan jian zhu* 列仙傳箋注. Beijing: Zhonghua Shuju, 2007.

Wang Yongping 王永平. *Dong Jin Nanchao jiazu wenhua shi luncong* 東晉南朝家族文化史論叢. Yangzhou: Guangling Shushe, 2010.

Wang Zhongling 王鍾陵. *Zhongguo zhonggu shige shi* 中國中古詩歌史. Nanjing: Jiangsu Jiaoyu Chubanshe, 1988.

Wang Zhongluo 王仲犖. *Wei Jin Nanbeichao shi* 魏晉南北朝史. 2 vols. Shanghai: Renmin Chubanshe, 1980.

Wei Jin Nanbeichao wenxue lunji 魏晉南北朝文學論集. Xianggang Zhongwen Daxue Zhongguo Yuyan Wenxue Xi 香港中文大學中國語言文學系, ed. Taipei: Wen Shi Zhe Chubanshe, 1994.

Wells, Matthew V. "From Spirited Youth to Loyal Official: Life Writing and Didacticism in the *Jin Shu* Biography of Wang Dao." *EMC* 21 (2015): 3–20.

Westbrook, Francis A. "Landscape Description in the Lyric Poetry and 'Fu on Dwelling in the Mountains' of Shieh Ling-yunn." Phd diss., Yale University, 1973.

————. "Landscape Transformation in the Poetry of Hsieh Ling-yün." *JAOS* 100, no. 3 (1980): 237–54.

Wilhelm, Hellmut. "The Scholar's Frustration: Notes on a Type of Fu." In *Chinese Thought and Institutions*, edited by John K. Fairbank, 310–19, 398–403. Chicago: Chicago University Press, 1973.

Wilhelm, Richard. *The I Ching or Book of Changes*. Translated by Cary F. Baynes. Princeton: Princeton University Press, 1969.

Williams, Nicholas Morrow. "The Brocade of Words: Imitation Poetry and Poetics in the Six Dynasties." PhD diss., University of Washington, 2010.

———. "A Conversation in Poems: Xie Lingyun, Xie Huilian, and Jiang Yan." *JAOS* 127, no. 4 (2007): 491–506.

———. "The Metaphysical Lyric of the Six Dynasties." *TP* 98, nos. 1–3 (2012): 65–112.

Wimsatt, W. K., and M. C. Beardsley. "Intentional Fallacy." *Sewanee Review* 54, no. 3 (1946): 468–88.

Wu Guanwen 吳冠文 and Chen Wenbin 陳文彬. *Miaotang yu shanlin zhijian: Xie Lingyun de xinlu lichen yu shige chuangzuo* 廟堂與山林之間：謝靈運的心路歷程與詩歌創作. Shanghai: Fudan Daxue Chubanshe, 2013.

Yang Bojun 楊伯峻 (1909–1992), comp. *Chunqiu Zuozhuan zhu* 春秋左傳注. Beijing: Zhonghua Shuju, 1990.

Yang Rur-Bin 楊儒賓. "Shanshui shi yeshi gongfu lun" 山水詩也是工夫論. *Zhengda zhongwen xuebao* 22 (2014): 3–41.

———. "'Shanshui' shi zenme faxian de: 'Xuan hua shanshui' xilun" 「山水」是怎麼發現的：「玄化山水」析論. *Taida zhongwen xuebao* 30 (2009): 209–54.

Yao Silian 姚思廉 (557–637), comp. *Liang shu* 梁書. Beijing: Zhonghua Shuju, 1973.

Ye Jiaying. *Han Wei Liuchao shi jiang lu* 漢魏六朝詩講錄. Shijiazhuang: Hebei Jiaoyu, 1997.

Yu, Pauline. *The Reading of Imagery in the Chinese Poetic Tradition*. Princeton: Princeton University Press, 1987.

Yu Ying-shih 余英時. "Life and Immortality in the Mind of Han China." *HJAS* 25, no. 1 (1964): 80–122.

———. *Shi yu Zhongguo wenhua* 士與中國文化. Shanghai: Shanghai Renmin Chubanshe, 1987.

Zhang Keli 張可禮. *Jian'an wenxue lungao* 建安文學論稿. Jinan: Shandong Jiaoyu, 1986.

Zhang Yihe 章義和. *Diyu jituan yu Nanchao zhengzhi* 地域集團與南朝政治. Shanghai: Huadong Shifan Daxue, 2002.

Zhang Yinan 張一南. "Xie Lingyun shiwen huayong *I* dian fangshi yanjiu" 謝靈運詩文化用《易》典方式研究. *Yunnan daxue xuebao (Shehui kexue)* 11, no. 2 (2011): 94–101.

Zhao Jianjun 趙建軍. "Jian'an ershier nian de wenyi dui wenxue de yingxiang" 建安二十二年的瘟疫對文學的影響. *Yinshan xuekan* 20, no. 1 (2007): 19–21.

Zheng Wei 鄭偉. "Xie Lingyun *Linzhong shi* yiwen zhuwen bianzheng" 謝靈運《臨終詩》佚文注文辨正. *Tushuguan lilun yu shijian* 圖書館理論與實踐, no. 9 (2011): 47–50.

Zhengtong daozang 正統道藏. Taipei: Xin Wen Feng, 1985.

Zhong Youmin 鍾優民. *Xie Lingyun lungao* 謝靈運論稿. Jinan: Qi Lu Shushe, 1985.

Zhou Xunchu 周勛初. "Lun Xie Lingyun shanshui wenxue de chuangzuo jingyan" 論謝靈運山水文學的創作經驗. *Wenxue yichan*, no. 5 (1989): 46–55.

Zhou Yiliang 周一良. *Wei Jin Nanbeichao shi lunji* 魏晉南北朝史論集. Beijing: Beida Chubanshe, 1997.

Zhu Jian 朱珔, comp. *Wen xuan jishi* 文選集釋. Taipei: Guangwen Shuju, 1966.

Zhu Qianzhi 朱謙之, comp. *Laozi jiaoshi* 老子校釋. Beijing: Zhonghua Shuju, 1984.

Zhu Ziqing 朱自清. *Shi yan zhi bian* 詩言志辨. Taipei: Taiwan Kaiming Shudian, 1964.

Ziporyn, Brook Anthony. *The Penumbra Unbound: The Neo-Taoist Philosophy of Guo Xiang*. Albany: State University of New York Press, 2003.

Zürcher, Erik E. *The Buddhist Conquest of China*. Leiden: Brill, 1972.

Index

aesthetics, 6, 80, 138, 154–55, 158, 165, 225n17, 247n35; *mei* (to entice), 86, 122, 132, 153, 241n97; *qing* (clear) as paradigm, 146–47, 157–61, 164, 174, 247n30; *shen* (divinely inspired) as principle, 71, 138–39

autumn: imagery of, 110, 112; lament of, 129–31, 137; seasonal transitions marked by Fire Star (Antares), 125, 127–28; as season of decline, 129–30; as trope, 128–31; in Xie's poetry, 110, 112, 177–78

Bao Zhao, 13, 78, 244n52; evaluation of Xie Lingyun's poetry, 143

"beauty of mountains and rivers," 67; as manifestation of the Way, 70–71, 77

Biographies of Eminent Monks (Gaoseng zhuan), 165

birds: as images of scholars, 43, 90, 112–13, 144, 158; in mountain poetry, 72, 74, 79, 92, 164; transformation of, in poem, 133, 135, 144, 245n4

Bo Juyi, 186–89; admiration for Xie Lingyun's "spring grass" couplet, 136–37

Buddhabhadra, 166

Buddhism: and Confucianism, 171–72; Daoist influences on, 175; in fifth-century China, 2, 165–75; meditation practice, 166, 173–74; Mount Lu retreat, 165–66; and nature imagery, 167–70; participation in events, 2; retreats built by Xie, 2, 172–75; sudden enlightenment (*dunwu*), 2, 171, 175;

and Xie's death poem, 184–85; Xie's interest in, 172; Xie's fourteen phonetic glossaries for, texts, 165. *See also* Huiyuan

Cao Cao, 31–34, 36, 39, 43–44, 144, 158; military campaigns of, 33–34, 37, 216n46; as regent of Han dynasty, 32–34

Cao family, 32–36, 40, 46–47; literary gatherings at Ye, 32–36, 46–47

Cao Pi, 32–33, 35–36, 38–40, 42, 46–47, 113, 158; letter to Wu Zhi, 42, 96–97; as patron of literary talents, 35–40

Cao Zhi, 28–30, 39, 100, 143, 157–58, 246n24, 248n62; literary excellence, 28–30, 45–47; "roaming immortals" poetry of, 71, 84–86

Chan, Timothy, 183–84

Chen Lin, 34, 38–39, 216n51

cheng (to cleanse, to purify), 120–21, 158

chiasmata (crossovers), 164

Classic of Changes, The, 4, 124; for divination, 115–17, 153; dragon imagery in, 132, 142, 153, 161–63; goose imagery in, 132, 135, 153, 163; "Great Domestication" (Daxu) hexagram, 80; hexagrams, 70, 115–17, 132, 139–41, 153, 163; "Inner Truth" hexagram, 81; "Modesty" (Qian) hexagram, 81; "Release" (Xie) hexagram, 83; "Rising" (Sheng) hexagram, 83

Classic of Poetry, The, 4, 27–30, 43–44, 51–56, 82–83, 110–23, 141, 145, 236n33; "The Fourth Month" poem, 129–30;

Classic of Poetry, The (continued)
imagery from, 48–49, 126–28, 139, 157;
influence on Xie, 124–28, 133–35, 139,
157; seasonal imagery, 125–28; "The
Seventh Month" poem, 125–28
cosmic time, 7, 124; in relation to natural
cycles, 124–29
critical reception of Xie Lingyun: Bao
Zhao's evaluation, 13, 78, 143; Bo
Juyi's assessment, 136–37, 186–89;
comparison with Yan Yanzhi, 143;
contemporary praise, 13, 17; Du
Fu's admiration, 6, 107; Ge Lifang's
commentary, 137; Hu Zi's commentary, 137; Li Bo's influence by, 14, 136;
Liu-Song History assessment, 11–24;
ranking in *Gradation of Poets*, 13, 30,
142–43; scholarly recognition, 5, 13–14,
142; Shen Yue's evaluation, 26–30;
Song dynasty appreciation, 137; Tang
dynasty influence, 13–14, 136–37,
186–89; Wang Hong's correspondence,
171; Xiao Gang's critique, 13; Yan Yu's
criticism, 154; Yuan Haowen's praise
of "spring grass" couplet, 137; Zhong
Rong's praise, 13, 30, 137, 142–43
Dao (the Way), 5, 62; and compliance
with natural order, 60; as manifested
in nature, 55, 62, 70–71
Daoism: and immortality, 68–69, 87,
180–81; influence of, on Buddhist
thought, 175; philosophy, 57–63, 68,
102, 124; and principle of compliance,
60; and Xie's early education under
Du Mingshi, 5, 87; in Xie's education,
2, 5, 87; and Zhuangzi, 57–63
Daoist aesthetics, 69–70, 138–39; influence on landscape poetry, 57–63,
92–93

da-ren (person of penetrating vision),
55–58, 62, 63
dragon: as aesthetic ideal and framework
for poetry, 142, 153; from hexagram
"Qian," 135, 142, 161–63, 242n23,
247n37; and hidden potential, 132,
135, 153, 161–63; imagery in *Classic of
Changes*, 132, 142, 153, 161–63; as metaphor for artistic excellence, 142; as
metaphor for poetic form, 142, 153–54;
in "The Pond," 132, 142, 153, 161–63,
242n25; as symbol of poetic transformation, 142, 153; as unifying literary
symbol, 142
Eastern Jin: aristocracy, 1–4, 11–13, 25–26,
63; culture, 2, 26, 74; displaced elites, 2,
48; *fengliu* (graceful detachment), 58;
literati, 63; nobility, 1, 13, 26; and Xie
clan, 48, 63
Eastern Mountain (Dongshan), 53–54,
209n29; Xie family estate in, 48–49
emotion: catharsis in poetry, 6, 36–37,
79–80; emotional journey in verse,
79–80, 90–91, 140–41; grief, 36–37,
94–97, 177–79; joy in nature, 67, 71,
79–80; lament, 94–97, 112, 128–31,
177–81; longing, 77, 94–97, 101, 177–79;
melancholy, 74, 90, 102, 178–79; nostalgia, 3, 33, 122, 177, 181; sorrow, 23–24,
36–37, 62, 94–97, 177–79; yearning,
36–37, 74, 94–97, 177–79
ethics, 105–6; Confucian and Daoist
approaches, 49–56, 61–63
exploration, 71, 74, 88–89; in *You mingshan zhi* (Roaming Famous Mountains), 67–69
Fan Tai, 17, 172
Faxian, 165–66, 248–49n5
fengliu (graceful detachment), 58

five-syllable line, 6, 144–47, 152–55, 186;
balanced/unbalanced foot, 145–47, 153;
composition of, 145–47; evolution of,
145–52; and intralinear parallelism,
155; pivot verb in, 6, 87, 144–45, 152–54,
163–64, 187; structure of, 145–47, 152;
syntax in, 147–52, 155–56
friendship: brotherhood, 97–101; homosocial relationships, 97–98, 100–101,
158–59; literary, 32–34, 37, 46–47,
93–97, 158–59; literary companionship, 32–34, 46–47, 83, 93–97; male
bonding, 96–97, 159; mutual appreciation, 96–97, 101; poems of, 93–101; and
reciprocity, 33, 96–97; support system,
97–103, 159; in Xie Huilian's poetry,
98–103; in Xie's life, 93–97, 101, 174–75
Frodsham, J. D., 5, 119, 136, 154, 171,
181–82
"*Fu* on Dwelling in the Mountains," 70,
172–74
Gong Sheng, 23, 97
goose imagery, 153, 163; in "The Pond,"
132, 135
Guo Pu, 84–85
Guo Xiang, 138
Han dynasty, 2, 27–28, 57, 62, 66, 134, 137;
end of, and chaos, 31–33
He Changyu, 18–19, 25
hexagrams, 132, 153, 163; in Xie's poetry as
philosophical framework, 70, 115–17,
139–41
hiking, 19–20; in Xie's poetic journeys,
68, 71
"hillside garden" (*qiuyuan*), 109, 117–18,
235n23
Huiyuan, 165–67, 171
Huizhong, Lake, 20
immortality, 69, 87, 180–81

intertextuality, 98, 110, 139, 144, 154; allusions to earlier texts, 82–83, 87, 133–34
Jian'an era, 4, 28, 46–47, 156–59; as literary golden age, 30, 32, 37, 96; literati,
31, 47; Lord's Feast category, 113; poets
of, 30, 32, 44, 46, 143–44; "Seven Masters of Jian'an," 32, 37, 46
Jin-Song transition, 64, 122; and poetry,
26, 30, 97; and political upheaval, 14, 97
journeys of exile, 12–13, 22–24, 132; to
Yongjia and Linchuan, 16–17, 176–82
Kang-i Sun Chang, 154
Knechtges, David R., 221n31, 233n4
Kong Jing: backed Liu Yu with military
and financial support, 109, 117; banquet in honor of, 115–17
Kwong, Charles, 136, 162; studies on parallelism in Xie's poetry, 154–55
landscape poetry, 14, 84; *shanshui* (mountains and rivers) tradition of, 2–3, 71,
76, 77, 187–88; Xie Lingyun as founder
of, 2–3, 5, 87
li (principle), 183–84; natural order, 5,
55–56, 70, 78; universal principle,
70–71, 80, 92
Liu Yizhen, 16–17; and friendship with
Xie Lingyun, 93, 96–97
Liu Yu, 18, 25, 27, 96, 107, 109, 124; as
founding emperor of Liu-Song dynasty, 11–12; military campaigns, 11–12,
15–16, 115; Xie Lingyun's relationship
with, 14–16, 25, 107, 115
loneliness: in poetry, 83, 158; and themes
of isolation, 93–103
Lord's Feast, 113–15
Lu Ji, 52–53, 71, 119, 225n18, 240n81,
240n87; as literary predecessor, 28–29,
146, 159–61
Lu Zhonglian, 54, 74, 88–89

Mahaparinirvana Sutra, 175

Meng Yi, 13; official who quarreled with
Xie Lingyun, 20–21, 24

metaphysical discourse, 78, 80, 86

moral modeling: ancestral exemplars,
48–56, 63, 107; ancient worthies,
54–56, 91, 176–77; exemplary deaths,
182–85; forefathers in poetry, 48–56,
63, 107; and heroes in "Dwelling in the
Mountains," 71; historical precedents,
50–56, 73–74, 89, 98, 182–84; Jian'an
writers as models, 31–47; paradigmatic figures, 41, 43–44, 54, 74, 88–89;
in personal conduct, 49–56, 63; in
political exile, 73–74, 88–89, 176–77;
reclusion, models of, 41, 45, 63–64,
74, 161–62; in "Recounting Ancestral
Virtues," 48–56; spiritual exemplars,
167–71, 173–75; through textual allusions, 50–56, 73–74, 88–89, 98

Mount Lu, 176; Buddhist retreat, 165–66;
Huiyuan's community, 165–66

mountain excursions, 67–73, 81–83,
180–81; documented in *You mingshan
zhi*, 67–69

mountains: Eastern Mountain (Dongshan) estate, 48–49; as home, 70, 77,
105–6; and humanity, 67, 70–71, 75,
91; imagery of, 72–73, 75, 78, 91, 188;
metaphysical significance, 75, 90; and
self-cultivation, 64, 74; and spiritual
freedom, 69–70; and Way (Dao), 64

nature: Buddhist view of, on, 167; civilization and, 70, 159–60; Daoist view
of, 57–60, 69, 72, 158, 161; imagery
of, 67, 77–78, 87, 91–93, 144, 164; law
of, 70–71, 92, 141; in Xie's poetry, 67,
77–78, 144, 152, 187–88

nostalgia, 3, 33, 122, 177, 181

Owen, Stephen, 5, 135, 162–63, 221n31,
241n98, 245n4, 246n10, 248n45

parallelism: balanced/unbalanced foot,
145, 153; inter/intralinear, 155–56; in
Xie's poetry, 154–56, 188

Peihuang, Lake, 20

philosophy: aesthetic theory, 138–39,
154–55; balance in nature, 71, 73, 82;
Buddhist thought, 2, 165–75; complementary principles, 71, 73, 82, 92;
cosmology, 55–56, 123, 124, 139–41;
Daoist aesthetics, 57–63, 69–70,
92–93, 138–39; ethics, 49–56, 61–63,
105–6; metaphysical discourse, 78,
139–41; natural law (*li*), 5, 55–56, 70,
78; principle (*li*), 5, 55–56, 70, 78,
183–84; self-cultivation, 49–56, 64, 74;
syncretism, 171–72, 175; truth and illusion, 61–62, 69, 76; universal principle,
70–71, 80, 92; yin-yang philosophy, 71,
73, 82, 92, 188

pivot verb, 163–64, 187; in pentasyllabic
line, 6, 87, 144–45, 152–54; structural
importance, 144–45, 152–54

pond imagery, 78, 142, 158; in "The Pond"
poem, 133–36

Qu Yuan, 27, 29, 30, 62, 74, 128–29, 177,
178, 223n59, 242n16, 252n44

reclusion, 41, 161–62; as life choice, 63–64,
69–70, 74

ritual, 163, 210n43, 220n24, 232n78; ceremonial aspects of, in poetry, 14, 84, 134

river journeys, 12, 19, 86–92, 94–122

"rivers and oceans" (*jianghai*), 22, 210n42

"roaming immortals" (*youxian*), 72,
84–85, 222n41, 228n3

seasons: in poetry, 60–62, 90, 103, 120,
124–31, 237n47, 245n9, 247n3

self-cultivation, 49–56, 74

"self-valuing" (vs. "self-casting"), 57–58, 117

Shen Yue, 2, 14, 24, 26–30, 51, 80, 142, 211n57; evaluative essay on Xie Lingyun and literary history, 27–29

shi (poetry), 2–3, 5, 30, 32, 139, 154, 187; evolution of, 3, 31–32, 146–52, 186; five-syllable line, 6, 144–47, 152–55, 186; Xie's influence on, 142, 186

sightseeing, 12, 33, 74, 80–83; documented in *You mingshan zhi*, 67–69

Songs of Chu (Chu ci), 4, 73, 74, 76–77, 83, 84, 124, 128–32, 139, 157

spiritual pilgrimage: 84, 87–89, 175; Buddhist elements in Xie's journeys, 87, 175

spring grass imagery, 143–44; in "The Pond," 133, 135–39, 141

Swartz, Wendy, 5, 70, 82, 136, 162–63, 245n4

syncretism: integration of Confucian, Daoist, and Buddhist thought, 171–72, 175

Tao Yuanming, 107, 122, 143, 159, 181, 242n25

Tian, Xiaofei, 142

"time": astronomical markers of, 125, 127–28, 135; cosmic cycles, 124, 153; as dynamic force, 124, 141; in early Chinese poetry, 124–32; as human experience, 124–25, 128–32; literary concepts of, 124–32; natural vs. political, 124–25, 128–32, 177–78; opportune moment (*shi*), 124–25, 130–32; seasonal rhythms, 125–28, 177–78; temporality in lyric poetry, 128–32; in Xie's poetry, 124–25, 132–41, 153

travel and roaming: exploration, 67–69, 71–74, 87–93; geographical interest, 67–69; hiking, 19–20, 68, 71; journeys of exile, 12–13, 16–17, 22–24, 132, 176–82; mountain excursions, 67–73, 81–83, 180–81; physical discomfort during, 89–91; river journeys, 12, 77–83, 88–89, 178–79; roaming immortals (*youxian*), 71–72, 84–87; sightseeing, 12, 74, 80–83; spiritual pilgrimage, 84, 87–89, 175

truth and illusion, 61–62

universal principle (*li*), 70–71

Wang Can, 18, 28–29, 34, 36–37, 143, 215n39, 215n42, 216n46, 243n37; "Seven Sorrows" poems, 29, 37, 215nn39–41

Wang Xizhi, 1

Warring States period, 74, 117, 184; historical context for ancient worthies, 54

water: aesthetic significance of, 77–83, 92–93; as agent of change, 92; cleansing property of, 80, 92; fluidity symbolism, 92–93; imagery in poetry, 78–83, 92–93, 133–35; lakes, 19–20, 78–79, 81–83, 133–41; metaphysical significance, 79–80, 92–93; Numinous Pond, 133–41; philosophical qualities, 79, 92–93; ponds, 78, 133–41, 158; purification function, 80, 92, 158; rivers, 12, 73, 75, 77–78, 88–92; as spiritual metaphor, 92–93, 133–41; and transformation, 73, 92–93; as Way (Dao) metaphor for, 92–93; and yin-yang balance, 71, 73, 92, 188. *See also* landscape poetry: *shanshui* tradition of

Wen xuan, 51–52, 72, 86, 95–97, 102, 110, 113–14, 121, 161, 185, 186; anthology containing poems by Xie Lingyun, 2, 51, 80

Westbrook, Francis, 5, 82–83, 136, 161, 163

wilderness exploration, 67–71, 92–93

wu (things), 132; Daoist concept of the myriad things, 57, 61

Xie An, 63, 89, 107, 209n29, 219n2, 219n4; established Eastern Mountain (Dongshan) estate, 48–49; as Xie Lingyun's great-great-uncle, 25, 48–53

Xie clan: aristocratic status, 11, 13–14, 48–49; cultural contributions, 2, 48–49; Eastern Jin influence, 48, 63; family estates, 12, 16, 19–20, 48, 121–22; heroic deeds of, 49–56; legacy of, 51–53, 63; "lofty way" (*yadao*), 63; military achievements, 11, 48–49, 107; moral exemplars as, 51, 55, 63; political influence, 11, 13, 48–49; scholarly accomplishments, 49, 55, 63; violent deaths among, 211n56; and virtue (*de*), 49–56; withdrawal from politics, 48–49, 63

Xie Huilian, 18–19, 80, 137, 231n48, 231n51, 231n55; death of, 101, 231n61; poetic exchanges with Xie Lingyun, 97–103; as Xie Lingyun's cousin, 18, 97–103

Xie Hun, 11, 24, 28, 30, 34, 80, 156–59, 214n17, 247n25; encouraged Xie Lingyun's poetic development, 28, 80; as Xie Lingyun's uncle, 11, 28, 80

Xie Lingyun: as aristocrat, 1–3; on beauty of mountain, 67–69; Buddhist phonological studies and fourteen phonetic glossaries, 165; as Buddhist scholar, 165–75; characterized as *bianji* (headstrong) and *shehao* (extravagant) in official accounts, 14, 18–19; death of, 182–85; exile of, 12–13, 16–17, 22–23, 132, 176; family background, 11, 14, 48–49; five-syllable line innovation, 145–54, 186; influence on Tang poetry, 13–14, 136, 186–89; literary talent, 1,

17, 142–43; on mountain journeys, 67, 71–106; novel words, use of, 73, 107, 137, 142; official account of life and career of, 14–23; penchant for using rare vocabulary like *ke* or *e* (illness), 73, 107, 137; place in literary history, 1, 13, 26–30, 142, 186; political exile, 16–21, 74, 176; public execution, 23–24, 101, 182; and religious communities, 165, 171–75; scholarly pursuits, 17, 165–76; on *shanshui* (mountains and waters), 71, 187–88; transformed landscape through development of his estates, 19–20, 70–71; tribute to Jian'an masters, 31–47; untrammeled heroism of, 48–64; voluntary change of identity from Chen to Shining Commandery, 48–49; *You mingshan zhi* (Roaming Famous Mountains) geographical work, 67–69

———, poems of, 32–47, 49–53, 71–72, 75–76, 79, 81–82, 86, 87–88, 89–90, 91–92, 94–95, 98–100, 103–5, 108–9, 118, 119–20, 121–22, 132–33, 176–77, 177–78, 178–79, 180–81, 182–83

Xie Xuan, 14, 22, 24, 48–55, 89, 107, 209n29, 227n58

Xie Zhan, 113–15, 209–10n19, 238n58

Yan Yu, 154

yin-yang philosophy, 82, 83, 120

You mingshan zhi (Roaming Famous Mountains), 68, 224n3

Yuanjia era, 13, 18, 24, 143, 244n53

Zhong Rong, 13, 30, 41, 51, 137, 142–43, 151, 244n52, 246n24

Zhu Daosheng, 171, 175, 250n26

Zhuangzi, 4, 6, 26, 28, 30, 58, 60, 61–63, 77–78, 85, 89, 105, 124, 138–39, 210n42, 211n61, 212n65, 223n53, 229n17,

229nn19–20, 232n71, 232n80, 234nn14–15, 240n88, 247n29, 249n11; on concepts of freedom, 57–60; on *da-ren* concept, 55–58; on death and immortality views, 59–62; on human nature, 61–63; on literati disengagement, 62–64; on nature perception, 59–62, 77–78; on self-oblivion, 61–62; on Xie's aesthetics, 138–39; on Xie's landscape representation, 77–78, 89

Zuo Si, 160, 161, 240n96